To Malcoln

wishe

D1795766

LIBRARY OF HEBREW BIBLE/
OLD TESTAMENT STUDIES

592

Formerly Journal for the Study of the Old Testament Supplement Series

FROM CREATION TO BABEL

Studies in Genesis 1–11

John Day

B L O O M S B U R Y
LONDON • NEW DELHI • NEW YORK • SYDNEY

Bloomsbury Academic
An imprint of Bloomsbury Publishing Plc

50 Bedford Square	1385 Broadway
London	New York
WC1B 3DP	NY 10018
UK	USA

www.bloomsbury.com
Bloomsbury is a registered trade mark of Bloomsbury Publishing Plc

First published 2013

British Library Cataloguing-in-Publication Data
A catalogue record for this book is available from the British Library.

ISBN: HB: 978-0-56721-509-3
         ePDF: 978-0-56737-030-3

Library of Congress Cataloging-in-Publication Data
From Creation to Babel / John Day p.cm
Includes bibliographic references and index.
ISBN 978-0-5672-1509-3 (hardcover)

Typeset by Forthcoming Publications Ltd (www.forthpub.com)
Printed and bound in Great Britain

CONTENTS

PREFACE

Although this volume is not a monograph in the strict sense, it consists of eleven chapters that hang together because of their common purpose of exploring issues relating to the interpretation and background of Genesis 1–11. It arises from the fact that in 2008 I was honoured by an invitation from Professor Graham Davies to prepare the ICC commentary on these chapters. In order to accomplish such a major task it seemed wise for me first to attempt to formulate my views on many of the main questions which these important chapters raise, and that is what the reader will find in these pages. Four of the chapters are completely new, whilst the other seven have either been previously published in Festschriften or elsewhere or represent expansions or reworkings of such articles. I believe the volume makes a significant contribution to the understanding of Genesis 1–11, and I hope the reader will enjoy reading it as much as I have enjoyed researching and writing it. As with several previous books of mine, I have greatly benefited from the meticulous attention of Dr Duncan Burns as copy editor and typesetter.

John Day

ACKNOWLEDGMENTS AND STATUS OF THE CHAPTERS

Chapter 1
THE MEANING AND BACKGROUND
OF THE PRIESTLY CREATION STORY (GENESIS 1.1–2.4A)
Previously unpublished.

Chapter 2
PROBLEMS IN THE INTERPRETATION OF THE STORY OF THE GARDEN OF EDEN
Previously unpublished.

Chapter 3
CAIN AND THE KENITES
Previously published in Gershon Galil, Mark Geller and Alan Millard (eds.), *Homeland and Exile: Biblical and Ancient Near Eastern Studies in Honour of Bustenay Oded* (VTSup, 130; Leiden: Brill, 2009), pp. 335-46. Reprinted by kind permission of Brill.

Chapter 4
THE FLOOD AND THE TEN ANTEDILUVIAN FIGURES
IN BEROSSUS AND IN THE PRIESTLY SOURCE IN GENESIS
Expanded version of article previously published in James K. Aitken, Katharine J. Dell and Brian A. Mastin (eds.), *On Stone and Scroll: A Festschrift for Graham Ivor Davies* (BZAW, 420; Berlin: W. de Gruyter, 2011), pp. 211-23. Overlapping parts reprinted by kind permission of W. de Gruyter.

Chapter 5
THE SONS OF GOD AND DAUGHTERS OF MEN AND THE GIANTS:
DISPUTED POINTS IN THE INTERPRETATION OF GENESIS 6.1-4
Previously published in *Hebrew Bible and Ancient Israel* 1.4 (2012), pp. 427-47. Reprinted by kind permission of Mohr Siebeck.

Chapter 6
THE GENESIS FLOOD NARRATIVE IN RELATION
TO ANCIENT NEAR EASTERN FLOOD ACCOUNTS
Previously published in Katharine J. Dell and Paul M. Joyce (eds.), *Biblical Interpretation and Method: Essays in Honour of Professor John Barton* (Oxford: Oxford University Press, 2013), pp. 74-88 Reprinted by kind permission of Oxford University Press.

Chapter 7
ROOMS OR REEDS IN NOAH'S ARK (GENESIS 6.14)?
Previously unpublished. To be republished by kind permission of Bloomsbury
T&T Clark as 'Rooms or Reeds in Noah's Ark? קנים in Genesis 6.14', in
Claire Gottlieb, Chaim Cohen and Mayer Gruber (eds.), *Visions of Life in
Biblical Times in Honor of Meir Lubetski—A Tribute to his Scholarship,
Teaching and Research* (Sheffield: Sheffield Phoenix Press, forthcoming).

Chapter 8
WHY DOES GOD 'ESTABLISH' RATHER THAN 'CUT' A COVENANT
WITH NOAH (AND ABRAHAM) IN THE PRIESTLY SOURCE?
Previously published as 'Why does God 'Establish' rather than 'Cut'
Covenants in the Priestly Source?', in A.D.H. Mayes and R.B. Salters (eds.),
Covenant as Context: Essays in Honour of E.W. Nicholson (Oxford: Oxford
University Press, 2003), pp. 91-109. Reprinted by kind permission of Oxford
University Press.

Chapter 9
NOAH'S DRUNKENNESS, THE CURSE OF CANAAN, HAM'S CRIME,
AND THE BLESSING OF SHEM AND JAPHETH (GENESIS 9.18-27)
Expanded version of article simultaneously published in David Baer and
Robert P. Gordon (eds.), *Leshon Limmudim: Essays on the Language and
Literature of the Hebrew Bible in Honour of Andrew Macintosh* (LHBOTS,
593; London: Bloomsbury T&T Clark, 2014), pp. 31-44. Overlapping parts
reprinted by kind permission of Bloomsbury T&T Clark.

Chapter 10
WHERE WAS TARSHISH (GENESIS 10.4)?
Reworked version of 'Where was Tarshish?', published in Iain Provan and
Mark J. Boda (eds.), *Let us Go up to Zion: Essays in Honour of Hugh William-
son on the Occasion of his Sixty-Fifth Birthday* (VTSup, 153; Brill: Leiden,
2012), pp. 359-69. Overlapping parts reprinted by kind permission of Brill.

Chapter 11
THE TOWER AND CITY OF BABEL STORY (GENESIS 11.1-9):
PROBLEMS OF INTERPRETATION AND BACKGROUND
Previously unpublished. To be republished by kind permission of Bloomsbury
T&T Clark in Shamir Yona, Ed Greenstein, Mayer Gruber, Peter Machinist
and Shalom Paul (eds.), *Marbeh Hokma: Studies in the Bible and the Ancient
Near East in Memory of Victor Avigdor Hurowitz* (Winona Lake, IN: Eisen-
brauns, forthcoming).

ABBREVIATIONS

AASOR	Annual of the American Schools of Oriental Research
AB	Anchor Bible
AfO	*Archiv für Orientfoschung*
AJA	*American Journal of Archaeology*
AJSL	*American Journal of Semitic Languages and Literatures*
AnBib	Analecta Biblica
ANET	J.B. Pritchard (ed.), Ancient Near Eastern Texts relating to the Old Testament (Princeton: Princeton University Press, 3rd edn with Supplement, 1969)
AOAT	Alter Orient und Altes Testament
AOS	American Oriental Society
ASV	American Standard Version
ATD	Das Alte Testament Deutsch
AThANT	*Abhandlingen zur Theologie des Alten und Neuen Testaments*
AThR	*Anglican Theological Review*
ATLA	American Theological Library Association
AuOr	*Aula Orientalis*
AUSS	*Andrews University Seminary Studies*
AV	Authorized Version
BA	*Biblical Archaeologist*
BAH	Bibliothèque archéologique et historique
BARev	*Biblical Archaeology Review*
BASOR	*Bulletin of the American Schools of Oriental Research*
BBR	*Bulletin for Biblical Research*
BDB	Francis Brown, S.R. Driver and Charles A. Briggs, *A Hebrew and English Lexicon of the Old Testament* (Oxford: Clarendon Press, 1907)
BeO	*Bibbia e Oriente*
BETL	Bibliotheca ephemeridum theologicarum lovaniensium
BHS	*Biblia Hebraica Stuttgartensia*
Bib	*Biblica*
BibInt	*Biblical Interpretation*
BibOr	Biblica et Orientalia
BJRL	*Bulletin of the John Rylands Library*
BKAT	Biblischer Kommentar: Altes Testament
BN	*Biblische Notizen*
BO	*Bibliotheca Orientalis*
BSacra	*Bibliotheca Sacra*
BSOAS	*Bulletin of the School of Oriental and African Studies*
BT	*Bible Translator*
BTB	*Biblical Theology Bulletin*

BWANT	Beiträge zur Wissenschaft vom Alten und Neuen Testament
BZ	*Biblische Zeitschrift*
BZAW	Beihefte zur *ZAW*
CBC	Cambridge Bible Commentary
CBQ	*Catholic Biblical Quarterly*
CBQMS	Catholic Biblical Quarterly Monograph Series
CHANE	Culture and History of the Ancient Near East
COS	W.W. Hallo (ed.), *The Context of Scripture: Canonical Compositions, Monumental Inscriptions, and Archival Documents from the Biblical World* (3 vols.; Leiden: Brill, 1997–2002)
DCH	D.J.A. Clines (ed.), *The Dictionary of Classical Hebrew* (8 vols.; Sheffield: Sheffield Phoenix Press, 2011)
DJD	Discoveries in the Judaean Desert
ET	English Translation
ETL	*Ephemerides Theologicae Lovanienses*
ExpTim	*Expository Times*
FAT	Forschungen zum Alten Testament
FOTL	Forms of Old Testament Literature
FzB	Forschung zur Bibel
HALAT	Ludwig Koehler *et al.* (eds.), *Hebräisches und aramäisches Lexikon zum Alten Testament* (5 vols.; Leiden: Brill, 1967-95)
HALOT	L. Koehler, W. Baumgartner, J.J. Stamm *et al.*, *Hebrew and Aramaic Lexicon of the Old Testament* (trans. and ed. M.E.J. Richardson; 5 vols.; Leiden: Brill, 1994–2000)
HeBAI	*Hebrew Bible and Ancient Israel*
HKAT	Handkommentar zum Alten Testament
HSM	Harvard Semitic Monographs
HTR	*Harvard Theological Review*
HUCA	*Hebrew Union College Annual*
ICC	International Critical Commentary
IDB	George Arthur Buttrick (ed.), *The Interpreter's Dictionary of the Bible* (4 vols.; Nashville: Abingdon Press, 1962)
IEJ	*Israel Exploration Journal*
IVP	InterVarsity Press
JAAR	*Journal of the American Academy of Religion*
JAOS	*Journal of the American Oriental Society*
JB	Jerusalem Bible
JBL	*Journal of Biblical Literature*
JCS	*Journal of Cuneiform Studies*
JEOL	*Jaarbericht ex oriente lux*
JHS	*Journal of Hebrew Scriptures*
JJS	*Journal of Jewish Studies*
JNES	*Journal of Near Eastern Studies*
JNSL	*Journal of Northwest Semitic Languages*
JPS	Jewish Publication Society
JQR	*Jewish Quarterly Review*
JRAS	*Journal of the Royal Asiatic Society*
JSJSup	Journal for the Study of Judaism Supplement Series

JSOT	*Journal for the Study of the Old Testament*
JSOTSup	*Journal for the Study of the Old Testament*, Supplement Series
JSS	*Journal of Semitic Studies*
JSSM	Monograph Journal of Semitic Studies Monograph
JTS	*Journal of Theological Studies*
KTU	M. Dietrich, O. Loretz, J. Sanmartín, *The Cuneiform Alphabetic texts from Ugarit, Ras Ibn Hani and Other Places (KTU: Second Enlarged Edition)* (Münster: Ugarit-Verlag, 1995). 2nd edn of M. Dietrich, O. Loretz, J. Sanmartín, *Die keilalphabetischen Texte aus Ugarit* (Neukirchen-Vluyn: Neukirchener Verlag, 1976)
LCL	Loeb Classical Library
LHBOTS	Library of Hebrew Bible/Old Testament Studies
LXX	Septuagint
MIO	*Miteilungen des Instituts für Orientforschung*
MT	Masoretic Text
NAB	New American Bible
NASV	New American Standard Version
NCB	New Century Bible
NCBC	New Cambridge Bible Commentary
NEB	New English Bible
NF	Neue Folge
NICOT	New International Commentary on the Old Testament
NIV	New International Version
NJB	New Jerusalem Bible
NJPSV	New Jewish Publication Society Version
NRSV	New Revised Standard Version
NS	New Series
NTS	*New Testament Studies*
OBO	Orbis biblicus et orientalis
OBT	Overtures to Biblical Theology
OLA	Orientalia lovaniensia analecta
OLP	*Orientalia lovaniensia periodica*
Or	*Orientalia*
OTL	Old Testament Library
OTS	Oudtestamentische studiën
PEQ	*Palestine Exploration Quarterly*
RA	*Revue d'Assyriologie et d'archéologie orientale*
RB	*Revue biblique*
REB	Revised English Bible
RevQ	*Revue de Qumran*
RHPR	*Revue d'histoire et de philosophie religieuse*
RHR	*Revue de l'histoire des religions*
RLA	*Reallexikon der Assyriologie*
RV	Revised Version
RSV	Revised Standard Version
SBL	Society of biblical Literature
SBLABS	Society of Biblical Literature Archaeology and Biblical Studies
SBLDS	Society of Biblical Literature Dissertation Series

SBLMS	Society of Biblical Studies Monograph Series
SBS	Stuttgarter Bibelstudien
SBT	Studies in Biblical Theology
SCM	Student Christian Movement
Sem	*Semitica*
SJLA	Studies in Judaism in Late Antiquity
SJOT	*Scandinavian Journal of the Old Testament*
SPCK	Society for Promoting Christian Knowledge
SVTP	Studia in Veteris Testamenti Pseudepigrapha
TBü	Theologische Bücherei
TSBA	*Transactions of the Society of Biblical Archaeology*
TynBul	*Tyndale Bulletin*
TZ	*Theoogische Zeitschrift*
UF	*Ugarit-Forschungen*
VT	*Vetus Testamentum*
VTSup	*Vetus Testamentum*, Supplements
WBC	Word Biblical Commentary
WMANT	Wissenschaftliche Monographien zum Alten und Neuen Testament
WO	*Die Welt des Orients*
WTJ	*Westminster Theological Journal*
ZA	*Zeitschrift für Assyriologie*
ZAH	*Zeitschrift für Althebraistik*
ZAW	*Zeitschrift für die alttestamentliche Wissenschaft*
ZDMG	*Zeitschrift der deutschen morgenländischen Gesellschaft*
ZNW	*Zeitschrift für die nutestamentliche Wissenschaft*

Chapter 1

THE MEANING AND BACKGROUND OF THE PRIESTLY
CREATION STORY (GENESIS 1.1–2.4A)

1. *The Structure of Genesis 1.1–2.4a*
and its Numerical Patterns

The Priestly Creation story in Gen. 1.1–2.4a has a clearly defined structure in which the second three days closely parallel the first three days, with God's resting on the seventh day providing a climax. It will be noted that there are eight divine actions spread over six days of creation, with days 3 and 6 having two divine actions instead of one, unlike the others. The parallels between the days are as follows:

Day 1. Creation of light	Day 4. Creation of heavenly lights
Day 2. Creation of firmament and separation of the waters	Day 5. Creation of birds and sea creatures
Day 3. Creation of (a) earth and sea (b) vegetation	Day 6. Creation of (a) land animals (b) man and woman

Day 7. God rests

This pattern appears to have been first discovered by J.G. von Herder[1] in the eighteenth century. It is to be observed that God's creating light on day 1 is mirrored by his creation of the heavenly lights (the sun, moon and stars) on day 4, and that God's creation of the firmament and separation of the waters to positions above the firmament and on the earth's surface is mirrored by the creation of birds which can fly near the firmament and sea creatures which swim in the earth's waters. As for day 3, there are here two divine acts of creation, just as there are on day 6.

---

1. J.G. von Herder, *Älteste Urkunde des Menschengeschlechts* (ed. J.G. Müller; 2 vols.; Tübingen: J.G. Cotta, 1806), I, pp. 129-30. Herder originally put forward the idea in the first edition of this work which appeared in 1774.

However, in terms of content the second act of creation on day 3, that of vegetation, relates not so much to the second divine act of day 6, the creation of man and woman, but rather specifically to the giving of vegetation on day 6 as the food for both humans and animals, which is mentioned immediately after the creation of humanity.

In other ways too the Priestly Creation story shows signs of having been carefully crafted. The number seven and multiples thereof seem to have been especially significant. Thus, in addition to the overarching seven-day scheme which pervades the narrative, acts of creation are declared 'good' seven times,[2] the word 'God' comes 35 times (7 × 5), and the word *haʾāreṣ* or *ʾereṣ*, whether to be translated '(the) earth' or '(the) land', occurs 21 times (7 × 3) if we restrict ourselves to Gen. 1.1–2.3 (see below on Gen. 2.4a as a probable later redactional addition). The account of the climactic seventh day (Gen. 2.1-3) also consists of 35 (7 × 5) words.

2. Genesis 1.1–2.4a and Science[3]

Contrary to what is often said by some popular apologists, there is no reason to doubt that the original writer of Genesis 1 intended his account to be taken literally. Although not a scientific account in our sense, it is not *simply* a theological account, as is sometimes claimed: the account reflects ancient views of the nature of the universe, for example, the notion of a firmament, that is, a solid dome above the earth (cf. Job 37.18, where the sky is said to be 'hard as a cast mirror'), with cosmic waters above it and below the earth. Occasionally, conservative scholars have tried to avoid the concept of a solid firmament by supposing that the Hebrew word *rāqîaʿ* should rather be translated 'expanse', meaning the

---

2. For some reason there is no declaration of goodness in connection with the second day (is this because the divine work *vis-à-vis* the waters is not yet complete?), but there are declarations of goodness regarding both acts of creation on the third day, thus compensating for the omission on the second day.

3. From the vast number of works which touch on various aspects of Gen. 1 and science, certain parts of the following may be noted: L.R. Bailey, *Genesis, Creation, and Creationism* (Mahwah, NJ: Paulist Press, 1993); R.L. Numbers, *The Creationists: From Scientific Creationism to Intelligent Design* (Cambridge, MA: Harvard University Press, 2006); W.H. Jennings, *Storms over Genesis: Biblical Battleground in America's Wars of Religion* (Minneapolis: Fortress Press, 2007); S.C. Barton and D. Wilkinson, *Reading Genesis after Darwin* (Oxford: Oxford University Press, 2009); W.P. Brown, *The Seven Pillars of Creation: The Bible, Science, and the Ecology of Wonder* (Oxford: Oxford University Press, 2010).

atmosphere (cf. NIV; J.H. Walton, R.W. Younker and R.M. Davidson[4]). However, against that stands the fact that the underlying verb *rqᶜ* means 'to beat out' (used in the hiphil of the sky in Job 37.18), and in the piel and pual forms is used in connection with objects of gold, bronze and silver (Exod. 39.3; Num. 17.4 [ET 16.39]; Isa. 40.19; Jer. 10.9); similarly the Phoenician word *mrqᶜ* is used of an object made of gold, possibly a bowl.[5] Again, the Septuagint's translation of *rāqîᶜa* as *stereōma*, literally 'solid body' (cf. Vulgate *firmamentum*) suggests the solid vault of heaven rather than the expanse of the atmosphere.

Moreover, the text clearly speaks of creation in seven, or rather six, days, and since each day has an evening and a morning it is hardly plausible that we should interpret the days as geological periods, as some apologists have sometimes supposed. Again, since the seventh day provides a precedent for the Sabbath, it has to be a literal day. However, even if we were to suppose that geological periods were intended, the order of creation would not always agree with that revealed by modern science, the alleged existence of the earth and its vegetable world before the sun and stars, for example, being inaccurate (cf. Gen. 1.2, 11-12, 14-18).[6]

Again, there can be no doubt, if we follow the Priestly and general biblical chronology, that the world is envisaged as having been created about 6,000 years ago (or 7,500 years if we follow the longer Septuagint chronology in Gen. 5 and 11). The chronology of James Ussher, Archbishop of Armagh and Primate of All Ireland, published in 1650, is the best known;[7] for many years it was included in the marginal notes of the

---

4. J.H. Walton, *The Lost World of Genesis One: Ancient Cosmology and the Origins Debate* (Downers Grove, IL: IVP Academic, 2009), pp. 155-61; R.W. Younker and R.M. Davidson, 'The Myth of the Solid Heavenly Dome: Another Look at the Hebrew רָקִיעַ (*RĀQÎAᶜ*)', *AUSS* 49 (2011), pp. 125-47. Walton, however, does not deny that *šᵉḥāqîm* denote a solid sky in Job 37.18.

5. Cf. *KAI* 38.1, part of a 391 BCE inscription from Idalion in Cyprus.

6. Long ago, S.R. Driver, *The Book of Genesis* (Westminster Commentaries; London: Methuen, 1904), pp. 19-26, made a very helpful comparison of the order of creation in Genesis with that revealed by modern science.

7. J. Ussher, *Annales veteris testamenti, prima mundi origine deducti* (London: J. Flesher, 1650), ET *The Annals of the World* (London: E. Tyler, 1658). On the principles underlying Ussher's chronology, see J. Barr, 'Why the World was Created in 4004 B.C.: Archbishop Ussher and Biblical Chronology', *BJRL* 67 (1984–85), pp. 565-608. Cf. too Barr's more general work, *Biblical Chronology: Legend or Science?* (Ethel M. Wood Lecture; London: University of London, 1987). Clearly few people read Ussher in the original Latin: Barr, 'Why the World was Created in 4004 B.C.', pp. 575-76, recounts how when he did this in 1981 in the Bodleian library in Oxford, the pages still needed cutting!

King James Bible. This estimated the date of creation as the nightfall preceding Sunday, October 23, 4004 BCE, but over the centuries there have also been many other attempts to date the creation precisely on the basis of the biblical data, including Sir Isaac Newton's 4000 BCE, Martin Luther's 3961 BCE, the traditional Jewish date of 3760 BCE, and the traditional Byzantine date (using the Septuagint) of 5009 BCE, just to mention a few.

Nevertheless, it may be accepted that the narrative's theological assertion that God is the creator of the universe and of humanity, which constitutes the climax of God's acts of creation, is the primary affirmation of the narrative. The fact that Gen. 2.4b-23 has a different order of creation highlights the fact that the precise order of events is not the most fundamental point, though many fundamentalists who claim to accept literally 'the biblical account of creation' seem unaware of the different order to be found there, where man is made before the vegetation, and woman after that, rather than (as in Gen. 1) the vegetation being created before man and woman, who are created together.

John Walton[8] has recently argued that Gen. 1.1–2.4a is not to be understood as an account of the creation of the material universe but rather as a narrative setting out the functions of the various aspects of creation, usually for the benefit of humanity. Moreover, he assumes that the account understands the world to be a cosmic temple, with God's resting on the seventh day implying his taking up residence in his temple. However, although Walton is right to emphasize that there is a functional element in the narrative, he is certainly wrong to understand it wholly in such terms, and it is quite unnatural to deny that Genesis 1 gives us an account of the creation of the material universe. That is the only natural way of taking the text, as is shown by the fact that this is the way all other interpreters have read it over the past two thousand years. For example, we cannot envisage the description of the vegetation on the third day as merely functional, since Gen. 1.11 declares, 'let the earth put forth vegetation', which can only refer to its creation, and it is only on the parallel sixth day (Gen. 1.29-30) that its function as food for humanity and animals is declared. Exodus 20.11 also provides a problem for Walton in that it states that God made (ʿāśâ) the heavens and the earth, the sea and all that is in them in six days, since ʿāśâ cannot here mean 'do', as Walton claims. Finally, the idea that the world is here depicted as a cosmic temple is something that Walton has read into Gen. 1.1–2.4a

---

8. Walton, *The Lost World of Genesis One*; idem, *Genesis 1 as Ancient Cosmology* (Winona Lake, IN: Eisenbrauns, 2011).

which is not present in the text, and it is pure eisegesis to suppose that God's cessation of work on the seventh day implies his taking up residence in his temple, a notion that Walton reads in from Ps. 132.7-8, 13-14.[9]

3. *The Meaning of bārāʾ: Create or Separate?*

The verb *bārāʾ* always has God as its subject in the Old Testament, and it has long been accepted that the meaning is 'to create'. Within the Priestly Creation account it occurs in Gen. 1.1, 21, 27 (×2); 2.3, 4. Recently, however, a Dutch Old Testament scholar, Ellen van Wolde, has claimed that the meaning is rather 'to separate'.[10] She notes that seven other ancient Near Eastern creation accounts have the idea of a deity separating heaven and earth. For example, in the prologue to 'Enkidu and the Underworld' in the Gilgamesh epic, we read of a time 'When the heavens had been separated from the earth; when the earth had been delimited from the heavens…'[11] She holds that the Hebrew verb *bārāʾ*, traditionally rendered 'create' in Genesis 1 and throughout the Old Testament, rather means 'separate'. Van Wolde's view was sensationally publicized in a British newspaper, *The Daily Telegraph* (October 8, 2009), with the dramatic headline, 'God is not the Creator, says academic'! However, her view has gained little support.[12] Among

9. Others have previously noted linguistic parallels between the end of the Priestly Creation story in Gen. 1–2 and the end of the Tabernacle narrative in Exod. 39–40; see, e.g., M. Weinfeld, 'Sabbath, Temple, and the Enthronement of the Lord—The Problem of the Sitz in Leben of Genesis 1:1–2:3', in A. Caquot and M. Delcor (eds.), *Mélanges bibliques et orientaux en l'honneur de M. Henri Cazelles* (AOAT, 212; Neukirchen–Vluyn: Neukirchener Verlag, 1981), pp. 501-12; J.D. Levenson, *Creation and the Persistence of Evil: The Jewish Drama of Divine Omnipotence* (San Francisco: Harper & Row, 1988), pp. 78-87. However, the parallels are not so remarkable and certainly do not justify seeing the creation as a kind of temple structure but merely illustrate common Priestly language used in connection with different creative activities.

10. E. van Wolde, *Reframing Biblical Studies: When Language and Text Meet Culture, Cognition and Context* (Winona Lake, IN: Eisenbrauns, 2009), pp. 184-200; *eadem*, 'Why the Verb ברא Does Not Mean "To Create" in Genesis 1.1–2.4a', *JSOT* 34 (2009), pp. 3-23. She and R. Rezetko replied to Becking and Korpel (see n. 12 below) in 'Semantics and the Semantics of ברא: A Rejoinder to the Arguments Advanced by B. Becking and M. Korpel', *JHS* 11 (2011), article 9.

11. Translation taken from *The Electronic Text Corpus of Sumerian Literature* (accessible at http://etcsl.orinst.ox.ac.uk).

12. See the convincing critique in B. Becking and M.C.A. Korpel, 'To Create, to Separate or to Construct: An Alternative for a Recent Proposal as to the Interpretation of ברא in Genesis 1.1–2.4a', *JHS* 10 (2010), article 3.

the objections that may be made are the following. First, all the ancient Versions render *bārāʾ* by 'create'; if the verb really meant 'separate' it is remarkable that the meaning of this not infrequent verb was universally forgotten so soon. Secondly, in the Hebrew Bible the verb *bārāʾ* occurs parallel with the verbs *ʿāśâ*, 'make', and *yāṣar*, 'form' (cf. Isa. 45.7). We may also compare Isa. 65.17 and 66.22, the former of which speaks of God creating (*bārāʾ*) new heavens and earth, and the latter refers to God's making (*ʿāśâ*) new heavens and earth. Thirdly, in Biblical Hebrew one does not separate things but separates between things or separates things from other things, as is the case with the verb *hibdîl* in Genesis 1, so if *bārāʾ* really meant 'separate' it should have been followed by *bên*, 'between', or *min*, 'from'. This, however, is never the case with *bārāʾ* in Gen. 1.1–2.4a or anywhere else in the Old Testament.

4. *Creation* ex Nihilo *or Not? The Translation of Genesis 1.1*

A more serious debate centres on the first word of Gen. 1.1, *bᵉrēʾšît*. Should we understand the text to be saying, '*In the beginning* God created the heavens and the earth. The earth was empty and void…', or '*In the beginning, when* God created the heavens and the earth, the earth being empty and void…' The beginning of Enuma elish (the so-called Babylonian Creation epic) and the opening of the J Creation story in Gen. 2.4b-7 have been urged in favour of the latter. If this translation is correct, it would appear to rule out *creatio ex nihilo* and imply the existence of pre-creation matter. It has been argued by some that if the text meant 'In *the* beginning God created the heavens and the earth' the Hebrew should read *bārēʾšît*, not *bᵉrēʾšît*. However, this is not so: Hebrew similarly regularly says *mērōʾš*, not *mēhārōʾš* for 'from the beginning' (cf. Isa. 40.21; 41.4, 26; 48.16), and interestingly *mērēʾšît*, not *mēhārēʾšît*, 'from the beginning' (cf. Isa. 46.10); other expressions of time, like *miqqedem* (cf. Isa. 46.10; Ps. 74.12) and *mᵉʿôlām* (cf. Isa. 46.9; Prov. 8.23), 'from of old', also lack the definite article. This is comparable to the fact that in British English we say 'in the light of', whereas American English is content to say 'in light of'. Even so, there are some scholars who prefer the translation 'In the beginning, when God created the heavens and the earth…',[13] and it has been claimed that the perfect

---

13. E.g. J. Skinner, *A Critical and Exegetical Commentary on Genesis* (ICC; Edinburgh: T. & T. Clark, 1910), pp. 12-14; E.A. Speiser, *Genesis* (AB, 1; Garden City, NY: Doubleday, 1964), pp. 12-13; Levenson, *Creation and the Persistence of Evil*, p. 121; R.S Hendel, *Genesis 1–11* (Anchor Yale Bible, 1A; New Haven: Yale University Press, forthcoming). I am deeply grateful to Ron for letting me see an advance copy of his manuscript.

tense of *bārā᾽* is not incompatible with this (cf., e.g., Hos. 1.2, *tᵉhillat dibber yhwh bᵉhōšēʿa*, 'When the Lord first spoke through Hosea'). However, this kind of construction is exceedingly rare, and by far the most natural translation is 'In the beginning God created the heavens and the earth'. Moreover, all the ancient Versions have the traditional translation, 'In the beginning God created the heavens and the earth', and none support the revisionist rendering; it was only in the mediaeval era with Rashi that this alternative translation 'In the beginning, when God created...' was suggested.

In accepting the translation 'In the beginning God created the heavens and the earth', the question still remains whether v. 1 is to be understood as chronologically preceding v. 2 or is rather to be seen as a heading to or summary of the whole chapter. The term 'heading' does not seem appropriate, since v. 1 is in the form of a complete sentence; if it were really a heading we should expect something like *rēšît bᵉrō᾽ ᵉlōhîm ᾽et-haššāmayim wᵊᵉt-hā᾽āreṣ*, 'The beginning of God's creating the heavens and the earth'. Is it therefore acceptable to regard v. 1 rather as a summary of the following creation account as a whole, the heavens and the earth denoting the final created universe? This seems to be the most popular view at the present time.[14] However, it seems to me more natural to suppose that the events of v. 1 immediately precede those of v. 2.[15] This would fit nicely with Gen. 2.4a, which refers to 'the generations (lit. begettings) of the heavens and the earth when they were created', a phrase which by analogy with all the other references to generations in Genesis (e.g. the generations of Noah, Gen. 6.9), suggests that the heavens and the earth were created first (in some inchoate form), and that the fullness of creation emerged from them. (Compare Gen. 1.11, 20, 24 where the earth is said to bring forth vegetation and various living creatures.) Indeed, in v. 2 the earth already exists in inchoate state. The fact that the sentence starts with 'and' makes it plausible to regard it as a continuation of v. 1, with its initial reference to the creation of the earth.

14. E.g. Driver, *The Book of Genesis*, p. 3; J. Barr, 'Was Everything that God Created Really Good? A Question in the First Verse of the Bible', in T. Linafelt and T.K. Beal (eds.), *God in the Fray: A Tribute to Walter Brueggemann* (Minneapolis: Fortress Press, 1998), pp. 55-65 (55-60); H. Seebass, *Urgeschichte (1,1–11,26)* (Neukirchen–Vluyn: Neukirchener Verlag, 3rd edn, 2009), p. 65.

15. E.g. J. Wellhausen, *Prolegomena zur Geschichte Israels* (Berlin: G. Reimer, 2nd edn, 1883), pp. 313, 411 n. 1, ET *Prolegomena to the History of Israel* (trans. J.S. Black and A. Menzies; Edinburgh: A. & C. Black, 1885), pp. 298, 387 n. 1; B.S. Childs, *Myth and Reality in the Old Testament* (SBT, 27; London: SCM Press, 2nd edn, 1962), pp. 31-43; G.J. Wenham, *Genesis 1–15* (WBC, 1; Waco, TX: Word Books, 1987), pp. 11-13.

This is certainly how the Septuagint, the oldest of the ancient Versions, understood the situation, since in v. 2 it continues '*But* the earth was...', and this was indeed the universal view of antiquity. This is quite compatible with the fact that 'earth' (without definite article) in the sense of dry land does not emerge till v. 10. In the same way, the creation of the dome of the 'sky' (without definite article) in v. 5 is compatible with the previous existence of the heavens (with the definite article) in some broader, inchoate sense in v. 1. The heavens were not confined to the firmament but included all the area above the earth,[16] and of course God had to dwell somewhere! However, although the translation and interpretation I have advocated here is compatible with belief in *creatio ex nihilo*, this was probably a philosophical question that P was not concerned with and only arose later (first explicitly about 100 BCE in 2 Macc. 7.28).

5. *Tōhû wābōhû*

Either descriptive of the earth after God's initial creation of the inchoate heavens and earth (as argued above) or alternatively as a description of the earth before anything of God's creative work had even begun, v. 2 states that the earth was *tōhû wābōhû*. This deliberately assonantal phrase has traditionally been rendered in English Bibles as 'without form and void' (RSV, NEB; AV [with a comma]) or 'waste and void' (RV, ASV), or other similar expressions. The word *bōhû* only occurs three times in the Hebrew Bible (Gen. 1.2; Isa. 34.11; Jer. 4.23), each time alongside *tōhû*, and is plausibly related to Arabic *bahiya*, 'to be empty'. On the other hand, *tōhû* occurs a fair number of times, so we have quite a lot of instances to help us tease out its meaning (in addition to the three references above, these are Deut. 32.10; 1 Sam. 12.21 (×2); Job 6.18; 12.24; 26.7; Ps. 107.40; Isa. 24.10; 29.21; 40.17, 23; 41.29; 44.9; 45.18, 19; 49.4; 59.4). From these references it is clear that the word's connotations in Biblical Hebrew range from the concrete 'desert' (e.g. Deut. 32.10; Job 12.24; perhaps also in Ugaritic in *KTU* 1.5.I.15) to the abstract 'non-entity' (e.g. Isa. 41.29; 44.9), the central meaning uniting these being that of 'empty' or 'nothing' (e.g. Jer. 4.23; Job 26.7).[17]

---

16. Cf. L.I.J. Stadelmann, *The Hebrew Conception of the World* (AnBib, 39; Rome: Biblical Institute Press, 1970), p. 61.

17. D.T. Tsumura, *Creation and Destruction: A Reappraisal of the* Chaoskampf *Theory in the Old Testament* (Winona Lake, IN: Eisenbrauns, 2005), pp. 9-35; T. Fenton, 'Chaos in the Bible? Tohu vabohu', in G. Abramson and T. Parfitt (eds.), *Jewish Education and Learning: Published in Honour of Dr David Patterson on the Occasion of his Seventieth Birthday* (Newark, NJ: Harwood Academic Publishers,

'Empty' seems to be the meaning we have in Gen. 1.2. In endeavouring to retain the Hebrew word play, Mark Smith suggests translating *tōhû wābōhû* in Gen. 1.2 as 'void and vacuum'.[18] Of course the world was not completely empty, since it was covered with water. What is meant is that the earth existed only in an inchoate state and was devoid of all its familiar features and inhabitants which are subsequently created in Genesis 1.

D.T. Tsumura and Terry Fenton are right in saying that *tōhû wābōhû* in Gen. 1.2 has sometimes been wrongly understood as chaos.[19] However, the term chaos is surely not inappropriately used of the raging waters that God has to do battle with in some parts of the Old Testament at the time of creation (e.g. Ps. 104.6-9), and which ultimately lies behind the waters of the deep in Gen. 1.2.

6. *Spirit of God, Wind of God or a Mighty Wind (Genesis 1.2)?*

In Gen. 1.2 we read that the *rûaḥ ᵊlōhîm* was hovering or sweeping over the waters. Opinion is divided as to whether this refers to the Spirit of God, the wind of God or merely a mighty wind. Curiously, in P's creation narrative it is mentioned only in Gen. 1.2. Everywhere else in the Old Testament the expression means 'Spirit of God', which at first sight might appear to provide a strong argument in favour of this, the traditional translation.[20] However, the verbal participle used in connection with it, *mᵉraḥepet*, means 'swept' or 'hovered', which might be thought to fit better with a reference to the wind. Elsewhere this verb is used in both Hebrew and Ugaritic of birds (Deut. 32.11; *KTU* 1.18.IV.20, 21, 31, 32), and in Jer. 23.9 the qal form of the verb means 'to shake', which certainly disproves the once held view that the verb means 'to brood', with the earth in Gen. 1.2 being conceived as a world-egg. But the really decisive argument in favour of a reference to the wind is the fact that Psalm 104, which is closely related to Genesis 1 and has a very similar order of creation, refers at this precise point (v. 3) to Yahweh

1994), pp. 203-19. Curiously, forms of the Hebrew expression have actually come through into ordinary French and German discourse with the meaning of chaos; see Fenton, 'Chaos in the Bible?', pp. 216-17.

18. M.S. Smith, *The Priestly Vision of Genesis 1* (Minneapolis: Fortress Press, 2010), p. 57.

19. See above n. 17.

20. Cf. AV, RV, RSV, REB, NIV. This traditional view is sometimes favoured by conservative scholars; see, e.g., V.P. Hamilton, *The Book of Genesis Chapters 1–17* (NICOT; Grand Rapids, MI: Eerdmans, 1990), pp. 103, 111-14.

riding on the wings of the wind prior to the conflict with the waters, which further implies that the 'wind' is birdlike.[21] This parallel thus not only clearly indicates the meaning wind but also explains the use of the verb *merahepet*, which is suggestive of a bird. Interestingly, the view that the wind is in view here provides a parallel with the Priestly flood narrative in Gen. 8.1, where we read that 'God made a wind blow over the earth, and the waters subsided', the flood thus constituting a resurgence of the primaeval waters, which again needed to be kept in check. But should we translate 'wind of God'[22] or 'mighty wind'[23] in Gen. 1.2? The latter view would imply that the divine name is being used in an intensive sense. The existence of such a usage in the Old Testament is, however, open to question, as I have shown elsewhere.[24] But what is decisive is that the 34 other references to Elohim in the Priestly creation story clearly refer to the deity. If the writer had intended otherwise here, this would have been more clearly indicated by using an expression like *rûaḥ seʿārâ* or *rûaḥ seʿārôt*, 'stormy wind' (Pss. 107.25; 148.8) or *rûaḥ qādîm*, 'east wind' (cf. Ps. 48.8 [ET 7]; Jer. 18.17).

7. The Creation of Light and the Heavenly Luminaries

The first day of creation saw what is generally referred to as the creation of light (Gen. 1.3-5). Mark Smith,[25] however, has recently queried whether light actually is created and prefers to envisage here rather an uncreated, primordial divine light. He notes that light is not explicitly stated to have been created, and compares the light with which Yahweh is wrapped in the related Ps. 104.2 as well as the light emanating from

21. Cf. J. Day, *God's Conflict with the Dragon and the Sea: Echoes of a Canaanite Myth in the Old Testament* (UCOP, 35; Cambridge: Cambridge University Press, 1985), p. 53.

22. Cf. NRSV, NJB; H.M. Orlinsky, 'The Plain Meaning of ruaḥ in Gen. 1.2', *JQR* 48 (1957–58), pp. 174-82; B. Janowski and A. Krüger, 'Gottes Sturm und Gottes Atem. Zum Verständnis von רוּחַ אֱלֹהִים in Gen 1,2 und Ps 104,29f', *Jahrbuch für Biblische Theologie* 24 (2009), pp. 3-29 (3-19).

23. Cf. NEB, NAB; Speiser, *Genesis*, pp. 3, 5 ('an awesome wind'); B. Vawter, *On Genesis: A New Reading* (London: Geoffrey Chapman, 1977), pp. 40-41.

24. Cf. J. Day, *The Recovery of the Ancient Hebrew Language: The Lexicographical Writings of D. Winton Thomas* (Hebrew Bible Monographs, 20; Sheffield: Sheffield Phoenix Press, 2013), Chapter 2.

25. Mark S. Smith, 'Light in Genesis 1:3—Created or Uncreated: A Question of Priestly Mysticism?', in C. Cohen *et al.* (eds.), *Birkat Shalom: Studies in Bible, Ancient Near Eastern Literature, and Postbiblical Judaism Presented to Shalom M. Paul on the Occasion of his Seventieth Birthday* (2 vols.; Winona Lake, IN: Eisenbrauns, 2008), I, pp. 125-34.

Marduk in Enuma elish (1.101-104). However, while I certainly see Ps. 104.2 as lying *behind* Gen. 1.3-5 (see below for evidence of the dependence of Gen. 1 on Ps. 104), the fact that God declares 'Let there be light', followed by the statement 'and there was light', can only mean that what was once not in existence now is, that is, we have here an act of creation.

Coming to the fourth day of creation (Gen. 1.14-18), there are two unusual things to be noted in connection with the creation of the heavenly luminaries there—the sun, moon and stars (which for the ancients would have included some of our planets). The first, as has often been noted before, is that light was already in existence from the first day (Gen. 1.3-5), although the sun, moon and stars were not created till the fourth day (contrast Job 38.7, where the morning stars already existed when the foundations of the earth were laid). The second is that the sun and moon are not directly mentioned, but are referred to obliquely as 'the two great lights—the greater light to rule the day and the lesser light to rule the night'. Scholars over the last century have repeatedly asserted that P refrained from mentioning them directly because the words for sun and moon in Hebrew were also divine names, and P did not want to leave open the possibility of their being seen as gods.[26] But it is difficult to see what real evidence there is for this view. Other parts of the Old Testament that are staunchly opposed to idolatry are perfectly happy to mention the sun and moon by name (e.g. Deut. 4.19; 2 Kgs 23.5, 11; Job 31.26). Most likely P simply spoke of the greater and lesser lights in order to heighten the parallel of their creation with that of the creation of light on the first day. This would be in keeping with P's general tendency to highlight connections between days 1–3 and 4–6, to which attention has already been drawn above.

8. *'Let Us Make Humanity'*

One of the questions that Gen. 1.26 raises is, Why does God say 'Let *us* make humanity in *our* image according to *our* likeness'? Some of the early Church Fathers supposed this was a reference to the Trinity,[27] but this is unacceptable since it involves reading back into the text a Christian

26. E.g. Wenham, *Genesis 1–15*, p. 21; J. McKeown, *Genesis* (Two Horizons Old Testament Commentary; Grand Rapids, MI: Eerdmans, 2008), p. 24; B.T. Arnold, *Genesis* (NCBC; Cambridge: Cambridge University Press, 2009), pp. 42-43.

27. Cf. G.T. Armstrong, *Die Genesis in der alten Kirche* (Promotionsarbeit, Heidelberg; Tübingen: J.C.B. Mohr [Paul Siebeck], 1962), pp. 39, 69-70; R.McL. Wilson, 'The Early History of the Exegesis of Gen 1:28', *Studia Patristica* 1 (1957), pp. 420-37.

theological idea which evolved only much later. Biblical Hebrew has no royal plural elsewhere, but H. Seebass nevertheless favours this interpretation here,[28] and C. Westermann's proposed 'plural of deliberation'[29] is elsewhere unattested in Biblical Hebrew. W.H. Schmidt and O.H. Steck favour a plural of self-exhortation,[30] but P.D. Miller has convincingly shown that there is no reliable evidence for such a form in Biblical Hebrew either.[31] Another minority view put forward by D.J.A. Clines is that God was addressing his own spirit,[32] though I have shown above that *rûaḥ* in Gen. 1.2 refers to God's wind, not spirit, and even apart from that it seems doubtful that in the pre-Trinitarian world of the Old Testament God would ever be represented as consulting his own spirit.

The dominant view nowadays is that there is a reference to the heavenly court which God addressed[33] (cf. Job 38.7, where 'all the sons of God shouted for joy' at the time of the creation, though admittedly it does not say that God consulted them). This view may also claim some support from Psalm 8, which stands very close to Gen. 1.26-28, as it also refers to humanity's lordship over the natural world. Now v. 6 says of humanity, 'Yet you have made them little less than the gods, and crowned them with glory and honour'. Everywhere else in this psalm God is referred to as Yahweh, which supports the view that *ʾelōhîm* here refers to gods, not God. Accordingly, Psalm 8 sees some resemblance between humans and the gods, which would link up with Gen. 1.26 if humanity is made in the image of the heavenly court and not just God. That God

28. Seebass, *Genesis*, I, p. 79. The royal plural is, however, perhaps found in the Aramaic of Ezra 4.18, where the Persian King Artaxerxes I refers to 'the letter that you sent to us'. However, later in the verse the king refers to the letter as being read 'before me', so it is not impossible that 'to us' refers to the royal court more generally.

29. C. Westermann, *Genesis. I. Genesis 1–11* (BKAT, 1.1; Neukirchen–Vluyn: Neukirchener Verlag, 1974), pp. 200-201, ET *Genesis 1–11: A Commentary* (trans. J.J. Scullion; London: SPCK, 1984), p. 145.

30. W.H. Schmidt, *Die Schöpfungsgeschichte der Priesterschrift* (WMANT, 17; Neukirchen–Vluyn: Neukirchener Verlag, 1964), p. 130; O.H. Steck, *Der Schöpfungsbericht der Priesterschrift* (FRLANT, 115; Göttingen: Vandenhoeck & Ruprecht, 1975), p. 140.

31. P.D. Miller, *Genesis 1–11: Studies in Structure and Theme* (JSOTSup, 8; Sheffield: Department of Biblical Studies, University of Sheffield, 1978), pp. 10-11.

32. Cf. D.J.A. Clines, 'The Image of God in Man', *TynBul* 19 (1968), pp. 53-103 (69), reprinted as 'Humanity as the Image of God', in *idem*, *On the Way to the Postmodern: Old Testament Essays, 1967–98* (2 vols.; JSOTSup, 292-93 [293]; Sheffield: Sheffield Academic Press, 1998), II, pp. 447-97 (464).

33. For a strong defence of the divine court understanding of 'let us make humanity', see Miller, *Genesis 1–11*, pp. 9-20.

addressed (what were referred to as) the angels is already attested in Philo and Targum Pseudo-Jonathan (but not the other Targums), as well as *Gen. R.* 8.4; *b. Sanh.* 38b (242). Polytheistic ideas probably ultimately lie in the background here. Scholars have sometimes compared Enuma elish and the Atrahasis epic, where humanity is created by the joint action of Ea and Marduk or Enki (= Ea) and the goddess Mami respectively. However, the evidence adduced above suggests a consultation between Yahweh and his heavenly court more generally, rather than simply with one other god. It might be objected that in Gen. 1.28 it was only God, not the heavenly court, who actually created humanity. However, it is arguable that the momentous decision to create humanity is envisaged as a joint act between God and his heavenly council, even if it was only God himself who finally enacted the decision.

9. *Humanity in the Image of God*

A second question raised by Gen. 1.26 is, What is the nature of 'the image of God' in which humanity is created?[34] Traditionally, for many centuries in Christian theology it was believed that the image implied a spiritual likeness between God and humanity.[35] However, the word *ṣelem*, 'image', is characteristically used of physical images in the Old Testament, in particular of pagan idols (cf. Num. 33.52; 2 Kgs 11.18 = 2 Chron. 23.17; Ezek. 7.20; Amos 5.26), but also of physical images of men (Ezek. 16.17; 23.14), or even of tumours and mice (1 Sam. 6.5, 11), and the cognate Aramaic word *ṣᵉlēm* occurs frequently of two different statues in Daniel (cf. Dan. 2.31, 32; 3.1, 2, etc.). Interestingly, both terms employed in Gen. 1.26, *ṣelem* and *dᵉmût*, traditionally rendered 'image' and 'likeness', are attested in Aramaic (*ṣlm* and *dmwtʾ*) with the meaning 'statue' in the ninth-century BCE bilingual Aramaic/Akkadian inscription from Tell Fekheryeh in Syria.[36] Moreover, the Hebrew word for 'image' is also employed by P of Seth's likeness to Adam (Gen. 5.3), following a repetition of Genesis 1's statement that humanity was created in the

34. For general surveys of this subject, see G.A. Jónsson, *The Image of God: Genesis 1:26-28 in a Century of Old Testament Research* (ConBOT, 26; Stockholm: Almqvist & Wiksell, 1988); W.R. Garr, *In his Own Likeness: Humanity, Divinity, and Monotheism* (CHANE, 15; Brill: Leiden, 2003); J.R. Middleton, *The Liberating Image: The* Imago Dei *in Genesis 1* (Grand Rapids, MI: Brazos Press, 2005).

35. Still maintained by H.H. Rowley, *The Faith of Israel* (London: SCM Press, 1956), p. 84.

36. A. Abou-Assaf, P. Bordreuil and A.R. Millard, *La statue de Tell Fekherye et son inscription assyro-araméenne* (Etudes assyriologiques, 7; Paris: Editions Recherche sur les civilisations, 1982), pp. 23-25, lines 1, 12, 15, 16 of the inscription.

likeness of God (Gen. 5.1), which further supports the notion that a physical likeness was included in P's concept. It is also noteworthy that the prophet Ezekiel, who was a priest as well as prophet at a time not so long before P, and whose theology has clear parallels with P's, similarly speaks of a resemblance between God and the appearance of man. As part of his call vision in Ezek. 1.26, he declares of God, 'and seated above the likeness of a throne was something that seemed like a human form' (the word *demût*, 'likeness', is used, as in Gen. 1.26). Accordingly, there are those who see the image as simply a physical one.[37] However, although the physical image may be primary, it is better to suppose that both a physical and spiritual likeness is envisaged, since the Hebrews saw humans as a psycho-physical totality.[38]

The usage of *ṣelem* elsewhere in Genesis and of *demût* in Ezekiel certainly tells against the view of those scholars who see the divine image in humanity as purely functional in nature, referring to humanity's domination over the natural world that is mentioned subsequently (Gen. 1.26, 28), an increasingly popular view in recent years.[39] Although the two ideas are closely associated, it is much more likely that humanity's rule over the world (Gen. 1.26-28) is actually a consequence of its being made in the image of God, not what the image itself meant.

The notion of humanity being made in the image of God seems to have its ultimate background in the idea attested in both Egypt and Mesopotamia according to which it was the king who was the image of a god, so that Gen. 1.26 would represent a democratization of this royal concept.[40] This would fit nicely with Ps. 8.5-8, which has some marked similarities with Gen. 1.26-28 in that it not only speaks of humanity's

37. Cf. P. Humbert, *Etudes sur le récit du Paradis et de la chute dans la Genèse* (Neuchâtel: Secrétariat de l'université, 1940), pp. 153-75.

38. So, e.g., H. Gunkel, *Genesis* (HKAT, 1.1; Göttingen: Vandenhoeck & Ruprecht, 3rd edn, 1910), p. 112, ET *Genesis* (trans. M.E. Biddle; Macon, GA: Mercer University Press, 1997), p. 113; Seebass, *Genesis*, I, p. 80.

39. Cf. Levenson, *Creation and the Persistence of Evil*, pp. 112-16; Middleton, *The Liberating Image, passim*; Arnold, *Genesis*, p. 45. Apparently this view is already found in John Chrysostom.

40. Cf. Schmidt, *Die Schöpfungsgeschichte der Priesterschrift*, pp. 127-49; H. Wildberger, 'Das Abbild Gottes. Gen. I, 26-30', *TZ* 21 (1965), pp. 245-59, 481-501, reprinted in *idem, Jahwe und sein Volk: Gesammelte Aufsätze zum Alten Testament. Zu seinem 70. Geburtstag am 2. Januar 1980* (ed. H.H. Schmid and O.H. Steck; TBü, 66; Munich: Chr. Kaiser, 1979), pp. 110-45. This democratization is already found in the third-millennium BCE Instruction for Merikare, which states regarding humans *vis-à-vis* a deity, 'They are his images, who came from his body'. See M. Lichtheim, *Ancient Egyptian Literature* (3 vols.; Berkeley: University of California Press, 1973-80 [1973]), I, p. 106.

closeness to the divine world ('You have made them little lower than the gods', v. 5) but also employs royal language to speak of its rule over the natural world ('You have crowned them with glory and honour. You have given them dominion over the works of your hands; you have put all things under their feet…', vv. 5-8).

10. *Humanity's Lordship over the World*

Following God's making of humanity in the image of God we are told that humans were told to subdue the earth and have dominion over the animal world (Gen. 1.26, 28). The verbs used here, *kābaš*, 'subdue', and *rādâ*, 'have dominion over', may at first sound rather harsh. Books and articles on this subject often cite an influential article of Lynn White as blaming Gen. 1.26-28 for the current ecological crisis and humanity's ruthless exploitation of nature.[41] I was therefore surprised to find that White nowhere directly refers to Gen. 1.26-28 in his article, though he clearly has the ideas of this passage in mind when he blames the ecological crisis on the Judaeo-Christian belief in humanity's duty to rule the world. However, immediately afterwards in Genesis God commands both humans and animals to exist on a vegetarian diet (Gen. 1.29-30), so it is clear that no ruthless dominion is intended at all but rather a benign rule over the natural order, what we should nowadays refer to as stewardship over creation.[42] It is only later, after the flood in Gen. 9.1-5, that humans are permitted to eat a diet of meat in P, provided the blood (the seat of the life) is avoided. The verb *rādâ*, meaning 'to have dominion over', alluded to above, refers to humanity's leadership over the animal world rather than ruthless exploitation of it. It should be noted that the verb *kābaš*, 'subdue', is not used with respect to the animals but to

41. L. White, 'The Historical Roots of our Ecologic Crisis', *Science* 155, no. 3767 (1967), pp. 1203-1207. White was not anti-Christian but a Churchman who preferred what he regarded as the Franciscan model of equality between humanity and animals rather than one lording it over the other.

42. Rightly emphasized in the studies of J. Barr, 'Man and Nature—The Ecological Controversy and the Old Testament', *BJRL* 55 (1972), pp. 9-32; J. Rogerson, 'The Creation Stories: Their Ecological Potential and Problems', in D.G. Horrell, C. Hunt, C. Southgate and F. Stavrakopoulou (eds.), *Ecological Hermeneutics: Biblical, Historical and Theological Perspectives* (London: T&T Clark International, 2010), pp. 21-31. Other important studies of this passage are U. Rütersworden, *Dominum Terrae: Studien zur Genese einer alttestamentlichen Vorstellung* (BZAW, 215; Berlin: W. de Gruyter, 1993), pp. 81-130; U. Neumann-Gersolke, *Herrschen in den Grenzen der Schöpfung: ein Beitrag zur alttestamentlichen Anthropologie am Beispiel von Psalm 8, Genesis 1 und verwandten Texten* (WMANT, 101; Neukirchen–Vluyn: Neukirchener Verlag, 2004).

the earth, and probably refers, as Barr argues, to humanity's task to till the soil.[43]

The picture of the world implied here is therefore one of paradisiacal peace and harmony in nature, with humanity (under God) in the lead. By virtue of the *Urzeit wird Endzeit* principle, according to which the first things correspond to the last things, this concept was later projected into the eschaton (cf. Isa. 11.6-9; 65.22).

11. *God's Resting on the Seventh Day and the Sabbath*

The Masoretic Hebrew text of Gen. 2.2 states that God completed his work of creation on the seventh day. However, the fact that God ceased from all his work on the seventh day, having finished his acts of creation on the sixth day, at first makes the reading in the Septuagint, Samaritan Pentateuch, Peshitta and the book of *Jubilees* (*Jub.* 2.16) seem more reasonable, according to which he completed his work on the sixth day. A minority of scholars therefore emend the Masoretic text to read 'sixth day'.[44] However, the concluding words of Gen. 1.31 imply that the events of day 6 were already over then, so it would be surprising for the sixth day to be returned to in Gen. 2.2. Rather, the concluding section in Gen. 2.1-3 should all be about the seventh day. This is reinforced by the fact that there are three parallel seven-word passages in Gen. 2.2-3a, each referring in the middle to the seventh day, and this parallelism would be lost if the first one is emended to allude rather to the sixth day. Moreover, U. (M.D.) Cassuto[45] has pointed out that there are a number of instances where the verb in question, the piel of *kālâ*, 'to finish', is used not in the sense of doing the final stages of something, but rather of putting an end to doing something (cf. Gen. 17.22; 24.19; Exod. 40.33). Accordingly, one may translate Gen. 2.2 as 'And on the seventh day God put an end to the work that he had done...' The meaning is thus analogous to God's cessation from work which is referred to immediately afterwards. S.R. Driver put it well over a century ago when he wrote that 'God formally brought His work to an end by not continuing it on the seventh day'.[46]

43.   Barr, 'Man and Nature', p. 22.

44.   Cf. NEB, REB, and see R.S. Hendel, *The Text of Genesis 1–11: Textual Studies and Critical Edition* (Oxford: Oxford University Press, 1998), pp. 32-34, for a defence of this rendering.

45.   U. (M.D.) Cassuto, *A Commentary on the Book of Genesis*. I. *From Adam to Noah, Genesis 1–VI 8* (trans. I. Abrahams; Jerusalem: Magnes Press, 1961), pp. 61-62.

46.   Driver, *The Book of Genesis*, p. 17.

Although the Sabbath did not become an institution for the Israelites till later on in the Pentateuch, the fact that already following the creation God rested on the seventh day provides an anticipation and justification of the Sabbath day. This is implicit in the reference to God blessing and sanctifying the seventh day in Gen. 2.3, while the use of the verb *šābat* to refer to God's ceasing from his work in Gen. 2.2, 3 is a clear echo of the Sabbath. (The verb *šābat* strictly means 'to cease' rather than 'to rest'.) That God's cessation from work on the seventh day provides the basis for the Sabbath is later made explicit in Exod. 20.11; 31.12-17. Philippe Guillaume is surely going too far, however, when he states that 'Gen. 1 [*sic*] is a sabbatogony more than a cosmogony'.[47] Important as the Sabbath is, the amount of space devoted to the preceding cosmogony—a whole lengthy chapter of Genesis 1—implies that this is the primary point of the narrative.

Although in P and subsequent Judaism the Sabbath is clearly a seventh-day affair, there is some evidence that the day might originally have been the day of the full moon. In Akkadian *šapattu* actually refers to the day of the full moon, the fifteenth day of a lunar month, which might then provide a ready explanation why the Sabbath is mentioned alongside the new moon in 2 Kgs 4.23; Isa. 1.13; Hos. 2.13; Amos 8.5. However, if this is so, the Sabbath day had already clearly become equivalent to the seventh day of the week by the time of the Priestly writer.

It has been suggested that there is a connection between God's resting on the seventh day in Genesis and the rest of the gods in the Sumerian work known as Enki and Ninmah,[48] as well as in the Akkadian Atrahasis epic and Enuma elish. However, although in both Genesis and the Mesopotamian works we read of divine rest following the creation of humanity, the cases are in fact totally different. In Genesis God alone rests on the seventh day as a result of his vast labours in creating the universe. In all the Mesopotamian works it is not the creator god/goddess who rests but the gods generally, who are spared future work as a result of the creation of humanity, who are to do their manual work instead.

47. P. Guillaume, *Land and Calendar: The Priestly Document from Genesis 1 to Joshua 18* (LHBOTS, 391; New York: T&T Clark International, 2009), p. 42.

48. See W.G. Lambert, 'A New Look at the Babylonian Background of Genesis', *JTS* 16 (1965), pp. 287-300 (297-98), reprinted in R.S. Hess and D.T. Tsumura (eds.), *'I Studied Inscriptions from before the Flood': Ancient Near Eastern, Literary, and Linguistic Approaches to Genesis 1–11* (Sources for Biblical and Theological Study, 4; Winona Lake, IN: Eisenbrauns, 1994), pp. 96-113 (107). For the text of Enki and Ninmah, see *The Electronic Text Corpus of Sumerian Literature* (accessible at http://etcsl.orinst.ox.ac.uk).

Moreover, this is a permanent rest for the gods generally, whereas in Genesis it is simply a one-day rest for the creator god. The matters seem entirely different.

12. *Is Genesis 2.4a the Conclusion of the P Account or the Introduction to the J Account?*

Are we to regard the words of Gen. 2.4a, 'These are the generations of the heavens and the earth when they were created', as the conclusion of the P account of Gen. 1.1–2.3 or the beginning of the J account of Gen. 2.4b–3.24? And are the words redactional or not? The traditional view has been that they are the conclusion of the P account, since the words employ the language of the previous P rather than the subsequent J account ('the heavens and the earth' rather than the 'the earth and the heavens' of 2.4b, and the verb *bārā*', which is repeatedly used in Gen. 1.1–2.3 but never in Gen. 2.4b–3.24).[49] This the first of a series of *tôlᵉdōt* ('generations') passages, the others being found in Gen. 5.1; 6.9; 10.1; 11.10, 27; 25.12, 19; 36.1, 4, 9; 37.2; Num. 3.1. All the other *tôlᵉdōt* passages, however, introduce rather than conclude the sections to which they relate, so in recent years a number of scholars, such as F.M. Cross, S. Tengström and M.A. Thomas, have argued against the earlier consensus, claiming that Gen. 2.4a should rather be seen as an introduction to the J account in Gen. 2.4b–4.26.[50] However, it is important to note that the expression 'the generations of the heavens and the earth' is much more appropriate for the content of P's account than it is of J's, since J focuses almost entirely on things going on in the earth, specifically life in the Garden of Eden, followed by the story of Cain and Abel and Cain's descendants, and has very little to say on heavenly matters at all. In contrast, P tells us of the creation of the firmament of heaven, and of the sun, moon and stars, which fits well the description of 'the generations of the heavens'. So the words of Gen. 2.4a are far more appropriate as the conclusion of the previous P narrative than as an introduction to the

49. Among those seeing Gen. 2.4a as P's original conclusion to his narrative are O.H. Steck, *Der Schöpfungsbericht der Priesterschrift* (Göttingen: Vandenhoeck & Ruprecht, 1975), pp. 241-43.

50. Cf. F.M. Cross, *Canaanite Myth and Hebrew Epic* (Cambridge, MA: Harvard University Press, 1973), p. 302; S. Tengström, *Die Toledotformel und die literarische Struktur der priesterlichen Erweiterungsschicht im Pentateuch* (ConBOT, 17; Lund: Gleerup, 1982), pp. 54-59; M.A. Thomas, *These are the Generations: Identity, Promise, and the 'Toledot' Formula* (LHBOTS, 551; New York: T&T Clark International, 2011), p. 127.

following J account. However, the words are probably redactional. As J.D. Levenson[51] has pointed out, the series of multiples of seven is disturbed if we include Gen. 2.4a in the original Priestly narrative, but is kept intact if we see the original story as comprising Gen. 1.1–2.3.[52] Furthermore, if the words of Gen. 2.4a are a redactional addition to P's account, rather than from P himself, this would explain both why the term *tôlᵉdōt* is used in a somewhat different sense from all the other *tôlᵉdōt* passages, which refer to literal rather than metaphorical generations, as well as why the passage does not introduce a new section, unlike all the others. It was not originally part of the same series, which will have begun with Gen. 5.1 ('This is the book of the generations of Adam'), but rather derivative from them.

13. *The Background of Genesis 1.1–2.4a*

A common view, argued in detail and almost for the first time by H. Gunkel in 1895,[53] has been that the account of creation in Genesis 1 represents a demythologization of the creation story in the so-called Babylonian Creation epic (Enuma elish). In both the universe has watery beginnings, in Enuma elish the chief Babylonian god Marduk defeating the sea monster Tiamat (whose name means 'sea'), who appears to be bovine in character, having udder and tail (Enuma elish 5.57, 59), making heaven and earth out of her, while in Genesis 1 God brings order to (rather than battles) the impersonal waters (called *tᵉhōm*, 'deep', in Gen. 1.2). However, although philologically cognate, the Hebrew word *tᵉhōm* is not directly dependent on Babylonian Tiamat, as the former's lack of a Hebrew feminine ending in *–ah* corresponding to Akkadian *-at*

---

51. Levenson, *Creation and the Persistence of Evil*, p. 67. Levenson further implies (pp. 67 and 165 n. 9) that there are 21 instances of *šāmayim* + *rāqîaᶜ* in Gen. 1.1–2.3 but 22 if one includes Gen. 2.4a. This, however, is based on faulty arithmetic: there are clearly 21 instances if one includes Gen. 2.4a (12 *šāmayim* + 9 *rāqîaᶜ*) but only 20 (11 *šāmayim* + 9 *rāqîaᶜ*) if one confines oneself to Gen. 1.1–2.3. But since *šāmayim* and *rāqîaᶜ* are not actually the same word, this is surely less significant than the fact that there are 21 instances of 'earth/land' in Gen. 1.1–2.3, for here it is the identical word throughout.

52. In seeing Gen. 2.4a as redactional but at the same time belonging with Gen. 1.1–2.3 I am in agreement with Schmidt, *Die Schöpfungsgeschichte der Priesterschrift*, pp. 91-93.

53. H. Gunkel, *Schöpfung und Chaos in Urzeit und Endzeit* (Göttingen: Vandenhoeck & Ruprecht, 1895), ET *Creation and Chaos in the Primeval Era and the Eschaton: A Religio-Historical Study of Genesis 1 and Revelation 12* (trans. K.W. Whitney, Jr; Grand Rapids, MI: Eerdmans, 2006).

shows (although the Hebrew word is feminine). The form of the Hebrew word *t^ehōm*, is moreover, already attested hundreds of years earlier at Ugarit as *thm* (cf. *KTU* 1.100.1).[54]

Furthermore, it is clear from the discovery of the Ugaritic texts from 1929 onwards (which were unknown to Gunkel) that the divine conflict with the dragon and the sea in the Old Testament,[55] of which Genesis 1 must represent a demythologization, reflects a Canaanite rather than Babylonian myth. For example, in Ps. 74.14 the sea monster defeated at creation is called Leviathan and has more than one head, which corresponds to a seven-headed sea serpent or dragon Litan (or Lotan), apparently an associate of Yam, defeated by Baal in Ugaritic myth (*KTU* 1.5.I.1-3; cf. *KTU* 1.3.III.40-42). Elsewhere in the Old Testament the sea monster defeated at creation is called Rahab (Ps. 89.11 [ET 10]; Job 26.12), and again this is also clearly a masculine creature like Leviathan and appears to be another name for it, since both are called 'the twisting serpent' (Job 26.12-13; cf. Isa. 27.1; *KTU* 1.5.I.1), and so clearly cannot be regarded as simply an appropriation from the Babylonian female bovine sea monster Tiamat. The biblical sea monster is also spoken of as *tannîn*, 'dragon' (e.g. Isa. 27.1; 51.9; Job 7.12; cf. Ps. 74.13), which again reflects Leviathan's description as *tnn* in Ugaritic (*KTU* 1.3.III.40).

Moreover, a point that tends to be overlooked is that whereas in Enuma elish Marduk makes heaven out of one half and earth out of the other half of Tiamat, in Genesis 1 the earth (in inchoate state) is already present when God controls the waters. The same is true in connection with God's defeat of the sea monster Leviathan (cf. Ps. 74.12-14).

Thorkild Jacobsen[56] conjectured that Marduk's victory over Tiamat may be derived from Baal's victory over Yam, the myth having been brought eastwards by the Amorites. He notes that the theme of the

---

54.   The fact that *t^ehōm* regularly lacks the definite article (except two rather late examples of the plural in Isa. 63.13; Ps. 106.9) would fit an originally mythological figure, and the fairly early poem in Gen. 49.25 (= Deut. 33.13) refers to 'blessings of the deep (*t^ehōm*) that lies beneath', suggesting that the Israelites were familiar with the idea of an animalic figure embodying the *t^ehōm*, since the verb 'to lie' (*rābaṣ*) is elsewhere used especially in connection with animals. However, this mythological figure would in my view have been Canaanite rather than Babylonian.

55.   The attempts of Tsumura, *Creation and Destruction*, pp. 191-95, and R.S. Watson, *Chaos Uncreated: A Reassessment of the Theme of "Chaos" in the Hebrew Bible* (BZAW, 341; Berlin: W. de Gruyter, 2005), to deny all traces in the Old Testament of a connection between creation and a divine conflict with the dragon and sea is forced. See, e.g., Pss. 74.12-17; 89.10-15 [ET 9-14]; 104.6-9.

56.   T. Jacobsen, 'The Battle between Marduk and Tiamat', *JAOS* 88 (1968), pp. 104-108.

victory of a god using the power of a thunderstorm over the sea is more appropriate to the Levant than to Mesopotamia. As Mark Smith notes,[57] this view perhaps now finds support in an eighteenth-century BCE text from Mari which speaks of Hadad defeating Tiamat. Hadad declared to Zimri-Lim, 'the weapons with which I battled against Sea (*têmtum*) I gave to you'.[58] It remains a problem that the Ugaritic text of Baal's victory over Yam does not appear to be connected with the creation, unlike Marduk's victory over Tiamat, but one may conjecture that there was a Canaanite version of the myth which did so associate it (El creating the world and Baal then subduing the waters), and these may have been drawn on by the biblical writers, eventually being demythologized in Genesis 1.[59]

However, for the more immediate background to Genesis 1 we should probably turn to Psalm 104, where the order of creation is closer than it is with Enuma elish:

Psalm 104		Genesis 1
vv. 1-4	Creation of heaven and earth	Cf. vv. 1-5
vv. 5-9	Waters pushed back	Cf. vv. 6-10
vv. 10-13	Waters put to beneficial use	Implicit in vv. 6-10
vv. 14-18	Creation of vegetation	Cf. vv. 11-12
vv. 19-23	Creation of heavenly luminaries	Cf. vv. 14-18
vv. 24-26	Creation of sea creatures	Cf. vv. 20-22
vv. 27-30	Creation of living creatures	Cf. vv. 24-31

There are also many striking linguistic parallels between the two passages, which it is not possible to spell out in detail here.[60] Just to cite one example, the expression *lemô‘adîm*, 'for seasons', is found in the Old Testament only in Ps. 104.19 and Gen. 1.14, in both cases with respect to the role of the heavenly luminaries.

That it is Genesis 1 which is dependent on Psalm 104, rather than the other way round,[61] is supported, among other things, by the fact that the

---

57. M.S. Smith, *The Ugaritic Baal Cycle*. I. *Introduction with Text, Translation and Commentary on KTU 1.1–1.2* (VTSup, 55; Leiden: Brill, 1995), pp. 111-12.

58. Cf. J.M. Durand, 'Le mythologème du combat entre le dieu de l'orage et la mer en Mésopotamie', *Mari: Annales de recherches interdisciplinaires* 7 (1993), pp. 41-61 (45).

59. Cf. Day, *God's Conflict with the Dragon and the Sea*, Chapter 1.

60. For these parallels see the article by van der Voort in the next footnote.

61. For a detailed presentation of the evidence that Gen. 1 is dependent on Ps. 104, see A. van der Voort, 'Genèse I, 1 à II, 4a et le Psaume 104', *RB* 58 (1951), pp. 321-47, *contra* P. Humbert, 'La relation de Genèse 1 et du Psaume 104 avec la liturgie du Nouvel-An israélite', *RHPR* 15 (1935), pp. 1-27.

latter is more mythological. Thus, Ps. 104.7 actually alludes to God's battle with the sea, whereas in Gen. 1.6-10 God's control of the waters is simply presented as a job of work. Again, Ps. 104.26 speaks of God's creation of Leviathan, using a highly mythological name, whereas Gen. 1.21 refers in demythologized terms of God's creation of 'great sea monsters'. Furthermore, Gen. 1.24 significantly uses a rare form of the word for 'beasts' (*hay^{e}tô*), attested elsewhere in the Hebrew Bible only in poetry, including Ps. 104.11, 20, suggesting that a poetic source underlies Genesis 1, presumably Psalm 104. Another point to note is that Ps. 104.9 speaks of God controlling the waters so that they will never cover the earth again. From the context this clearly refers to the control of the waters at the time of creation, not Noah's flood.[62] In view of that, it seems impossible to suppose that Psalm 104 is dependent on Genesis, or the writer would have been familiar with the story of Noah's flood there, where the waters do cover the earth again.

Moreover, Ps. 104.6 uses the word *t^{e}hōm* to denote the primaeval waters, suggesting that this rather than Babylonian mythology is the immediate source of the allusion in Gen. 1.2. Again, as already mentioned above, the reference in Psalm 104 to God's riding on the wings of the wind at the time of the conflict with the sea explains Gen. 1.2's allusion to the wind of God sweeping over the deep, which, as noted earlier, is similarly birdlike language.

Although the chaos-conflict element in Psalm 104 probably depends on Canaanite rather than Babylonian myth, a significant part of the rest of Psalm 104 (esp. vv. 20-30) is dependent on the fourteenth-century BCE Egyptian pharaoh Akhenaten's Hymn to the Sun god Aten. As I have recently pointed out,[63] these parallels almost all come in the same order:

> Ps. 104.20-21, cf. Akhenaten lines 27-37: when darkness comes the lions leave their dens.
> Ps. 104.22, cf. Akhenaten lines 38-45: at sunrise people go to work.
> Ps. 104.24, cf. Akhenaten lines 76-82: how manifold are the deity's works!
> Ps.104.26, cf. Akhenaten lines 53-58: ships go their way and the deity frolics with a sea creature.
> Ps. 104.27-28, cf. Akhenaten lines 85-86: the deity provides food for all.
> Ps. 104.29-30, cf. Akhenaten lines 127-28: the deity is the source of life and death.

62. *Contra* D.G. Barker, 'The Waters of the Earth: An Exegetical Study of Psalm 104:1-9', *Grace Theological Journal* 7 (1986), pp. 57-80.
63. J. Day, 'Psalm 104 and Akhenaten's Hymn to the Sun', in S. Gillingham (ed.), *Jewish and Christian Approaches to the Psalms: Conflict and Convergence* (Oxford: Oxford University Press, 2013), pp. 211-28.

Consequently, through Ps. 104 an ultimately Egyptian source partly lies behind Genesis 1, probably mediated to Israel by the Canaanites,[64] and this is still reflected in Genesis 1 in the creation of the sun on day 4, sea creatures on day 5, and the provision of food on day 6.

64. We have also seen above that humanity made in the image of God also has a possible Egyptian as well as Babylonian background. However, the attempt of J. Atwell, 'An Egyptian Source for Genesis 1', *JTS* 51 (2000), pp. 441-77, to find a much more extensive influence from Egypt on Gen. 1 seems unjustified.

Chapter 2

PROBLEMS IN THE INTERPRETATION
OF THE STORY OF THE GARDEN OF EDEN

1. *Introduction*

The story of the Garden of Eden is one of the best-known narratives
of the Old Testament and has had a great impact on Western culture.
No other story in the Old Testament, for example, has been represented
so many times in Christian art.[1] However, the story is the subject of a
number of popular misconceptions on the part of ordinary readers, as
well as presenting many disputed points of interpretation for the scholar.
For example, the ordinary reader is prone to think of the story as that of
Adam and Eve without further ado, not realizing that the original Hebrew
text never speaks of Adam but simply 'the man'. It is also commonly
assumed that it was Satan who tempted Eve to eat of the forbidden fruit,
and that the latter is to be equated with an apple. However, both these
understandings represent cases of later interpretation that are not in the
biblical text. For the scholar, disputed points include the precise location
of the Garden of Eden (assuming the writer intended one), the question
why the first couple did not die on the day they ate of the forbidden fruit
as God had declared, the meaning of the knowledge of good and evil
which the humans acquired, the background of the serpent, whether the
first humans are deemed to be immortal or mortal while in the garden,
and the question whether the expulsion from Eden is to be understood as
an allegory of the Jewish exile in Babylon. All these and many other
questions will be considered in this chapter.

2. *The Garden of Eden Story as a J Narrative*

The account in Gen. 2.4b–3.24 is often spoken of as the second Creation
account in Genesis, following on that of P in Gen. 1.1–2.4a. This is true,
but the second account very much centres on the Garden of Eden and the

---

1. So J. Snyder, 'Jan van Eyck and Adam's Apple', *Art Bulletin* 58 (1976),
pp. 511-15 (511).

first man and woman, and apart from that there is little on the creation of the world more generally, referred to as 'the earth and the heavens' rather than P's 'the heavens and the earth' (cf. Gen. 2.4b-6).

This second narrative is generally attributed to the Yahwist (J) source, sometimes spoken of as non-P by those who do not see it as one continuous source throughout the Tetrateuch. In common with other J stories in Genesis 1–11, it is replete with anthropomorphisms (Gen. 2.7; 3.8; cf. 7.17; 11.5) and word plays (Gen. 2.7; 2 25–3.1; 3.20; cf. 4.1; 5.29; 11.9), is concerned with the transcendence of divine/human boundaries (Gen. 3.5, 22; cf. 6.1-4; 11.4), and ends with an expulsion (Gen. 3.23-24; cf. 4.13-16; 11.7-9). In addition, the Garden of Eden narrative uses the name Yahweh for the deity. But unlike everywhere else in Genesis (and indeed elsewhere in the Pentateuch except Exod. 9.30), we find throughout Gen. 2.4b–3.24 the joint form Yahweh Elohim rather than simply Yahweh. How are we to explain that? Various views have been suggested.[2] Although it has sometimes been suggested that the joint name reflects the combination of two different accounts in the narrative,[3] it seems more natural to suppose that since J uses the name Yahweh everywhere else, this was what the text originally had here, but that as it provided the first instances of the name Yahweh, a later redactor added Elohim to Yahweh throughout this narrative so as to make perfectly clear in the polytheistic environment of the ancient world that Yahweh was the same deity as Elohim referred to in the previous narrative of Gen. 1.1–2.4a.[4]

3. *The Origin of the Names Eden and Paradise*

What does the name Eden mean? In the past it was sometimes supposed that we have here a word cognate with Sumerian *edin* and Akkadian *edinu*, meaning 'steppe, plain, desert', a view first suggested by Friedrich Delitzsch.[5] However, not only does this meaning seem inappropriate in

---

2. See the survey in P.J. Titus, *The Second Story of Creation (Gen 2:4–3:24): A Prologue to the Concept of the Enneateuch?* (European University Studies, 23.912; Frankfurt: Peter Lang, 2011), pp. 144-53.

3. E.g. K. Budde, *Die biblische Urgeschichte (Gen. 1–12,5)* (Giessen: J. Ricker, 1883), pp. 233-34, and others since.

4. Cf. U. (M.D.) Cassuto, *A Commentary on the Book of Genesis*. I. *From Adam to Noah, Genesis 1–VI 8* (trans. I. Abrahams; Jerusalem: Magnes Press, 1961), p. 88, among others.

5. Cf. Friedrich Delitzsch, *Wo lag das Paradies?* (Leipzig: J.C. Hinrichs, 1881), pp. 4, 6, 79-80; A.H. Sayce, 'Eden', in J. Hastings (ed), *Dictionary of the Bible*

view of the Garden of Eden's association elsewhere with fertility (cf. Gen. 13.10; Isa. 51.3; Ezek. 31.16; Joel 2.3) and a mountain (Ezek. 28.14, 16), but it has been noted by A.R. Millard[6] that the Akkadian word *edinu* is *extremely* rare, occurring only once in a syllabary, unlike other Akkadian loan words which we know were actually taken up into Hebrew. In addition, there is no evidence that the Akkadian word was preceded by an ayin (Sumerian does not have an ayin). Accordingly, this meaning seems unlikely. More recently, both A.R. Millard and J.C. Greenfield[7] have proposed that Eden means 'luxury' or 'delight'. This root ʿ*dn* is attested elsewhere in Biblical Hebrew (e.g. ʿ*ednâ*, 'delight', ʿ*ēdānîm*, 'luxury dainties', 'delights') and it is the meaning assigned to Eden by the Septuagint and Vulgate translations (Greek *truphē* and Latin *voluptas* respectively; Gen. 2.15; 3.23). Moreover, the verbal root ʿ*dn* is attested in Aramaic in the ninth-century BCE bilingual Aramaic/ Akkadian Tell Fekheryeh inscription with regard to the god Hadad, provider of water, 'who makes all lands luxuriant' (*mʿdn mt kln*;[8] cf. too Baal at Ugarit, *KTU* 1.4.V.6-7). This fits in well with Gen. 13.10 and Ezek. 31.16, where the Garden of the Lord is expressly described as 'well watered' and Isa. 51.3 and Joel 2.3, where the Garden of the Lord/ Eden is contrasted with a desolate wilderness/desert.

It has long been customary to refer to the Garden of Eden as Paradise. This term for Eden is first attested in the Greek Septuagint translation in the third century BCE, where it regularly translates the Hebrew word *gan*, 'garden', in this narrative, as well as occurring in some other passages in the Septuagint. The form of the word in Greek, as also in Hebrew (*pardēs*, Neh. 2.8; Eccles. 2.5; Song 4.13), reflects the Median spelling *paridaiza* rather than the Old Persian *paridaida*, and was taken over into both languages during the Persian period. Literally the Old

(5 vols.; Edinburgh: T. & T. Clark, 1898–1904 [1898]), I, pp. 643-44 (643), though he admits that it came to mean 'delight' in Hebrew; E.A. Speiser, *Genesis* (AB, 1; Garden City, NY: Doubleday, 1964), pp. 16, 19.

6. A.R. Millard, 'The Etymology of Eden', *VT* 34 (1984), pp. 103-106.

7. Millard, 'The Etymology of Eden'; J.C. Greenfield, 'A Touch of Eden', in *Acta Orientalia J. Duchesne-Guillemin emerito oblata* (Acta Iranica, 23; Leiden: Brill, 1984), pp. 219-24, reprinted in ʿ*Al Kanfei Yonah: Collected Studies of Jonas C. Greenfield* (ed. S.M. Paul, M.E. Stone and A. Pinnick; 2 vols.; Leiden: Brill; Jerusalem: Magnes Press, 2001), II, pp. 750-55.

8. A. Abou-Assaf, P. Bordreuil and A.R. Millard, *La statue de Tell Fekherye et son inscription assyro-araméenne* (Etudes assyriologiques, 7; Paris: Editions Recherche sur les civilisations, 1982), pp. 23-24, lines 4-5 of the Aramaic inscription.

Persian/Median word means 'surrounding wall', and it was used to denote a walled orchard. The Septuagint probably preferred this term for the Garden of Eden rather than the ordinary Greek word *kēpos*, 'garden', because of its more grandiose associations.[9] By the principle whereby the last things return to the state of the first things (*Urzeit wird Endzeit*), Paradise eventually became a term for heaven, as in Luke 23.43, where Jesus says to the thief on the cross, 'Truly, I tell you, today you will be with me in Paradise', and in 2 Cor. 12.4 for the third heaven (cf. 2 Cor. 12.2). In Rev. 2.7 we read of the tree of life in the heavenly Paradise, and for this idea, without the word Paradise, see Rev. 22.2, 14, 19.

4. *The Location of Eden*

Where was the Garden of Eden? I shall refrain from discussing here the crazier ideas that have sometimes been suggested, such as the Mormon view (going back to its founder Joseph Smith) which locates it in Jackson Co, Missouri, or the view of William R. Warren, a former President of Boston University, that it is to be located at the North Pole,[10] and will confine myself to serious scholarly views.

Although for modern readers the Garden of Eden is not a literal place, for the ancients it surely was, in view of the precise geographical indications given in Gen. 2.10-14. These geographical data are sufficient to refute the thesis of Claus Westermann[11] that the Yahwist did not have some particular location in mind. Its location at the source of the rivers

9. For more on the origins of the word Paradise, see J.N. Bremmer, 'Paradise: From Persia, via Greece, into the *Septuagint*', in G.P. Luttikhuizen (ed.), *Paradise Interpreted: Representations of Biblical Paradise in Judaism and Christianity* (Themes in Biblical Narrative, 2; Leiden: Brill, 1999), pp. 1-20.

10. For these two views see B. Wilensky-Lanford, *Paradise Lust: Searching for the Garden of Eden* (New York: Grove Press, 2011), pp. 132-38, 221-35. Other works dealing with the history of attempts to locate the Garden of Eden include A. Scafi, *Mapping Paradise: A History of Heaven on Earth* (London: British Library, 2006), and the relevant parts of J. Delumeau, *Une histoire du Paradis: le jardin des délices* (Paris: Fayard, 1992), ET *History of Paradise: The Garden of Eden in Myth and Tradition* (trans. M. O'Connell; New York: Continuum, 1995). See too E.H. Cline, *From Eden to Exile: Unravelling Mysteries of the Bible from Eden to Exile* (Washington, DC: National Geographic, 2007), pp. 1-15, with endnotes on pp. 196-99.

11. C. Westermann, *Genesis 1–11* (BKAT, 1.1; Neukirchen–Vluyn: Neukirchener Verlag, 1974), p. 294, ET *Genesis 1–11: A Commentary* (trans. J.J. Scullion; London: SPCK, 1984), pp. 215-16.

Tigris ('which flows east of Assyria'[12]) and Euphrates suggests either Armenia (at their western end) or near the Persian gulf (at their eastern end). Sometimes modern scholars have presumed it to be located at the Persian gulf end of the Tigris and Euphrates, a view advocated already in the sixteenth century by John Calvin and followed later by scholars such as A.H. Sayce, E.A. Speiser and M. Dietrich.[13] The Mesopotamian paradise, Dilmun, has on occasion been appealed to, but it is now generally accepted that this was located on the island of Bahrain in the Persian gulf, not on the mainland, whereas nothing in Genesis 2 suggests that the Garden of Eden was set on an island. Furthermore, Gen. 2.10 states that the river flowing from Eden became four headwaters ($r\bar{a}$'$\check{s}\hat{i}m$), indicating that the rivers were flowing from there. Since waters flow down, not up, the indications are that the mountainous western end of the rivers in Armenia is in mind, not the flat end near the Persian gulf in the east.[14]

12.   The Hebrew word here in Gen. 2.14 is '*aššûr*. Scholars have debated whether this means Assyria or the city of Asshur. In favour of the former is the fact that on every other occasion within the Hebrew Bible '*aššûr* undoubtedly means Assyria, as well as the fact that Asshur is not included in J's list of Assyrian cities in Gen. 10.11-12, which would be surprising if Asshur was thought worthy of special mention in Gen. 2.14. Nor is it mentioned anywhere else in the Old Testament. It should be borne in mind that the city of Asshur was in decline at the likely time of J, c. 800 BCE. The fact that the Tigris was not to the east of all of Assyria (but only some of it), unlike the city of Asshur, is not a significant counter-argument, since, as will become clear from our discussion, not all of Gen. 2.10-14 is geographically accurate.

13.   J. Calvin, *Commentaries on the First Book of Moses Called Genesis* (trans. J. King; 2 vols.; Calvin Translation Society; Edinburgh: The Edinburgh Printing Co., 1847–60 [1847]), I, pp. 118-24 (with Calvin's map on p. 120); Sayce, 'Eden', pp. 643-44; E.A. Speiser, 'The Rivers of Paradise', in R. von Kienle, A. Moortgat, H. Otten, E. von Schuler and W. Zaumseil (eds.), *Festschrift Johannes Friedrich* (Heidelberg: Carl Winter, Universitätsverlag, 1959), pp. 473-85, reprinted in J.J. Finkelstein and M. Greenberg (eds.), *Oriental and Biblical Studies: Collected Writings of E.A. Speiser* (Philadelphia: University of Pennsylvania Press, 1967), pp. 23-34; *idem, Genesis*, p. 20; M. Dietrich, 'Das biblische Paradies und der babylonische Tempelgarten: Überlegungen zur Lage des Garten Eden', in B. Janowski and B. Ego (eds.), *Das biblische Weltbild und seine altorientalischen Kontexte* (Tübingen: Mohr Siebeck, 2001), pp. 281-323 (302-20). On the other hand, Delitzsch, *Wo lag das Paradies?*, *passim*, located Eden further inland, between the Tigris and Euphrates in between Baghdad and Babylon.

14.   Advocates of Armenia include A. Calmet, *Commentaire litteral sur tous les livres de l'Ancien et du Nouveau Testament* (16 vols.; Paris: Pierre Emery, 2nd edn, 1709–30 [1715]), I, p. 57 (though he wrongly equates it with biblical Beth-Eden); P. Haupt, 'Wo lag das Paradies?', in *Ueber Land und Meer* 15 (1894–95), pp. 3-8 (7-8); Driver, *Genesis*, pp. 59-60; G. von Rad, *Das erste Buch Mose: Genesis* (ATD,

Moreover, in keeping with this, Ezek. 28.14, 16 actually sets Eden on a mountain (though this doubtless had Mt Lebanon in mind; cf. Ezek. 31.8, 16 and see below).

Interestingly, we have evidence that the supreme Canaanite god El—equated with Yahweh in the Old Testament—was thought of as dwelling at the source of the river Euphrates (called the Mala river) in the Hittite-Canaanite Elkunirsha myth[15] (cf. the Ugaritic texts, where El, who resides on a mountain, lives a long way away at the source the rivers; e.g. *KTU* 1.6.I.33). Sometimes in the Old Testament the Garden of Eden is called 'the Garden of the Lord' (Gen. 13.10; Isa. 51.3) or 'the Garden of God' (Ezek. 31.9), which would make sense if it was thought of as his dwelling place (cf. God taking a stroll in the garden in Gen. 3.8). Moreover, El was not only the supreme god, but also the creator god and wise, which would fit in with the presence of the themes of creation and wisdom in Genesis 2–3. (Compare too Job 15.7-8, where the first man was said to be in the council of God, the latter concept deriving from El's heavenly court dwelling on his sacred mountain.)

But what of the other two rivers, the Gihon and the Pishon? Interestingly, Genesis 2 feels the need to say a bit more about them, which indicates that they were also less familiar to the ancient Israelites and not just to us. The river Gihon is surely the Nile, since it is stated that it 'flows around the whole land of Kush (Nubia)' (Gen. 2.13). In addition to being the natural interpretation of the text, this view also has the support of ancient Jewish sources, since Gihon explicitly denotes the Nile in LXX Jer. 2.18; Ecclus 24.27 (Greek); Genesis Apocryphon; and Josephus, *Ant.* 1.1.3. There is confused geography here, of course, since the Nile does not actually join up with the Tigris and Euphrates, but we should recall that Pausanias (*Description of Greece* 2.5.3) reports the 'story that the Nile is the Euphrates, which disappears into a marsh, rises again beyond Ethiopia and becomes the Nile'! Again, Arrian (*Anabasis Alexandria* 6.1.2-6) reports that when he was in India Alexander the Great at first believed that he had found the upper course of the Nile,

24; Göttingen: Vandenhoeck & Ruprecht, 1958), p. 64, ET *Genesis* (OTL; London: SCM, 2nd edn, 1963), p. 77 (von Rad has a question mark by Armenia, but is certain Eden is in the north); E. Lipiński, 'El's Abode: Mythological Traditions Related to Mount Hermon and to the Mountains of Armenia', *OLP* 2 (1971), pp. 13-69 (54).

15. For the Elkunirsha myth, see, for convenience, *ANET*, p. 519, or *COS* 1, p. 149. This was originally published by H. Otten, 'Ein kanaanäischer Mythus aus Boğazköy', *MIO* 1 (1953), pp. 125-50, and there was also a translation by H. Hoffner, 'The Elkunirsa Myth Reconsidered', *Revue hittite et asianique* 23 (1965), pp. 5-16.

when it was in fact the Indus (cf. Strabo, *Geography* 15.1.25). The view
that Kush here rather stands for the Kassites, thus facilitating the Gihon
being a river in Mesopotamia, western Iran[16] or a Babylonian canal,[17] is
improbable. If this unusual meaning were really intended, one feels a
way would have been found to distinguish the name from the well-
known Kush. As for the river Pishon, this is not the Ganges (Josephus,
Ant. 1.1.3; a view dominant from Augustine till the Renaissance[18]) or the
Indus,[19] a river in western Iran,[20] or even a Babylonian canal.[21] None of
these fit the biblical text, which states that the Pishon 'flows around the
whole land of Havilah, where there is gold...', which seems to denote
the southern part of the Arabian peninsula (lit. 'sand land', cf. Khawlan
in Yemen). It seems most likely, therefore, that this represents the
Persian gulf/Indian ocean/Red Sea, misconceived as a river.[22] We have
evidence that the Persian gulf was so regarded.

Gihon is also used in the Old Testament as the name of the spring in
Jerusalem (1 Kgs 1.33, 38, 45; 2 Chron. 32.30; 33.14). Because of this a
number of scholars have recently located Eden in Jerusalem.[23] However,

---

16. Cf. Speiser, 'The Rivers of Paradise', pp. 479-82, repr. pp. 31-34, who
regards it as the river Kerkha or Diyala; Dietrich, 'Das biblische Paradies', pp. 313-
14, followed by A. van der Kooij, 'The Story of Paradise in the Light of Mesopotamian Culture and Literature', in K.J. Dell, G.I. Davies and Y.V. Koh (eds.), *Genesis,
Isaiah and Psalms: A Festschrift to Honour Professor John Emerton for his Eightieth
Birthday* (VTSup, 135; Leiden: Brill, 2010), pp. 1-22 (13), regards it as the river
Kerkha.

17. Cf. Delitzsch, *Wo lag das Paradies?*, pp. 75-76, who equated it with the
Shatt en-Nil, which he regarded as the ancient Arahtu.

18. Scafi, *Mapping Paradise*, p. 13.

19. Cf. Hippolytus, *Chronicle* (Codex Matritensis) 237.1; Cosmas Indicopleustes,
Christian Topography 2.81, who presents this as one alternative, the other being the
Ganges; A. Dillmann, *Die Genesis* (Kurzgefasstes exegetisches Handbuch zum
Alten Testament; Leipzig: S. Hirzel, 5th edn, 1886), p. 60.

20. Speiser, 'The Rivers of Paradise', pp. 479-82, repr. pp. 31-34, regards it as
either the river Kerkha, Karun or Wadi er-Rumma; Dietrich, 'Das biblische
Paradies', pp. 308-12, followed by van der Kooij, 'The Story of Paradise', p. 13,
regards it as the river Karun.

21. Delitzsch, *Wo lag das Paradies?*, pp. 71, 77 (the Pallakopas canal).

22. Cf. Haupt, 'Wo lag das Paradies?', pp. 6-7; Driver, *Genesis*, pp. 59-60;
T. Stordalen, *Echoes of Eden: Genesis 2–3 and Symbolism of the Eden Garden in
Biblical Hebrew Literature* (Contributions to Biblical Exegesis and Theology, 25;
Leuven: Peeters, 2000), p. 279.

23. Cf. L.E. Stager, 'Jerusalem and the Garden of Eden', in B.A. Levine, P.J.
King, J. Naveh and E. Stern (eds.), *Eretz-Israel* 26 (Frank Moore Cross Volume;
Jerusalem: Israel Exploration Society, 1999), pp. 183*-94*, with popular adaptation

this is impossible, since, as we have seen above, Gen. 2.13 states that the Gihon 'flows around the whole land of Kush', that is, Nubia. Although having faulty geographical knowledge, the Israelites were fully aware that Jerusalem did not link up with the Tigris and Euphrates, anymore than it linked up with the likely identification of the Pishon noted above. Nevertheless, the name Gihon coheres with a number of other pieces of evidence indicating that Zion could be conceived in paradisiacal terms.[24]

While not arguing for the location of Eden in Jerusalem, Gordon Wenham nevertheless claims that the Garden of Eden is depicted as a temple.[25] It is true that the Garden was undoubtedly seen as the divine dwelling place (elsewhere in the Old Testament called the Garden of God and the Mountain of God), which coheres with its location by the source of rivers (cf. El), and the cherubim mentioned at the end of the story also functioned as divine guardians in the Jerusalem temple and elsewhere. However, it seems going too far to describe it as an actual temple: there is no mention of the word 'temple' or equivalent term or of any building on the site, no allusion to an altar or other cultic appurtenances apart from the cherubim, and no reference to worshippers. And

in L.E. Stager, 'Jerusalem as Eden', *BARev* 20.3 (May/June 2000), pp. 37-47, 66. However, in his article in the Stager Festschrift, R.S. Hendel, 'Other Edens', in J.D. Schloen (ed.), *Exploring the Long Durée: Essays in Honor of Lawrence E. Stager* (Winona Lake, IN: Eisenbrauns, 2008), pp. 185-89, notes that the relationship between Eden and Jerusalem is more complicated than Stager implies. The view that Eden is Jerusalem was further publicized in a British TV programme in 2011 by Francesca Stavrakopoulou entitled 'The Real Garden of Eden' on BBC 2 (downloadable through BBC i-Player). In addition M. Ottosson, 'Eden and the Land of Promise', in J.A. Emerton (ed.), *Congress Volume: Jerusalem 1986* (VTSup, 40; Leiden: Brill, 1986), pp. 177-86, equated Eden with the Holy Land as a whole, bordered on the north-east side by the Tigris and Euphrates and on the south-west by the Pishon and Gihon, which he identified with the Nile and the River of Egypt (the Naḥal Besor, south of Gaza) respectively. However, these latter identifications do not cohere with the data given in the biblical text.

24. Cf. J.D. Levenson, *Sinai and Zion: An Entry into the Jewish Bible* (Minneapolis: Winston, 1985), pp. 128-32.

25. G.J. Wenham, 'Sanctuary Symbolism in the Garden of Eden Story', in *Proceedings of the Ninth World Congress of Jewish Studies, Division A: The Period of the Bible* (Jerusalem: World Union of Jewish Studies, 1985), pp. 19-25, reprinted in R.S. Hess and D.T. Tsumura (eds.), *"I Studied Inscriptions from before the Flood": Ancient Near Eastern, Literary, and Linguistic Approaches to Genesis 1–11* (Sources for Biblical and Theological Study, 4; Winona Lake, IN: Eisenbrauns, 1994), pp. 399-404. So too P.T. Lanfer, *Remembering Eden: The Reception History of Genesis 3:22-24* (New York: Oxford University Press, 2012), pp. 127-57, though curiously he fails to mention Wenham.

Wenham's attempt to relate the reference to the man's tilling the soil
(ʿbd) in Gen. 2.15 with the cultic meaning of ʿbd, 'to serve', found elsewhere in the Old Testament seems overly midrashic.

However, returning to the country of location of the Garden of Eden,
we must accept that there was also an alternative tradition that Eden was
rather to be located in Phoenicia. Ezekiel 28.13 speaks of the king of
Tyre as having been in Eden, Ezek. 31.8 speaks of cedars in the Garden
of God, and Ezek. 31.16 similarly speaks of 'all the trees of Eden, the
choice and best of Lebanon'. We should probably compare the cedar
forest and dwelling of the Anunnaki in the Gilgamesh epic.[26] Since it was
not a Mesopotamian concept that gods dwelt on mountains, this must
reflect an underlying north-west Semitic concept.

5. *Adam [sic] and Eve*

People often speak of the human subjects of the story as Adam and Eve.
However, the Hebrew text repeatedly speaks not of Adam but of
hāʾādām, 'the man', in Gen. 2.7, 8, 15, 16, 21, 22 (×2), 23, 24; 3.8, 9, 12,
20, 22, 24, and only three times in the Masoretic text do we have 'Adam'
(in Gen. 2.20; 3.17, 21).[27] However, in these latter three instances it
is merely a matter of a vowel point in lᵉʾādām, 'to Adam', and since the
Masoretic text continues to speak of 'the man' (haʾādām) after this
(Gen. 3.22, 24), it is natural to suppose these also originally read lāʾādām,
'to the man'. This supposition is rightly followed in most modern Bible
translations (in contrast to the earlier AV, RV, RSV), though the NEB
still renders Adam in Gen. 3.21, and the NIV not only retains Adam in
both Gen. 3.17 and 3.21 but even introduces it in one place where the
Masoretic text has 'the man' (Gen. 3.20). In this regard it is following
the AV. It is in Gen. 4.25 that we first find Adam employed as a personal
name in J,[28] doubtless reflecting the fact that there were now other men

---

26. Lipiński, 'El's Abode', pp. 18-19. See OB IM, lines 17-18 in A.R. George,
The Babylonian Gilgamesh Epic: Introduction, Critical Edition and Cuneiform Texts
(2 vols.; Oxford: Oxford University Press, 2003), I, pp. 268-69.

27. The word ʾādām also occurs without the definite article in Gen. 2.5, but
without specific reference to the first man: 'and there was no one (ʾādām ʾayin) to
till the ground'.

28. Sometimes Gen. 4.25-26 is attributed to the Redactor (R) rather than J.
However, there are multiple pointers to J authorship. First, the use of the passive qal
yullad (cf. Gen. 3.19, 23; 6.1); secondly, the use of the hiphil of the verb *ḥālal*, 'to
begin' (cf. Gen. 6.1; 9.20); thirdly, the word play on Seth's name (cf. Gen. 2.7; 3.20;
4.1; 5.29); and fourthly, the fact that Seth and Cain (Sheth and Qayin) appear closely

around on earth.[29] Likewise in P, at Gen. 5.1, 3-5, we find *ʾādām* used as a personal name, Adam. It should also be noted that it is only towards the end of the story that the woman is named Eve (*ḥawwâ*, Gen. 3.20), so called because she was the mother of all living (*ḥāy*, a typical J word play); prior to that she is simply 'the woman' or the man's 'wife'.

Phyllis Trible has proposed that the *ʾādam* that God makes is initially an 'earth creature' who only becomes a man in the sense of a male when the woman is created, and this view has been followed by others, including Carol Meyers and Mieke Bal.[30] Although this may seem logical, it is nevertheless to be rejected. First of all, it should be noted that if one were seeking for a sex-neutral translation of *hāʾādām* it would have to be 'the human', rather than 'the earth creature'; the connection between *hāʾādām* and the earth (*ʾadāmâ*) is only one of word play (Gen. 2.7).[31] However, it is quite certain that this creature was understood to be male from the beginning. Not only is it spoken of identically as the *hāʾādām* both before and after the creation of the woman, but Gen. 2.23 specifically states of Eve, 'this one shall be called Woman, for out of Man (*ʾîš*) this one was taken'.[32] This is decisive, since *ʾîš* can only refer to a male. A further point is that logically, if Trible's position is correct, it would be the sexless earth creature that needed a helper and counterpart, but this is clearly not the case. The original *ʾādam* is certainly a man, though with one more rib than subsequently!

With none of the animals proving appropriate for the task, we read that Eve is created to be a 'helper' for the man (Gen. 2.18-25). Trible argues that this does not mean she is inferior, pointing out how the term 'helper' is sometimes even used of God himself in the Old Testament.[33] David Clines, however, returns to the view of Augustine and Aquinas

together again (with ethnic overtones) in Num. 24.17, 22, part of the Balaam oracles generally attributed to the Yahwist.

29. As suggested by R.S. Hendel, *Genesis 1–11* (Anchor Yale Bible, 1A: New Haven: Yale University Press, forthcoming). I am most grateful to Ron for letting me see the typescript of this excellent work.

30. P. Trible, *God and the Rhetoric of Sexuality* (OBT; Philadelphia: Fortress Press, 1978), pp. 80, 98; C.L. Meyers, *Discovering Eve: Ancient Israelite Women in Context* (New York: Oxford University Press, 1988), pp. 81-82; M. Bal, *Lethal Love: Feminist Literary Readings of Biblical Love Stories* (Indiana Studies in Biblical Literature; Bloomington, IN: Indiana University Press, 1989), pp. 112-14.

31. Meyers, *Discovering Eve*, p. 82 accepts 'the human' as an alternative translation, insisting that this figure is 'not inherently gendered'.

32. As rightly pointed out by J.J. Collins, *The Bible after Babel: Historical Criticism in a Postmodern Age* (Grand Rapids, MI: Eerdmans, 2005), p. 88.

33. Trible, *God and the Rhetoric of Sexuality*, p. 90.

that Eve is a helper only in the sense that she can procreate; for any other purpose a man would have been of more use.[34] But I feel this is interpreting 'helper' in too narrow a sense: even in a patriarchal society the woman would surely be seen as helping in more ways than this, such as offering companionship, running the home, as well as perhaps assisting with light work (here, on the farm). Moreover, a work like the Song of Songs shows that the purpose of a woman's sexuality was not understood to be confined to procreation. Accordingly, God's earlier words in Gen. 2.18, 'It is not good that the man should be alone', are surely not limited to the man's need for a procreator, although we may fully accept that procreation was one important way in which the woman helps.

In Gen. 3.12, when confronted by God, the man blames the woman and the woman blames the man for eating the forbidden fruit. The picture of human nature here displayed is true to life. The text clearly regards both the man and woman as culpable—hence both are cast out of the garden—though it was the woman who was tempted first. Over time, increasing blame was fastened on Eve by some (e.g. Ecclus 25.24, 'From a woman sin had its beginning, and because of her we all die').[35] This viewpoint is followed by the pseudo-Pauline 1 Tim. 2.14, 'Adam was not the one deceived; it was the woman who was deceived and became a sinner', which contrasts with the authentic Paul, who interestingly twice mentions the name of Adam in connection with the fall, not Eve (Rom. 5.14; 1 Cor. 15.22), though he does refer very briefly to Eve being tempted by the serpent in 2 Cor. 11.3.[36] Similarly in the rabbis the main

---

34. D.J.A. Clines, 'What Does Eve Do to Help? And Other Irredeemably Androcentric Orientations in Genesis 1–3', in D.J.A. Clines, *What Does Eve Do to Help? And Other Readerly Questions to the Old Testament* (JSOTSup, 94; Sheffield: JSOT Press, 1990), pp. 25-48 (27-37). The references are to Augustine, *De Genesi ad litteram libri duodecim* 9.5.9, and Aquinas, *Summa Theologiae* Part 1a, Q. 92, art. 1. Clines quotes these passages in English translation on p. 37.

35. The view of J.R. Levison, 'Is Eve to Blame? A Contextual Study of Sirach 25:24', *CBQ* 47 (1985), pp. 617-23, that Ecclus 25.24 is not referring to Eve is unconvincing. Noting that the passage comes in the context of Ben Sira's discussion of bad wives he attempts to argue that we should understand the verse as saying, 'From the [evil] wife is the beginning of sin, and because of her we [husbands] all die', death being a hyperbolic reference to the devastating effect a wife has on her husband! But this is to read into the text what is simply not there, and it is much more natural to assume from the language used that we have here a brief aside to Eve.

36. For the figure of Adam in Paul, see C.K. Barrett, *From First Adam to Last: A Study in Pauline Theology* (London: A. & C. Black, 1962); R. Scroggs, *The Last Adam: A Study in Pauline Anthropology* (Oxford: Blackwell, 1966).

emphasis tends to fall on Adam, and the same is true of the late first-century apocalyptic works *4 Ezra* (*2 Esdras*) 7.116-18 (46-48) and *2 Bar.* 54.15, 19.[37]

One feminist scholar, Jean Higgins, has attempted to exonerate Eve altogether from the common view that she tempted the man, claiming that this has to be read between the lines into the text.[38] But this is surely to go too far. Although what the text says on this subject is admittedly brief and there is no detailed temptation scene comparable to the interaction between the serpent and Eve (Gen. 3.1-5), we not only read that Eve gave the man some of the forbidden fruit (Gen. 3.6, 12), but the man is specifically condemned by God for listening to the voice of his wife in connection with this (Gen. 3.17), which can only mean that she encouraged him to eat of the fruit that she gave him.

6. *The Serpent*

The serpent was not Satan (the devil) in J's understanding. The concept of Satan developed later, and we find him first equated with the Eden serpent in the apocryphal book of Wisdom (Wis. 2.24, 'but though the devil's envy death entered the world'). Compare Rev. 12.9 and 20.2, where we read of 'that ancient serpent, who is [called] the Devil and Satan'. Less well known is the fact that the serpent is equated in *1 En.* 69.6 with Gader'el, one of the wicked angels involved with the descent to have sex with human women. Genesis 3.1, however, refers to the Eden serpent as one of Yahweh's creatures, a 'beast of the field'. It is certainly the case that it is the prototype of later ordinary serpents known to humanity (cf. Gen. 3.14-15), but in its original pre-cursed state the serpent not only has the capacity to speak but also to have supernormal knowledge, which makes it more than an ordinary serpent at that point. We may recall Balaam's donkey in Num. 22.22-30 for the only other example of a talking animal in the Old Testament, one moreover with comparable supernatural awareness, a passage which has likewise been traditionally ascribed to the J source. This attribution gains further support from the fact that the Balaam narrative in Num. 24.17, 22 similarly knows a Cain and a Seth (here with clear ethnic overtones), just as in the J source in Genesis 4.

37. For Jewish interpretations of Adam from the second century BCE to the first century CE, see J.R. Levison, *Portraits of Adam in Early Judaism: From Sirach to 2 Baruch* (JSOTSup, 1; Sheffield: JSOT Press, 1988).

38. J.M. Higgins, 'The Myth of Eve: The Temptress', *JAAR* 44 (1976), pp. 639-47.

Turning to the ancient Near Eastern background, it should be noted that a few scholars have tried to see the Eden serpent as symbolic of Canaanite religion. Thus, F.F. Hvidberg saw it as symbolic of the god Baal, a view recently adopted by B.T. Arnold,[39] while N. Wyatt[40] understands it rather as symbolic of El. Both views are unconvincing. Baal was never symbolized by a serpent in Canaanite religion (or anywhere else in the Old Testament)—indeed, it was Baal who defeated the sea serpent Leviathan—and nor is El, who is viewed positively throughout the Old Testament (*contra* Wyatt). Again, in a BBC TV programme broadcast in 2011, Francesca Stavrakopoulou (see above, n. 19) claimed the serpent symbolized snake worship; she seems to be thinking of Nehushtan. She follows Nick Wyatt in thinking that the expulsion of the man symbolizes the destruction of Jerusalem and exile of 586 BCE. But Nehushtan had already been destroyed a century earlier (2 Kgs 18.4). Moreover, Genesis 3 does not speak of worship of the serpent. More generally, J. Coppens and J.A. Soggin[41] saw the serpent as symbolic of the Canaanite fertility cult, but this is not presented elsewhere as a strong concern of the Yahwist, so it would be surprising to find it depicted as the archetypal sin at the time of creation.

Recently James Charlesworth has written a massive book entitled *The Good and Evil Serpent*[42] in which he argues that in the ancient Near East the serpent is mostly viewed positively, not negatively, and he claims this is also true of the Bible, including the serpent of Genesis 3.[43] However, while his ancient Near Eastern material is fascinating, I would argue that in the Bible the serpent is mostly viewed negatively, and certainly in Genesis 3. Charlesworth claims that the serpent does not tempt Eve (it merely asks her a question!), it tells the truth (unlike God), is described as wise (not crafty), and is not a symbol of evil. However, if

39. F.F. Hvidberg, 'The Canaanitic Background of Gen. i–iii', *VT* 10 (1960), pp. 285-94 (287-90); B.T. Arnold, *Genesis* (NCBC; Cambridge: Cambridge University Press, 2009), pp. 62-63.

40. N. Wyatt, 'Interpreting the Creation and Fall Story in Genesis 2–3', *ZAW* 93 (1981), pp. 10-21 (18-20).

41. J. Coppens, *La connaissance du bien et du mal at le péché du paradis* (Gembloux: J. Duculot, 1948), *passim*; J.A. Soggin, 'The Fall of Man in the Third Chapter of Genesis', in *idem, Old Testament and Oriental Studies* (Rome: Biblical Institute Press, 1975), pp. 88-111 (94-100).

42. J.H. Charlesworth, *The Good and Evil Serpent* (Anchor Yale Bible Reference Library; New Haven: Yale University Press, 2010).

43. Charlesworth, *The Good and Evil Serpent*, pp. 275-324. On the serpent in Gen. 3, see too K.R. Joines, *Serpent Symbolism in the Old Testament* (Haddonfield, NJ: Haddonfield House, 1974), pp. 16-41.

all this is true it becomes difficult to understand why the serpent should be so thoroughly cursed towards the end of the story. Again, the fact that Eve declares 'the serpent beguiled me' (Gen. 3.13) indicates that 'crafty' rather than 'wise' is the better translation of the Hebrew word ʿārûm used to describe the serpent in Gen. 3.1.[44] Charlesworth also holds that the serpent was deprived of its legs by God. This suggestion has been made before and serpents with legs are attested elsewhere in ancient Near Eastern symbolism, but since nothing explicitly is said of the serpent's legs here it is perhaps preferable to think of the serpent as originally having a good sense of balance so that it could move upright without legs.

Can the ancient Near East shed any light on the Eden serpent? Probably it can. In the Mesopotamian Gilgamesh epic we read that it was a serpent[45] that snatched and ate the plant of life which Gilgamesh had been seeking in order to obtain immortality, thereby rejuvenating itself (Gilgamesh 11.305-307). When we bear in mind that the Gilgamesh epic tablet 11 has three points in common with Genesis 2–3—namely, a serpent responsible for depriving humans of immortality, a plant or tree of life that conveys immortality, and the theme of humanity not quite achieving immortality (in this life)—it becomes at least possible to suppose that these elements in the Garden of Eden narrative are a reworking of the same elements in the Gilgamesh epic. We have evidence that the Gilgamesh epic was known in Palestine and the Levant from a fragment found at Megiddo dating to the fourteenth century BCE, as well as Late Bronze Age fragments found at Ugarit and Emar.

Finally, some words are in order about the conversation between the serpent and Eve in Gen. 3.1-5, which unusually uses the name Elohim for God rather than Yahweh Elohim (originally Yahweh). Why should this be? It has been suggested that it was inappropriate for one giving evil counsel to mention the personal name of God or that the serpent was

44. The word ʿārûm clearly has negative overtones in the book of Job (cf. Job 5.12; 15.5), 'crafty', and positive overtones in Proverbs (cf. Prov. 12.16, 23; 13.16; 14.8, 15, 18; 22.3; 27.12), 'wise', 'shrewd', 'sensible', 'prudent', 'clever'. Note further the Yahwist's liking for word play in referring to the first couple as 'naked' (ʿarûmmîm) in Gen. 2.25, the verse immediately preceding the allusion to the serpent as crafty (ʿārûm). Contrast Gen. 3.7, 10, 11, where the word 'naked' is spelled ʿêrummîm and ʿêrōm.

45. Å.W. Sjöberg, 'Eve and the Chameleon', in W.B Barrick and J.R. Spencer (eds.), *In the Shelter of Elyon: Essays on Ancient Palestinian Life and Literature in Honor of G.W. Ahlström* (JSOTSup, 31; Sheffield: JSOT Press, 1984), pp. 217-25 (221-23), claimed that the Gilgamesh epic and even perhaps Gen. 3 referred to a chameleon rather than a serpent, but this view has rightly failed to gain acceptance.

keeping his distance from Yahweh.[46] Neither seems particularly convincing. It should be noted that in J speeches elsewhere, as opposed to narratives, people do on occasion use Elohim rather than Yahweh.[47] In addition to Gen. 3.1-5, such passages include Gen. 4.25; 9.27; 27.28, as well as possibly some in the Joseph narrative. But that still leaves the question why Elohim is used in this particular instance. Most likely it is because at this early stage in the history of humanity the name Yahweh was not known to Eve. This would fit in with the fact that we have a further speech of Eve from J in Gen. 4.25 in which she again uses the name Elohim for God, saying 'God has appointed for me another child instead of Abel, because Cain killed him'. The very next verse, Gen. 4.26, then implies that it was in the days of Seth's son Enosh that humans started calling on the name of Yahweh, thus explaining why Lamech then uses the name Yahweh when speaking of the birth of his son Noah in Gen. 5.29. The only objection which might be raised against this is that Eve does use the name Yahweh in connection with the birth of Cain in Gen. 4.1. However, as I have already argued elsewhere,[48] there are strong signs that the story of Cain and Abel originally had a later context. Cain has a wife (Gen. 4.17) and fears that someone might kill him (Gen. 4.14), which are both problematic in the present setting near the beginning of human existence when there are supposedly no other people around. The Yahwist has thus failed to integrate the story properly into its current context. The same may therefore be true with regard to Eve's use of the name Yahweh before it has officially been revealed.

7. Why Do the First Humans Not Die Immediately after Their Disobedience, as God Had Predicted?

God states that on the day that Adam and Eve eat of the tree of knowledge, they will surely die (Gen. 2.17). But as the serpent predicts (Gen. 3.4-5), they do not die that day (though they do later). How are we to explain this?

---

46. For these two views see, respectively, Cassuto, *A Commentary on the Book of Genesis*, I, p. 88; Titus, *The Second Story of Creation*, p. 326.

47. As pointed out by R.E. Friedman, *Who Wrote the Bible?* (London: Cape, 1988), p. 265 n. 17.

48. J. Day, 'Cain and the Kenites', in G. Galil, M. Geller and A.R. Millard (eds.), *Homeland and Exile: Biblical and Ancient Near Eastern Studies in Honour of Bustenay Oded* (VTSup, 130; Leiden: Brill, 2009), pp. 335-46 (342), reprinted in Chapter 3 below.

(1)   Some interpret death as metaphorical, referring to the alienation from God implied by the expulsion from the garden (e.g. G.J. Wenham, R.W.L. Moberly, R.P. Gordon),[49] but this view is unconvincing since it is not the most natural way of taking what is said. As James Barr pointed out,[50] there are about forty other instances in the Hebrew Bible where we read that someone will surely die, and these all imply imminent literal death.

(2)   It has occasionally been proposed that *môt tāmût* means 'you will surely become mortal'. This view is found, for example, already in Targum Pseudo-Jonathan ('you shall incur the death penalty'), Symmachus (*thnētos*) and in Jerome (*mortalis*), who followed him,[51] as well as by many subsequent Christian interpreters, and in modern times it has been followed by a few scholars.[52] However, although providing a seemingly simple solution to the problem, this view is unlikely, since this meaning is nowhere else attested for this verb, and in addition it would appear that the first humans are already mortal, since Gen. 3.22 implies that they have not eaten of the tree of life (even though they had not originally been forbidden from doing so).

(3)   Should we see God as a liar and the serpent as telling the truth? This provocative view has been held by several scholars recently, including John Gibson and James Charlesworth.[53] This seems unlikely, however, since it is natural to suppose that the reader is meant to identify with God over against the serpent, the latter

49. G.J. Wenham, *Genesis 1–15* (WBC, 1; Waco, TX: Word Books, 1987), p. 90; R.W.L. Moberly, 'Did the Serpent Get it Right?', *JTS* 39 (1988), pp. 1-27 (16-18); *idem*, 'Did the Interpreters Get it Right?', *JTS* 59 (2008), pp. 22-40 (34-37); R.P. Gordon, 'The Ethics of Eden: Truth-Telling in Genesis 2–3', in K.J. Dell (ed.), *Ethical and Unethical in the Old Testament: God and Humans in Dialogue* (LHBOTS, 528; London: T&T Clark International, 2010), pp. 11-33 (22).

50. J. Barr, 'Is God a Liar? (Genesis 2–3)—and Related Matters', *JTS* 57 (2006), pp. 1-22 (12).

51. A. Salvesen, *Symmachus in the Pentateuch* (JSSMS, 15; Manchester: Manchester University Press, 1991), pp. 9-10; Jerome, gloss on Gen. 2.17 in *Liber Hebraicarum Quaestionum in Genesim* 308 (*PL* 23, col. 941).

52. Cf. Cassuto, *A Commentary on the Book of Genesis*, I, pp. 124-25; Speiser, *Genesis*, pp. 15, 17; D. Jobling. 'The Myth Semantics of Genesis 2.4b–3.24', *Semeia* 18 (1980), pp. 41-49 (47); A. LaCocque, *The Trial of Innocence: Adam, Eve, and the Yahwist* (Eugene, OR: Cascade Books [Wipf & Stock], 2006), pp. 99, 101, translates 'deserve to die'.

53. E.g. J.C.L. Gibson, *Genesis* (2 vols.; Daily Study Bible; Edinburgh: Saint Andrew Press, 1991–92 [1991]), I, pp. 113-14; Charlesworth, *The Good and Evil Serpent*, pp. 275-324.

being cursed in the end. Moreover, we should observe that the serpent is telling only a half-truth in stating that their eyes will be opened but they will not die. For death is clearly depicted as the ultimate result of their disobedience, since the couple no longer have the possibility of accessing the tree of life following their expulsion from the garden (cf. Gen. 3.19, 22, 24). Although death does not happen immediately, the couple's fate is sealed from the moment they disobey God.

(4)   It has occasionally been pointed out that *b^eyôm* can mean not only literally 'on the day that' but also more broadly 'when', so that one might render 'for when you eat of it you will surely die'.[54] For example, Jer. 7.23; 11.4, 7 refer to things God is supposed to have said when he led the Israelites out of Egypt, but the subject matter concerns God's commandments to the Israelites to obey, which sounds more to do with the Sinai covenant than anything happening on the literal day of deliverance from Egypt. There is also other evidence that *yôm* could sometimes mean 'time' rather than a specific day, though the latter is most frequently intended. Indeed, a specific day does appear to be intended in Genesis 2–3, since the serpent takes up the expression *b^eyôm* in Gen. 3.5, saying to the first humans, 'You will not die; for God knows that on the day you eat of it your eyes will be opened, and you will be like gods,[55] knowing good and evil', and as we see from Gen. 3.6-7, this happened immediately on the very same day.

(5)   Finally, it has sometimes been claimed that Adam and Eve did not die immediately because of God's grace and mercy (so, e.g., Hermann Gunkel, John Skinner, Gerhard von Rad, David Clines, James Barr and Johnson Lim), a view already implied in Milton's *Paradise Lost*.[56] By a process of elimination of other

54. So NIV; similarly God's Word translation.
55. The Hebrew *kē^ʾlōhîm* is ambiguous, but on balance the translation 'like gods' seems preferable to 'like God', since in Gen. 3.22 God states that the humans have come to know good and evil 'like one of us', including both God and his heavenly court. The translation 'like gods' is also supported by the LXX, the oldest translation we have (in addition to the Vulgate). It is also sometimes argued in favour of the plural 'gods' that the verb in the immediately following expression *yōd^{eʿ}ê ṭôb wārāʿ*, 'knowing good and evil', is in the plural. Since, however, the 'you' being addressed here is also in the plural it is difficult to feel totally confident about this particular argument.
56. H. Gunkel, *Genesis* (HKAT, 1.1; Göttingen: Vandenhoeck & Ruprecht, 3rd edn, 1910), p. 10, ET *Genesis* (trans. M.E. Biddle; Macon, GA: Mercer University

views noted above, none of which seem to be likely, I find this view the most plausible. It fits well with the theme of divine grace operating alongside judgment that we find throughout the early chapters of Genesis, though it has to be admitted that in this instance it is not specifically drawn attention to as an act of grace.

8. *The Two Trees in the Garden and the Meaning of the Knowledge of Good and Evil*

Two trees in particular are singled out for special mention in the Garden of Eden, the tree of life (immortality) and the tree of the knowledge of good and evil (wisdom)—the first humans attaining the latter but not the former. This reminds one of the Babylonian myth of Adapa, the first sage, who similarly obtained wisdom but not immortality. As one of the first lines of the text states, 'To him he (Ea) gave wisdom, he did not give him eternal life' (Adapa A, col. 1, line 4).[57] Moreover, as with first man in Eden, Adapa's fate is symbolic of humanity generally.[58] It is entirely appropriate, therefore, that there were two special trees in the Garden of Eden, one symbolizing wisdom and the other immortality, and attempts to claim that there was originally only one (the tree of knowledge) are now rightly generally abandoned.[59]

Whereas the meaning of the tree of life is clear—its fruit conveys immortality, like the plant of life in the Babylonian Gilgamesh epic—the precise meaning of the tree of the knowledge of good and evil is debated.

Press, 1997), p. 10; J. Skinner, *A Critical and Exegetical Commentary on Genesis* (ICC; Edinburgh: T. & T. Clark, 1910), p. 67; von Rad, *Das erste Buch Mose*, p. 77, ET *Genesis*, p. 92; D.J.A. Clines, *The Theme of the Pentateuch* (JSOTSup, 10; Sheffield: JSOT Press, 2nd edn, 1997), p. 70; Barr, 'Is God a Liar?', p. 22; J.T.K. Lim, 'Did the Scholar(s) Get it Right?', in R. Boer, M. Carden and J. Kelso (eds.), *The One Who Reads May Run: Essays in Honour of Edgar W. Conrad* (LHBOTS, 553; London: T&T Clark International, 2012), pp. 69-79. Cf. J. Milton, *Paradise Lost* III.38-42 (cited in Gordon, 'The Ethics of Eden', p. 20).

57.   Cf. S. Izre'el, *Adapa and the South Wind: Language Has the Power of Life and Death* (Winona Lake, IN: Eisenbrauns, 2001), pp. 10-11.

58.   Compare the god Anu's words following Adapa's refusal to eat and drink the food and water of life offered to him, 'Come, Adapa, why did you not eat or drink! Hence you shall not live. Alas for inferior humanity' (Adapa B, lines 67-68). Cf. Izre'el, *Adapa and the South Wind*, pp. 20-21.

59.   Cf. T.N.D. Mettinger, *The Eden Narrative: A Literary and Religio-Historical Study of Genesis 2–3* (Winona Lake, IN: Eisenbrauns, 2007), pp. 5-11, *contra* Budde, *Die biblische Urgeschichte*, pp. 46-65, and others who followed after him.

Coming first of all to the nature of the fruit, the popular idea that it was an apple can be traced as far back as the fifth century CE, when it is first attested in Cyprian of Gaul, *Heptateuchus* 1.66-67, 77, 106 (cited as Pseudo-Tertullian, *PL* 2, cols. 1097-1100), and Alcimus Avitus, Bishop of Vienne, also in Gaul, *Carmina* 2, 203-37 (*PL* 59, col. 334),[60] and it subsequently became the dominant view in Western Christianity in the mediaeval era as well as afterwards. Although it is impossible to prove from mediaeval and patristic sources that the identification with the apple derived from word play between the Latin words for apple and apple tree, *malus* and *malum*, and the Latin adjective *malus/a/um*, 'evil', found in the Vulgate's description of the tree of knowledge as *lignum scientiae boni et mali*, this nevertheless remains a plausible hypothesis. It is noteworthy that the identification of the fruit with an apple is first attested in western, Latin Christianity in the decades following the publication of the Vulgate, and continued to dominate in that area.[61] In contrast, in Greek Christianity the fruit was generally equated with the fig, and the same is true of Syriac Christianity, though the grape is also sometimes attested there. The fig or grape are also the dominant views in the Jewish tradition, the former deriving from the fact that the first humans are said to have sewn themselves fig leaves for loin cloths (Gen. 3.7).[62] It is, however, surely a complete error to attempt to identify the fruit of the tree with any known fruit, since the whole point of the tree and what it bestows is that it is unique.

   Three broad views have been held by modern scholars about the meaning of the knowledge of good and evil: (1) that it refers to the ethical discernment of good and evil;[63] (2) that it means knowledge of everything, 'good and evil' constituting a merism;[64] and (3) that the

---

60. I am deeply indebted to Professor Brian Murdoch of Stirling University for this information.

61. See H.-G. Leder, 'Arbor scientiae. Die Tradition vom paradiesischen Apfelbaum', *ZNW* 52 (1961), pp. 156-89 (181-87) for objections to this view.

62. For a list of different views among Jews and Christians on the identity of the fruit, see L. Ginzberg, *Legends of the Jews* (7 vols.; Philadelphia: Jewish Publication Society of America, 1968), V, pp. 97-98 n. 70; H.M. von Erffa, *Iconologie der Genesis: die christlichen Bildthemen aus dem Alten Testament und ihre Quellen* (2 vols.; Munich: Deutscher Kunstverlag, 1989–95 [1989]), I, pp. 120-22.

63. Driver, *Genesis*, p. 41; J. Barr, *The Garden of Eden and the Hope of Immortality* (London: SCM Press, 1992), p. 62.

64. Cf. von Rad, *Das erste Buch Mose*, p. 65, ET *Genesis*, p. 79; R.A. Oden, 'Divine Aspirations in Atrahasis and in Genesis 1–11', *ZAW* 93 (1981), pp. 197-216 (211-13); H. Wallace, *The Eden Narrative* (HSM, 32; Atlanta: Scholars Press, 1983), pp. 115-30.

knowledge in question is sexual knowledge.[65] Engnell regarded it specifically as knowledge of procreation.[66]

Option 3 is the easiest to refute. Although 'to know' can be used of carnal knowledge, as in Gen. 4.1, there is no evidence elsewhere that the phrase 'knowledge of good and evil' was ever used to denote sexual knowledge alone. Moreover, the view that the tree of knowledge conveyed simply sexual knowledge is also unlikely on the grounds that the man and woman are already implied to be one flesh in Gen. 2.24, and God, whom they become like after acquiring the knowledge of good and evil (Gen. 3.22), is not a sexual being in the view of the biblical writers. But one can understand how this view arose, since we are informed that after the human couple had eaten of the tree they became aware of their nakedness.

Clearly the tree of knowledge bestowed wisdom of some kind (cf. Gen. 3.6, which states that 'the woman saw...that the tree was to be desired to make one wise'). This has led to view 2, the idea that the tree conveyed special divine wisdom akin to omniscience (e.g. by extrapolating 2 Sam. 14.17 and 20[67]). This view might claim support from Job 15.7-8 and Ezek. 28.12 (cf. v. 3), which suggest that the first man was superlatively wise. However, it would be out of keeping with other things in Genesis 3, which provides aetiologies of the state of humanity as the Israelites knew it, which was not omniscient. So, while this view may well represent one strand of understanding of the first man in ancient Israel, it cannot represent the viewpoint of Genesis 3.

So this brings us to the first view, the idea that the tree of knowledge conveyed the ability to distinguish ethically between good and evil. This acquisition may be seen as symbolizing the wisdom of a mature adult as opposed to a child (Deut. 1.39; cf. Isa. 7.15-16), which explains why the

65. E.g. H. Schmidt, *Die Erzählung von Paradies und Sündenfall* (Tübingen: J.C.B. Mohr [P. Siebeck], 1931), pp. 26-28; Coppens, *La connaissance du bien et du mal et le péché du paradis, passim*; B. Reicke, 'The Knowledge Hidden in the Tree of Paradise', *JSS* 1 (1956), pp. 193-202; L. Hartman, 'Sin in Paradise', *CBQ* 20 (1958), pp. 26-40.

66. I. Engnell, '"Knowledge" and "Life" in the Creation Story', in M. Noth and D.W. Thomas (eds.), *Wisdom in Israel and in the Ancient Near East Presented to Professor Harold Henry Rowley* (VTSup, 3; Leiden: Brill, 1955), pp. 103-19 (116).

67. The wise woman of Tekoa there flatters King David by saying both that he 'is like the angel of God, discerning good and evil' (2 Sam. 14.17) and also that he has 'wisdom like the wisdom of the angel of God to know all things that are on the earth' (2 Sam. 14.20). These are not identical but complementary matters. The former refers to the king's fine moral discernment, which is important for his judicial role (cf. 1 Kgs 3.9), while the latter exaggeratingly attributes omniscience to him.

first humans became aware of their nakedness in contrast to their previous childlike state of innocence. Some Church Fathers such as Theophilus of Antioch and Irenaeus saw Adam and Eve as being like children,[68] a view also shared by modern scholars such as H. Gunkel.[69] This view has the advantage of taking the phrase 'knowledge of good and evil' in the sense that it is employed elsewhere in the Old Testament. However, it raises the question why God should want humans to remain ignorant of basic, mature wisdom. Elsewhere in the Old Testament the acquisition of wisdom is thought of as a good thing, as throughout the book of Proverbs, for example. Indeed, in the light of the Old Testament as a whole, it is difficult to see why God should want humans to remain ignorant of the knowledge of good and evil for ever. The most likely explanation is that God disapproves of the first humans acquiring the knowledge of good and evil by the assertion their human autonomy in disobedience to his explicit command.[70] Rather, this knowledge should be acquired through obedience to God. 'The fear of the Lord is the beginning of knowledge/wisdom', as Prov. 1.7 and 9.10 say.

9. *The Story as an Explanation of the Origin of Sin and Death?*

Traditionally the story in Genesis 2–3 has been known in Christian theology as 'the Fall'.[71] In recent years, however, a number of scholars[72] have rejected this understanding. Carol Meyers and James Barr, for example, emphasize that the word for 'sin' is nowhere to be found in it, Barr regarding the story as rather describing a missed opportunity to obtain immortality. But this is surely a false dichotomy, and the fact that the word for 'sin' is not present is irrelevant, since what we have here is

68.   Cf. Theophilus of Antioch, *Ad Autolycum* 2.24; Irenaeus, *Adversus haereses* 4.38.1.

69.   Gunkel, *Genesis*, p. 30, ET *Genesis*, p. 30.

70.   W.A.M. Clark, 'A Legal Background to the Yahwist's Use of "Good and Evil" in Genesis 2–3', *JBL* 88 (1969), pp. 266-78 (277); J. Van Seters, *Prologue to History: The Yahwist as Historian in Genesis* (Louisville, KY: Westminster/John Knox Press, 1992), pp. 126, 133 n. 71.

71.   Two older works still worthy of attention are F.R. Tennant, *The Sources of the Doctrines of the Fall and Original Sin* (Cambridge: Cambridge University Press, 1903); N.P. Williams, *The Ideas of the Fall and Original Sin: A Historical and Critical Study* (London: Longmans, Green & Co., 1927).

72.   Meyers, *Discovering Eve*, p. 87; Barr, *The Garden of Eden and the Hope of Immortality*, p. 6.

clearly a case of disobedience to the divine will, followed by punishment. The idea of sin is there, even if the word is absent, as is also the case in some other Old Testament passages. But interestingly, the verb *ḥṭ'*, 'to sin' is actually used of the man in Eden in the parallel account in Ezek. 28.16, and a word for 'iniquity' (*ʿawlātâ*) is likewise found in the preceding verse. Overall, it is difficult to see why the Garden of Eden story should not be understood as one of sin and judgment, comparable to others which follow in Genesis 4–11. Indeed, it is the first one, resulting in the loss of Paradise. However, it is wrong to read into the story all the ideas contained in the later full-blown Augustinian concept of original sin, and within the Old Testament it clearly does not have the centrality that it later acquired in Christianity or even certain parts of Judaism at the turn of the era.

Genesis 3.14-19 contains not merely one but a whole series of aetiologies, and this is typical of the Yahwist's narratives in Genesis 1–11, explaining why serpents crawl on their bellies, female labour pains and subordination to men, the laboriousness of man's toil, and apparently death. This last raises the question whether the man and woman are conceived of as immortal or mortal in the Garden of Eden. Traditionally in Christian theology they have been seen as immortal, their disobedience leading to their mortality (Rom. 5.12; cf. Gen. 3.19, 'You are dust, and to dust you shall return'), and there are still scholars in recent years who have taken this view.[73] On the other hand, James Barr[74] has argued that the language used in Gen. 3.22 ('lest he reach out his hand and take also from the tree of life, and eat, and live for ever') implies that the man is mortal and has not yet eaten of the tree of life, and God wishes to prevent the possibility of his living for ever, so he expels them from

---

73. Cf. J. Gertz, 'Von Adam zu Enosch: Überlegungen zur Entstehungsgeschichte von Genesis 2–4', in M. Witte (ed.), *Gott und Mensch im Dialog: Festschrift für Otto Kaiser zum 80. Geburtstag* (BZAW, 345 1; Berlin: W. de Gruyter, 2004), pp. 215-36 (230-31 and n. 42); E. Blum, 'Von Gottesunmittelbarkeit zu Gottesähnlichkeit: Überlegungen zur theologischen Anthropologie der Paradieserzählung', in G. Eberhardt and K. Liess (eds.), *Gottes Nähe im Alten Testament* (SBS, 202; Stuttgart: Katholisches Bibelwerk, 2004), pp. 9-29 (22-25); A. LaCocque, *The Trial of Innocence: Adam, Eve, and the Yahwist* (Eugene, OR: Cascade Books [Wipf & Stock], 2006), pp. 100-101.

74. Barr, *The Garden of Eden and the Hope of Immortality*, p. 58 with p. 135 n. 2. Cf. too K. Schmid, 'Loss of Immortality: Hermeneutical Aspects of Genesis 2–3 and its Early Reception', in *idem* (ed.), *Beyond Eden: The Biblical Story of Paradise (Genesis 2–3) and its Reception History* (FAT, 2.34; Tübingen: Mohr Siebeck, 2008), pp. 58-78, for a defence of the idea that the first couple were mortal in Eden.

the garden. This appears to be the majority scholarly view nowadays. However, we can probably reconcile the implications of Gen. 3.19 and 3.22 by seeing the first man and woman as potentially immortal in the garden—that is, God intends them to have immortality, but they have not eaten of the tree of life, even though it has not been barred to them and their subsequent disobedience deprives them of it. The fact that the series of divine curses climaxes with the words 'you are dust, and to dust you shall return' (Gen. 3.19) fits best with the view that the first man and his wife's disobedience did indeed finalize their fate to die, but the fact that it is not further elaborated is consistent with mortality having been their previous default state. What has happened is that they have missed out on a chance of immortality.

10. *Does the Expulsion from Eden Symbolize the Babylonian Exile?*

In recent years a number of scholars have claimed that the expulsion of the first humans from Eden symbolizes the exile of the Jews in 586 BCE.[75] Some even suppose that the story was the original beginning of an Enneateuch (the nine books from Genesis to 2 Kings).[76] I see little evidence for this. As I have already noted, it is difficult to envisage the serpent as a symbol of the idolatry that led Judah astray before the exile. The serpent is nowhere a symbol of Baal, and serpent worship does not feature in the Old Testament's depiction of the monarchical period apart from the cult of Nehushtan, something already eliminated by Hezekiah over 100 years before the exile (2 Kgs 18.4). Furthermore, the serpent in Genesis 3 is not actually worshipped. Again, the crime of the first humans was in seeking the knowledge of good and evil by eating the forbidden fruit, and it is difficult to relate that to Judah's situation before the exile. Nowhere does the Old Testament represent the fall of Judah as being due to seeking after forbidden wisdom. We have, moreover, already seen that the case for the identification of Eden with Jerusalem in

---

75. E.g. J. Vermeylen, Le récit du paradis et la question des origines du Pentateuque', *Bijdragen: Tijdschrift voor filosofie en theologie* 41 (1980), pp. 230-50 (245), and J.-M. Husser, 'Entre mythe et philosophie: La relecture sapientielle de Genèse', *RB* 107 (2000), pp. 232-59 (244-45), have seen here an evocation of the Babylonian exile. Wyatt, 'Interpreting the Creation and Fall Story in Genesis 2–3', pp. 10-21, sees the story as originally referring to the exile of the final king of the Northern Kingdom, and subsequently applied to the last king of Judah.

76. For an exhaustive survey and ultimate rejection of this view, see Titus, *The Second Story of Creation (Gen 2:4–3:24): A Prologue to the Concept of Enneateuch?*

Gen. 2.10-14 is extremely weak, and the theme of expulsion is characteristic of other J stories in Genesis 1–11 which clearly have nothing to do with the Babylonian exile (cf. Gen. 4.13-16; 11.7-9). Moreover, the expulsion from Eden sounds final and irreversible, which is in contrast to what the Old Testament elsewhere says about the Babylonian exile. It seems better, therefore, to regard the story as relating simply to the first humans and the human situation generally, as its surface meaning suggests, rather than to Judah and the exile. The latter historicizing interpretation is ultimately no more convincing than the alternative historicizing view of W. von Soden, M. Görg and K. Holter[77] that we have in Genesis 2–3 a critique of Solomon's foreign policy!

Finally, it should be noted that we actually possess an interpretation of the Eden story written not long after 586 BCE in Ezekiel 28, and significantly this does not relate it to Judah and its exile (in spite of Ezekiel's great focus on this subject throughout his prophecy) but rather to the fate of the king of Tyre. There is also evidence that J is a pre-exilic source. So this brings us to our next topic.

11. *Ezekiel 28, its Relationship to Genesis 2–3, and the Date of J*

Ezekiel 28 and Genesis 2–3 sound like different versions of the same myth. In both we read of a man who was in the Garden of Eden, and who was subsequently cast out by God because of sin. In Gen. 3.24 the cherubim guard the way to the tree of life after the man's expulsion, while in Ezek. 28.16 it is a cherub who casts the man out. There is also an association of the man with wisdom in both versions: in Ezekiel the man is already wise in the garden from the beginning until he is cast out because of pride, whereas in Genesis 3 the man acquires wisdom as a result of eating the forbidden fruit, immediately prior to his expulsion from the garden.

---

77. W. von Soden, 'Verschlüsselte Kritik an Salomo in der Urgeschichte des Jahwisten?', *WO* 7 (1974), pp. 228-40 (233-36), reprinted in H.-P. Müller (ed.), *Bibel und alter Orient: Altorientalische Beiträge zum Alten Testament von Wolfram von Soden* (BZAW, 162; Berlin: W. de Gruyter, 1985), pp. 174-86 (179-82); M. Görg, 'Die Sünde Salomos. Zeitkritische Aspekte der jahwistischen Sündenfallerzählung', *BN* 16 (1981), pp. 42-59; idem, 'Weisheit als Provokation: Religionsgeschichtliche und theologische Aspekte der Sündenfallerzählung', in A.E. Hierold *et al.* (eds.), *Die Kraft der Hoffnung. Gemeinde und Evangelium. Festschrift für Alterzbischof DDr. Josef Schneider zum 80. Geburtstag* (Bamberg: St Otto-Verlag, 1986), pp. 19-34; K. Holter, 'The Serpent in Eden as a Symbol of Israel's Political Enemies: A Yahwistic Criticism of the Solomonic Foreign Policy?', *SJOT* 4 (1990), pp. 106-12.

Among the points listed above is that of a cherub casting out the man in Ezek. 28.16. This is the view that we find in the Septuagint and Peshitta, whereas the MT rather equates the man with the cherub. Similarly, the Septuagint and Peshitta of Ezek. 28.14 imply that the man is 'with (Hebrew *ʾet*) the cherub', whereas the MT addresses the man, 'you (Hebrew *ʾatt*) are a...cherub'. The following reasons may be given for supporting the Septuagint and Peshitta understanding. First, the parallels between Genesis 2–3 and Ezekiel 28 are in general such that it is most likely that they are alternative versions of the same myth, in which case the cherub would not be identical with the man but set over against him. Secondly, it is unparalleled in the whole of Old Testament and Jewish literature for there to be a wicked cherub or a cherub who is cast out of Eden. On the other hand, James Barr[78] has argued that it is easier to understand how the MT's *ʾatt*, 'you', was corrupted to *ʾet*, 'with', rather than the other way round. However, this view is open to question. In both the previous and succeeding verses of Ezekiel 28 the king is addressed in the second person, and it is, moreover, rare to start a sentence with *ʾet*, 'with', so it is quite easy to imagine how a scribe might have misunderstood *ʾet* as *ʾatt*, 'you'.

Both J. Van Seters and T.N.D. Mettinger have claimed that Genesis 2–3 is dependent on Ezekiel 28.[79] This would make Genesis 2–3 exilic or post-exilic. It has in fact become quite fashionable in recent years to date J to the exilic period, but I remain unconvinced. First, with regard to content, nowhere in J do we find clear evidence of the doom and gloom of the exilic era that manifests itself in all indisputably exilic works, the toleration of a multitude of local sanctuaries in the patriarchal narratives bespeaks a date before Deuteronomy, and the positive attitude to Esau (Edom) in Genesis 33 (see, e.g., vv. 3, 10) is quite out of keeping with the hatred of the exilic and post-exilic period.[80] Moreover, within

78. J. Barr, '"Thou Art the Cherub": Ezekiel 28.14 and the Post-Ezekiel Understanding of Genesis 2–3', in E.C. Ulrich *et al.* (eds.), *Priests, Prophets and Scribes: Essays on the Formation and Heritage of Second Temple Judaism in Honour of Joseph Blenkinsopp* (JSOTSup, 140; JSOT Press, 1992), pp. 213-22.

79. J. Van Seters, 'The Creation of Man and the Creation of the King', *ZAW* 101 (1989), pp, 333-42; *idem, Prologue to History*, pp. 19-22; Mettinger, *The Eden Narrative*, pp. 85-98.

80. For powerful defences of a pre-exilic J, see E.W. Nicholson, *The Pentateuch in the Twentieth Century: The Legacy of Julius Wellhausen* (Oxford: Clarendon Press, 1998), pp. 132-60; J.A. Emerton, 'The Date of the Yahwist', in J. Day (ed.), *In Search of Pre-Exilic Israel: Proceedings of the Oxford Old Testament Seminar*

Genesis 1–11, Calah is described as 'the great city' in Gen. 10.12, which would be particularly apt between c. 880 and c. 700 BCE when it was the capital of Assyria, prior to Nineveh taking over that role, but not during the exile when Calah was destroyed and abandoned. Within that period, my hunch would be that J dates somewhere between c. 850 and c. 730 BCE, since Gen. 27.40 shows knowledge of Judah's loss of Edom at the former date and Hosea seems aware of J traditions at the later date (cf. Hos. 12).

Secondly, linguistically, the evidence also points to a pre-exilic date. More than any other part of the Old Testament the J source shows a preference for *ʾānōkî* over *ʾªnî* for 'I' (including Gen. 3.10), the latter form becoming the norm during the post-exilic period, so J ought to be one of the earliest parts of the Old Testament. By contrast, Ezekiel, always uses *ʾªnî*, with but one exception.[81] Similarly, J employs the qal *yālad* rather than the hiphil *hôlîd* to mean 'to beget', and as R.S. Hendel has shown, the qal is the older form, whereas P (probably sixth century BCE), employs the later hiphil form.[82] It is also interesting to note that J has a liking for the passive qal (including Gen. 3.19, 23), which later became replaced by the niphal. It has been demonstrated that J is written uniformly in Classical, not Late, Biblical Hebrew,[83] and there are good reasons for believing that the exile provides the dividing point between the two, as the former strongly parallels what is attested in pre-exilic Hebrew inscriptions.[84] On the other hand, the exilic Ezekiel represents a transitional stage in the development of Hebrew.[85] Accordingly, it is unlikely that Genesis 2–3 is dependent on Ezekiel 28, the former rather appearing to be earlier.

(JSOTSup, 406; London: T&T Clark International, 2004), pp. 107-29; R.S. Hendel, 'Historical Context', in C.A. Evans, J.N. Lohr and D.L. Petersen (eds.), *The Book of Genesis: Composition, Reception, and Interpretation* (VTSup, 152; Leiden: Brill, 2012), pp. 51-81.

81. See the data in BDB, p. 59.

82. R.S. Hendel, '"Begetting" and "Being Born" in the Pentateuch: Notes on Historical Linguistics and Source Criticism', *VT* 50 (2000), pp. 38-46.

83. R.M. Wright, *Linguistic Evidence for the Pre-Exilic Date of the Yahwistic Source* (LHBOTS, 419; London: T&T Clark International, 2005).

84. See J. Joosten, 'The Operation of Syntactic Rule in Classical Biblical Hebrew and in Hebrew Inscriptions of the Monarchic Period', in J.K. Aitken, K.J. Dell and B.A. Mastin (eds.), *On Stone and Scroll: A Festschrift for Graham Ivor Davies* (BZAW, 420; Berlin: W. de Gruyter, 2011), pp. 493-50.

85. See M.F. Rooker, *Biblical Hebrew in Transition: The Language of the Book of Ezekiel* (JSOTSup, 90; Sheffield: JSOT Press, 1990).

12. *Permanent Value?*

The story of the Garden of Eden is a myth. But is there any enduring message that one may take away from it? I would suggest that there is. The events of the Garden of Eden do not depict an actual historical one-off event of bygone times when our first ancestors fell from grace and were cast out of Paradise as was once supposed, since we know that human beings were imperfect creatures from the beginning who evolved out of lower forms of life. Nevertheless, there came a time, or countless times, when primitive human beings developed the first stirrings of conscience, an awareness of falling short of a higher moral law, and we may regard the story of the Garden of Eden as a mythical reflection of this experience.[86] Furthermore, whether we care to use the religious language of 'sin' or not, there is no doubt that the story lays bear uncomfortable truths about human nature. As already mentioned earlier, the way the man blames the woman and the woman blames the serpent is very true to much human experience as we know it: the tendency to blame others rather than take responsibility ourselves for our actions. Each of us, if we are honest, has to admit that we fall short of what we could be. And here the words of the Syriac Apocalypse of Baruch, *2 Bar.* 54.19, come to mind, 'Each of us has been the Adam of his own soul'. And just as Adam's sin resulted in his being cast out of the garden, so our own evil actions are fraught with consequences both for ourselves and for others. In the words of St Paul, whatsoever a man sows, that shall he reap (Gal. 6.7).

86. Cf. G.A. Barton, *Christ and Evolution: A Study of the Doctrine of Redemption in the Light of Modern Knowledge* (Philadelphia: University of Pennsylvania Press, 1934), pp. 1-26.

Chapter 3

CAIN AND THE KENITES

The purpose of this chapter is to reargue the case for understanding the story of Cain in Genesis 4 as being an aetiology of the tribe of the Kenites. This was first argued in the nineteenth century by H. Ewald, J. Wellhausen and B. Stade and taken up by others,[1] but a glance at commentaries on the book of Genesis in recent decades indicates that

---

1. H. Ewald, 'Erklärung der Biblischen urgeschichte. 4. Die geschlechter des ersten Weltalters', *Jahrbücher der Biblischen wissenschaft* [*sic*] 6 (1853–54), pp. 1-19 (esp. pp. 5-6); B. Stade, 'Das Kainszeichen', *ZAW* 14 (1894), pp. 250-318; H. Zeynder, 'Kainszeichen, Keniter und Beschneidung', *ZAW* 18 (1898), pp. 120-25; J. Wellhausen, *Die Composition des Hexateuchs* (Berlin: G. Reimer, 3rd edn, 1899), p. 9, but already in earlier editions; E. Meyer, *Die Israeliten und ihre Nachbarstämme* (Halle: Max Niemeyer, 1906), pp. 219, 394-99; H. Gunkel, *Genesis* (HKAT, 1.1; Göttingen: Vandenhoeck & Ruprecht, 3rd edn, 1910), p. 48, ET *Genesis* (trans. M.E. Biddle; Macon, GA: Mercer University Press, 1997), p. 48, in contrast to earlier editions of his commentary; W. Vischer, *Jahwe der Gott Kains* (Munich: Chr. Kaiser Verlag, 1929), pp. 1-28; S. Mowinckel, *The Two Sources of the Predeuteronomic Primeval History (JE) in Gen. 1–11* (Avhandlinger utgitt av Det Norske Videnskaps-Akademi i Oslo, II. Hist.-Filos. Klasse 1937, no. 2; Oslo: J. Dybwad, 1937), pp. 25-43; G. von Rad, *Das erste Buch Mose: Genesis* (ATD, 2.4; Göttingen: Vandenhoeck & Ruprecht, 5th edn, 1958), pp. 87-88, 90, ET *Genesis* (trans. J.H. Marks; OTL; London: SCM Press, 2nd edn, 1963), pp. 104-105, 107 (though von Rad envisages the originally tribal figure of Cain as having been universalized in its current primaeval setting); H. Heyde, *Kain, der erste Jahwe-Verehrer* (Stuttgart: Calwer Verlag, 1965). S.R. Driver, *Genesis* (Westminster Commentaries; London: Methuen, 1904), p. 72, regarded the Kenite view as possible. Among more recent commentators J.A. Soggin, *Genesis 1–11* (Commentario storico ed esegetico all'Antico e al Nuovo Testamento, AT 1.1; Turin: Marietti, 1991), p. 99, also regards it as possible, but J.J. Scullion, *Genesis: A Commentary for Students, Teachers, and Preachers* (OT Studies, 6; Collegeville, MN: Liturgical Press, 1992), p. 52, is the only Genesis commentary in recent decades I have discovered that asserts categorically that Cain is the eponymous ancestor of the Kenites.

this standpoint is now largely overlooked or even rejected,[2] though without good reason, as I shall argue.

The most obvious argument for seeing a connection between Cain and the Kenites is the very name, since the Hebrew word *qayin* is used for both. That *qayin* denotes the Kenites is clear from Num. 24.22 and Judg. 4.11. The latter passage states, 'Now Heber the Kenite had separated from the Kenites (*qayin*), the descendants of Hobab the father-in-law of Moses…' In Num. 24.21-22 we read of Balaam, 'And he looked on the Kenite, and took up his discourse, and said, "Enduring is your dwelling place, and your nest is set in the rock; nevertheless Kain (*qayin*) shall be wasted. How long shall Asshur take you away captive?"' In each case the context makes it indubitable that *qayin* is a collective singular name referring to the Kenites. Incidentally, in the latter passage Asshur clearly refers to the Assyrians, not to the Arab tribe of the Asshurim, since in the Hebrew Bible Asshur occurs numerous times in the singular and never in the plural with reference to Assyria (e.g. Gen. 2.14; 10.11, 22; Isa. 8.4; 10.5, 12; Hos. 5.13; 7.11; 8.9; Nah. 3.18), whereas the Arab tribe appears only in the plural as Asshurim (Gen. 25.3).[3] We thus appear to have here

---

2.   Commentators on the book of Genesis who fail even to mention the Kenite view include E.A. Speiser, *Genesis* (AB, 1; Garden City, NY: Doubleday, 1964); J.C.L. Gibson, *Genesis* (2 vols.; Daily Study Bible; Edinburgh: Saint Andrew Press, 1981–82 [1981]), I; G.W. Coats, *Genesis with an Introduction to Narrative Literature* (FOTL; Grand Rapids, MI: Eerdmans, 1983); G.J. Wenham, *Genesis 1–15* (WBC, 1; Waco, TX: Word Books, 1987); V.P. Hamilton, *The Book of Genesis Chapters 1–17* (NICOT; Grand Rapids, MI: Eerdmans, 1990); R. Alter, *Genesis* (New York: W.W. Norton, 1996); J. McKeown, *Genesis* (Two Horizons OT Commentary; Grand Rapids, MI: Eerdmans, 2008). N.M. Sarna, *Genesis* (JPS Torah Commentary; Philadelphia: Jewish Publication Society, 1989), does not mention the Kenite hypothesis in his discussion of the Cain story (Gen. 4.1-16), though he subsequently indicates awareness of the possible Midianite–Kenite connection of Cain's son Enoch on p. 36. R. Davidson, *Genesis 1–11* (CBC; Cambridge: Cambridge University Press, 1973), p. 50, regards this and all other attempts to trace the Cain story's prehistory as 'purely speculative'. U. (M.D.) Cassuto, *A Commentary on the Book of Genesis. I. From Adam to Noah, Genesis 1–VI 8* (trans. I. Abrahams; Jerusalem: Magnes Press, 1961), pp. 179-83, and C. Westermann, *Genesis 1–11* (BKAT, I.1; Neukirchen–Vluyn: Neukirchener Verlag, 1974), pp. 385-88, 428-32, ET *Genesis 1–11* (trans. J.J. Scullion; London: SPCK, 1984), pp. 282-284, 315-18, explicitly reject the Kenite interpretation. An older commentator who rejected the view that Cain was an aetiology of the Kenites was J. Skinner, *A Critical and Exegetical Commentary on Genesis* (ICC; Edinburgh: T. & T. Clark, 1910), pp. 111-15, though he accepted that Gen. 4.13-16 was an aetiology of nomadic life more generally.

3.   *Contra* J. de Vaulx, *Les Nombres* (Sources bibliques; Paris: J. Gabalda, 1972), pp. 295-96; G.J. Wenham, *Numbers* (Tyndale Commentary; Leicester: Inter-Varsity

a reference to the Assyrians taking the Kenites into captivity. In my view the line about the Kenites' captivity could well be a later gloss since it conflicts both with the positive tone regarding the Kenites in the first line as well as all the surrounding verses that speak of Israel's victories over her enemies in the time of David and Saul, when the Kenites were rather a friendly tribe that was spared (cf. 1 Sam. 15.6). Although we have no explicit reference to the Kenites being carried away captive in the Assyrian records, the reference to this most naturally fits into the period of the eighth century or possibly seventh century BCE, when the Assyrians were most aggressive in their policy of deportation of various

Press, 1981), p. 181; J. Milgrom, *Numbers* (JPS Torah Commentary; Philadelphia: Jewish Publication Society, 1990), p. 209; T.R. Ashleigh, *The Book of Numbers* (NICOT; Grand Rapids, MI: Eerdmans, 1993), p. 508, who claim that Asshur in Num. 24.22 refers to the Arab tribe. Occasionally it has been supposed that Asshur in Ps. 83.9 (ET 8) also refers to the Arab tribe rather than to Assyria (e.g. H. Gunkel, *Die Psalmen* [HKAT, 11.2; Göttingen: Vandenhoeck & Ruprecht, 1925–26], p. 365; de Vaulx, *Les Nombres*, p. 296), but not only does the singular form tell against this but the fact that Asshur is said there to be 'the (strong) arm of the children of Lot' (i.e. of the Moabites and Edomites just referred to; cf. Gen. 19.30-38; Deut. 2.9, 19), language appropriate for the mighty Assyria but not the insignificant Arab tribe of the Asshurim. That 'arm' is a metaphor for 'strength' or 'power' is indicated by various biblical references (e.g. Exod. 6.6; 15.16; 2 Kgs 17.36; Job 22.8; Isa. 33.2; Jer. 21.5; Dan. 11.6). Yet again, it has occasionally been supposed that 2 Sam. 2.9 refers to these Arab Asshurim (e.g. de Vaulx, *Les Nombres*, p. 296), where we read that 'He [Abner] made him [Ishbaal] king over Gilead, the Ashurites, Jezreel, Ephraim, Benjamin, and over all Israel'. However, since all the other places alluded to are in northern Israel or Transjordan, a reference to the Arab Asshurim seems out of place (as would even more, of course, a reference to Assyria). Most likely the text is slightly corrupt and we should emend *hāᵖᵃšûrî* to *hāʾāšērî*, the Asherites (cf. Judg. 1.32), i.e. the northern Israelite tribe of Asher (cf. Targum 'the house of Asher'). Cf. J.A. Soggin, 'The Reign of ʾEšbaʿal, Son of Saul', in *Old Testament and Oriental Studies* (Biblica et Orientalia, 29; Rome: Biblical Institute Press, 1975), pp. 31-49 (41-43); B. Oded, 'Ish-bosheth', in *Encyclopaedia Judaica* (22 vols.; Detroit: Thomson Gale [Macmillan Reference USA], 2nd edn, 2007), X, pp. 80-81 (81); though D. Edelman, 'The "Ashurites" of Eshbaal's State', *PEQ* 117 (1985), pp. 85-91, thinks in terms of an Asherite enclave further south. The reading 'Geshurites' (*haggᵉšûrî*), presupposed by the Peshitta and Vulgate, is less likely, since 2 Sam. 3.3 implies that Geshur was an independent kingdom at this time. The LXX B text has *Thaseirei*, the A text reads *Thasour*, while the Lucianic recension has *Ezri*: the first two readings imply the corruption of the initial Hebrew letter *he* to *taw*. W. Wifall, 'Asshur and Eber, or Asher and Heber? A Commentary on the Last Balaam Oracle, Num 24 21-24', *ZAW* 80 (1970), pp. 110-14, implausibly emends the text so as to find a reference to the Israelite tribe of Asher also in Num. 24.22, 24, and Eber is emended to Heber in Num. 24.24, but these speculations have found no following.

peoples of the Levant (including Arabs), the standard volume on which has been written by Bustenay Oded.[4]

Not only does the name *qayin*[5] suggest a connection between Cain and the Kenites, but the lifestyle to which Cain is destined—a life of wandering—also fits the semi-nomadic lifestyle of the Kenites. Cain is described as becoming 'a fugitive and a wanderer (*nāʿ wānād*) on the earth' (Gen. 4.14), the hiphil of the first of these verbs being used elsewhere of the Israelites wandering in the wilderness for forty years (Num. 13.32). That the Kenites were semi-nomadic is attested, for example, by Judg. 5.24, where Jael, the wife of Heber the Kenite, is described as 'of tent-dwelling women most blessed', and one of Cain's descendants, Jabal, is referred to in Gen. 4.20 as 'the father of those who dwell in tents'. It has also often been believed in the past that the Rechabites, who lived in tents rather than houses, as well as refusing to drink wine, sow seed or plant vineyards long after the time of the Israelite settlement (Jer. 35.1-19, esp. 7-10),[6] are represented as being descendants of the Kenites in 1 Chron. 2.55, but this interpretation now appears unlikely.[7] Anyway,

---

4.   See B. Oded, *Mass Deportations and Deportees in the Neo-Assyrian Empire* (Wiesbaden: O. Harrassowitz, 1979). Cf. too I. Eph'al, *The Ancient Arabs* (Jerusalem: Magnes Press, 1982).

5.   The name *qayin* is most naturally to be seen as cognate with Arabic *qayn* as well as Aramaic *qynyʾ*, 'smith', the latter being attested with several different vocalizations. (Hebrew *qayin*, 'spear', in 2 Sam. 21.16 is related to this.) This gains support from the fact that Cain's descendant, Tubal-Cain, is said to have 'made all kinds of bronze and iron tools' (Gen. 4.22). The Yahwist's connection of the name with the root *qnh*, 'to create' (Gen. 4.1), is, of course, in the nature of a popular etymology and is comparable to J's other suggested etymologies for Seth, Noah, Babel, Levi and Judah (Gen. 4.25; 5.29; 11.9; 29.34, 35).

6.   It is interesting to note that the lifestyle of the Nabataean Arabs, who lived in the wilderness not so far away from the earlier Kenites, is described in remarkably similar terms in Diodorus Siculus, *Univ. Hist.* 19.94.3 (deriving from the fourth century BCE historian Hieronymus of Cardia): 'It is their custom neither to plant grain, set out any fruit-bearing tree, use wine, nor construct any house...' Moreover, just as the Rechabites kept to this lifestyle in obedience to the command of Jonadab son of Rechab (Jer. 35.6, 8, 14, 16, 18), so Diodorus presents the Nabataeans' lifestyle as a legal obligation (disobedience to which was punishable by death).

7.   On the one hand, 1 Chron. 2.55 makes reference to certain 'Kenites, who came from Hammath, father of *bêt-rēkāb*'. By analogy with other references in this chapter the last expression must allude to a personified place name, Beth-rechab, rather than to the 'house of Rechab', contrary to what has often been supposed in the past. This is perhaps to be equated with Beth-markaboth, apparently near Beersheba, attested in Josh. 19.5; 1 Chron. 4.31. On the other hand, the Rechabites are repeatedly described as being descended from Jonadab son of Rechab (Jer. 35.6, 8, 14, 16, 19; cf. 2 Kgs 10.15, 23), Rechab surely being a reference to Jonadab's actual

the combination of the name Cain (*qayin*) and the life of wandering which is his fate makes it attractive to see the story of Cain as an aetiology of the Kenites. This coheres with Genesis more generally, which is noteworthy for the large number of aetiologies (both ethnic and otherwise) that it contains.

An additional two arguments for a Kenite background to the figure of Cain in Genesis 4, which have been generally overlooked in recent years, emerge from the names of his brother Seth and his son Enoch. Thus, first, it can hardly be due to chance that the oracles of Balaam, which allude to the Kenites as Cain in Num. 24.22 refer only a few verses earlier (Num. 24.17) to another tribal group as Seth (literally Sheth).[8] We there read that what is clearly the Davidic monarchy 'will smite the foreheads of Moab, the scalps[9] of all the sons of Seth'. The tribal name Seth here is identical in spelling to the figure of Seth in Genesis 4, but this has been somewhat concealed in English Bibles, which inconsistently follow the Greek spelling Seth in Genesis 4 but the Hebrew spelling Sheth in Numbers 24. It is clear from Num. 24.17 that the 'sons of Seth' are to be located in the area of Moab, and so a bit further north than the Kenites. It is generally accepted that 'the sons of Seth' are to be equated with the tribe of the Shutu, the name of a nomadic people in Transjordan attested in the Egyptian execration texts from the early second millennium BCE, as well as in other texts.[10] This view was first

father. Evidence is lacking that 'son of Rechab' might mean 'coming from Beth-rechab', not that I have seen anyone suggest that (see J. Day, *Yahweh and the Gods and Goddesses of Canaan* [JSOTSup, 265; Sheffield: Sheffield Academic Press, 2000], pp. 133-35, for a critique of alleged comparable examples of 'son of Anat' and 'son of Rehob'). See further C.H. Knights, 'Kenites = Rechabites? 1 Chronicles ii 55 Reconsidered', *VT* 43 (1993), pp. 1-18.

8.   Wenham, *Genesis 1–15*, p. 115, states dogmatically that 'There is certainly no connection between Seth and the tribe of Shut mentioned in Num 24:17', failing to take account of the fact that the tribal names Seth and Cain are mentioned in close proximity in Num. 24, just as the primaeval individuals Seth and Cain are closely associated in Gen. 4.

9.   Reading *wᵉqodqod* for MT *wᵉqarqar*, following the Samaritan version and Jer. 48.45. 'Scalp' makes an excellent parallel to 'forehead', and interestingly *qodqod*, 'scalp', is similarly found as the object of the verb *mḥṣ*, 'smite', in Ps. 68.22 (ET 21).

10.   Cf. A.H. Sayce, 'Ur of the Chaldees', *ExpTim* 13 (1901–1902), pp. 64-66 (64), which should be contrasted with his earlier view in 'Balaam's Prophecy (Numbers xxiv.17-24) and the God Sheth', *Hebraica* 4 (1887), pp. 1-6, where he thought Sheth was a Moabite god; W.F. Albright, 'The Land of Damascus between 1850 and 1750 B.C.', *BASOR* 83 (1941), pp. 30-36 (34 n. 8); *idem*, 'The Oracles of Balaam', *JBL* 63 (1944), pp. 207-33 (220 n. 89); de Vaulx, *Les Nombres*, p. 290; J. Milgrom,

put forward by A.H. Sayce and has been widely accepted since.[11] Jeremiah 48.45 echoes Num. 24.17, stating that 'it [a fire] has destroyed the forehead of Moab, the scalp of the sons of tumult (*šāʾôn*)', reading 'sons of tumult (*šāʾôn*)' instead of 'sons of Seth (*šēt*)', but this must represent either a misunderstanding of an expression that had become obscure with the passage of time or alternatively a tendentious alteration of the original allusion.[12] Either way, what is clear from the poetic parallelism in Num. 24.17 is that the phrase *bᵉnê šēt*, 'sons of Seth', must originally have been an ethnic designation for a tribal group in the area of Moab, just as the immediately preceding and following lines use the parallel ethnic names Jacob/Israel and Edom/Seir respectively.

Secondly, as for Enoch, the name of Cain's son in Gen. 4.17, it is noteworthy that the identical name (Hebrew *hᵃnōk*) occurs as one of the sons of Midian in Gen. 25.4 and 1 Chron. 1.33,[13] presumably denoting a Midianite clan, just as Ephah, another son of Midian mentioned in the same verse, is attested as a north-west Arabian tribal name in Assyrian inscriptions as *Ha-a-a-ap-pa-a-a* (Tiglath-pileser III, 734 BCE) or *Ha-ia-pa-a* (Sargon II, 716 BCE). Bearing in mind the evidence for the association of the Kenites with the Midianites (e.g. Moses's father-in-law is

Numbers (JPS Torah Commentary; Philadelphia: Jewish Publication Society, 1990), p. 208; E.W. Davies, *Numbers* (NBC; London: Marshall Pickering, 1995), p. 275. Von Rad, *Das erste Buch Mose*, p. 92, also shares this view, the English translation (*Genesis*, p. 109) wrongly refers to 'Guti' instead of 'Suti' owing to the translator misreading the Gothic script letter 'S' as 'G'!

11. For the references to the Shutu in the Execration texts, see K. Sethe, *Die Ächtung feindlicher Fürsten, Völker und Dinge auf altägyptischen Tongefässscherben der mittleren Reiches* (Berlin: Akademie der Wissenschaften in Kommission bei W. de Gruyter, 1926), pp. 46-47, 56 (texts e4-6, f5); G. Posener, *Princes et pays d'Asie et de Nubie* (Brussels: Fondation égyptologique reine Elisabeth, 1940), pp. 89-90 (texts E52-53); Y. Koenig, 'Les textes d'envoûtement de Mirgissa', *Revue d'Egyptologie* 41 (1990), pp. 101-25 (111; texts F4, G5); cf. *ANET*, p. 329, and *COS* 1, p. 51 for some of these. This tribal group is also attested in Akkadian under the name Suti in texts such as those from Mari. Cf. J.R. Kupper, 'Sutéens et Hapiru', *RA* 55 (1961), pp. 197-205. It has sometimes been proposed that there is a connection between the Shutu and the Shosu, but I cannot go into this question here.

12. For the former view, see, e.g., Albright, 'The Oracles of Balaam', p. 220 n. 89, and for the latter opinion, see, e.g., B.A. Levine, *Numbers 21–36* (AB, 4A; New York: Doubleday, 2000), p. 202.

13. The only difference, insignificant in importance, is that the MT spells the Midianite name as *hᵃnōk* in Gen. 25.4, whereas the antediluvian figure's name includes the vowel letter (*hᵃnôk*). However, the vowel letter waw is included in the other occurrence of the Midianite name in 1 Chron. 1.33. It should also be noted that Hanoch (Enoch) appears additionally as the name of a Reubenite clan in Gen. 46.9; Exod. 6.14; Num. 26.5; 1 Chron. 5.3.

described as both a Midianite in Exod. 3.1; 18.1 [Jethro]; Num. 10.29 [Hobab], and a Kenite in Judg. 1.16; 4.11 [Hobab]), it seems difficult to view this as merely due to coincidence. It is no objection to Cain's equation with the Kenites/Midianites that his son Enoch had a city named after him (Gen. 4.17),[14] since 1 Sam. 30.29 specifically makes mention of 'the cities of the Kenites' in the Negeb (cf. too a town in Judah named Kain in Josh. 15.57). It may be that Enoch is to be equated with the Hanikites, a tribal group in north Arabia, as E.A. Knauf has suggested.[15] If one follows the natural and generally accepted understanding that Genesis 4 is from J and Genesis 5 is from P, and that the former is earlier than the latter, it is plausible to suppose that P deliberately transferred the position of Enoch to its special seventh place so as to correspond to the seventh figure of Enmeduranki in the antediluvian Mesopotamian King list.[16] In this way we can explain how traditions about Enmeduranki as a seer with solar associations became attached to the figure of Enoch, whose name originally denoted a Midianite clan name (cf. Enoch's 365-year length of life in Gen. 5.24 and his promotion of the solar calendar in *1 En.* 72–82).[17]

14. Although the MT states that Cain named the city after his son Enoch and there is no textual evidence to the contrary, some scholars wish to emend the text so as to read either that Enoch named the city after himself or that Enoch named it after his son, that is, Irad (supposedly denoting Eridu). However, against the last view it may be noted that it is not till the next verse that we read that Enoch begat a son Irad, so a reference to a city being named after him already in v. 17 seems premature. Also, an allusion to Eridu in Mesopotamia seems out of place in this context. So the city will have been called Enoch (Hanoch), whether we retain the MT or follow the first emendation.

15. Cf. E.A. Knauf, *Midian: Untersuchungen zur Geschichte Palästinas und Nordarabiens am Ende des 2. Jahrtausends v. Chr.* (Abhandlungen der deutschen Palästinavereins; Wiesbaden: O. Harrassowitz, 1988), pp. 81-84.

16. There are various versions of the Mesopotamian antediluvian King list. Not all of them have ten kings (some have eight or nine) and the position of Enmeduranki also differs slightly between them. However, Enmeduranki does occur as the seventh out of ten names in Berossus, who has a number of particularly striking parallels with the Priestly source both here and in their accounts of the flood over against other versions. See below, Chapter 4, for more information on this.

17. On the Mesopotamian background to the Enoch traditions generally, see J.C. VanderKam, *Enoch and the Growth of an Apocalyptic Tradition* (CBQMS, 16; Washington, DC: Catholic Biblical Association, 1984), esp. pp. 33-75; H.S. Kvanvig, *Roots of Apocalyptic: The Mesopotamian Background of the Enoch Figure and of the Son of Man* (WMANT, 61; Neukirchen–Vluyn: Neukirchener Verlag, 1988), pp. 15-342.

A further point may now be noted that coheres with the Kenites being around since near the beginning of humanity, such as we are arguing is implied in Genesis 4. This is the fact that the Kenites were closely associated with the Amalekites (cf. Judg. 1.16; 1 Sam. 15.6) and that in the course of Balaam's oracles we read: 'First of the nations was Amalek, but his end is to perish for ever' (Num. 24.20). Different opinions have been expressed as to whether 'first of the nations' means that the Amalekites were the first in importance or the first that existed.[18] The evidence clearly suggests, however, that it is the latter meaning that is intended. First, the Amalekites were such a tiny tribal group that it would have been ludicrous for anyone ever to imagine that they could be regarded as the first in importance.[19] Secondly, the words 'first' ($r\bar{e}$'$\check{s}\hat{\imath}t$) and 'end' ('$ah^{a}r\hat{\imath}t$) clearly stand in antithetical parallelism, and since the word 'end' has a temporal reference this must likewise be the case with 'first', as in all the other instances where the words $r\bar{e}$'$\check{s}\hat{\imath}t$ and '$ah^{a}r\hat{\imath}t$ stand in opposition (Deut. 11.12; Isa. 46.10; Job 8.7, 42.12; Eccl. 7.8). It is plausible to suppose that there is a connection between the tradition that Amalek was the most ancient of nations and the implication of Genesis 4 that the closely associated Kenites arose in the second generation of humanity.[20] This must reflect an alternative view to the one found in Gen. 36.12, 16 according to which Amalek was the grandson of Esau/Edom, but it should be noted that Gen. 14.7 likewise attests the notion that the Amalekites existed at an earlier date.

18.   Some have seen a reference to Amalek's antiquity (e.g. Meyer, *Die Israeliten*, p. 395), whereas others have understood a reference to Amalek's pre-eminence (e.g. D. Edelman, 'Saul's Battle against Amaleq', *JSOT* 35 [1986], pp. 71-84 [74], who originally proposes that the reference is to Amalek's pre-eminence in a long-standing rivalry with Israel for control of the Ephraimite hills, but her thesis about such a conflict, which she also sees in 1 Sam. 15, is highly speculative). Again, Levine (*Numbers 21–36*, p. 204) claims that both meanings are implied, but this seems unlikely, as is his view that the antiquity part refers to Amalek's being the first to do battle with Israel (Exod. 17.8-16), a view found already in the Targum.

19.   Some mediaeval Arab historians believed that the Amalekites had once been pharaohs of Egypt, an idea that was taken up in Immanuel Velikovsky's eccentric reconstruction of ancient history in *Ages in Chaos* (London: Sidgwick & Jackson, 1953), pp. 55-101, which equated them with the Hyksos. However, T. Nöldeke, *Ueber die Amalekiter und einige andere Nachbarvölker der Israeliten* (Göttingen: Dieterich, 1864), had already shown in the nineteenth century how implausible it was to suppose that these historians had access to authentic information going back thousands of years.

20.   Cf. Meyer, *Die Israeliten*, p. 395.

If we accept that the story of Cain was intended as an aetiology of the Kenites, there seems no natural reason why this should *originally* have been regarded as taking place so soon after the creation of the world and the first man. It is much more likely that this has been projected back from a later time. In this way we can answer the old problem of where Cain got his wife from (Gen. 4.17): the story originally came from a later period when lots of women were around.[21] Similarly, the danger that someone might slay Cain (Gen. 4.14-15) presupposes the existence of other people, which is not the case with the story in its current primaeval setting. Again, the genealogy of Cain's descendants that follows (Gen. 4.17-24), which describes the acquisition of various aspects of civilization, is ignorant of the flood that subsequently destroyed civilization—this too fits an originally later setting. One may recall that in Gen. 25.4 Midian and various Midianite clans are still represented as emerging at a later time as descendants of Abraham.

But are we to assume that by being projected back to primaeval times the tribal figure of Cain has been transformed into merely a primaeval individual divorced of ethnic overtones?[22] It is true that Cain is depicted as a primaeval individual and that his story is now part of the early history of humanity, not just that of a tribe. However, that of itself does not prevent his being understood at the same time as the eponymous ancestor of the Kenites, just as the various individual sons of Shem, Ham and Japheth in Genesis 10 are at the same time symbolic of various nations and cities, Esau is the ancestor of the Edomites (Gen. 36, etc.) and so on. Even less does it mean, as C. Westermann[23] supposed, that we have here an argument against the whole concept of an original connection of Cain with the Kenites. In favour of the view that the narrative retained its tribal overtones we may point to the fact that the story of Cain is followed immediately afterwards in Gen. 4.17-24 by a genealogy of his descendants from Enoch to Lamech, and what is there stated is suggestive of a tribal understanding. We have already noted that Enoch was the name of a Midianite clan. Moreover, Cain's descendants include Jabal, the father of those who dwell in tents and have livestock, Jubal, the father of those who play the lyre and harp, and Tubal-Cain, who made all kinds of tools of bronze and iron (Gen. 4.20-22). This is a

---

21. A later Jewish solution to this problem was to claim that Cain married his sister (*Jub.* 4.9; *b. Sanh.* 58b). This might have been influenced by P's statement in Gen. 5.4 that Adam 'had other sons *and daughters*' (in addition to Seth), though the earlier J account says nothing of his having had daughters.

22. Cf. von Rad, *Das erste Buch Mose*, pp. 87-88, ET *Genesis*, pp. 104-105.

23. Westermann, *Genesis 1–11*, ET *Genesis 1–11*, *loc cit.*

rather limited range of professions, much less than what we find, say, in the technogony section of Philo of Byblos's *Phoenician History*,[24] and hardly constitutes an aetiology of the full range of human activities. Rather, what we have here would appear to be occupations typical of the Kenites. Thus, just as Jabal was the father of those who dwell in tents, so we know the Kenites to have been tent dwellers (Judg. 5.24), and just as Tubal-Cain was a metal worker, so the Kenites must have been a tribe of smiths, as their very name indicates. As for Jubal, the father of those who play the lyre and pipe, it should be noted that music is often associated elsewhere with wandering herdsmen, as in Greek mythology where it was the shepherd god Pan who invented the pipe. Moreover, even in the final form of the text it cannot be claimed that Cain is an ancestor of the whole human race, since we are not informed of his descendants beyond Genesis 4. Most scholars support the likelihood that J's Noah, the ancestor of the world's nations, was understood to be rather a descendant of Seth, just as in P (notwithstanding the resemblances in names between the J Cainite genealogy in Gen. 4 and P's Sethite genealogy in Gen. 5). This is supported by the fact that in Gen 9.20 J depicts Noah as a tiller of the soil, thereby becoming the first to discover wine, the fruit of the vine (anticipated in the fragmentary J genealogical insertion in the Genesis P's narrative in 5.29), which does not cohere so well with the nomadic genealogy of Cain.

In conclusion, a strong case can be made for assuming that the figure of Cain is to be regarded as the eponymous ancestor of the tribe of the Kenites, and that this is true as much of the final form of the text of Genesis as it is of the original story lying behind it. Commentators writing on Genesis in recent decades have been wrong to overlook or reject this.

24. For a comparison of the early advances in civilization recounted in Gen. 1–11, including our passage in Gen. 4, and those in Philo of Byblos, see J. Ebach, *Weltentstehung und Kulturentwicklung bei Philo von Byblos* (BWANT, 108; Stuttgart: W. Kohlhammer, 1979), pp. 278-354.

Chapter 4

THE FLOOD AND THE TEN ANTEDILUVIAN FIGURES
IN BEROSSUS AND IN THE PRIESTLY SOURCE IN GENESIS

It has long been recognized by modern scholars that there is a connection between the account of Noah's flood in Genesis 6–8 and the Mesopotamian flood tradition. Not so many scholars realize, however, that this was already recognized almost two thousand years ago by the Jewish historian Josephus, who knew the Mesopotamian story from the account written in Greek by the Babylonian priest Berossus, and who clearly implies that this and the Genesis account refer to the same event (*Ant.* 1.93; *Ag. Ap.* 1.130).[1] With the advent of archaeological discoveries in the Near East in the nineteenth century and subsequently and the discovery of the much earlier Mesopotamian version of the flood story in tablet 11 of the Gilgamesh epic,[2] as well as the even earlier accounts in the Atrahasis epic[3] and brief Sumerian version,[4] it is not surprising that the later version in Berossus has tended to be somewhat neglected by Old Testament scholars. It is, however, Berossus on whom I wish to focus in

1. Josephus, *Ant.* 1.94-95, then goes on to mention other historians of antiquity who had alluded to the flood: Hieronymus the Egyptian, Mnaseas and Nicolaus of Damascus.

2. Many translations of Gilgamesh are available, but see now the massive edition and commentary of A.R. George, *The Babylonian Gilgamesh Epic: Introduction, Critical Edition and Cuneiform Text* (2 vols.; Oxford: Oxford University Press, 2003), as well as his shorter volume, *The Epic of Gilgamesh: The Babylonian Epic Poem and Other Texts in Akkadian and Sumerian* (London: Allen Lane, 1999).

3. W.G. Lambert and A.R. Millard, *Atra-ḥasīs: The Babylonian Story of the Flood* (Oxford: Clarendon Press, 1969); S. Dalley, *Myths from Mesopotamia* (Oxford: Oxford University Press), pp. 1-38; B.R. Foster, *Before the Muses: An Anthology of Akkadian Literature* (Bethesda, MD: CDL Press, 3rd edn, 2005), pp. 227-80.

4. M. Civil, in Lambert and Millard, *Atra-ḥasīs*, pp. 138-45; T. Jacobsen, in *The Harps that Once... Sumerian Poetry in Translation* (New Haven: Yale University Press, 1987), pp. 145-50. Cf. too Jacobsen's article, 'The Eridu Genesis', *JBL* 100 (1981), pp. 513-29.

this chapter, and to draw attention to the fact that the Priestly version of the flood story in Genesis 6–8 stands closer to that found in Berossus in certain respects than it does to the earlier known Mesopotamian flood accounts. Similarly, the preceding list of ten antediluvian patriarchs in Genesis 5 stands closer to Berossus's version of the ten antediluvian kings in certain respects than it does to earlier known versions of the Sumerian King List. That this should be the case ought not to surprise us, since P (c. 500 BCE) and Berossus (c. 280 BCE) are both late works, standing relatively close in time.

It would be as well to begin here by citing Berossus's account of the flood,[5] which refers to the flood hero under the name of Xisouthros, a Greek form of the original Sumerian name of the flood hero, Ziusudra:[6]

> Kronos appeared to Xisouthros in a dream and revealed that on the fifteenth day of the month Daisios mankind would be destroyed by a flood. Therefore, he ordered Xisouthros to bury the beginnings and the middles and the ends of all writings in Sippar, the City of the Sun. Then,

5. The translation is taken from S.M. Burstein, *The* Babyloniaca *of Berossus* (Sources and Monographs: Sources from the Ancient Near East, 1.5; Malibu, CA: Undena Publications, 1978), pp. 20-21, except for a couple of minor stylistic changes and a more significant point referred to below in n. 7. (The words in square brackets in the translation occur only in the citations from Berossus found in Abydenus.) Another English translation may be found in G.P. Verbrugghe and J.M. Wickersham, *Berossos and Manetho: Introduced and Translated; Native Traditions in Ancient Mesopotamia and Egypt* (Ann Arbor: University of Michigan Press, 1996). The Greek text of Berossus, together with a German version of excerpts from the Armenian, is to be found in P. Schnabel, *Berossos und die babylonisch-hellenistische Literatur* (Leipzig: B.G. Teubner, 1923), as well as in F. Jacoby, *Die Fragmente der griechischen Historiker* IIIC.1 (14 vols.; Leiden: Brill, 1923–58 [1958]), pp. 364-97 (no. 680).

6. This could indicate that Berossus was dependent on the Sumerian flood account, as G. Komoróczy, 'Berossus and the Mesopotamian Literature', *Acta Antiqua* 21 (1973), pp. 125-52 (133-35) argues, but if so it was certainly not his only source. As Burstein, *The* Babyloniaca *of Berossus*, p. 20 n. 51 points out, Berossus's account of the announcement of a flood coming to the flood hero in a dream stands contrary to the Sumerian flood account, lines 149-50, but appears to agree with the Atrahasis epic, 3.1.13-14 (though the text is broken). He could have added that revelation of the coming flood by a dream is also attested in the Gilgamesh epic, 11.197, where using the name Atrahasis to denote Utnapishtim, Ea declares, 'I let Atrahasis see a dream and so he heard the gods' secret'. Again, Berossus's implication that Sippar was spared the flood implies knowledge of the tradition attested in the brief account of the flood in the Erra epic (see L. Cagni, *The Poem of Erra* [Sources and Monographs: Sources from the Ancient Near East, 1.3; Malibu, CA: Undena Publications, 1977], where Sippar is similarly spared (Erra epic 4.50-51, cf. 1.130-48); Marduk rather than Enlil is there the bringer of the flood.

he should build a boat and embark on it with his kin and his closest friends. Food and drink should be placed in it. He was to load into it also the winged and four-footed creatures and to make ready to sail. If asked where he was sailing, he should reply, 'To the gods to pray for good things for men'. Heeding him, he built a boat 5 stades in length and 2 stades in breadth. He collected everything he had been ordered, and he embarked his wife and his children and his closest friends; [and straightway the things from the god came upon him.]

[On the third day] after the flood had come and swiftly receded, Xisouthros released some of the birds [to determine if they might see somewhere land which had arisen from the waters] But finding neither food nor a place on which to alight, the birds returned to the ship. After a few days Xisouthros again released the birds and these again returned to the ship but with their feet covered with mud. On being released a third time, they did not again return to the ship. Xisouthros understood that land had reappeared. Tearing apart a portion of the seams and seeing that the boat had landed on a mountain, he disembarked with his wife and his daughter and the pilot. After performing obeisance to the earth and setting up an altar and sacrificing to the gods, he and those who had disembarked from the ship with him disappeared. When Xisouthros and the others did not come back in, those remaining in the boat disembarked and searched for him calling out his name. Xisouthros was no longer visible to them, but a voice from the sky ordered them to be reverent. Because of his piety, he had gone to live with the gods; and his wife, daughter[7] and the pilot were to share the same honour. The voice also told them that they were to return to Babylon and that it was decreed that they were to dig up the writings from (the city) of the Sipparians and distribute them to mankind. It also said that the land in which they found themselves was Armenia. After hearing these things, they sacrificed to the gods and proceeded to Babylon on foot.

A portion of the ship which came to rest in Armenia still remains in the mountains of the Korduaians of Armenia, and some of the people, scraping off pieces of bitumen from the ship, bring them back and use them as talismans.

When these people came to Babylon, they dug up the writings at (the city) of the Sipparians and founded many cities and rebuilt shrines and founded anew Babylon.

The first distinctive point of connection between Berossus and P that I wish to draw attention to is that, unlike the earlier Mesopotamian flood accounts found in the Atrahasis and Gilgamesh epics, Berossus gives a precise date for the beginning of the deluge, just as P does, in contrast to the earlier J source. Remarkably, the Priestly flood account is the only

---

7. The reference to 'daughter' here is accidentally missing from Burstein's translation, so I have added it here. Cf. Jacoby, *Die Fragmente der griechischen Historiker* IIIC.1, pp. 380-81.

event in Genesis that receives precise dates in terms of both days and months. Stephanie Dalley has previously noted that Berossus and P have in common that they give a date for the start of the flood,[8] but so far as I am aware no one hitherto has pointed out that their dates are remarkably similar. For Berossus, the flood commenced on the fifteenth day of Daisios, Daisios being the second month in the Macedonian calendar corresponding precisely to Babylonian Ayyaru, Hebrew Iyyar (April/May).[9] Likewise, the Priestly source informs us in Gen 7.11 that Noah's flood began on the seventeenth day of the second month, which was similarly in April/May, that is, Iyyar 17, only two days later than the date given in Berossus. (The Septuagint refers rather to the twenty-seventh day of the month, but R.S. Hendel[10] argues convincingly that the MT's seventeenth day is original.) This similarity would seem to be too great to be due to a chance coincidence, even granting that the period from March to May is the general period for flooding in Mesopotamia. Berossus is hardly dependent on Genesis here, so it seems natural to suppose that Berossus was indebted to a late Babylonian tradition similar to that on which P also drew. That this parallel has gone unnoticed up till now is perhaps in part attributable to the fact alluded to above that less attention has been paid by Old Testament scholars to classical sources like Berossus since the advent of archaeological discoveries of more ancient Near Eastern texts.[11] But additionally, nineteenth- and early twentieth-century biblical scholars, who were doubtless more prone than

8. Dalley, *Myths from Mesopotamia*, p. 6.

9. On Daisios see, e.g., W. Dittenberger, 'Daisios', in G. Wissowa (ed.), *Paulys Real-Encyclopädie der classischen Altertumswissenschaft* 4 (Stuttgart: J.B. Metzlerscher Verlag, 1901), pp. 2014-15. In the Seleucid period when Berossus wrote the Macedonian and Babylonian calendars were completely meshed together; see A.E. Samuel, *Greek and Roman Chronology: Calendars and Years in Classical Antiquity* (Handbuch der Altertumswissenschaft, 1.7; Munich: C.H. Beck, 1972), pp. 139-44.

10. R.S. Hendel, *The Text of Genesis 1–11: Textual Studies and Critical Edition* (New York: Oxford University Press, 1998), pp. 54-55, points out that not only does the Septuagint differ from all other ancient Versions and ancillary sources (*Jubilees*; 4QCommGenᵃ) in reading 'twenty-seventh' rather than 'seventeenth', but its reading may easily be explained as due to a simple misreading of עשר יום as עשרים (the Septuagint lacks a reference to 'day' here).

11. Cf. my observations in J. Day (ed.), *William Robertson Smith: Lectures on the Religion of the Semites, Second and Third Series* (JSOTSup, 183; Sheffield: Sheffield Academic Press, 1995), p. 30, where I note the rich use of classical Greek and Latin sources made by the great nineteenth-century scholar William Robertson Smith and express the view that modern Old Testament scholars have much to gain by giving such sources renewed attention.

subsequent scholars to read Berossus, often assumed that P's second month meant the second month of the autumnal rather than the spring calendar (e.g. A. Dillmann, Franz Delitzsch, A.H. Sayce, S.R. Driver;[12] similarly Josephus, *Ant.* 1.80; Targum Pseudo-Jonathan[13]), which thus obscured the parallel with Berossus. It is, however clear that P employed the spring calendar throughout his work (e.g. Exod. 12.2; Lev. 16.29-30; cf. H in Lev. 23.5, 6, 27, 34, 39; 25.9).

Another point on which the Priestly version of the flood narrative agrees with Berossus over against earlier Mesopotamian tradition is the landing place of the ark. According to the Gilgamesh epic 11.140-44, the ark landed at Mt Nimush (previously read Niṣir[14]). As a result of another reference to Mt Nimush in the annals of Ashurnaṣirpal II it is generally accepted that this is to be equated with the impressive mountain now known as Pir Omar Gudrun, located south of the lower Zab in southern (Iraqi) Kurdistan, near Suleimaniyah.[15] In another text Mt Nimush is referred to as 'the mountain of Gutium', which confirms its location in the Zagros range, as A.R. George has noted.[16] The Priestly source in Gen. 8.4, however, locates the landing of the ark considerably further north-west on 'the mountains of Ararat'. Ararat is the name the Old Testament gives to Armenia, corresponding to the country known in Assyrian sources as Urartu (cf. 2 Kgs 19.37 = Isa. 37.38; Jer. 51.27). But in spite

12. Cf. A. Dillmann, *Die Genesis* (Kurzgefasstes exegetisches Handbuch zum Alten Testament; Leipzig: S. Hirzel, 5th edn, 1886), p. 130; Franz Delitzsch, *Neuer Commentar über die Genesis* (Leipzig: Dörffling & Franke, 1887), p. 176; A.H. Sayce, *The Early History of the Hebrews* (London: Rivingtons, 1897), p. 126; S.R. Driver, *The Book of Genesis* (Westminster Commentaries; London: Methuen, 1904), p. 90.

13. The version of the flood story in Targum Neofiti 1 is not clear in this regard, and support for seeing either the autumnal or the spring calendar here is found in later glossators. See M. McNamara, *Targum Neofiti 1: Genesis Translated, with Apparatus and Notes* (The Aramaic Bible, 1A; Edinburgh: T. & T. Clark, 1992), p. 78 n. j (on Gen. 8.13).

14. Cf. W.G. Lambert, 'Note brève, Niṣir or Nimuš?', *RA* 80 (1986), pp. 185-86; Dalley, *Myths from Mesopotamia*, p. 133 n. 135; George, *The Babylonian Gilgamesh Epic*, I, p. 516 n. 252.

15. Cf. E.A. Speiser, 'Southern Kurdistan in the Annals of Ashurnasirpal and Today', *AASOR* 8 for 1926–27 (1928), pp. 1-41 (17-18); M. Liverani, *Studies in the Annals of Ashurnasirpal II, 2: Topographical Analysis* (Quaderni di Geografia Storica, 4; Rome: Università di Roma 'La Sapienza', Dipartimento di Scienze storiche, archeologiche e antropologiche dell'Antichità, 1992), p. 48.

16. George, *The Babylonian Gilgamesh Epic*, I, p. 516 n. 252, referring to the text published by Erica Reiner, '*Lipšur* Litanies', *JNES* 15 (1956), pp. 129-49 (134-35, no. 41).

of Gen. 8.4's reference to 'the mountains of Ararat' in the plural, leaving the precise mountain undesignated, the singular term 'Mt Ararat' later became used of the landing place of the ark and came to be identified with a particular impressive Armenian mountain otherwise known as Ağri Daği, situated in the east of modern Turkey. However, this equation is simply a mediaeval supposition arising no earlier than the eleventh or twelfth century CE[17] but it has led to a widespread popular misconception that the mountain now known as Mt Ararat is where the ark is supposed to have landed (not to mention occasional misguided attempts to discover fragments of the ark there!). Earlier sources had located the landing place of the ark much further south in Armenia or in northern Kurdistan in an area variously known as Qardu (e.g. Targums Neofiti 1, Onqelos, Pseudo-Jonathan, and Peshitta) or the mountains of the Korduaians of Armenia (Berossus).[18] Now it is interesting to observe that Berossus mentions both Armenia and the mountains of the Kordyaians (Gordyene) in connection with the landing of the ark—indeed he clearly regards the latter as included within the former—thus indicating that he had the most southerly part of Armenia in mind. He states that 'It is also said that the land in which they found themselves was Armenia... A portion of the ship which came to rest in Armenia still remains in the mountains of the Korduaians of Armenia...'[19] Since Berossus is hardly dependent on Genesis it seems that, as in the case of the dating of the onset of the deluge noted above, both the Priestly writer and Berossus depended on a variant Babylonian tradition locating the landing place of the ark in Armenia rather than much further to the south-east at Mt Nimush. Interestingly, the first-century BCE historian Nicolaus of Damascus, whose account, reported in Josephus, *Ant.* 1.94-95, appears to be independent of both Berossus and Genesis, also implies that the ark landed in Armenia.[20]

17. See the evidence from the sources usefully collated by L.R. Bailey, *Noah: The Person and the Story in History and Tradition* (Columbia, SC: University of South Carolina Press, 1989), pp. 68-79, 81.

18. Cf. Bailey, *Noah*, pp. 65-68.

19. Cf. Burstein, *The* Babyloniaca *of Berossus*, pp. 20-21.

20. According to Nicolaus the ark landed on 'a great mountain in Armenia, over Minyas, called Baris'. Minyas must be identical with Minni in Jer. 51.27, mentioned there adjacent to Ararat (Urartu), and attested also in Assyrian inscriptions as Mannai; it denotes an area south of Lake Urmia. G.L. Huxley, 'Nikolaos of Damascus on Urartu', *Greek, Roman and Byzantine Studies* 9 (1968), pp. 319-20, is wrong in equating Baris with the mountain now known as Mt Ararat, following H. Kiepert, *Formae Orbis Antiqui* (Berlin: D. Reimer, 1902), p. v, and H. Treidler, 'Βάρις ὄρος', in K. Ziegler and W. Sontheimer (eds.), *Der kleine Pauly Lexikon der Antike*

A further point that Berossus and P have in common over against the earlier Mesopotamian flood accounts, unnoticed hitherto so far as I am aware, is that they both reject the depiction of the ark in the Gilgamesh epic (11.30) and apparently the Atrahasis epic (see the fragmentary passage in 3.1.26) as a perfect cube and envisage it rather as analogous to a raft, with the length much greater than the breadth. Thus, in the Gilgamesh epic (11.28-30, 57-59), Ea informs the flood hero, Utnapishtim, 'The boat that you are going to build, her dimensions should all correspond: her breadth and length should be the same...one "acre" was her area. 10 rods (= 60 yards) each her sides stood high, 10 rods (= 60 yards) each, the edges of her top were equal'. However, in contrast Berossus[21] claims that the boat was 5 stades (= 1,000 yards) long and 2 stades (= 400 yards) wide, and P states (Gen. 6.15) that the ark was 300 cubits (= 150 yards) long, 50 cubits (= 25 yards) wide and 30 cubits (= 15 yards) high. Although the precise figures in P and Berossus are quite different, these authors agree in envisaging the ark as having longer and shorter sides, over against earlier known Mesopotamian sources.

Yet another parallel between the Priestly account and Berossus is that in both (prior to the flood narrative) the flood hero is cited as the tenth in a series of ten remarkably long-lived antediluvian figures, and this has its background in the earlier Sumerian King List.[22] Most modern scholars accept that Genesis 5 is ultimately dependent on some version of this list.[23] However, a small number of scholars, including

(5 vols. Stuttgart: A. Druckenmüller, 1964–75), I, pp. 825-26. Further, the name Baris may be related to that of Mt Lubar, attested in *Jub*. 5.28 and 7.1 (cf. 7.17; 10.15) as the landing place of the ark, as originally suggested by A.H. Sayce, 'The Cuneiform Inscriptions of Van, Deciphered and Translated', *JRAS* 14 (1882), pp. 377-732 (389 n. 1).

21. Cf. Burstein, *The* Babyloniaca *of Berossus*, p. 20.

22. For the antediluvian rulers in the Sumerian King List, see T. Jacobsen, *The Sumerian King List* (Assyriological Studies, 11; Chicago: University of Chicago Press, 1939), pp. 70-77; J.J. Finkelstein, 'The Antediluvian Kings: A University of California Tablet', *JCS* 17 (1963), pp. 39-54 (45-46); J.-J. Glassner, *Mesopotamian Chronicles* (SBL Writings from the Ancient World; Leiden: Brill, 2004), pp. 57-59. There is also a most helpful chart in J.C. VanderKam, *Enoch and the Growth of an Apocalyptic Tradition* (CBQMS, 16; Washington, DC; Catholic Biblical Association, 1984), pp. 36-37. Cf. too H.S. Kvanvig, *Roots of Apocalyptic: The Mesopotamian Background of the Enoch Figure and of the Son of Man* (WMANT, 61; Neukirchen–Vluyn: Neukirchener Verlag, 1988), pp. 160-72 for valuable comparative material relating to the different versions of the King List.

23. Cf. H. Zimmern, 'Urkönige und Uroffenbarung', in E. Schrader (ed.), *Die Keilinschriften und das Alte Testament* (Giessen: Reuther & Reichard, 3rd edn, 1902–1903), pp. 530-43, who originally proposed the idea. A selection of the many

Gerhard Hasel and Claus Westermann,[24] have rejected such a connection, both emphasizing that the precise number of antediluvian figures varies in different texts. Earlier versions of the Sumerian King List vary between seven/eight, eight, nine and ten kings: UCBC 9-1819 has seven or eight, WB 444 has eight, K 12054 has nine, while only WB 62 has ten[25] (a later version, W 20030, 7 has seven). It is mistaken and rather illogical of Westermann[26] to reject the notion that Genesis 5 is dependent on the King List on the grounds that most earlier lists have eight rather than ten figures, since not only do earlier versions of the King List vary between seven/eight, eight, nine or ten names, but it is precisely the fact that P is late that would lead one to expect that it would follow a late version of the King List tradition such as that attested in Berossus, which has ten figures.[27] Hasel's main argument is to emphasize the differences between the Mesopotamian and biblical lists (e.g. the former has Sumerian names, the latter Semitic, the former lists kings but the latter has figures who are not kings, the former has lengths of life and the latter

who followed include G. von Rad, *Das erste Buch Mose: Genesis* (ATD, 2.4; Göttingen: Vandenhoeck & Ruprecht, 5th edn, 1958), p. 56, ET *Genesis* (OTL; London: SCM Press, 2nd edn, 1963), p. 69; W.G. Lambert, 'A New Look at the Babylonian Background of Genesis', *JTS* 16 (1965), pp. 287-300 (292-93), reprinted in R.S. Hess and D.T. Tsumura (eds.), *"I Studied Inscriptions from before the Flood": Ancient Near Eastern, Literary, and Linguistic Approaches to Genesis 1–11* (Sources for Biblical and Theological Study, 4; Winona Lake, IN: Eisenbrauns, 1994), pp. 96-113 (102); VanderKam, *Enoch and the Growth of an Apocalyptic Tradition*, pp. 23-51; Dalley, *Myths from Mesopotamia*, p. 6.

24. G.F. Hasel, 'The Genealogies of Gen 5 and 11 and their Alleged Babylonian Background', *AUSS* 16 (1978), pp. 361-74; C. Westermann, *Genesis 1–11* (BKAT, 1.1; Neukirchen–Vluyn: Neukirchener Verlag, 1974), pp. 471-77, 485-86, ET *Genesis 1–11* (London: SPCK, 1984), pp. 348-52, 358.

25. In a letter dated December 2, 2001, W.G. Lambert informed me that an Old Babylonian version of the Sumerian King List which had been on the market also has ten names, though he did not know where it was to be found. As of 2009, when I contacted him again about this, he still did not know.

26. Westermann, *Genesis 1–11*, p. 475, ET *Genesis 1–11*, p. 350.

27. Curiously, in addition to Berossus, which is the latest form of the King List, the earliest King List of all (WB 62), which dates from c. 2000 BCE, also has ten names. However, Kvanvig, *Roots of Apocalyptic*, pp. 170-71, interestingly notes that the names of the antediluvian kings in Berossus correspond most closely by far to those found in K 12054, and K 12054 is also the only cuneiform version of the King List which relates directly to the flood story, like Berossus. K 12054 dates from c. 650 BCE and is the latest attested version of the King List prior to the time of Berossus (and P). Of the remaining King Lists, W 20030, 7 is even later than Berossus (c. 165 BCE), while two others date from the Old Babylonian period (WB 444 from c. 1817 BCE and UCBC 9-1819 from c. 1700 BCE).

lengths of reign, etc.), but this is no problem, since the Priestly writer was clearly free to transform the tradition, just as J and P were able to do with the Mesopotamian flood story.

Continuing our discussion of the antediluvian figures, we should note that the special character Enoch, seventh in the list of the ten antediluvian patriarchs in Genesis 5,[28] has his origin in Enmeduranki,[29] who is listed seventh out of the ten antediluvian kings in Berossus, whom he calls Euedorankhos. Enmeduranki is listed seventh in two other versions of the King List (WB 444; W 20030, 7) but only in Berossus is he seventh out of ten, making the parallel with Genesis 5 particularly striking. This again strongly supports the view that P and Berossus shared some common traditions. (In UCSC 9-1819 Enmeduranki is sixth out of seven or eight, in K 12054 he is sixth out of nine, in WB 444 he is seventh out of eight, in W 20030, 7 he is seventh out of seven, and in WB 62 he is eighth out of ten.) It is also striking that Enoch is said to have lived for 365 years, 365 being the number of days in a solar year. Enoch's solar connection is further highlighted later in the so-called Astronomical Book of Enoch, *1 Enoch* 72–82, where he appears as an advocate of the solar calendar. As has often been noted, this finds a ready explanation in the fact that Enmeduranki was specifically associated with Sippar, the city of the sun god Shamash, and is also said to have entered the presence of Shamash as well as of Adad.[30] The alternative explanation of the 365 years of Enoch's life sometimes offered, that it implies that he lived a full life, is unconvincing,[31] since his earthly lifespan is actually much less than that of all the other figures in Genesis 5. Again, Enmeduranki's intimacy with the gods referred to above doubtless lies behind the statement in Gen. 5.22, 24 that 'Enoch walked with God'.[32]

28. In J's genealogy in Gen. 4 a figure called Enoch is of the third generation of humanity, and it seems clear that his transferral to seventh place in P's genealogy in Gen. 5 (involving the reversal of Enoch and Mehujael/Mahalalel) highlights his significance. On the importance of the seventh place in certain biblical genealogies, see J.M. Sasson, 'A Genealogical "Convention" in Biblical Chronography?', *ZAW* 90 (1978), pp. 171-85; *idem*, 'Generation, Seventh', in *IDBSup*, pp. 354-56.

29. See VanderKam, *Enoch and the Growth of an Apocalyptic Tradition*, esp. pp. 33-75; Kvanvig, *Roots of Apocalyptic*, pp. 15-342.

30. W.G. Lambert, 'Enmeduranki and Related Matters', *JCS* 21 (1967), pp. 126-38, esp. pp. 130, 132.

31. *Contra* Westermann, *Genesis 1–11*, p. 485, ET *Genesis 1–11*, p. 358.

32. Bearing in mind this polytheistic background, VanderKam, *Enoch and the Growth of an Apocalyptic Tradition*, pp. 31, 44, has argued that this should rather be rendered 'Enoch walked with the angels'. However, the more usual translation 'walked with God' should be retained here. This is supported by the fact that the

Further, these gods are said to have taught Enmeduranki various kinds of divination, knowledge of which he subsequently passed on to other humans, something which fits in with the fact that in the later Enochic literature Enoch became regarded as an apocalyptic visionary and seer (similarly *Jub.* 4.17-26). The reference to Enoch's being taken up to heaven at the end of his life is admittedly not paralleled in what is said anywhere about Enmeduranki, though as noted above, it is reported that he was privileged to have access to the divine assembly during his lifetime. Rather, it is plausible to suppose that the motif of Enoch's being taken up at the end of his life was appropriated from the comparable taking up of the Mesopotamian flood hero, which is attested in the Sumerian flood story, Gilgamesh, Atrahasis (preserved in the fragment from Ugarit and a later Neo-Babylonian fragment), and Berossus, but specifically rejected for Noah in Genesis, unlike many other aspects of the Mesopotamian flood story which are appropriated.[33] (Incidentally, both Noah and Enoch are described by P as having 'walked with God' [Gen. 5.22, 24; 6.9], a phrase used of nobody else in the book of Genesis; this indicates that P saw a resemblance between the two.) Nevertheless, although the figure of Enoch is certainly modelled in many ways on Enmeduranki, and though these figures are uniquely the seventh out of ten antediluvian figures only in P and Berossus, the specifically solar

identical phrase is also used by P of Noah in Gen. 6.9 (including speaking of *hā'elōhîm*, as in Gen. 5.22, 24, rather than *'elōhîm*), where it is indubitable that the meaning is 'walked with God' rather than 'walked with the angels'; cf. Gen. 6.11, which just afterwards similarly uses *hā'elōhîm* of the deity, and the fact that Noah is nowhere else associated with angels.

33.   Cf. VanderKam, *Enoch and the Growth of an Apocalyptic Tradition*, pp. 49-50. This seems more likely than the theory of R. Borger, 'Die Beschwörungsserie *bīt mēseri* und die Himmelfahrt Henochs', *JNES* 33 (1974), pp. 183-96, according to which Enoch's ascension derives from that of Utu-abzu, Enmeduranki's apkallu (sage). However, this seems less likely than derivation from the Mesopotamian flood hero. First, traditions pertaining to the Mesopotamian flood hero would have been much better known in Israel than those concerning Utu-abzu. Secondly, the same verb 'take' (Hebrew *lāqaḥ*, Akkadian *leqû*) is used in connection with the disappearance of both Enoch and the Mesopotamian flood hero; compare Gen. 5.24, 'Enoch...was no more, because God took him', with Gilgamesh epic 11.196, where Utnapishtim states, 'So they took me and caused me to dwell in the distance, at the mouth of the rivers'. Contrast Utu-abzu, of whom it is simply stated that 'he ascended to heaven'. Interestingly, the parallel with the flood hero in Gilgamesh is even closer in *Jub.* 4.23, where we read, 'He [Enoch] was taken from human society, and we led him to the Garden of Eden...', for the Garden of Eden similarly lay at the mouth of the rivers; cf. Gen. 2.10-14.

connections of Enmeduranki are absent from Berossus, where he is associated with the city of Pautibiblon (= Badtibira) rather than Sippar, the city of the sun god. Here, therefore, P must have been indebted to the more usual tradition associating Enmeduranki with Sippar and the sun rather than that which is attested in Berossus.

It has also occasionally been claimed that there is a precise mathematical relationship between the length of time attributed to these ten long-lived figures in P and in Berossus. This was first argued by Jules Oppert[34] in the nineteenth century, who noted that in Berossus the ten antediluvian kings reigned for 432,000 (= 86,400 × 5) years, whereas the ten antediluvian figures in P lived for 1,656 years, which he claimed was equivalent to 86,400 weeks. On this view one must assume that in order to reduce the Babylonian figures P divided the Babylonian numbers underlying Berossus by five, and then converted the resulting number into weeks, thus yielding 1,656 years instead of 432,000 years. If Oppert is correct, this would support the originality of the Masoretic figures over against those found in the Septuagint and Samaritan Pentateuch, which instead of 1,656 years report the length of the period as 2,242 and 1,307 years respectively, as well as over various modern scholarly estimates as to what the original length of the antediluvian period in P was intended to be. However, there are two reasons why we should reject Oppert's view. First, although Berossus's 432,000 years is indeed the equivalent of 86,400 × 5 years, it is only possible to make the Masoretic text's 1,656 years equivalent to exactly 86,400 weeks by presuming that a very precise length of the solar year was in view, just a fraction above 365.217 days, but no independent grounds are given for believing that P had this precise length in mind. Oppert would appear to have decided on the particular length that he did in order to make it fit his theory! Secondly, as a result of a comparison of the Masoretic figures with those given in the Septuagint and the Samaritan Pentateuch, it is generally accepted nowadays that the Masoretic figures for the antediluvian period do not always represent the original ones, but have in certain places been

---

34. J. Oppert, 'Die Daten der Genesis', *Nachrichten von der Königlichen Gesellschaft der Wissenschaften in Göttingen* (1877), pp. 201-23 (205-209); also later more briefly in *idem*, 'Chronology (I)', in *The Jewish Encyclopedia* (12 vols.; New York: Funk & Wagnalls, 1903–1906 [1903]), IV, pp. 64-68 (66-67). Although noted in some older Genesis commentaries, it appears to have been overlooked since the commentary of J. Skinner, *A Critical and Exegetical Commentary on Genesis* (ICC; Edinburgh: T. & T. Clark, 1910), p. 135, who sits on the fence regarding its veracity; but cf. more recently Dalley, *Myths from Mesopotamia*, p. 6, who supports Oppert.

deliberately modified in order to avoid a number of anomalies in the
original chronology in which certain of the antediluvian patriarchs had
inappropriately outlived the flood.[35] Overall, therefore, Oppert's claim
that there is a precise mathematical relationship between the numbers in
Berossus and Genesis 5 must be rejected.[36]

Similarly, older attempts[37] to find precise correlations between some
of the names of the ten antediluvian figures in Genesis 5 and Berossus
have long been abandoned. Thus, Berossus's third name, Amelon, was
connected with Akkadian *amēlu*, 'man', and compared with the third
name in Genesis 5, Enosh, 'man', Berossus's fourth name, Ammenon,
understood to be related to Akkadian *ummānu*, 'workman', was connected with the fourth name in Genesis 5, Kenan, supposedly meaning

---

35. See, e.g., the discussions in R.W. Klein, 'Archaic Chronologies and the
Textual History of the Old Testament', *HTR* 67 (1974), pp. 255-63; Hendel, *The
Text of Genesis 1–11*, pp. 61-71; *idem*, 'A Hasmonean Edition of MT Genesis? The
Implications of the Editions of the Chronology in Genesis 5', *HeBAI* 1 (2012), pp.
448-64.

36. Incidentally, it should be noted that a more recent scholar, J.H. Walton, 'The
Antediluvian Section of the Sumerian King List and Genesis 5', *BA* 44 (1981),
pp. 207-208, has also attempted to find a correlation between the numbers given in
Gen. 5 and those in the antediluvian King List, but unlike Oppert he is not thinking
in terms of Berossus but rather an earlier version of the Sumerian King List, WB
444. However, his arguments also fail to carry conviction. He speculates that both
this Sumerian King List and Gen. 5 were dependent on an older list, the former interpreting the numbers given there according to the sexagesimal system and the latter
according to the decimal system. In this way, the 241,200 years of the eight antediluvian figures in WB 444 are 36 times the length of the lives of the eight figures
from Seth to Lamech in Gen. 5 (he excludes Adam and Noah since WB 444 lacks
the flood hero, Ziusudra, and allegedly also the first man), provided we round up
the 6,695 years of the latter to 6,700 (but why should we?). However, having done
this, Walton is forced to concede that none of the individual numbers that result
for the length of life of the eight figures from Seth to Lamech correspond with those
actually given in Gen. 5. He attributes this to 'internal fluidity' (p. 208), that is,
corruption, which does not encourage confidence in his theory. In fact there is no
reason whatsoever to suppose that Gen. 5 and the Sumerian King List were both
dependent on an earlier unattested, conjectural source rather than that Gen. 5 was
ultimately dependent on a version of the Sumerian King List itself. To suppose
otherwise is to multiply entities beyond necessity.

37. E.g. Zimmern, 'Urkönige und Uroffenbarung', pp. 531-32, 539-40;
H. Gunkel, *Genesis* (Göttinger Handkommentar zum Alten Testament, 1.1; Göttin-
gen: Vandenhoeck & Ruprecht, 3rd edn, 1910), p. 132, ET *Genesis* (Macon, GA:
Mercer University Press, 1997), p. 134; Skinner, *A Critical and Exegetical
Commentary on Genesis*, p. 137.

'smith', and Berossus's eighth name, Amempsinos, taken to represent Akkadian Amēl-Sin ('man of Sin'), was held to underlie the name Methuselah ('man of Shelah' [allegedly a god's name]), the eighth figure in Genesis 5. However, all these attempts were based on the misconception that the names of the antediluvian Mesopotamian kings in Berossus were Akkadian, whereas earlier forms of the Sumerian King List have shown that they are Sumerian. Thus, Amelon actually represents the name Ammeluanna, Amempsinos derives from Ensipazianna, and Ammenon perhaps represents Enmenunna.[38]

Several times above I have mentioned that it is scarcely possible that the parallels between Berossus and the P flood and antediluvian figures to which I have drawn attention were due to Berossus's dependence on Genesis. Berossus was a Babylonian priest of Bel (Marduk) writing an account of Mesopotamian history for the benefit of a Greek-speaking audience, and throughout his work he was clearly dependent on earlier Mesopotamian sources. This is supported by the fact that ancient cuneiform texts provide numerous parallels to points in his narratives, both in general and with specific reference to the flood and the antediluvian figures.[39] Nowhere is there any obvious dependence on the Old Testament in his work. The particular parallels to which I have drawn attention above are therefore most naturally similarly to be attributed to dependence on earlier Mesopotamian sources, even if we do not now have access to them. Again, when we consider the nature of the particular parallels to which I have drawn attention, they are not so blatant as to suggest the direct dependence of Berossus on Genesis. Thus, while Genesis and Berossus give very similar dates for the beginning of the flood, they are not identical, and while they both present an ark that is

38. Cf. Jacobsen, *The Sumerian King List*, pp. 73 n. 18, 74 n. 25, though he prefers to see Ammenon as a doublet of Amēlon; VanderKam, *Enoch and the Growth of an Apocalyptic Tradition*, pp. 27-28. Already H. Zimmern, who first proposed identifying some of the names as Akkadian (see previous footnote), came to reject this view in 'Die altbabylonischen vor- (und nach-)sintlichen Könige nach neuen Quellen', *ZDMG* 78 NF 3 (1924), pp. 19-35 (24).

39. For Berossus's cuneiform sources, in addition to various footnotes in Burstein, *The Babyloniaca of Berossus*, see A. Heidel, *The Babylonian Genesis* (Chicago: University of Chicago Press, 2nd edn, 1951), pp. 77-81; Komoróczy, 'Berossus and the Mesopotamian Literature', pp. 125-52; Verbrugghe and Wickersham, *Berossos and Manetho*, pp. 15-27; R.J. van der Spek, 'Berossus as a Babylonian Chronicler and Greek Historian', in *idem* (ed.) *Studies in Ancient Near Eastern World View and Society: Presented to Marten Stol on the Occasion of his 65th Birthday* (Bethesda, MD: CDL Press, 2008), pp. 277-318 (290-314).

longer than it is broad, the figures again do not correspond precisely. Further, although the landing place of the ark in both P and Berossus is in Armenia, P uses the Hebrew name Ararat and Berossus the Greek name Armenia, and P also goes on to specify the Korduaian mountains of Armenia (i.e. Gordyene), something unheard of in P. Again, although Berossus has ten antediluvian figures like P, the names and years of the figures in Berossus tend to follow various older Mesopotamian versions of the King List and do not agree with P at all (for which latter, of course, the figures were not even kings). Moreover, while we know that P's seventh figure, Enoch, derives from the Mesopotamian Enmeduranki, known as Euedorankhos in Berossus where he also appears in seventh place, the seventh placing is not unique in Mesopotamian sources (only his placing in Berossus as seventh out of ten names, comparable to P's placing of Enoch, is unique) and nothing actually said about Euedorankhos in Berossus suggests dependence on P. As we have already seen, the solar connections of this seventh figure, still visible in P, are absent from Berossus. Moreover, in general it is unlikely that Berossus even knew the Pentateuch: we have no evidence that he was familiar with Hebrew, and the Septuagint translation of the Pentateuch, undertaken far away in Egypt, had almost certainly not yet appeared when he wrote in c. 280 BCE. Berossus's dependence on Genesis is thus extremely unlikely.

Finally, we should mention the recent book by Russell E. Gmirkin,[40] which puts forward a completely new and audacious thesis about the relationship of Berossus to Genesis. He argues at great length, but totally unconvincingly, that the Hebrew Pentateuch was not compiled until about 273–272 BCE in Alexandria, not long before the Greek Septuagint translation undertaken there, with Genesis 1–11 being dependent on Berossus's *Babyloniaca* (dated to 278 BCE) and Exodus on Manetho's *Aegyptiaca* (c. 285–280 BCE). Gmirkin's position thus represents the ultimate in terms of a minimalist late dating of the Old Testament, fully accepting the Copenhagen school's view that it is a Hellenistic book. By focusing so narrowly on Genesis 1–11 and the story of the Exodus and their alleged dependence on Berossus and Manetho, however, Gmirkin overlooks many important matters relevant to the dating of the Pentateuch, including pointers to a far more extended process of composition. Just to cite one important point, John Van Seters, in a critical review, notes that for Gmirkin 'All references to the stories of Genesis or Exodus

---

40. R.E. Gmirkin, *Berossus and Genesis, Manetho and Exodus: Hellenistic Historians and the Date of the Pentateuch* (LHBOTS, 433; London: T&T Clark International, 2006).

in the rest of the Hebrew Bible, such as the numerous allusions in Second Isaiah to creation, to the flood story, to the patriarchs, to the exodus and sea crossing, to the wilderness journey, are disqualified as unreliable for dating the Pentateuch and are therefore not even considered'.[41]

With regard to the specifics of the accounts of the flood and the antediluvian figures, Gmirkin is guilty of both omissions and inaccuracies. Although striving to find all possible parallels between Berossus and Genesis 1–11 so as to support dependency, he fails to note most of the parallels pointed out above. Thus he is unaware that Berossus and P have very similar dates for the beginning of the flood. Again he fails to note that Berossus and P are distinctive in depicting the ark as more like a raft, greater in length than breadth, in contrast to earlier known Mesopotamian flood accounts in which it was a perfect cube. He further fails to note that Berossus and P agree in locating the landing of the ark in Armenia, wrongly claiming that the Gilgamesh epic likewise situated it there,[42] whereas the latter rather placed it further south-east in southern Kurdistan, as was noted earlier. Moreover, even by concentrating on the flood narrative and the preceding genealogy of ten long-lived figures alone it is easy to see serious problems with Gmirkin's daring thesis that Genesis was dependent on Berossus. For example, Berossus's account of the sending out of the birds envisages a threefold sending out of birds in the plural, unlike Genesis, which has rather a threefold sending out of one bird at a time (Gen. 8.8-12, J), comparable (though not identical) to the Gilgamesh epic, in addition to the initial sending out of another bird (Gen. 8.7, probably P).[43] Moreover, the account of Noah's sacrifice following the flood (Gen 8.20-21, J), in which Yahweh smells the sweet savour of the sacrifice, clearly echoes what we read in the Atrahasis and Gilgamesh epics, where the gods gather round like flies and smell the sweet savour of the sacrifice. However, Berossus's account, while mentioning the sacrifice, makes no reference to the deities smelling it. Again, Enoch's life of 365 years finds its explanation, as we have seen above, in Enmeduranki's association with Sippar, the city of the sun god. However, Berossus's version of the King List does not even associate

---

41. J. Van Seters, Review of Russell E. Gmirkin, *Berossus and Genesis, Manetho and Exodus, JTS* 59 (2008), pp. 212-14 (212). Other critical reviews of Gmirkin include L.L. Grabbe in the *Society for Old Testament Study Book List 2007* (London: Sage, 2007), p. 117, and J.R. Wood in the online *JHS* 8 (2008).

42. Gmirkin, *Berossus and Genesis, Manetho and Exodus*, p. 111.

43. Gmirkin, *Berossus and Genesis, Manetho and Exodus*, p. 112, curiously reverses the consensus as to the source attribution without discussion, attributing Gen. 8.8-12 to P (and Gen. 8.7 to J, though this latter view does have supporters).

Enmeduranki with Sippar, but rather with Pautibiblon (= Badtibira), so
P must have been dependent on the more usual Mesopotamian tradition
associating Enmeduranki with Sippar and the sun god for his attribution
of 365 years to Enoch, not on Berossus. Overall, therefore, it is incon-
ceivable that Genesis was dependent on Berossus,[44] and the parallels
between Berossus and Genesis are rather to be attributed to the sharing of
certain common traditions.

   In conclusion, Berossus and the Priestly source in Genesis have a
number of distinctive points in common which are not found in earlier
known Mesopotamian accounts of the flood and the antediluvian figures. These are most naturally to be explained on the supposition that
P and Berossus shared a common knowledge of certain late Babylonian
traditions.[45]

44.   Gmirkin attempts to get round the problem that closer parallels to Gen. 1–11
can sometimes be found in earlier Mesopotamian sources than in Berossus by
proposing that our current text of Berossus represents an abbreviation of an earlier,
fuller version of Berossus, which would have had the material in question. This,
however, smacks of special pleading. In addition, it fails to explain cases noted
above in which Berossus has a version contradictory to what we find in Genesis,
while at the same time earlier Mesopotamian sources are more in agreement with
Genesis.

45.   It has been suggested to me that the details in Berossus might have been
deliberately corrupted in the course of Christian transmission so as to bring them
into line with Genesis. However, this is extremely unlikely. First, the correspon-
dences are not so blatant as to lead one to such a conclusion. Secondly, of the two
Christian transmitters of Berossus's account of the flood (via Alexander Polyhistor),
Eusebius and George Synkellos, the second actually goes out of his way to emphasize the differences between the account in Berossus and in Genesis, so may hardly
be suspected of bringing the texts closer together. He states regarding Berossus's
flood story: 'All of the above is from Alexander Polyhistor, who in turn took it from
Berossus, the false prophet of the Chaldeans. It is possible for those wishing to
understand correctly what really happened to refer to the holy writings of Genesis
to see how much they differed from the above account of the Chaldeans, full of
unbelievable stories.' The translation here is from Verbrugghe and Wickersham,
Berossos and Manetho, p. 51; cf. W. Adler and P. Tuffin, *The Chronography of
George Synkellus: A Byzantine Chronicle of Universal History from the Creation*
(Oxford: Oxford University Press, 2002), p. 41.

Chapter 5

THE SONS OF GOD AND DAUGHTERS OF MEN
AND THE GIANTS: DISPUTED POINTS
IN THE INTERPRETATION OF GENESIS 6.1-4

Genesis 6.1-4, the strange story of the sons of God and daughters of men, is a remarkably short narrative encompassing only four verses. However, it has given rise a surprisingly large number of disputed questions which I shall endeavour to deal with in this chapter.

1. *The Identity of the Sons of God*

One subject on which there is now widespread, though not universal, agreement is the identity of the sons of God. It is now generally held that they denote God's heavenly court, what were originally seen as gods but later, with the emergence of absolute monotheism, became regarded as angels.[1] The basic argument in favour is that this is clearly what 'sons of God' (*bᵉnê hāᵃᵉlōhîm*) and comparable phrases mean in all other places in the Hebrew Bible.[2] Moreover, such an understanding coheres very well with two other elements in the story: first, the fact that humans were seemingly in danger of becoming immortal as a consequence of the marriages (Gen. 6.3); secondly, the fact that the Nephilim giants were doubtless originally understood as being the offspring of the unions between the sons of God and daughters of men, even though, as I shall argue below, Gen. 6.4 now rejects this concept.

Furthermore, such an understanding is also in line with the earliest attested interpretation found in *1 Enoch* 6–11 and *Jub.* 5.1 (cf. 4.15), where the sons of God are depicted as angels. The view that the sons of God were judges or nobles, frequently found in the rabbis from Simeon b. Yoḥai (c. 140 CE) onwards, was clearly a way of avoiding the angelic

---

1. See all the main recent Genesis commentaries on this passage.
2. Cf. J. Day, *Yahweh and the Gods and Goddesses of Canaan* (JSOTSup, 265; Sheffield: Sheffield Academic Press, 2000), pp. 22-24.

interpretation, which had come to be regarded as offensive.[3] The same is true of the view often found in the Church Fathers from Julius Africanus (early second century CE) onwards, that the sons of God were the descendants of Seth, who had sexual intercourse with the descendants of Cain.[4] This interpretation continued to be held by many Catholic Old Testament scholars up till the twentieth century, but failed to do justice to the contrast between the sons of *God* and the daughters of *men*.[5] More recently, Lyle Eslinger has proposed the reverse idea that the sons of God were the descendants of Cain and that it was the daughters of men who were the descendants of Seth.[6] However, the same objection applies, and additionally no plausible reason can be found to explain why the descendants of Cain would be called 'the sons of God'. Again, Sven Fockner has recently claimed that the sons of God are the human followers of God and the daughters of men are the daughters of the rest of humanity, that is, the unbelievers, but this does not correspond to the meaning of 'sons of God' elsewhere in the Old Testament.[7] During the course of the twentieth century, the minority of scholars who have objected to the divine/angelic interpretation have tended to suppose that the sons of God were kings or heroes.[8] But although the Davidic king can be called 'son

3. See P.S. Alexander, 'The Targumim and Early Exegesis of "Sons of God" in Genesis 6', *JJS* 23 (1972), pp. 60-71, who shows that the older angelic interpretation was originally found in Targum Pseudo-Jonathan (now partly corrupted) and is attested in the Targum Neofiti margin, whereas the later view that the sons of God were judges or nobles is found in Targums Neofiti and Onqelos respectively.

4. For a survey of the interpretation of Gen. 6.1-4 in both early Jewish and Christian sources, see F. Dexinger, 'Jüdisch-Christliche Nachgeschichte von Gen 6,1-4', in S. Kreuzer and K. Luthi (eds.), *Zur Aktualität des Alten Testaments: Festschrift für Georg Sauer zum 65. Geburtstag* (Frankfurt: Peter Lang, 1992), pp. 155-75. See too L.R. Wickham, 'The Sons of God and Daughters of Men: Genesis vi 2 in Early Christian Exegesis', in A.S. van der Woude (ed.), *Language and Meaning: Studies in Hebrew Language and Biblical Exegesis* (OTS, 19; Leiden: Brill, 1974), pp. 135-47.

5. E.g. J. Scharbert, 'Traditions- und Redaktionsgeschichte von Gn 6,1-4', *BZ* NF 11 (1967), pp. 66-78; L. Ruppert, *Genesis. I. Gen. 1,1–11,26* (FzB, 70; Würzburg: Echter Verlag, 1992), pp. 272-79. However, Scharbert and Ruppert restrict this meaning to the final form of the text and grant that the 'sons of God' had a polytheistic meaning in the text's *Vorlage*.

6. L. Eslinger, 'A Contextual Identification of the *bene ha'elohim* and *benoth ha'adam* in Genesis 6.1-4', *JSOT* 13 (1979), pp. 65-73.

7. S. Fockner, 'Reopening the Discussion: Another Contextual Look at the Sons of God', *JSOT* 32 (2008), pp. 435-56 (448-51).

8. F. Dexinger, *Sturz der Göttersöhne oder Engel vor der Sintflut? Versuch eines Neuverständnisses von Genesis 6,2-4 unter Berückschtigung der religionsvergleichenden und exegesegeschichtlichen Methode* (Wiener Beiträge zur Theologie,

of God' (cf. Ps 2.7), nowhere in the Old Testament is a non-Israelite king referred to in this way, and as noted above, the plural 'sons of God' is confined to gods and later angels.

Apart from Gen. 6.2, 4, there are two other places where we find the expression *bᵉnê hā*ᵉlōhîm*, namely Job 1.6 and 2.1, while *bᵉnê *ᵉlōhîm* is found in Job 38.7 and was the original reading in Deut. 32.8. Should this expression actually be translated 'sons of God', as we have been doing, or rather 'sons of (the) gods'? As for Deut. 32.8, the original text read that the Most High divided the nations according to the number of the *bᵉnê *ᵉlōhîm* (4QDeutʲ *bny *lwhym*, LXX; MT has 'sons of Israel').⁹ This number was seventy, for we know that there were deemed to be seventy nations (Gen. 10), and with the growth of absolute monotheism the seventy gods of the nations became seventy angels of the nations in *1 En.* 89.59, 90.22-25 and Targum Pseudo-Jonathan on Deut. 32.8. A strong case can be made that this concept derives from the Canaanite concept of the sons of El (*bn *il*), a term for the gods well attested in the Ugaritic texts. Not only are the terms virtually identical, but significantly the sons of El also numbered seventy deities, since the Baal epic (*KTU* 1.4.VI.46) refers to the seventy sons of Athirat (El's consort). Now the sons of El were regarded as being 'biologically' the offspring of him and Athirat (cf. Athirat explicitly as 'progenitress of the gods' [*qnyt *ilm*] and 'mother of the gods' [*ʾum *ilm*] and El as 'father of the sons of El' [*ʾab bn *il*] at Ugarit). We may therefore be confident that in origin the Israelite expression was 'sons of God' and that this referred to deities having God as their father, rather than meaning 'the sons of the gods', that is, beings belonging to the god category by analogy with the expression 'the sons of the prophets'. I think we may also be confident that at the end of the biblical period the term similarly meant 'sons of God'. The three latest

13; Vienna: Herder, 1966), p. 131 ('heroes', comparing the Ugaritic Keret as 'son of El'; a view he later retracted in Dexinger, 'Jüdisch-Christliche Nachgeschichte von Gen 6,1-4', p. 157); D.J.A. Clines, 'The Significance of the "Sons of God" Episode (Genesis 6.1-4) in the Context of the "Primeval History" (Genesis 1–11)', *JSOT* 13 (1979), pp. 33-46. M.G. Kline, 'Divine Kingship and Genesis 6:1-4', *WTJ* 24 (1962), pp. 187-204, is an example of a conservative scholar who saw the sons of God here as dynastic rulers, specifically of the line of Cain. However, for W. Wifall, 'Genesis 6:1-4—A Royal Davidic Myth', *BTB* 5 (1975), pp. 294-301, it is the Nephilim/mighty men who are the rulers (pre-Davidic Canaanite kings of cities like Jerusalem).

9. For the 4QDeutʲ fragment's reading *bny *lwhym*, see E. Ulrich *et al.*, *Qumran Cave 4. IX. Deuteronomy, Joshua, Judges, Kings* (DJD, 14; Oxford: Clarendon Press, 1995), p. 90, and plate XXIII, col. XII, 34. It is now universally accepted that the MT reflects an attempt to avoid the polytheistic overtones of the original.

references in the Old Testament in Job 1.6, 2.1 and 38.7 date from the post-exilic period when absolute monotheism had been achieved, so 'sons of (the) gods' seems unlikely there, and the LXX uniformly renders these and comparable phrases with expressions including 'God' in the singular. Probably we should similarly understand Gen. 6.2, 4 as referring to 'the sons of God', implying that these gods have God for their father. We may compare examples of 'son of God' in the singular—both with regard to the Davidic monarch and to Israel—which clearly envisaged God as the father (cf. Ps. 2.7; Hos. 11.1). We should also draw attention to Ps. 82.6, which uses the variant expression 'sons of the Most High (Elyon)' for the gods. This surely cannot mean 'those belonging to the Most High category', for only one god can be the Most High. It makes more sense if the reference is to gods who have the Most High as their father.

However, we have to grant that in two or three places in the Old Testament we find the related expression $b^e n\hat{e}\ {}^{\circ}\bar{e}l\hat{i}m$, 'sons of gods' (Pss. 29.1; 89.7 [ET 6]; possibly also Ps. 58.2 [ET 1]), which presumably does mean 'beings belonging to the god category'. However, the analogy of the comparable expression 'sons of the prophets' shows that even this term may include subordination as well as classification.[10] Thus, 1 Sam. 10.12 indicates that the sons of the prophets have a 'father', and when Elijah is taken up into heaven, Elisha cries, 'My father. My father!...' The same words are uttered on the death of Elisha (2 Kgs 13.14). Accordingly, the $b^e n\hat{e}\ {}^{\circ}\bar{e}l\hat{i}m$, 'sons of the gods', may well still have been envisaged as having God as their father, and the same would be true of the $b^e n\hat{e}\ h\bar{a}^{\circ e}l\bar{o}h\hat{i}m$, even if we were to render this expression as 'sons of (the) gods'; rather than 'sons of God'.

2. The Daughters of Men as ṭōbōt: Morally Good or Good Looking?

Whereas the identity of the sons of God has been debated for the last two thousand years, the next topic to be considered has been the subject of dispute only recently. This concerns the precise nuance of the word ṭōbōt used to describe the daughters of men. The ancient Versions rendered the word as 'beautiful' or 'fair', and this is widely followed in modern translations. Such an understanding seems natural, since the text states that the sons of God *saw* that the women were good, prior to taking them

10. Cf. G. Cooke, 'The Sons of (the) God(s)', *ZAW* 76 NF 35 (1964), pp. 22-47 (24).

as wives. Even in English we can say 'she looks good', meaning attractive. However, both Ellen van Wolde and Carol Kaminski have argued that we should understand *ṭōbōt* to have its literal meaning of 'good' rather than 'fair' or 'beautiful', when Gen. 6.2 says of the women that 'the sons of God saw that they were *ṭōbōt*'.[11] Van Wolde simply states that it is mistaken to suppose that the women were attractive as opposed to good. Kaminski, however, goes beyond that and argues that the sons of God's fundamental mistake was that they thought that the daughters of men were good when they were not, as God's punishment of humanity subsequently showed. She maintains that *ṭōbâ* of itself never means 'fair' or 'beautiful', but only when it is followed by *marʾeh* or *tōʾar*. In response, we may argue that while *ṭōb* or *ṭōbâ* throughout the Hebrew Bible basically means good, the nature of the goodness varies according to the context, and in the context of the sons of God seeing the women prior to choosing them for wives it seems far more natural to assume that the sense is that of attractiveness rather than moral goodness. Perhaps the best way to preserve the nuance of the Hebrew word in English is to render it as 'good looking'. A similar instance of *ṭōbâ* by itself meaning attractive when used of women (*pace* Kaminski) is in Judg. 15.2, where Samson's first wife's father says of her to Samson, 'I was sure you had rejected her; so I gave her to your companion. Is not her younger sister more good looking (*ṭōbâ*) than her. Why not take her instead?' It is most unlikely that *ṭōbâ* means morally good here.

3. *The Nephilim and their Relationship to the Sexual Unions*

Genesis 6.4 declares, 'The Nephilim were on the earth in those day—and also afterwards—when the sons of God used to go in to the daughters of men, who bore children to them. They were the mighty men that were of old, men of renown'. It is clear that the Nephilim are to be understood as giants. This emerges from Num. 13.33, where they were among the original inhabitants of Canaan, in contrast to whom the Israelites appeared as mere grasshoppers. The high stature of the pre-Israelite inhabitants of Canaan is also attested in Amos 2.9, where it is said of the Amorite that his 'height was like the height of cedars, and who was as strong as oaks'; similarly Deut. 2.10, 20-21; 3.11. Now it is entirely

---

11. E. van Wolde, *Words become Worlds: Semantic Studies of Genesis 1–11* (BibInt, 6; Leiden: Brill, 1994), pp. 73-74; *eadem, Stories of the Beginning: Genesis 1–11 and Other Creation Stories* (trans. J. Bowden; London: SCM Press, 1996), p. 113; C.M. Kaminski, 'Beautiful Women or "False Judgment?": Interpreting Genesis 6.2 in the Context of the Primaeval History', *JSOT* 32 (2008), pp. 457-73.

natural that the union of gods (or angels) and humans should be understood as leading to the creation of giants. This is indeed explicitly stated to be the case in the later books of *1 Enoch* and *Jubilees* (see below). Many scholars believe this is also the case in Genesis 6.[12] However, close attention to the wording of the biblical text indicates that J (otherwise known as non-P) has distanced himself from such an understanding. Genesis 6.4 states that 'The Nephilim were on the earth in those days—and also afterwards—when the sons of God used to go in to the daughters of men...'[13] This makes it quite clear that the Nephilim were already in existence at the time of these unions.[14] It has been suggested to me that we might be able to evade this conclusion by noting that the Hebrew verb is in the imperfect, implying repeated sexual liaisons between the sons of God and daughters of men (hence the rendering 'when the sons of God used to go in to the daughters of men'), and that this might be compatible with the idea that the Nephilim were both around at the time of the unions as well as being offspring from them. However, this does not seem to me to be the most natural way of taking the text, which suggests that the existence of the Nephilim was prior to the unions, not the other way round. Moreover, if the Nephilim were the product of the unions, they cannot already have been in existence at the time of the very first unions. Further, if J had intended to say that the Nephilim were the offspring of the unions, he would surely have phrased it otherwise to make this clear. We may contrast *1 En.* 7.2, which states explicitly, 'And the women became pregnant and gave birth to great giants whose heights were three hundred cubits', and *Jub.* 5.1, 'And they took wives for themselves from all of those whom they chose.

12.   This widespread view hardly needs documenting, but see, e.g., R.S. Hendel, 'Of Demigods and the Deluge: Towards an Interpretation of Genesis 6:1-4', *JBL* 106 (1987), pp. 13-26 (14); E. Hamori, *"When Gods Were Men": The Embodied God in Biblical and Near Eastern Literature* (BZAW, 384; Berlin: W. de Gruyter, 2008), p. 123.

13.   That *ᵃšer* means 'when' here is generally accepted. It is well attested that *ᵃšer* means 'when' when it occurs after expressions of time and this is particularly common after *yôm*, 'day' (see the examples in BDB, p. 82). The closest parallel I have found is in 1 Kgs 22.25, where we have *bayyôm hahû* ᵃ*šer*, 'in that day when', paralleling *bayyāmîm hahēm* ᵃ*šer*, 'in those days when', in Gen. 6.4. (As noted below, 'and also afterwards' in Gen. 6.4 is a later gloss.)

14.   So rightly G. von Rad, *Das erste Buch Mose: Genesis* (ATD, 2.4; Göttingen: Vandenhoeck & Ruprecht, 5th edn, 1958), p. 94, ET *Genesis* (trans. J.H. Marks; OTL; London: SCM Press, 2nd edn, 1963), p. 111; B.S. Childs, *Myth and Reality in the Old Testament* (SBT, 27; London: SCM Press, 2nd edn, 1962), pp. 56-58; Fockner, 'Reopening the Discussion', pp. 452-54; H. Seebass, *Genesis. I. Urgeschichte (1,1– 11,26)* (Neukirchen–Vluyn: Neukirchener Verlag, 3rd edn, 2009), pp. 189, 191.

And they bore children for them; and they were the giants'. Verse 4's reference to the Nephilim being around at the time thus functions as a kind of antiquarian note, comparable to other references to the pre-Israelite inhabitants of Canaan (including giants) in the book of Deuteronomy (cf. Deut. 2.10-12, 20-23; 3.11, 13b), as well as J's own references to the Canaanites being in the land at that time in Gen. 12.6 and 13.7.

Granted that the Nephilim were not the offspring of the sons of God and the daughters of men in our current text, in contrast to the underlying myth, what are we to make of the words 'These were the mighty men (*gibbōrîm*) that were of old, men of renown'? Are they to be equated with the Nephilim or to be seen rather as the offspring of the sons of God and daughters of men? It all depends how we understand the ambiguous 'These' (*hēm*). In the underlying myth, of course, both were the case; there was no difference. In the text as we now have it, however, it is more natural to equate the mighty men with the Nephilim, so that they are no longer understood as the offspring of the sexual liaisons referred to. We know that the Nephilim were seen as giants (Num. 13.33), so it makes good sense that they should be described as 'the mighty men that were of old, men of renown'. If the mighty men were the sons of the sexual liaisons, but distinct from the Nephilim, the Nephilim would then be laconically referred to in Gen. 6.4 without any further explanation, which would be very strange.

It is possible that the Nephilim are also alluded to in Ezek. 32.27, where we read of the presence in Sheol of 'the mighty men (*gibbôrîm*), those who fell of old (*nōpᵉlîm mēᶜôlām*)', language which is reminiscent of Gen. 6.4.[15] However, this is uncertain, and even if they are in mind we should probably not actually emend *nōpᵉlîm* to *nᵉpilîm*, since reference to 'those who fell' (*nōpᵉlîm*) is a constant refrain of this passage (Ezek. 32.22, 23, 24; cf. 32.20). Nevertheless, this passage does encourage the thought that the term Nephilim, 'fallen ones', was a name given retrospectively to denote the giants because they had fallen and were no more. As we shall see later, a related term for Canaanite giants, Rephaim, seems to have arisen in a similar manner, since it originated as a term for the dead.

---

15. In the first part of Ezek. 32.27 it is widely agreed that we should follow the LXX in reading 'They lie with the mighty men, those who fell of old' rather than the MT's 'They do not lie with the mighty men, those who fell among the uncircumcised'. This involves reading *mēᶜôlām*, 'of old', for MT's *mᵉᶜᵃrēlîm*, 'uncircumcised', as well as omitting MT's 'not' at the beginning of the verse. With regard to the latter, we should more naturally expect the dead in Ezek. 32.27 to share the same fate as the mighty men of old, as this is much more in keeping with the general thrust of the chapter as a whole, where distinctions among the dead are not found.

4. *Genesis 6.1-4 and the Tradition of the Watchers in 1 Enoch*

The standard view has been that the detailed account of the Watchers in *1 Enoch* is a later midrashic elaboration of the story in Gen. 6.1-4 (so, e.g., M. Delcor, G.W.E. Nickelsburg, D. Dimant, and J.J. Collins).[16] However, in more recent years a number of scholars, including J.T. Milik, M. Black (in part), P.R. Davies and M. Barker, have argued that Gen. 6.1-4 already presupposes something akin to what we find in the more elaborate account in *1 Enoch*.[17] This has doubtless been encouraged on the one hand by the discovery of the Aramaic text of much of *1 Enoch* in the Dead Sea Scrolls, which showed that the Enoch traditions about the Watchers are older than previously thought (going back to the third century BCE), and on the other hand by the tendency of many to date J later than previously supposed.

What are we to make of all this? It is certainly the case that the account in Gen. 6.1-4 is remarkably brief, and doubtless presupposes a fuller story than is recounted there. Further, we have already shown that, whereas the Nephilim are not the offspring of the sons of God and daughters of men in our current narrative in Genesis 6, they certainly were in the myth underlying it, just as they are in *1 Enoch*. It therefore seems that *1 Enoch* preserves the original mythical understanding at this

---

16. M. Delcor, 'Le mythe de la chute des anges et de l'origine des géants comme explication du mal dans le monde dans l'apocalyptique juive. Histoire des traditions', *RHR* 190 (1976), pp. 3-53; G.W.E. Nickelsburg, 'Apocalyptic and Myth in 1 Enoch 6–11', *JBL* 96 (1977), pp. 383-405; D. Dimant, 'Use and Interpretation of Mikra in the Apocrypha and Pseudepigrapha', in M.J. Mulder (ed.), *Mikra: Text, Translation, Reading of the Hebrew Bible in Ancient Judaism and Early Christianity* (Assen: Van Gorcum, 1988), pp. 404-406; J.J. Collins, 'The Sons of God and the Daughters of Men', in M. Nissinen and R. Uro (eds.), *Sacred Marriages: The Divine–Human Sexual Metaphor from Sumer to Early Christianity* (Winona Lake, IN: Eisenbrauns, 2008), pp. 259-74 (264).

17. J.T. Milik (ed. with the collaboration of M. Black), *The Book of Enoch: Aramaic Fragments of Qumrân Cave 4* (Oxford: Clarendon Press, 1976), pp. 30-32; M. Black, *The Book of Enoch or 1 Enoch: A New English Edition with Commentary and Textual Notes* (SVTP, 7; Leiden: Brill, 1985), pp. 14, 124-25; P.R. Davies, 'Sons of Cain', in J.D. Martin and P.R. Davies (eds.), *A Word in Season: Essays in Honour of William McKane* (JSOTSup, 42; Sheffield: Sheffield Academic Press, 1986), pp. 35-56 (46-50); *idem*, 'And Enoch Was Not, for Genesis Took Him', in C. Hempel and J.M. Lieu (eds.), *Biblical Traditions in Transmission: Essays in Honour of Michael A. Knibb* (Leiden: Brill, 2006), pp. 97-107 (100-104); M. Barker, 'Some Reflections upon the Enoch Myth', *JSOT* 15 (1980), pp. 7-29; *eadem*, *The Older Testament: The Survival of Themes from the Ancient Royal Cult in Sectarian Judaism and Early Christianity* (London: SCM Press, 1987), pp. 18-19.

point, though whether this was due to direct dependence on the pre-biblical myth or simply an accidental deduction from the biblical text, is uncertain. However, there are so many respects in which the account in *1 Enoch* 6–11 is manifestly later than Gen. 6.1-4 that we must conclude that, whatever precise source underlies Genesis, it cannot simply be the version we now have in *1 Enoch*. Take for example the following parallel passages in Genesis and *1 Enoch*:

> When the people began to multiply on the face of the ground, and daughters were born to them, the sons of God saw that they were good looking; and they took wives for themselves of all that they chose. (Gen. 6.1-2)

> In those days, when the children of men multiplied, it happened that there were born unto them handsome and beautiful daughters. And the angels, the children of heaven, saw them and desired them; and they said to one another, 'Come, let us choose wives for ourselves from among the daughters of man and beget us children'. (*1 En.* 6.1-2)

Two points here immediately catch the eye as evidence of the priority of Genesis over against the account in *1 Enoch*. First, *1 Enoch* speaks of 'the angels' and 'the children of heaven' in contrast to Genesis's 'the sons of God'. The latter refers to the gods, and *1 Enoch*'s speaking of them as 'the angels' clearly indicates a later interpretation. Secondly, *1 Enoch*'s mention of 'the children of heaven' rather than 'the sons of God' is easily understood in the light of the later euphemistic habit of referring to 'heaven' rather than 'God'.

Among other points we should also note the multitude of angelic watcher names found in *1 Enoch*, in contrast to the anonymous mass of the sons of God referred to in Genesis, the former being a well-known characteristic of late, apocalyptic works. And of course, the very term 'watcher' (*ʿîr*) is attested of angels in the Bible only in the late book of Daniel (Dan. 4.10, 14, 20 [ET 13, 17, 23]). Moreover, the whole pre-supposition of *1 Enoch* 1–36 that we have here a vision of Enoch about the watchers (and other mysteries) is most obviously explained as coming about as a result of reflection on the fact that the originally separate allusions to Enoch in Gen. 5.22-24 (P) and the sons of God incident in Gen. 6.1-4 (J) now stand close together in our biblical text.

5. *Genesis 6.1-4 and the Flood*

What is the relationship between the incident in Gen. 6.1-4 and the flood story that follows? A strong case can be made that they were originally quite independent. First, we should note that nothing comparable to the sons of God incident is attested in the Mesopotamian flood tradition which lies behind the biblical flood story, and which is closely followed in many ways in Genesis. Secondly, it is generally agreed that the words 'and also afterwards', used of the Nephilim in v. 4, were added by a later redactor, conscious of the fact that the Nephilim were still around later (cf. Num. 13.33, at the time of the Israelite settlement). However, the flood story states that the only humans to survive the flood were Noah and his family, which makes problematic the survival of the Nephilim, 'men of renown'. Consequently, we must assume that the sons of God incident was originally quite independent of the flood story, doubtless set at some later time; we may compare the story of Cain and Abel, which also contains signs that it was originally set later, when more human beings were on the earth.[18] This, in my view, makes it unlikely that Ron Hendel was correct in supposing that the sons of God incident was originally understood as *the* cause of the flood in the pre-J tradition, parallel to the divine/human marriages in Hesiod's *Catalogue of Women* leading to Zeus's decision to bring about the Trojan war.[19] Similarly, we should reject the view of Gordon Wenham that the basic unit is not Gen. 6.1-4 but 6.1-8, which thereby implies a very close connection between the sons of God incident and the subsequent flood; he holds that humanity was guilty in Gen. 6.1-4 because the women and their parents consented to the marriages.[20] However, the current position of the story of the sons of God and daughters of men immediately before the flood account is presumably not due to chance. It highlights the way in which things were going wrong prior to the flood. Nevertheless, the way in which Gen. 6.1-4 is only loosely related to the flood story that follows probably explains why *1 Enoch* felt the need to elaborate further the

18. Cf. J. Day, 'Cain and the Kenites', in G. Galil, M. Geller and A.R. Millard (eds.), *Homeland and Exile: Biblical and Ancient Near Eastern Studies in Honour of Bustenay Oded* (VTSup, 130; Leiden: Brill, 2009), pp. 335-46 (342), reprinted above as Chapter 3.

19. Hendel, 'Of Demigods and the Deluge', pp. 14-16. For the Hesiodic *Catalogue of Women*, see M.L. West, *The Hesiodic Catalogue of Women: Its Nature, Structure, and Origins* (Oxford: Clarendon Press, 1985). More recently, R.S. Hendel, 'The Nephilim Were On the Earth: Genesis 6:1-4 and its Ancient Near Eastern Context', in C. Auffarth and L.T. Stuckenbruck (eds.), *The Fall of the Angels* (Themes in Biblical Narrative: Jewish and Christian Traditions, 6; Leiden: Brill, 2004), pp. 11-34 (29), has nuanced his position, saying that this is a possible combination of motifs, but is not found in any of the traditions, including the biblical.

20. G.J. Wenham, *Genesis 1–15* (WBC, 1; Waco, TX: Word Books, 1987), pp. 135, 141, 146. According to the *Testament of Reuben* 5.5-6 the women actually lured the Watchers into illicit sexual relations.

story of the sons of God and daughters of men, greatly magnifying the evil that resulted on the earth as a consequence, so as to make God's sending of the flood more comprehensible. (Compare *Jub.* 5.1-5; 7.21; Josephus, *Ant.* 1.3.1-2, which similarly connect Gen. 6.1-4 with the flood.)

6. *Genesis 6.3: Translation Problems, Authenticity, and the Question of the 120 Years*

We shall now turn to the problems raised by Gen 6.3, starting with two translation problems.

a. *yādôn*

At the beginning of Gen. 6.3 we read, 'The Lord said, "My spirit shall not *yādôn* in man for ever…"' The meaning of *yādôn* is disputed. Older views that *yādôn* meant 'strive with' (AV, RV), 'rule' (Hans Bauer and Pontus Leander; cf. Symmachus, 'judge')[21] or 'contend with' (NIV) have only limited support nowadays; these are based on the assumption that the verb is *dûn*, and that this is a by-form of *dîn*, literally 'judge'. However, no such by-form is elsewhere attested, and in any case a verb *dûn* would have the imperfect form *yādûn*, not *yādôn*. Two other minority views may now be noted. The first is that of JB, 'be disgraced', following scholars such as A. Dillmann and J. Scharbert, which is based on the Arabic root *dûn*, 'be humbled, humiliated, brought lo'.[22] However, while one could understand God being angered by the goings on, it is difficult to think that he would be spoken of as being humiliated.[23] The second was that of E.A. Speiser, who appealed to the Akkadian verbal base *dnn*, attested in the nouns *dinānu, andurānu*, 'personal substitute, surrogate, scapegoat', from which he derived the verbal sense 'expiate, atone for' and hence 'shield, protect' for Hebrew *yādôn*.[24] This has been

---

21. E.g. H. Bauer and P. Leander, *Historische Grammatik der hebräischen Sprache des Alten Testaments* (Halle: Niemeyer, 1922), p. 398.

22. A. Dillmann, *Die Genesis* (Kurzgefasstes exegetisches Handbuch zum Alten Testament; Leipzig: S. Hirzel, 5th edn, 1886), p. 121; Scharbert, 'Traditions- und Redaktionsgeschichte von Gn 6,1-4', p. 68.

23. So, rightly, V.P. Hamilton, *The Book of Genesis Chapters 1–17* (NICOT; Grand Rapids, MI: Eerdmans, 1990), p. 266.

24. E.A. Speiser, '*YDWN*, Gen 6:3', *JBL* 75 (1956), pp. 126-29, reprinted in E.A. Speiser, *Oriental and Biblical Studies: Collected Writings of E.A. Speiser* (ed. J.J. Finkelstein and M. Greenberg; Philadelphia: University of Pennsylvania Press, 1967), pp. 35-40; cf. *idem*, *Genesis* (AB, 1; Garden City, NY: Doubleday, 1964), p. 44.

followed by NJB, 'be responsible for'. However, this does not really make sense in the context of the earlier chapters of Genesis, where God has not shielded the guilty, and human beings have already taken responsibility for their own actions since Genesis 3.[25] The LXX, Targum Onqelos, Vulgate and Peshitta rendered 'dwell' (cf. *Jub.* 5.8) and this is widely followed in modern translations (cf. RSV, NRSV and NJPSV read 'abide'; NAB, NEB and REB read 'remain'). The context suggests that this general meaning cannot be very far off the mark, but it is difficult to find convincing philological support for this precise meaning in other Semitic languages.[26] This rendering may presuppose the reading *yādûr*, which is actually attested in 4Q252 1.2.[27] However since *yādôn* is the harder reading, it should probably be preferred as more original. It is supported by the Samaritan Pentateuch, Targums Neofiti and Pseudo-Jonathan, and Pseudo-Philo. Presumably the reading *yādûr* arose either through scribal corruption or guesswork as to the meaning of *yādôn*.

It was first pointed out by Karl Vollers that *yādôn* presupposes a verb *dānan*, and that this could be cognate with Akkadian *danānu*, a common verb meaning 'to be/become strong, powerful', a view which has gained increasing support from scholars in recent years, though it has yet to make headway in modern Bible translations.[28] This makes excellent

25. So rightly, Hamilton, *The Book of Genesis Chapters 1–17*, p. 266.

26. U. (M.D.) Cassuto, 'The Episode of the Sons of God and the Daughters of Men', in *idem, Biblical and Oriental Studies* (trans. I. Abrahams; 2 vols.; Jerusalem: Magnes Press, 1973–75 [1973]), I, pp. 17-28 (25-26), claimed that there was comparative Semitic evidence for this, and he is cited by Wenham, *Genesis 1–15*, p. 142, but careful scrutiny of the alleged evidence shows that this is dubious.

27. So G.J. Brooke, 'Some Remarks on 4Q252 and the Text of Genesis', *Textus* 19 (1998), pp. 1-25 (8-9); R.S. Hendel, *The Text of Genesis 1–11: Textual Studies and Critical Edition* (New York: Oxford University Press, 1998), p. 132; T.J. Lim, 'Biblical Quotations in the Pesharim', in E.D. Herbert and E. Tov (eds.), *The Bible as a Book: The Hebrew Bible and the Judaean Desert Discoveries* (London: The British Library, 2002), pp. 71-79 (72-75). However, M.J. Bernstein, 'לא ידור רוחי באדם לעולם: Biblical Text or Biblical Interpretation?', *RevQ* 16 (1994), pp. 421-27, regards *yādûr* not as a textual variant but as a paraphrase of *yādôn* in 4Q252.

28. K. Vollers, 'Zur Erklärung des ידון Gen 6,3', *ZA* 14 (1899), pp. 349-56; G.R. Berry, 'The Interpretation of Gen. 6:3', *AJSL* 16 (1899–1900), pp. 47-49; B. Jacob, *Das erste Buch der Tora: Genesis* (Berlin: Schocken Books, 1934), pp. 173-74, ET *The First Book of the Bible: Genesis Interpreted* (abridged, edited and translated by E.I. Jacob and W. Jacob; New York: Ktav, 1974; reprinted Jersey City, NJ: Ktav, 2007), p. 45, but lacking the detailed notes of the German original; R. Bartelmus, *Heroentum in Israel und seiner Umwelt: Eine traditionsgeschichtliche Untersuchung zu Gen. 6, 1-4 und verwandten Texten im Alten Testament und der*

sense, since it is understandable that God should have regarded the infusion of divine spirit into humanity resulting from the marriages of the sons of God and daughters of men, leading to potential immortality, as too strong. Hence we should render, 'My spirit shall not be strong in man for ever...' Moreover, this view coheres with the place name Dannah (Josh. 15.49), which plausibly means 'stronghold' or 'fortress', as pointed out by Vollers, Berry and Hendel.[29] Berry went further and noted that the Akkadian equivalent *dannatu* actually has this very same meaning.[30] Moreover, long before the decipherment of Akkadian, in a quite different context, when commenting on a passage in the Talmud, the mediaeval commentator Rashi shows awareness of a Hebrew verb *dānan* meaning 'be strong', since he explains an imperative *dûnû* as having the meaning 'be strong'.[31] It should also be noted that J.A. Emerton has plausibly argued that this verb occurs in Gen. 49.16.[32] He points out that it is difficult to give meaningful sense to the traditional translation, 'Dan shall judge (*yādîn*) his people as one of the tribes of Israel', since it either presupposes Dan judging itself or unaccountably judging the whole of Israel, depending on the meaning of 'his people'. Emerton therefore proposed rendering 'Dan—his people will be strong (*yādôn*), as one of the tribes of Israel', something that makes sense in the light of its small size, but at the same time strength, implied by its comparison to a biting snake in v. 17.

altorientalischen Literatur (AThANT, 65; Zurich: Theologischer Verlag, 1979), p. 19; Hendel, 'Of Demigods and the Deluge', p. 15 n. 10; *idem*, 'The Nephilim Were On the Earth', p. 15; H.S. Kvanvig, *Roots of Apocalyptic: The Mesopotamian Background of the Enoch Figure and of the Son of Man* (WMANT, 61; Neukirchen–Vluyn: Neukirchener Verlag, 1988), p. 286; M. Vervenne, 'All they Need is Love: Once More Genesis 6.1-4', in J. Davies, G. Harvey and W.G.E. Watson (eds.), *Words Remembered, Texts Renewed: Essays in Honour of John F.A. Sawyer* (JSOTSup, 195; Sheffield: Sheffield Academic Press, 1995), pp. 19-40 (27); H.R. Page, *The Myth of Cosmic Rebellion: A Study of its Reflexes in Ugaritic and Biblical Literature* (VTSup, 65; Leiden: Brill, 1996), p. 113; Seebass, *Genesis*, I, p. 188.

29. Vollers, 'Zur Erklärung des ידון Gen. 6,3', p. 354; Berry, 'The Interpretation of Gen. 6:3', p. 48; Hendel, 'Of Demigods and Deluge', p. 15 n. 10. At that time Hendel was unaware that Vollers and Berry had previously noted this.

30. Berry, 'The Interpretation of Gen. 6:3', p. 48.

31. Cf. L. Blau, *Das altjüdische Zauberwesen* (Budapest: Landes-Rabbinerschule, 1898), p. 67 with n. 5; C. Levias, 'Blau on Ancient Jewish Magic', *AJSL* 15 (1898–99), pp. 191-92 (191).

32. J.A. Emerton, 'Some Difficult Words in Genesis 49', in P.R. Ackroyd and B. Lindars (eds.), *Words and Meanings: Essays Presented to David Winton Thomas* (Cambridge: Cambridge University Press, 1968), pp. 81-93 (88-91).

b. *bᵉšaggam*
There is broad agreement nowadays that this is best understood as *bᵉ* + *ša* + *gam*, 'in that also', that is, 'since also', thus leading to the translation 'My spirit shall not be strong in man for ever, since he is also flesh', that is, in addition to spirit, just mentioned. The meaning 'since, because' was already supported by the LXX, Vulgate, Targum Neofiti and the Peshitta. *Bᵉ* + *ša* here can be compared with the more common *baᵃšer* (Gen. 39.9, 23; Jonah 1.8; Eccl. 7.2; 8.4) with this same meaning. Some Hebrew manuscripts read *bᵉšaggām*, which led to the view of some that we should render 'in their erring/transgression', from the verb *šāgag* or *šāgâ*, 'to err, transgress'. This is usually rejected nowadays because of the inconsistency between singular *hûʾ* and the plural ending in *bᵉšaggām*.

Kvanvig proposed to relate this to Akkadian *šagāmu*, 'to bellow', hence translating 'in/because of the noise', referring to humanity's noise prior to the flood alluded to in the Atrahasis epic.[33] This bold theory, however, has gained no following: this verb is attested nowhere else in the Hebrew Bible, and the Atrahasis epic does not even use this precise verb in that connection but rather the noun *rigmu*, 'noise'.[34] Moreover, Kvanvig's rendering would be surprising, appearing out of the blue, since the text hitherto has not said a word about any noise emanating from humanity, and as we have seen, the story in Gen. 6.1-4 appears originally to have been independent of the flood narrative.

But if the generally accepted view of *bᵉšaggam* is correct, the question is raised why this unusual form is used. Most often *še*, which became regular in Mishnaic Hebrew, is an indication of late Hebrew, but Ron Hendel has pointed out that we have here not *še* but *ša*, the latter being found already twice in Judg. 5.7, generally seen as one of the earliest poems in the Hebrew Bible (cf. *šā* before guttural in Judg. 6.17).[35] It is possible, therefore, that this is an old rather than a late feature. We may

33. Kvanvig, *Roots of Apocalyptic*, pp. 287-88; *idem, Primeval History: Baby-lonian, Biblical, Enochic* (JSJSup, 149; Leiden: Brill, 2011), p. 285. Clines, 'The Significance of the "Sons of God" Episode (Genesis 6:1-4)', p. 40 had previously suggested this possibility but doubted that it was true for the final form of the text.
34. The verb *šagāmu* is attested in Atrahasis, but only of the god Adad's roaring in the thunder (Atrahasis 3.2.53; cf. 3.2.49), on which latter see W.G. Lambert and A. R. Millard, *Atra-ḥasīs: The Babylonian Story of the Flood* (Oxford: Clarendon Press), p. 160.
35. Cf. Hendel, 'The Nephilim Were On the Earth', p. 15. See too the discussion in R.S. Hendel, *Genesis 1–11* (Anchor Yale Bible, 1A; New Haven: Yale University Press, forthcoming). I am deeply indebted to Ron for letting me see an advance copy of the manuscript of this excellent commentary.

compare the use of the qal form, *yālad*, rather than the hiphil *hôlîd* (the latter regular in P and post-exilic works) for 'beget' in vv. 1, 4, as well as consistently throughout J, which is also suggestive of a relatively early, and certainly pre-P date, as Ron Hendel has again noted.[36]

c. *The Authenticity of Genesis 6.3*

Some have seen the whole of v. 3 as a later addition.[37] This, however is to be rejected. Thus, first, for J to introduce an intervention by Yahweh at this point is entirely to be expected, since that is precisely what he does in the other comparable instances in Genesis 1–11 where the divine and human are improperly mixed (Gen. 3.22; 11.5-8). Secondly, the use of the rare form *yādôn* in this verse is more readily explicable if the text is ancient rather than being part of a late redaction, and the same, I have just argued, may be the case for *beˇsaggam*. Having said that, one must admit that the text reads a little strangely, in that the contents of Gen. 6.4 would more logically have come before v. 3 rather than after it. However, that does not mean that v. 3 is an interpolation. Rather, as noted above, J was wanting to separate the origin of the Nephilim from the sexual unions between the sons of God and daughters of men which existed in the original myth, and placing it in v. 4 helped in this regard.

d. *The Meaning of the 120 Years*

In this verse we read, 'Then the Lord said, "My spirit shall not be strong in man for ever, for he is flesh; his days shall be 120 years"'. The general consensus today is that this refers to God's shortening of humanity's lifespan to 120 years, a view already found in Josephus, *Ant.* 1.3.2, Pseudo-Philo, *L.A.B.* 3 and *Gen. R.* 16.6 on Gen. 5.3. In the context this shortening is most naturally seen as God's response to the danger of humans living for ever as a result of the infusion of the divine spirit from the marriages with the sons of God. This relates to the theme of Gen. 3.22-24, where God was earlier concerned at the possibility of

---

36. Cf. R.S. Hendel, ' "Begetting" and "Being Born" in the Pentateuch: Notes on Historical Linguistics and Source Criticism', *VT* 50 (2000), pp. 38-46.

37. E.g. J. Wellhausen, *Die Composition des Hexateuchs* (Berlin: G. Reimer, 3rd edn, 1899), pp. 307-309; C. Westermann, *Genesis 1–11* (BKAT, 1.1; Neukirchen–Vluyn: Neukirchener Verlag, 1974), p. 495, ET *Genesis 1–11: A Commentary* (trans. J.J. Scullion; London: SPCK, 1984), p. 366; Bartelmus, *Heroentum in Israel und seiner Umwelt*, pp. 25-28; L. Perlitt, *Riesen im Alten Testament* (Nachrichten von der Akademie der Wissenschaften in Göttingen, Philologisch-Historische Klasse, 1990, no. 1; Göttingen: Vandenhoeck & Ruprecht, 1990), p. 43. In contrast, Collins, 'The Sons of God and the Daughters of Men', p. 260, rightly defends the originality of v. 3.

the humans becoming immortal and had therefore denied their access to the tree of life. Incidentally, we may note that the idea that 120 years is the ultimate lifespan of humanity is also attested in a text from Emar in Syria which states, '120 years (are) the years of mankind—verily it is their bane'.[38] A minority, however, maintains that the reference to 120 years in Gen. 6.3 is rather to a period of grace prior to the flood. This view is already found at Qumran in 4Q252, 1.2-3, dating from the second half of the first century BCE, and it became the dominant Jewish under-standing (cf. Targums Neofiti, Fragment, Onqelos, Pseudo-Jonathan; *Mekhilta de Rabbi Ishmael*, Shirta 5; *Gen. R.* 30.7; *b. Sanh.* 108a; *ARN* A 32). It is still followed by a few scholars today, especially con-servative ones.[39] However, this cannot have been the original meaning, since within Gen. 6.1-4 the flood is not yet in view. Further, if a period of grace were in mind we should more naturally expect the text to have read, 'his *remaining* years shall be 120 years'. Moreover, the idea that a 120-year period of grace was in view could easily have arisen later in order to deal with the problem that human beings are still depicted living much longer than 120 years later on in Genesis 11 (though less than in Gen. 5). However, this is readily explicable as yet another inconsistency between J and P (who compiled the genealogy in Gen. 11) that the redac-tor has retained, either through oversight or possibly on the understand-ing that the 120 years maximum lifespan took time to come into effect. Alongside other discrepancies that can be observed within Genesis 1–11, this highlights the problem of trying to read Genesis 1–11 in a *completely* holistic way.[40]

38. See J. Klein, 'The "Bane" of Humanity: A Lifespan of One Hundred and Twenty Years', *Acta Sumerologica* 12 (1990), pp. 58-70 (59)—the text cited is from line 23. On the other hand, the claim sometimes made, for example, by Childs, *Myth and Reality in the Old Testament*, p. 54, that this is also found in Herodotus, *Hist.* 1.163 and 3.23 seems unjustified. Herodotus 1.163 merely states that King Argan-thonius of Tartessos lived to be 120, and 3.23 declares that most of the Ethiopians lived to be 120, *and some even more*, which clearly implies that 120 years was not thought to be the absolute limit. Incidentally, 122 years is the longest any human capable of providing adequate documentation has so far been known to have lived (a French woman, Jeanne Calment, 1875–1997).

39. E.g. A. Heidel, *The Gilgamesh Epic and Old Testament Parallels* (Chicago: University of Chicago Press, 2nd edn, 1949), p. 230, still retained in the 1975 reprint; Hamilton, *The Book of Genesis Chapters 1–17*, p. 269; H.S. Kvanvig, 'Gen 6,1-4 as an Antediluvian Event', *SJOT* 16 (2002), pp. 79-112 (98-99); Fockner, 'Reopening the Discussion', pp. 451-52.

40. Cf. the attempted holistic reading of Gen. 1–11 in J.T.K. Lim, *Grace in the Midst of Judgment: Grappling with Genesis 1–11* (BZAW, 314; Berlin: W. de Gruyter, 2002).

7. Ancient Near Eastern Mythical Background
and Parallels to Genesis 6.1-4

Genesis 6.1-4 clearly reports a mythical story, but so far there is no agreement as to its source. Among the proposals are the following:

a. *The Rebellion in Heaven Myth*
It has sometimes been supposed that the story in Gen. 6.1-4 is part of a larger myth involving a revolt of the gods against the supreme deity in heaven. For example, E.A. Speiser curiously compared the Hurrian myth (preserved in Hittite) of the overthrow in turn of the god Alalu by Anu, Anu by Kumarbi, and of Kumarbi by Teshub, which has clear echoes in the myth of the successive generations of Elioun, Ouranos, Kronos, and Zeus reported by Philo of Byblos in his *Phoenician History*, and of Ouranos, Kronos, and Zeus recounted by Hesiod in his *Theogony*.[41] But it is very difficult to see why this should have any connection with the myth reported in Gen. 6.1-4, which is quite different. Again, more recently, H.R. Page[42] has related Gen. 6.1-4 to other Old Testament passages referring to a rebellion against the supreme deity by the god, for example, Isa. 14.12-15; Ezek. 28.1-10, 12-19 and Psalm 82, as well as Daniel 11–12 and Job 38.13-15. However, these passages seem to be speaking of different things. While Isa. 14.12-15 probably derives from a myth about the rise and fall of the Canaanite god Athtar, equated with the morning star Venus, as has often been supposed, a passage that has doubtless influenced Daniel 11–12, there is no reason to believe this for the other passages.[43] Thus, Ezek. 28.12-19 is a variant of the story of the first man's disobedience in the Garden of Eden in Genesis 2–3, and Ezek. 28.1-10 appears to relate to that, while in Psalm 82 the gods of the nations are simply condemned to death for failing to ensure justice in their various countries. As for Job 38.13-15, there are no good reasons for believing that this refers to the rebellion of an astral deity at all, as Page speculates. Finally, Gen. 6.1-4 concerns not an ascent by one deity but a descent by the sons of God more generally. Page curiously wishes to relate the Nephilim here to the god Athtar, but there is no evidence for this.

---

41. Speiser, *Genesis*, pp. 45-46. Cf. P.D. Hanson, 'Rebellion in Heaven, Azazel, and Euhemeristic Heroes in 1 Enoch 6–11', *JBL* 96 (1977), pp. 195-233.

42. Page, *The Myth of Cosmic Rebellion*, pp. 110-208.

43. On Isa. 14.12-15 and Athtar/Venus, cf. Day, *Yahweh and the Gods and Goddesses of Canaan*, pp. 166-80.

b. *Mesopotamia*

Helge Kvanvig has attempted to find connections between Gen. 6.1-4 and the Atrahasis epic. However, the evidence adduced is rather tenuous and unconvincing. Thus, there is no story in Atrahasis about gods and women having sexual intercourse, in contrast to the many parallels which do exist between the flood stories in Atrahasis and Genesis. As we have already seen, Kvanvig's view is that *bešaggam* in Gen. 6.3 means 'in/because of the noise', cognate with the Akkadian verb *šagāmu*, 'to roar, bellow', which could then relate to the noise humanity was making prior to the flood.[44] To this notion various objections may be made. First, as noted above, no verb *šagāmu*, 'to roar, bellow', is otherwise attested in the Hebrew Bible, and the Atrahasis epic itself nowhere employs the verb *šagāmu* to denote the noise made by humanity; rather it uses the noun *rigmu*, 'noise'. Secondly, a reference to humanity's noise is totally unexpected and out of place in Gen. 6.1-4. Coming to another of Kvanvig's suggestions, it seems fanciful to hold that the 120 years of Gen. 6.3 derives from the 12,000-year intervals of time recorded in the Atrahasis epic, several such periods leading up to the flood.[45] As we have seen, the former refers to the future maximum human lifespan rather than to a specific period before the flood. Kvanvig further claims that Gen 6.3's allusion to human immortality refers back to the antediluvian characters generally, by analogy with the Atrahasis epic on W.G. Lambert's understanding.[46] However, Gen. 6.3 more naturally refers to immortality resulting from the immediate context of the sons of God and daughters of men's marriages, and Kvanvig's view further conflicts with the mortality implied by J for the previous antediluvian figures (cf. Gen. 3.22-24), as well as by P (Gen. 5), though Kvanvig is one of those who sees Gen. 6.1-4 as a post-J and post-P addition to the text. Against that, however, it may be noted that there are numerous linguistic parallels between Gen. 6.1-4 and the Primaeval J narrative elsewhere in Genesis 1–11, strongly supporting the traditional view that Gen. 6.1-4 is from J.[47] The only

44. See the references to Kvanvig in n. 33.
45. Kvanvig, 'Gen 6,1-4 as an Antediluvian Event', pp. 98-99.
46. Kvanvig, 'Gen 6,1-4 as an Antediluvian Event', pp. 97-98.
47. Cf. Hendel, 'The Nephilim Were On the Earth', p. 13. Besides Kvanvig, other scholars who see Gen. 6.1-4 as a late addition include H. Gese, 'Der bewachte Lebensbaum und die Heroen: Zwei mythologische Ergänzungen zur Urgeschichte der Quelle J', in H. Gese and H.P. Rüger (eds.), *Wort und Geschichte: Festschrift für Karl Elliger zum 70. Geburtstag* (AOAT, 18; Neukirchen–Vluyn: Neukirchener Verlag, 1973), pp. 77-85 (85); M. Witte, *Die biblische Urgeschichte: Redaktions- und theologiegeschichtliche Beobachtungen zu Genesis 1,1–11,26* (BZAW, 265; Berlin: W. de Gruyter, 1998), p. 72.

possible influence on Gen. 6.1-4 from the Atrahasis epic that I can conceive is the reference to the multiplication of humanity in Gen. 6.1, but even that is uncertain, since this is the kind of thing one might expect anyway in an account of the early development of humanity, and there is no hint that the multiplication of humanity was regarded as excessive, unlike in Atrahasis.

We may note, however, that there is a certain parallel in Mesopotamia in the figure of the hero Gilgamesh, for he was regarded as two-thirds god and one-third man, the son of Lugalbanda, king of Uruk, and the goddess Ninsun. However, this was insufficient to guarantee his immortality, as the Gilgamesh epic makes apparent, unlike what is initially presupposed in Gen. 6.3, and there is no real connection between the stories. Nevertheless, it is interesting to note that Gilgamesh did become the name of one of the giants in the Qumran Book of the Giants.[48]

c. *Greece*

The closest analogies attested so far appear to be in classical Greek literature. There are, for example, a number of instances of a woman having intercourse with a god, thereby giving birth to a noteworthy person, such as Zeus who was held in this way to have begotten Herakles, Perseus and Alexander the Great, and Apollo who similarly begat Ion, Asclepius, Pythagoras, Plato and Augustus. More relevant to the case in hand, however, is the *Catalogue of Women*, traditionally ascribed to Hesiod but now generally agreed to be later, from the sixth century BCE.[49] The parallels with Gen. 6.1-4 have been particularly emphasized by Ron Hendel and John Van Seters.[50] However, Hendel's earlier view that there was probably a genetic connection between this and Gen. 6.1-4, and that the flood originally constituted *the* reason for the flood in the pre-J tradition, analogous to the Trojan war in the *Catalogue of Women*, seems unduly speculative and indeed improbable.[51] As we have seen above, Gen. 6.1-4 appears originally to have had no connection at all with the flood story. Whereas Hendel does not speculate on whether the myth originated in the Greek or Semitic world, Van Seters sees the parallels

---

48. See L.T. Stuckenbruck, *The Book of the Giants from Qumran* (Texte und Studien zum Antiken Judentum, 63; Tübingen: Mohr Siebeck, 1997), *passim* (see references in index).

49. Cf. West, *The Hesiodic Catalogue of Women*, pp. 130-37.

50. Hendel, 'Of Demigods and the Deluge', pp. 15-20; J. Van Seters, 'The Primeval Histories of Greece and Israel Compared', *ZAW* 100 (1988), pp. 1-21 (4-9); *idem*, *Prologue to History*, pp. 155-58.

51. As pointed out above (n. 19), Hendel later nuanced his position.

as evidence that Gen. 6.1-4 is ultimately dependent on a Greek source, though probably mediated through the Phoenicians or Canaanites. However, in the pre-Hellenistic period the primary influence was from the orient to Greece rather than vice versa.[52] In addition to drawing attention to the Greek adoption of the Phoenician alphabet and the orientalizing period in Greek art, we may note, for example, that the authentic Hesiod is known to have taken up oriental mythological traditions (cf. Hesiod's Typhon myth's dependence on the Hurrian Ullikummi myth, and Hesiod's dependence for the generations of the gods on the Hurrian Kumarbi myth).[53]

d. *Canaan*
It has sometimes been suggested that we have a Ugaritic parallel to Gen. 6.1-4 in El's seduction of two women in the Shaḥar and Shalim myth (*KTU* 1.23).[54] However, this seems to be incorrect, since the women are probably goddesses, not human beings. This is supported by the fact that the offspring of these unions, Shaḥar and Shalim (Dawn and Dusk), are both gods, not giants. Contrary to what has sometimes been claimed, the term 'women' is used elsewhere of goddesses at Ugarit, as Mark Smith has noted.[55]

From a later time in the Canaanite, or more precisely Phoenician, world, Philo of Byblos (in Eusebius, *Praep. Ev.* 1.10.9) recounts the birth of giants who give their names to the mountains Kassios, Lebanon, Anti-Lebanon and Brathy. Albert I. Baumgarten has speculated that this is related to the myth in Gen. 6.1-4.[56] However, Philo's giants are the

---

52. A. Schüle, 'The Divine–Human Marriages (Genesis 6:1-4) and the Greek Framing of the Primeval History', *TZ* 65 (2009), pp. 116-28, has also recently argued for Greek influence on Gen. 6.1-4 and appeals in particular to the evidence of the knowledge of Greek mythology in Cypriot art between the seventh and fifth centuries BCE. However, this is not surprising, since it is widely accepted that there was enormous Greek influence in Cyprus in the pre-Hellenistic period, unlike in Palestine.

53. See P. Walcot, *Hesiod and the Near East* (Cardiff: University of Wales Press, 1966).

54. Cassuto, 'The Episode of the Sons of God and the Daughters of Man', p. 23; Westermann, *Genesis 1–11*, pp. 512-13, ET *Genesis 1–11*, p. 380.

55. Cf. M.S. Smith, *The Rituals and Myths of the Feast of the Goodly Gods of KTU/CAT 1.23: Royal Constructions of Opposition, Intersection, Integration, and Domination* (SBL Resources for Biblical Study, 51; Atlanta: SBL, 2006), pp. 89-92.

56. A.I. Baumgarten, *The* Phoenician History *of Philo of Byblos: A Commentary* (Etudes préliminaires aux religions orientales dans l'empire romain; Leiden: Brill, 1981), pp. 156-57.

offspring of humans (Light, Fire and Flame), and even if we assume that Philo's euhemerism is at work here, there is no evidence that the giants were originally seen as the offspring of gods and humans.

e. *An Israelite Myth Utilizing and Transforming Canaanite Concepts*
Finally, my own view is that it is likely that behind Gen. 6.1-4 there lies not so much a Canaanite myth as an Israelite myth utilizing and transforming Canaanite concepts. First, the reference to the heavenly sons of God is a concept taken over by the Israelites from the Canaanites, as noted above. Secondly, if, as seems likely, the story lying behind our text arose as an aetiology to explain the origin of the Canaanite giants, the Nephilim, we may be sure that the myth arose in Palestine. Furthermore, in Num. 13.33 the Anakim (lit. 'sons of Anak') are said to be descended from the Nephilim, and these Anakim are included among the Rephaim in Deut. 2.10-11. Elsewhere I have pointed out that the concept of these Canaanite giant Rephaim is somehow derivative from that of the Ugaritic *rpʾum*, a term used of divine underworld shades, especially dead kings, just as the term Rephaim is also used to denote the shades of the dead in the Hebrew Bible.[57] Thus, both the Canaanite giant Rephaim in the Old Testament and a Ugaritic divine figure called *rpʾu*, the singular of *rpʾum*, are stated to have dwelt at Ashtaroth (cf. Gen. 14.5; *KTU* 1.108.1-3), and both *rpʾu* and King Og, 'one of the last of the Rephaim', are said to have dwelt at Ashtaroth and Edrei, which were in Bashan (cf. Josh. 12.4; 13.12; *KTU* 1.108.1-3).[58] All this can hardly be due to coincidence. The giant Rephaim are presumably so called because they are now long dead, a thing of the past, having been wiped out by the Israelites (Josh. 11.21-22; 12.4-6; 13.12; 15.4; Judg. 1.20; 1 Sam. 21.18-21 = 1 Chron. 20.4-8). In a similar way it seems that the closely related Nephilim were viewed retrospectively as 'fallen ones'.

---

57. Day, *Yahweh and the Gods and Goddesses of Canaan*, pp. 223-25.
58. That the Ugaritic refers to the place names Ashtaroth and Edrei is now generally accepted. See the references and discussion in Day, *Yahweh and the Gods and Goddesses of Canaan*, p. 221 n. 102.

Chapter 6

THE GENESIS FLOOD NARRATIVE IN RELATION
TO ANCIENT NEAR EASTERN FLOOD ACCOUNTS

1. *Introduction and General Methodological Considerations*

One of the methods of Old Testament study that has grown up over the last century and a half has been that of comparing the Bible with other ancient Near Eastern texts. This approach has been enormously successful in shedding new light on the background of Scripture and thus enabling us to read it in its original setting. Comparative ancient Near Eastern study can come in various forms. The particular type with which I am concerned here is that where an ancient Near Eastern text may actually have been a source lying behind what we find in the Old Testament.

There is a danger in this kind of study of what has been called 'parallelomania'.[1] How are we to know what the significance of a particular parallel is? Is the parallel without any real significance or is there a definite connection with the biblical text? If the latter, does the parallel betoken direct influence on the Bible from the text in question or is the relationship more indirect? Could it be that both have a common source rather than one being dependent on the other? And if there was influence, when and how should we suppose this took place? Finally, if we conclude that there is a genetic relationship between the Bible and an ancient Near Eastern text, and we have established the priority in date of the extra-biblical source and how and when it could have influenced the Bible, we need to consider the ways in which the Bible has dealt with its source: how has it transformed it?

I shall now discuss these questions with special reference to the flood story in Genesis 6–9. In pursuing the story of the flood and its background there are two further methodological considerations we need to consider that scholars have sometimes failed to observe. The first is that the Mesopotamian flood story is not all of a piece but is found in various recensions, so we cannot assume without more ado that it is the Gilgamesh epic version that lies behind Genesis. Similarly, the Genesis flood

---

1. Cf. S. Sandmel, 'Parallelomania', *JBL* 81 (1962), pp. 1-13.

account is not a seamless garment, but is widely agreed to be composed of two separate accounts that have been joined together. We need, therefore, to pay attention to each account separately when comparing the underlying Mesopotamian tradition.

2. *Ancient Near Eastern Flood Accounts*

As mentioned above, it is first necessary to establish that a parallel really does have a genetic connection with the biblical text. In the case of the flood story, we have to take account of the fact that there are flood stories all over the world,[2] so in seeking the origin of the biblical flood account, why should we single out the Mesopotamian tradition? In reply we may say that Palestine is not an area particularly prone to floods but rather to excessive dryness, so the story must have originated elsewhere in the ancient Near East, and furthermore, it is the flood story from Mesopotamia—an area very much subject to floods—which is overwhelmingly the closest in content to the biblical account. What these parallels are will be examined in detail below. As for other ancient Near Eastern flood narratives, although there is an Egyptian flood story, it is unrelated to the biblical story,[3] while the Greek flood story of Deucalion is unattested before the fifth century BCE and appears dependent on the Mesopotamian,[4] and the version in Lucian of Samosata is even later and considerably dependent on Genesis.[5]

The Mesopotamian flood story was known in antiquity from the Greek account of Berossus,[6] a Babylonian priest c. 280 BCE, and already

---

2. J.K.R. Riem, *Die Sintflut in Sage und Wissenschaft* (Hamburg: Agentur des Rauhen Hauses, 1925), pp. 10-160, recounts over 300 flood stories; cf. T.H. Gaster, *Myth, Legend, and Custom in the Old Testament* (London: Duckworth, 1969), pp. 82-131.

3. Cf. Gaster, *Myth, Legend, and Custom in the Old Testament*, p. 84.

4. See M.L. West, *The East Face of Helicon: West Asiatic Elements in Greek Poetry and Myth* (Oxford: Clarendon Press, 1997), pp. 489-93.

5. See R.A. Oden, *Studies in Lucian's* De Syria Dea (HSM, 125; Missoula, MT: Scholars Press, 1977), pp. 26-29; West, *The East Face of Helicon*, p. 492 n. 162; *idem*, 'The Flood Myth in Ovid, Lucian, and Nonnus', in Juan Antonio López Férez (ed.), *Mitos en la literatura griega helenística e imperial* (Madrid: Ediciones Clásicas, 2003), pp. 254-57; J.L. Lightfoot, *Lucian, On the Syrian Goddess* (Oxford: Oxford University Press, 2003), pp. 339-42. Contrast E.G. Kraeling, 'Xisouthros, Deucalion and the Flood Traditions', *JAOS* 67 (1947), pp. 177-83, who thought both Genesis and Lucian shared a common tradition.

6. For Berossus, see S.M. Burstein, *The Babyloniaca of Berossus* (Sources and Monographs: Sources from the Ancient Near East, 1.5; Malibu: Undena Publications,

Josephus (*Ant.* 1.93; *Ag. Ap.* 1.130) recognized its connection with the biblical account. Here the flood hero is called Xisouthros (cf. the Sumerian name Ziusudra below), whom Berossus has earlier named as the tenth in a line of long-reigned antediluvian kings. The coming of a flood on 15 Daisios is revealed to Xisouthros in a dream by Kronos (Berossus's name for Ea), who instructs him to build a boat five stades long and two stades wide, and embark on it with kin and closest friends. After the waters had receded, Xisouthros sent out some birds on three separate occasions, which returned the first two times but disappeared on the third. The ark landed in the Korduaian mountains of Armenia, where Xisouthros offered sacrifice. Finally, together with his wife, daughter and pilot Xisouthros went to live with the gods.

However, the first discovery of a cuneiform account of the flood was of tablet 11 of the Gilgamesh epic in the nineteenth century.[7] It was discovered at Nineveh in the library of Ashurbanipal, the seventh-century Assyrian king, but it is now generally accepted that it was part of the Gilgamesh epic from the latter part of the second millennium BCE.[8] The story, which was recounted to Gilgamesh by the flood hero, Utnapishtim, in connection with the former's quest for immortality, goes as follows.[9] Having been forewarned of a flood by Ea, Utnapishtim built an ark, Enlil and the gods brought the flood for six days and seven nights, after which the ark landed on Mt Nimush.[10] After seven days Utnapishtim released a dove, which returned, then a swallow which also returned, and finally a raven, which disappeared. Utnapishtim then sacrificed on the mountain, the gods gathering round like flies to smell the sacrifice. Finally, Utnapishtim was made immortal.

1978), pp. 20-21. For an older study with Greek text, see P. Schnabel, *Berossos und die babylonisch-hellenistische Literatur* (Leipzig: B.G. Teubner, 1923). For the text of Berossus pertaining to the flood, see above, Chapter 4, pp. 62-63.

7.   G. Smith, 'The Chaldean Account of the Deluge', *TSBA* 2 (1873), pp. 213-34, reprinted in Alan Dundes (ed.), *The Flood Myth* (Berkeley: University of California Press, 1988), pp. 29-48.

8.   J.H. Tigay, *The Evolution of the Gilgamesh Epic* (Philadelphia: University of Pennsylvania Press, 1982), pp. 238-39.

9.   For translations of Gilgamesh tablet 11, see A.R. George, *The Epic of Gilgamesh* (London: Penguin Books, 1999), pp. 88-99; *idem*, *The Babylonian Gilgamesh Epic: Introduction, Critical Edition and Cuneiform Texts* (2 vols.; Oxford: Oxford University Press, 2003), I, pp. 700-725; S. Dalley, *Myths from Mesopotamia* (Oxford: Oxford University Press, 1989), pp. 109-20.

10.   Previously read Niṣir. See W.G. Lambert, 'Note brève, Niṣir or Nimuš', *RA* 80 (1986), pp. 185-86.

However, an even earlier form of the Mesopotamian flood story was later discovered in the form of the Atrahasis epic.[11] This is attested in various recensions from the second and first millennia BCE and all are fragmentary, but the best preserved and earliest is the Old Babylonian version from the seventeenth century BCE, which we shall summarize here. This flood story is the climax of a larger work. Originally the gods were like men, performing labour on the earth, but eventually man was created to relieve the gods. However, as humanity increased, so noise increased, which disturbed the chief god Enlil's sleep, so he brought first a plague, then drought, next a famine, and finally a flood to eliminate humanity. Enki (Ea), however, by ostensibly addressing a reed hut communicated to Atrahasis the coming of a flood in seven days and the necessity of building an ark (of wood, reeds and pitch). The flood subsequently came for seven days and seven nights and afterwards Atrahasis offered sacrifice and the gods gathered round like flies to smell the sacrifice. After the flood a new order of society was established by Enki which allowed humanity to continue but various restraints were put on human reproduction to stop numbers getting out of control again.[12]

Unfortunately, parts of the Atrahasis epic are missing. But we know from both a Ugaritic and a Neo-Babylonian fragment that Atrahasis was made immortal following the flood. It is particularly unfortunate that the Old Babylonian Atrahasis epic is lost at the point where the sending out of the birds was presumably mentioned. But it is generally agreed that some form of the Atrahasis epic (presumably the Middle Babylonian version from the second half of the second millennium BCE) lies behind the flood narrative in Gilgamesh epic tablet 11, since the versions are generally so similar, including much common wording.[13] Interestingly, on two occasions Utnapishtim is actually called Atrahasis (Gilgamesh 11.49, 197). However, whereas in Atrahasis the flood story is reported in its original primaeval context following the creation and growth of humanity, in Gilgamesh it is wrenched from its original context.

---

11. For various recensions of Atrahasis, see W.G. Lambert and A.R. Millard, *Atra-ḥasīs: The Babylonian Story of the Flood* (Oxford Clarendon Press, 1969); B.R. Foster, *Before the Muses: An Anthology of Akkadian Literature* (Bethesda, MD: CDL Press, 3rd edn, 2005), pp. 227-80. Dalley, *Myths from Mesopotamia*, pp. 1-38, translates just the Old Babylonian version.

12. If the restoration of W.G. Lambert is correct in 'The Theology of Death', in B. Alster (ed.), *Death in Mesopotamia: Papers Read at the XXVIᵉ Rencontre assyriologique internationale* (Copenhagen: Akademisk forlag, 1980), pp. 52-66 (58), Nintu also decreed death for humans at this point (Atrahasis 3.6.47-50).

13. See Tigay, *The Evolution of the Gilgamesh Epic*, pp. 215-17.

A further Mesopotamian version, the Sumerian flood story (seventeenth century BCE),[14] is preserved only in a fragmentary text from Nippur. Following the creation of man, the institution of kingship and the first cities, the decision of the divine assembly to bring a flood is revealed (presumably by Enki) to King Ziusudra. This lasts seven days and seven nights but Ziusudra is saved in a boat, after which he offers sacrifice to the gods and is made immortal in Dilmun.

Clearly the version in Berossus is too late to have directly influenced Genesis, but as we shall see later, the Priestly source did share some common traditions with it. As for the Sumerian version, the fact that it is attested only in one seventeenth-century text in Sumerian probably means that we do not need to consider it further when seeking influences on the Bible.[15] The main question to consider, therefore, is whether it was the version in the Gilgamesh or Atrahasis epic which ultimately lies behind the biblical flood narrative. However, before we consider that we need to note that the biblical flood story is itself made up of different sources.

3. *The Two Biblical Accounts*

It is widely accepted that the biblical flood story is composed of two sources, J[16] and P. The J account consists of Gen. 6.5-8; 7.1-5, 7-10, 12, 16b-17, 22-23; 8.2b-3a, 6, 8-12, 13b, 20-22. Here the deity is called Yahweh (the Lord), seven pairs of clean and a pair of unclean animals enter the ark, and the flood lasts forty days and forty nights. Noah sends out a dove three times to see whether the waters have subsided. Afterwards he offers a sacrifice to the Lord, who smells the sweet savour of the sacrifice. Finally the Lord promises no further flood.

The P account is in Gen. 6.9-22; 7.6, 11, 13-16a, 18-21; 7.24–8.2a; 8.3b-5, 7, 13a, 14-19; 9.1-17. Here the deity is called Elohim (God), we learn that Noah has three sons, Shem, Ham and Japheth, and a pair of all

---

14. For the Sumerian flood story, see Civil in Lambert and Millard, *Atra-ḫasīs*, pp. 138-45; also T. Jacobsen, 'The Eridu Genesis', *JBL* 80 (1981), pp. 513-29, reprinted in R.S. Hess and D.T. Tsumura (eds.), *"I Studied Inscriptions from before the Flood": Ancient Near Eastern, Literary, and Linguistic Approaches to Genesis 1–11* (Sources for Biblical and Theological Study, 4; Winona Lake, IN: Eisenbrauns, 1994), pp. 129-42.

15. *Contra* Jacobsen, 'The Eridu Genesis', who speculatively combines the Sumerian flood story with other texts which overall provide a better parallel to Gen. 1–9.

16. I continue to prefer the designation 'J' rather than the currently fashionable 'non-P'.

animals enter the ark. The ark is made of gopher wood, reeds[17] and pitch, and is 300 cubits long, 50 cubits broad and 30 cubits high. Noah is 600 years old when the flood comes, the waters bursting forth for 150 days, but the earth is not dry till one (lunar) year and ten days have passed (the flood having commenced on the seventeenth day of the second month and ended the following year on the twenty-seventh day of the second month). The ark lands on the mountains of Ararat and Noah sends out a raven from the ark.[18] After Noah and his family leave the ark, God blesses Noah, commands his descendants to be fruitful and multiply, and gives other regulations, making a covenant with him and setting his rainbow in the cloud as a sign that there will never be another universal flood.

In spite of the many challenges to the documentary hypothesis in recent years, the case for this source division is overwhelming, since the flood story is replete with doublets using two different divine names, Yahweh and Elohim, and containing discrepancies, for example, over the number of animals going into the ark and the length of the flood.[19] Those who oppose source division have no convincing response to these points.[20] For example, Wenham's much-cited attempt[21] to demonstrate the unity of the narrative by arguing it has an impressive chiastic structure is flawed, since as Emerton[22] has shown, some of the alleged chiastic parallels are arbitrary, weakening the overall pattern. In any case, a degree of parallelism between the two halves of the flood narrative was inevitable.

17. Reading *qānîm* for *qinnîm* in Gen. 6.14; see the discussion below, and in greater detail in the next chapter of this volume.

18. The sending out of the raven (Gen. 8.7) is often attributed to J (cf. Gen. 8.8-12). However, the minority view that it is from P is preferable, since if v. 7 is also from J, it is odd that the reason for the sending out of the various birds is not stated here at the beginning, but only later with the sending out of the first dove (v. 8). This suggests that v. 7 is not from J.

19. Incidentally, the contradictions are a strong argument in favour of P being a source rather than the redactor, since though it might appear strange for a redactor to combine two contradictory sources, it would be far odder for P as a redactor to introduce contradictions into his own account. On P as a source, see E.W. Nicholson, *The Pentateuch in the Twentieth Century: The Legacy of Julius Wellhausen* (Oxford: Clarendon Press, 1998), pp. 196-221.

20. See J.A. Emerton, 'An Examination of Some Attempts to Defend the Unity of the Flood Narrative in Genesis. Part I', *VT* 37 (1987), pp. 401-20; *idem*, 'An Examination of Some Attempts to Defend the Unity of the Flood Narrative. Part II', *VT* 38 (1988), pp. 1-21.

21. G.J. Wenham, 'The Coherence of the Flood Narrative', *VT* 28 (1978), pp. 336-48.

22. Emerton, 'An Examination of Some Attempts to Defend the Unity of the Flood Narrative. Part II', pp. 6-13.

However, Wenham and Rendsburg[23] have further claimed that it is odd that the full range of parallels with the Mesopotamian story—all occurring in the same order—is found only in the complete account, the alleged J and P sources each having only some of the parallels. This, they claim, supports the unity of the biblical narrative. However, Emerton's reply to Wenham[24] on this point (overlooked by Rendsburg) shows that this argument for unity is also unconvincing. The case for distinguishing J and P is too strong to be so summarily dismissed. Each probably had a more or less complete account, the redactor sometimes choosing one in preference to the other, sometimes citing both.

Anyway, the upshot is that we need to consider the J and P accounts separately when attempting to evaluate the Bible's relationship to Mesopotamian sources.

4. *The J Account and Mesopotamian Parallels*

Although there are several references in the Old Testament to sacrifices constituting a sweet savour to the Lord (e.g. Lev. 1.9; Num. 29.2), the flood story is the only place where Yahweh is actually spoken of as smelling the sweet savour of a sacrifice (Gen. 8.21). However, it has a striking parallel in both Atrahasis (3.5.31-35) and Gilgamesh (11.157-63), where we read that after the flood the gods gathered round like flies to smell the sweet savour of the flood hero's sacrifice.

Another striking parallel concerns the sending out of the birds (Gen. 8.6, 8-12). The passage is not currently preserved in Atrahasis (the text is broken) but is well preserved in Gilgamesh (11.147-56). Gilgamesh sends out first a dove, then a swallow and finally a raven to establish whether the flood has ended, while J has a dove sent out three times. In both Gilgamesh and J the first two birds return and the third disappears. Moreover, in both accounts this happens after the ark has landed on a mountain, and in both there is a reference to seven days. In Gilgamesh (11.147-50) it is on the seventh day after the ark's landing on Mt Nimush that the dove is sent out, while in Genesis the second and third doves are

---

23. Wenham, 'The Coherence of the Flood Narrative', pp. 345-47; G.A. Rendsburg, 'The Biblical Flood Story in the Light of the Gilgameš Flood Account', in J. Asize and N. Weeks (eds.), *Gilgameš and the World of Assyria: Proceedings of the Conference Held at Mandelbaum House, The University of Sidney, 21–23 July 2004* (Ancient Near Eastern Studies, Supplement 21; Leuven: Peeters, 2007), pp. 115-27.

24. Emerton, 'An Examination of Some Attempts to Defend the Unity of the Flood Story. Part II', pp. 14-15.

sent out after successive periods of seven days (Gen. 8.10-12). Many scholars think the first dove was also sent out after seven days, the words having fallen out of v. 8 (cf. *BHS*), since the second dove was sent out after '*another* seven days' (v. 10). This would make the Mesopotamian parallel even closer.

Both these striking parallels clearly indicate that J was dependent on the Mesopotamian flood tradition. But which version was he using? Scholars most frequently compare the Genesis account with the version known from Gilgamesh tablet 11.[25] But as we have seen, the Mesopotamian story is actually attested in several versions. Is J really closest to the Gilgamesh version, as is sometimes supposed, or is this supposition simply the result of the Gilgamesh version being better preserved and therefore more prone to produce parallels? I believe this latter to be the case and will argue that J knew some version of the Atrahasis epic.

First, in both Genesis and Atrahasis the flood story is set in the context of a primaeval narrative of the origins of the world, starting with creation and continuing with the multiplication of humanity prior to the flood. This contrasts with Gilgamesh tablet 11, where the flood story is wrenched from its original context and recounted by Utnapishtim to Gilgamesh in connection with the latter's quest for immortality. Secondly, related to this, it should be noted that the biblical account, like that in Atrahasis, reports the story in the third person, whereas in the Gilgamesh epic Utnapishtim recounts the flood story in the first person.

Thirdly, a point rarely noted, in J Yahweh specifically announces to Noah that the flood will take place after seven days (Gen. 7.4; cf. 7.10), which is in exact agreement with the Atrahasis epic (3.1.37), where we read that 'He [Enki] announced to him [Atrahasis] the coming of the flood for the seventh night'. Although in Gilgamesh the flood similarly began seven days after the start of the building of the ark, this timescale is not announced in advance to Utnapishtim. Moreover, it is only apparent that the flood comes after seven days in Gilgamesh when one pays extremely close attention to the text.[26]

25. E.g. Rendsburg. 'The Biblical Flood Story in the Light of the Gilgameš Flood Account'; C. Dykgraaf, 'The Mesopotamian Flood Epic in the Earliest Texts, the Bible, and the Qur'an', in R.S. Sabbath (ed.), *Sacred Tropes: Tanakh, New Testament and Qur'an as Literature and Culture* (BiblInt Series, 98; Leiden: Brill, 2009), pp. 233-43 (233).

26. G.J. Wenham, *Genesis 1–15* (WBC, 1; Waco, TX: Word Books, 1987), p. 177, fails to note that this is explicit in Atrahasis but says 'The Gilgamesh epic seems to envisage that seven days were needed to *build* the ship (11:76)...' However, this line (= George line 77, '[before] sundown the boat was finished') is

Fourthly, in contrast to Gilgamesh, there is a statement towards the end of the Atrahasis epic, in a recently discovered Neo-Babylonian fragment, that there will never be another worldwide flood. Ea declares:

> Henceforth let no flood be brought about,
> But let the people last forever.[27]

George[28] compares this passage with Gen. 9.8-17 (P), but it would have been equally, if not more relevant, to compare the earlier J account in Gen. 8.21-22, where the promise of no more flood follows on immediately at the corresponding point following the flood, unlike P's, which is somewhat separated by Gen. 9.1-7.

5. *The P Account and Mesopotamian Parallels*

Unlike J there is evidence that P knew some later Mesopotamian traditions also attested in Berossus. This should not surprise us, since they are both relatively late sources. I have already discussed this in detail elsewhere,[29] so will be brief here. First, the flood has a precise starting date which is similar in both, the seventeenth day of the second month in P (Gen. 7.11) and the fifteenth day of the second month (Daisios) in Berossus.[30] Secondly, in P the ark lands on the mountains of Ararat, that is, Armenia (Gen. 8.4), just as in Berossus it lands on Armenian mountains, in contrast to Mt Nimush (in Iraqi Kurdistan) in the earlier tradition (Gilgamesh 11.142-46; Atrahasis is broken at this point). Thirdly, the ark has dimensions more suggestive of a raft in both P (Gen. 6.15) and Berossus, rather than the cube-shaped object in the earlier tradition (Atrahasis 3.1.25-26; Gilgamesh 11.28-30). Fourthly, in both P and

---

actually referring to the sixth day (cf. line 57's previous reference to 'the fifth day'). It is only in line 88 that we read 'In the morning he will rain down...', referring to what is presumably the seventh day. This is finally recounted in line 97 onwards.

27.   Lambert, in I. Spar and W.G. Lambert (eds.), *Cuneiform Texts in the Metropolitan Museum of Art*. II. *Literary and Scholastic Texts of the First Millennium B.C.* (Metropolitan Museum of Art, New York: Brepols, 2005), p. 199, reverse, col. 5, lines 13-14.

28.   George, *The Babylonian Gilgamesh Epic*, I, p. 527.

29.   J. Day, 'The Flood and the Ten Antediluvian Figures in Berossus and in the Priestly Source in Genesis', in J.K. Aitken, K.J. Dell and B.A. Mastin (eds.), *On Stone and Scroll: A Festschrift for Graham Ivor Davies* (BZAW, 420; Berlin: W. de Gruyter, 2011), pp. 211-23. See above, Chapter 4, for an expanded version of this essay.

30.   For this and the subsequent references to Berossus, see Burstein, *The Babyloniaca of Beossus*, pp. 20-21, reproduced above in Chapter 4.

Berossus the flood hero is the tenth of a line of ten long-lived ante-diluvian figures of whom the seventh was Enoch/Euedoranchos = Enmeduranki (Gen. 5). These parallels are best explained by supposing that both P and Berossus had access to similar late Babylonian traditions.

That P also knew the flood story through some form of the Atrahasis epic rather than Gilgamesh is supported, as in the case of J, by the fact that his story is set in the context of the primaeval history of the world, starting with creation, in third-person narrative form. A further sugges-tive point is that P has a series of divine regulations for the new era following the flood (Gen. 9.1-7), which is also the case in Atrahasis but not in Gilgamesh. However, whereas in Atrahasis (3.6.45–7.11, only partly preserved) these regulations are concerned with limiting the future growth of the human population in various ways, P emphasizes the need for humans to be fruitful and multiply (Gen. 9.1, 7; cf. 8.17), repeating the original divine command at creation (Gen. 1.26, 28). This supports the contention[31] that P is polemicizing against the Atrahasis epic, where the flood is a draconian response to the noise resulting from the growth in the human population. In addition, like J, P has a divine promise that there will no more universal flood (Gen. 9.8-17), something which, as noted above, is attested in a Neo-Babylonian fragment of the Atrahasis epic, but not in Gilgamesh.

Some other parallels between P and the Mesopotamian flood tradition are attested in both Atrahasis and Gilgamesh, but in the light of the above comments we may assume Atrahasis to have been the source. Thus, in Gen. 6.14, referring to the construction of the ark, God says to Noah, 'pitch it inside and out with pitch'. Strikingly, the word used for 'pitch' here is *kōper*, a noun attested nowhere else in the Bible (the denominative verb 'pitch' here is also unique). Interestingly, the cognate Akkadian word *kupru* is specifically mentioned in Mesopotamian accounts of the building of the ark (Atrahasis 3.2.51; Gilgamesh 11.55, 66).[32] We thus have good evidence of the Mesopotamian background of P's reference here.[33]

---

31. W.L. Moran, 'Atrahasis: The Babylonian Story of the Flood', *Bib* 52 (1971), p. 61; A.D. Kilmer, 'The Mesopotamian Concept of Overpopulation and its Solution as Reflected in the Mythology', *Or* 41 (1972), pp. 160-77 (174-75); T. Frymer-Kensky, 'The Atrahasis Epic and its Significance for Understanding Genesis 1–9', *BA* 40 (1977), pp. 147-55 (150), reprinted in Dundes (ed.), *The Flood Myth*, pp. 61-73 (66).

32. Cf. H.R. (Chaim) Cohen, *Biblical Hapax Legomena in the Light of Akkadian and Ugaritic* (SBLMS, 37; Missoula, MT: Scholars Press, 1978), pp. 33-34, 53-54.

33. The view of J. Van Seters, *Prologue to History: The Yahwist as Historian in Genesis* (Louisville, KY: Westminster/John Knox, 1992), p. 165, that Gen. 6.13-16

Immediately before the reference to pitch in Gen. 6.14 we are told that the ark is also to be made with gopher wood and *qnym*. The word *qnym* was vocalized *qinnîm* by the Masoretes, and is generally rendered 'rooms' in modern translations, although elsewhere the singular *qēn* means 'nest', with reference to birds, even if it can be used metaphorically of a human dwelling in poetic passages (e.g. Hab. 2.9). However, a strong case can be made that we should read *qānîm*, 'reeds', rather than *qinnîm*, 'rooms', a view supported by a minority of scholars,[34] the NEB, REB and NJB. First, both Atrahasis (3.2.12; CBS 13532, rev. 7) and the Gilgamesh epic (11.51) imply that reeds were used in the making of the ark. Secondly, the reference to *qnym* in Gen. 6.14 is mentioned in between gopher wood and pitch, suggesting it was one of the materials used in the ark's construction, just as Atrahasis 3.2.11-13 and Gilgamesh 11.50-55 refer to reeds in between wood and pitch. Thirdly, the division of the ark into sections does not come till Gen. 6.16, so a reference to 'rooms' would be premature in v. 14. The use of reeds in the making of the ark was thus not merely a part of P's Mesopotamian *Vorlage* but also intended by P himself.[35]

A further parallel to P in both Atrahasis and Gilgamesh has been claimed by A.D. Kilmer.[36] She argues that the Mistress of the gods' lapis lazuli fly necklace mentioned after the flood, which serves to remind her of the flood (Atrahasis 3.6.2-4; Gilgamesh 11.164-67), denotes the rainbow, thus providing an analogy with Gen. 9.12-17, where the rainbow is a sign of God's covenant promise that he will never bring another

is from J is unconvincing. Not only is Elohim the only divine name found in this context (Gen. 6.11-13, 22), but the precise figures given for the dimensions of the ark in 6.15 are the kind of thing we should expect from P, not J.

34.   This view was proposed almost simultaneously by C.H. Gordon, *Introduction to Old Testament Times* (Ventnor, NJ: Ventnor Publishers, 1953), p. 38 n. 31; E. Ullendorff, 'The Construction of Noah's Ark', *VT* 4 (1954), pp. 95-96, reprinted in *idem, Is Biblical Hebrew a Language? Studies in Semitic Languages and Civilizations* (Wiesbaden: Harrassowitz, 1977), pp. 48-49, and G.R. Driver, 'Problems and Solutions', *VT* 4 (1954), pp. 225-45 (243), and has been followed by a few others, e.g. Wenham, *Genesis 1–15*, pp. 149, 152, 173.

35.   For a thorough consideration of the *qānîm/qinnîm* question, see Chapter 7 below.

36.   A.D. Kilmer, 'The Symbolism of the Flies in the Mesopotamian Flood Myth and Some Further Implications', in F. Rochberg-Halton (ed.), *Language, Literature, and History: Philological and Historical Studies Presented to Erica Reiner* (AOS Series, 67; New Haven, CT: American Oriental Society, 1987), pp. 175-80; also H.S. Kvanvig, *Primeval History: Babylonian, Biblical, and Enochic: An Intertextual Reading* (JSJSup, 149: Leiden: Brill, 2011), p. 232.

universal flood. However, Kilmer's arguments are rather tangential, and we have no explicit evidence anywhere that the Mother goddess's necklace symbolized a rainbow. Consequently, if a rainbow were envisaged here, we should expect the narrator to have spelled this out clearly. Nevertheless, it is quite attractive to suppose that P's rainbow has been constructed on the basis of this allusion in the Mesopotamian account. Not only do they occur at the same point in the narrative following the flood, but just as we read that the Mother goddess's necklace will remind her for ever of the flood (which she now regrets having consented to), so the rainbow will remind God for ever not to bring another flood.

It is intriguing that P declares Noah to have been 600 years old at the beginning of the flood (Gen. 7.6), since the Babylonians employed a sexagesimal numerical system, unlike the Israelites. This figure is therefore suggestive of a Babylonian background. Indeed, it suggests knowledge of the antediluvian King List, something already utilized by P in Genesis 5. In the Weld-Blundell 62 version of the King List the flood hero (Ziusudra) reigned for 36,000 years. If P or his source knew this figure, they could have divided it by 60 and applied it to Noah's life at the time of the flood.[37] (Division by sixty is, of course, central to the Babylonian sexagesimal system, and it is to the Babylonians that we ultimately owe our sixty seconds in a minute and sixty minutes in an hour.) In Berossus's version, the flood hero (Xisouthros) reigned 64,800 years,[38] which is 18 × 600 years, so alternatively this figure could have been divided by 18 (a much rounder number in the sexagesimal system than in ours) and applied it to Noah's age. Either way, P's figure of 600 years had a Babylonian background.

6. *How and When Were Mesopotamian Traditions Absorbed?*

There have been a few scholars who have claimed that the biblical flood account is not dependent on the Mesopotamian but that both are dependent on a common earlier tradition or event. These scholars tend to be

---

37. Cf. U. (M.D.) Cassuto, *A Commentary on the Book of Genesis. II. From Noah to Abraham* (trans. I. Abrahams; Jerusalem: Magnes Press, 1964), pp. 17, 22, 81. He was followed by L.R. Bailey, *Noah: The Person and the Story in History and Tradition* (Columbia, SC: University of South Carolina Press, 1989), p. 167, but the latter wrongly gives 36,000 years as Ziusudra's age rather than length of reign and does not note the precise Mesopotamian source.

38. J.C. VanderKam, *Enoch and the Growth of an Apocalyptic Tradition* (CBQMS, 16; Washington, DC: Catholic Biblical Association of America, 1984), p. 37, normally a most meticulous scholar, mistakenly says that Berossus attributed a 36,000-year reign to Xisouthros.

extremely conservative, such as Heidel and Millard,[39] seeking to avoid the unpalatable notion that the Bible is dependent on a pagan source. However, bearing in mind the certainty that the Mesopotamian tradition is much earlier than the biblical—even on the most conservative dating of Genesis 6–9—this supposition is unwarranted and reflects the logical fallacy known as positing entities beyond necessity.

We cannot know for certain how and when the Mesopotamian flood traditions were appropriated. However, Lambert[40] has suggested that these traditions spread westwards about the time of the Amarna age (fourteenth century BCE), which is plausible since Akkadian was the *lingua franca* of the ancient Near East at that time, and copies of various Akkadian literary works are attested in the west then, for example, Atrahasis at Ugarit,[41] Gilgamesh at Megiddo and the Hittite capital, Hattusa, and various other works at Amarna itself. If so, it is likely that the Mesopotamian flood story was originally mediated to the Israelites through the Canaanites. This, I have argued above, was in the form of the Atrahasis epic. Eventually the story reached J, whom I hold to have written c. 800 BCE.[42] In addition, P also seems to have had independent access to Mesopotamian flood traditions, including a version of the Atrahasis epic as well some traditions found later in Berossus. In view of the fact that P is generally dated to the sixth century BCE, it is plausible to suppose that these traditions were derived by P from a Babylonian source in the exile.[43]

39. A. Heidel, *The Gilgamesh Epic and Old Testament Parallels* (Chicago; University of Chicago Press, 2nd edn, 1949), p. 267; A.R. Millard, 'A New Babylonian "Genesis" Story', *TynBul* 18 (1967), pp. 3-18 (17-18), reprinted in Hess and Tsumura (eds.), *"I Studied Inscriptions from before the Flood"*, pp, 114-28 (127-28).

40. W.G. Lambert, 'A New Look at the Babylonian Background of Genesis', *JTS* NS 16 (1965), pp. 287-300 (299-300), reprinted in Hess and Tsumura (eds.), *"I Studied Inscriptions from before the Flood"*, pp. 96-113 (109).

41. The fragmentary Atrahasis text from Ugarit contains only the flood story and has Atrahasis speaking in the first person, thus providing a parallel to Gilgamesh tablet 11. See Lambert and Millard, *Atra-ḫasīs*, pp. 131-33.

42. Cf. Gen. 10.12, where Calah is 'the great city', Calah being the capital of Assyria from c. 880–c. 700 BCE.

43. Contrast Van Seters, *Prologue to History*, for whom it was J who appropriated Babylonian traditions in exile.

7. How Genesis Has Theologically Transformed
the Mesopotamian Flood Tradition

There are numerous details in which the biblical writers have transformed the underlying Mesopotamian flood tradition, for example, the
name of the flood hero and the length of the flood, but the four most
fundamental theological differences are as follows.

First, the Bible has 'monotheized' the Mesopotamian flood story.
Whereas in the Mesopotamian account Enlil and the gods bring the flood
and Enki/Ea delivers the flood hero, in Genesis there is simply one deity
who does both. Other polytheistic references have also been eliminated.
This 'monotheization' is of a piece with the way in which the Bible
transforms other ancient Near Eastern traditions, for example, those
concerning Enoch, Balaam and Daniel.

Secondly, the story has been ethicized. In the Atrahasis epic the flood
was brought by Enlil because he could not get to sleep at night as a result
of the noise of humanity which resulted from its increase; the claim
of Pettinato[44] that this refers to a rebellion on the part of humanity is
unjustified, and is now generally rejected.[45] In Gilgamesh no reason is
given for the flood, though we know it was a decision of the gods
(11.14), especially Enlil, something not only Ea but also the Mother
goddess later felt lacked wisdom (11.170, 184). The biblical flood story
thus represents a new development in the motivation for the flood, both J
and P attributing it to humanity's sin. P refers particularly to humanity's
violence and corruption (Gen. 6.11-13), whereas J speaks more generally
of wickedness and evil (Gen. 6.5).

Thirdly, a point that biblical scholars often overlook is that towards
the end of the Mesopotamian flood story, in both Atrahasis (3.5.36–6.40)
and Gilgamesh (11.164-206), some divine sympathy is expressed for the
victims of the flood in speeches from the Mother goddess and Enki/Ea.
In contrast, the Bible regards the flood as a just punishment for wicked
humanity, so there is no need for God to show regret.

Finally, in all versions of the Mesopotamian flood story (Sumerian,
Atrahasis [as preserved in Ugaritic and Neo-Babylonian fragments],
Gilgamesh, Berossus) the flood hero is made immortal after the flood. It
was therefore a deliberate move on the part of the biblical writers or their

---

44. G. Pettinato, 'Die Bestrafung des Menschengeschlechts durch die Sintflut:
die erste Tafel des Atramḥasīs-Epos eröffnet eine neue Einsicht in die Motivation
dieser Strafe', *Or* 37 NS (1968), pp. 165-200.

45. W.L. Moran, 'Atrahasis: The Babylonian Story of the Flood', *Bib* 52 (1971),
pp. 51-61; Kilmer, 'The Mesopotamian Concept of Overpopulation'.

sources to omit this part of the story. Probably P transferred this motif to Enoch (Gen. 5.24), who uniquely with Noah is described by P as having walked with God (Gen. 5.24; 6.9).[46] As for J, after the flood he goes on to present a very human Noah—one who becomes drunk and naked in the process of discovering wine (Gen. 9.20-27)—a story which Baumgarten[47] hypothesizes was placed here deliberately by way of rejection of the traditional apotheosis of the flood hero. This is possible but cannot be proved. The suggestion[48] that the name Noah derives from a root cognate with Ethiopic *nōḥa*, 'to be long' (especially of time), by analogy with the names Ziusudra ('Life of long days') and Utnapishtim ('He found life') therefore seems unlikely, since Noah is depicted as mortal.[49] Conceivably, of course, the Hebrew name Noah might have arisen with this etymology prior to the rejection of the immortality motif, and the etymology might subsequently have become forgotten. However, this is unlikely since a Hebrew verb with this meaning is otherwise unattested, whereas Akkadian and Amorite personal names based on *nwḥ*, 'rest, be satisfied' are well known.[50]

46. VanderKam, *Enoch and the Growth of an Apocalyptic Tradition*, p. 31; Day, 'The Flood and the Ten Antediluvian Figures', p. 218. Contrast R. Borger, 'Die Beschwörungsserie *bīt mēseri* und die Himmelfahrt Henochs', *JNES* 33 (1974), pp. 183-96, reprinted in English translation as 'The Incantation Series *Bīt Mēseri* and Enoch's Ascension to Heaven' in Hess and Tsumura (eds.), *"I Studied Inscriptions from before the Flood"*, pp. 234-53.

47. A.I. Baumgarten, 'Myth and Midrash: Genesis 9:20-29', in J. Neusner (ed.), *Christianity, Judaism and Other Greco-Roman Cults: Studies for Morton Smith at Sixty. III. Judaism before 70* (SJLA, 12; Leiden: Brill, 1975), pp. 55-71 (58-61).

48. G. Hilion, *Le déluge dans la Bible et les inscriptions akkadiennes et sumériennes* (Paris: Geuthner, 1925), pp. 50-53; G.R. Driver, 'L'interprétation masorétique à la lumière de la lexicographie hébraïque', *ETL* 26 (1950), pp. 337-53 (350); J. Barr, *The Garden of Eden and the Hope of Immortality* (London: SCM Press, 1992), p. 75. Cf. Bailey, *Noah*, pp. 165-67.

49. Even less likely is the view of M. Schwartz, 'Qumran, Turfan, Arabic Magic, and Noah's Name', in R. Gyselen (ed.), *Charmes et sortilèges: Magie et magicians* (Res Orientales, 14; Bures-sur-Yvette: Groupe pour l'Etude de la Civilisation du Moyen-Orient, 2002), pp. 231-38 (236-37), that the name Noah, 'rest', derived from that of Utnapishtim via Aramaic *ʾtnbš* (understood as reflexive of *npš*, 'he refreshed himself, rested').

50. Cf. Tigay, *The Evolution of the Gilgamesh Epic*, p. 230 n. 41.

Chapter 7

ROOMS OR REEDS IN NOAH'S ARK (GENESIS 6.14)?

In Gen. 6.14, part of the Priestly account of God's command to build the ark, Noah is instructed to make the ark with *qinnîm*, in between references to using gopher wood and pitch in its construction.[1] The Masoretic text reads, 'Make yourself an ark of gopher wood, with *qinnîm* make the ark, and daub [lit. pitch] it inside and out with pitch'. The majority of Bible translations, including all the ancient ones and most of the modern, render *qinnîm* as 'rooms' or 'cells' or the like (literally 'nests', plural of *qēn*); so the LXX ('nests'), the Vulgate, the Targums and Peshitta among ancient Versions and the AV, RV, RSV, NRSV, JB, NAB, NJPSV and NIV among English translations. However, in the modern scholarly literature, a minority have proposed that the original Hebrew text rather read *qānîm*, 'reeds'. This view was first put forward by Cyrus Gordon.[2]

---

1. It is generally agreed that Gen. 6.14-16 is from P. The only exception I have come across is in J. Van Seters, *Prologue to History: The Yahwist as Historian in Genesis* (Louisville, KY: Westminster/John Knox Press, 1992), p. 165, who curiously attributes these verses to J. However, I can see no convincing evidence for this. Not only is Elohim the only divine name found in this context (Gen. 6.11-13, 22), but the interest in the precise dimensions of the ark (Gen. 6.15) is exactly what we should expect from P rather than J. Moreover, the expression *mibbayit ûmiḥûṣ*, 'inside and out' (Gen. 6.14), is also attested elsewhere in P in connection with the construction of the ark of the covenant in Exod. 25.11, but never in J.

2. Even earlier A.S. Yahuda, *Die Sprache des Pentateuch in ihren Beziehungen zum Aegyptischen* (Berlin: W. de Gruyter, 1929), pp. 200-201, ET *The Language of the Pentateuch in its Relation to Egyptian* (London: Oxford University Press, 1933), pp. 206-207, followed by B. Jacob, *Das erste Buch der Tora: Genesis übersetzt und erklärt* (Berlin: Schocken Verlag, 1934), p. 188, had suggested the meaning 'reeds', but retained MT *qinnîm*, seeing it rather as the plural of what he regarded as an Egyptian-inspired word *qēn*, 'reed'. (The ET of B. Jacob, *The First Book of the Bible: Genesis Interpreted* [abridged, ed. and trans. Ernest I. Jacob and Walter Jacob; New York: Ktav, 1974; reprinted Jersey City, NJ: Ktav, 2007], pp. 48-49,

However, it was also independently suggested shortly afterwards by Edward Ullendorff, followed by Godfrey R. Driver, and more recently it has been supported by Sean E. McEvenue, Eva Strömberg Krantz and Gordon J. Wenham, among others, as well as by the NEB, REB and NJB translations.[3] In this chapter I shall undertake a detailed review of the question and will conclude that 'reeds' was indeed the original meaning intended.

This view is supported by the following considerations. First of all, elsewhere in Biblical Hebrew the word *qēn* (attested only in the singular) is used of a bird's nest (Deut. 22.6; 32.11; Job 39.27; Ps. 84.4 [ET 3]; Prov. 27.8; Isa. 10.14; 16.2), and although it is also used figuratively of a human dwelling in a few poetic passages (Num. 24.21; Jer. 49.16; Obad. 4; Hab. 2.9), attention to the context in each case shows that the origin of the imagery in a bird's nest is never lost sight of. Thus, in Jer. 49.16 and Obadiah 4 a comparison with an eagle is specifically mentioned in connection with the Edomites' 'nest', in Num. 24.21 the Kenites' 'nest' is set in the rock (just like the eagle's nest in Jer. 49.16), while in Hab. 2.9 the Babylonians' 'nest' is on high (cf. again the eagle's nest in Job 39.27;

retains the translation but lacks the detailed notes.) However, the underlying Egyptian word to which Yahuda and Jacob appealed, *qni*, means 'sheaf' rather than 'reed'; see Alan H. Gardiner, *Egyptian Grammar* (Oxford: Griffith Institute, Ashmolean Museum, 3rd edn, 1957), p. 596.

3.   C.H. Gordon, *Ugaritic Literature* (Rome: Pontifical Biblical Institute, 1949), p. 6 n. 1; *idem, Introduction to Old Testament Times* (Ventnor, NJ: Ventnor Publishers, 1953), p. 38 with n. 31, reprinted as *The Ancient Near East* (New York: W.W. Norton, 3rd edn, 1969), p. 50 with n. 37, and C.H. Gordon and G.A. Rendsburg, *The Bible and the Ancient Near East* (New York: W.W. Norton, 4th edn, 1997), p. 48 with n. 34; *idem*, 'Homer and Bible: The Origin and Character of East Mediterranean Literature', *HUCA* 26 (1955), pp. 43-108 (50 n. 21), reprinted as *Homer and Bible: The Origin and Character of East Mediterranean Literature* (Ventnor, NJ: Ventnor Publishers, 1967), p. 14 n. 21; E. Ullendorff, 'The Construction of Noah's Ark', *VT* 4 (1954), pp. 95-96, reprinted in *idem, Is Biblical Hebrew a Language? Studies in Semitic Languages and Civilizations* (Wiesbaden: O. Harrassowitz, 1977), pp. 48-49; G.R. Driver, 'Problems and Solutions', *VT* 4 (1954), pp. 225-45 (243); S.E. McEvenue, *The Narrative Style of the Priestly Writer* (AnBib, 50; Rome: Biblical Institute Press, 1971), p. 44 n. 36; E. Strömberg Krantz, *Des Schiffes Weg mitten im Meer: Beiträge zur Erforschung der nautischen Terminologie des Alten Testaments* (ConBOT, 19; Lund: C.W.K. Gleerup, 1982), pp. 171-73; G.J. Wenham, *Genesis 1–15* (WBC, 1; Waco, TX: Word Books, 1987), pp. 149, 152, 173. R.S. Hendel also follows this view in his *Genesis 1–11* (Anchor Yale Bible, 1A; New Haven: Yale University Press, forthcoming). I am grateful to Professor Hendel for letting me see a copy of his manuscript.

Obad. 4; Jer. 49.16).[4] The only exception is Job 29.18, but here the Masoretic text appears to be corrupt.[5] The use of the word *qēn* in Biblical Hebrew to denote a cell or room for humans and animals generally without bird's nest associations, and specifically in Biblical Hebrew prose such as is claimed for Gen. 6.14, is elsewhere unattested. Similarly, the denominative verb *qnn*, 'to make a nest', is used in the piel exclusively of birds (Isa. 34.15; Ezek. 31.6; Jer. 48.28; Ps. 104.17), and although the pual is used once in Jer. 22.23 of the human inhabitants of Lebanon, the reference to them as 'nested among the cedars' suggests that the bird's

4. It is for this reason that I am unconvinced by James Barr's questioning of the widely held consensus in his article, 'Is Hebrew ‍קן "Nest" a Metaphor?', in A.S. Kaye (ed.), *Semitic Studies in Honour of Wolf Leslau* (Wiesbaden: O. Harrassowitz, 1991), pp. 150-61. Barr held that the original meaning of *qēn* was 'habitation', that the specific meaning 'nest' was a secondary development, and that the generally accepted bird's nest background is not always present in the Bible. However, the only place in the Bible where I would concede that there is no bird's nest imagery in the background is Job 29.18, but here the text is corrupt (see n. 5 below). Barr also cites Ecclus 14.26, 36.31 and 37.30 in support of his claim that *qēn* can be used of a habitation without any suggestion of a bird's nest background. However, these are late postbiblical passages, and while there is nothing explicit to support a bird's nest background in Ecclus 36.31 and 37.30, this is surely the case in Ecclus 14.26, where the Hebrew reads that the wise man 'builds his nest in her leafage and lodges in her branches'.

5. The second line of Job 29.18, 'and I shall multiply my days like the sand', most naturally suggests that there should be a parallel allusion in the first line to Job's attaining old age, but this is not the case with the MT's *wā'ōmar 'im-qinnî 'egwā'*, 'I said, "I shall die with my nest"'. Rather, the LXX reading, 'And I said, "My manhood will see old age"', appears to reflect the original Hebrew here. We should therefore probably presuppose the original text to have read *wa'ōmar 'immi zāqēn 'egwā'*, 'And I said to myself, "I shall die in a ripe old age"' (cf. Job 42.17) with E. Dhorme, *Le livre de Job* (Etudes bibliques; Paris: V. Lecoffre, 1926), p. 389, ET *A Commentary on the Book of Job* (trans. H. Knight; London: Thomas Nelson, 1967), p. 426, and H.H. Rowley, *Job* (NCB; London: Thomas Nelson, 1970), p. 238, or possibly *wā'ōmar beziqnî 'egwā*, 'I thought, "In ripe age I shall expire"', with M.H. Pope, *Job* (AB, 15; Garden City, NY: Doubleday, 3rd edn, 1973), p. 213. It should further be noted that it has sometimes been maintained that bird's nest imagery is in the background of Job 29.18 by appealing to the second line, 'I shall multiply my days like the *ḥôl*', on the understanding that *ḥôl* means 'phoenix', not 'sand'. For this translation, see, e.g., L.L. Grabbe, *Comparative Philology and the Text of Job: A Study in Methodology* (SBLDS, 34; Missoula, MT: Scholars Press, 1977), pp. 98-101. However, the fact that Job elsewhere disavows belief in resurrection (cf. Job 14.7-14) makes it most unlikely that he would compare his fate to that of a phoenix, which was believed to rejuvenate itself after death. We should therefore take *ḥôl* in its common meaning, 'sand', which is used elsewhere in comparisons to denote a large amount (cf. Gen. 22.17; 2 Sam. 17.11, etc.), just as is postulated for Job 29.18.

nest background is again not lost sight of (cf. Ps. 104.16-17, where the cedars of Lebanon are cited as a site for birds' nests). All this creates an initial suspicion that the rendering of *qnym* by 'rooms' in Gen. 6.14 is incorrect. However, James Barr has argued on the basis of comparative Semitic philology that 'rooms' is a plausible meaning for *qnym* in Gen. 6.14. He notes that 'Akkadian *qinnu* means "family" as well as "nest"; so does Mandaean *qina* ("nest, brood, home, family, group", Drower–Macuch, p. 411); Arabic *qunn*, hardly separable from Hebrew *qen*, means "chicken-coop"; the common-Arabic word for "nest", *ʿuss̆s̆*, also means a hut or the like'.[6] Although none of these parallels denotes exactly a 'room' or 'cell', it must be conceded that the meaning which Barr thinks likely in Gen. 6.14 cannot be ruled out in principle, even though it remains unproven in reality. Accordingly, we need further evidence in order to adjudicate decisively between the renderings 'rooms' or 'reeds' in Gen. 6.14. Fortunately, as I shall now show, the case for understanding 'reeds' here is indeed supported by other compelling considerations.[7]

Thus secondly, there is repeated evidence in the Mesopotamian flood tradition, which ultimately underlies the biblical account, that reeds were used in the construction of the ark. For example, in one version of the Atrahasis epic, the Akkadian word *qá-ne-e*, 'reeds', is actually found in connection with the construction of the flood hero's boat (CBS 13532):[8]

---

6.   J. Barr, Review of Edward Ullendorff, *Is Biblical Hebrew a Language?*, *JSS* 26 (1981), pp. 115-22 (120). By 'Drower–Macuch' Barr is referring to Ethel S. Drower and Rudolf Macuch, *A Mandaic Dictionary* (Oxford: Clarendon Press, 1963).

7.   However, we should not use as an argument Ullendorff's claim in 'The Construction of Noah's Ark', p. 95, repr. p. 48, that if the correct reading were *qinnîm* we should expect the repeated distributive *qinnîm qinnîm*, since this is not necessary. Moreover, his statement that the alleged need for this repetition was already sensed by Philo of Alexandria in *Quaest. in Gen.* 2.3, is invalid. The text of Philo reads, 'Why does (Scripture) say, "Nests, nests thou shalt make the ark"?' In this connection p. 70 note c points out, 'The Arm. and Palest. Syriac versions of Scripture repeat the word…LXX MSS have only a single occurrence of νοσσιάς in this verse. Probably the Armenian translator of Philo has added the second occurrence to make Philo agree with his version of Scripture.'

8.   Cf. W.G. Lambert and A.R. Millard, *Atra-ḫasīs: The Babylonian Story of the Flood* (Oxford: Clarendon Press, 1969), pp. 126-27. Curiously, the only scholars hitherto to note this parallel were S. Loewenstamm, 'Should Qinnîm (Gen 6:14) be Amended to Read Qanîm?', in *Beer-Sheva* 1 (Jerusalem: Kiryat Sepher, 1973), pp. 135-36 (135) (Hebrew), and 'The Flood', in *idem, Comparative Studies in Biblical and Oriental Literature* (AOAT, 204; Neukirchen–Vluyn: Neukirchener Verlag, 1980), pp. 93-121 (115-16 n. 34), and Barr, Review of Edward Ullendorff,

...] build a big boat.
Let its structure be [...] entirely of reeds.[9]
...] let it be a *maqurqurrum*-boat with the name, The Life Saver.

However, significantly there is also another version of the Atrahasis epic in which it is implied that wood, reeds, and pitch were all used in the construction of this boat (Atrahasis 3.2.11-14):[10]

> The carpenter [carried his axe],
> the reed-worker [carried his stone],
> [The rich man (?) carried] the pitch,
> The poor man [brought what was needed].

The reconstructed words, which are certain, are based on the parallel passage in Gilgamesh 11.50-56, where we read as follows:[11]

> The carpenter carried [his] axe,
> the reed-worker carried [his] stone,
> [...carried his] *agasilikku* axe.
> The young men [...],
> the old men bore rope of palm-fibre.
> The rich man (?) carried the pitch,
> the poor man brought [...] what was needed.

It will be noted that the Atrahasis parallel with Genesis is particularly striking, since it implies that the ark was made specifically of wood, reeds and pitch, exactly as in Gen. 6.14 (if we are correct in reading *qānîm*). Gilgamesh 11, which is dependent on Atrahasis, while retaining the order of these three elements, has clearly chosen to add further, secondary items to the list. Curiously, these parallels with the underlying Mesopotamian flood tradition, which add particular weight to understanding *qnym* as 'reeds' in Gen. 6.14, were overlooked by Gordon,

---

Is Biblical Hebrew a Language?, p. 120, both of whom explicitly rejected the meaning 'reeds' in Gen. 6.14. However, they failed to note the other Mesopotamian parallels which I cite in this chapter.

9. This reading is not quite certain, B.R. Foster, *Before the Muses: An Anthology of Akkadian Literature* (Bethesda, MD: CDL Press, 3rd edn, 2005), p. 254 rendering 'good (?) reed' for 'entirely of reeds'. This would imply reading *ṭā-bi*, 'good' instead of *gáb-bi*, 'entire'.

10. For slightly varying translations, cf. Lambert and Millard, *Atra-ḥasīs*, pp. 90-91; S. Dalley, *Myths from Mesopotamia* (Oxford: Oxford University Press, 1989), p. 30; Foster, *Before the Muses,* p. 248.

11. For slightly varying translations, cf. Dalley, *Myths from Mesopotamia*, p. 111; A.R. George, *The Epic of Gilgamesh* (London: Penguin Books, 2000), p. 90; *idem, The Babylonian Gilgamesh Epic: Introduction, Critical Edition and Cuneiform Texts* (2 vols.; Oxford: Oxford University Press, 2003), I, pp. 706-707.

Ullendorff, Driver and others. However, Gordon did note another
passage in which Utnapishtim was instructed to cut down his reed hut
when making his boat in Gilgamesh 11.21-26, indicating that reeds were
used in its construction, though he overlooked the similar passage about
Atrahasis in Atrahasis 3.1.20-23.[12]

Incidentally, as Chaim Cohen has noted, the word used for pitch in
Gen. 6.14, *kōper*, occurs only here in the whole of the Hebrew Bible.[13]
The usual Hebrew word for pitch is *ḥēmār* (Gen. 11.3; 14.10; Exod. 2.3)
or *zepet* (Exod. 2.3; Isa. 34.9). This again strongly indicates a Mesopotamian background, since in addition to being unique in the Hebrew
Bible, its Akkadian equivalent, *kupru*, 'pitch', similarly occurs in connection with the flood hero's boat in both Atrahasis 3.2.51 and Gilgamesh
11.55, 66.[14] We therefore have good evidence that P was dependent on a
Mesopotamian source at this point.

But, it might be asked, granted that P's Mesopotamian *Vorlage* spoke
of the ark being made with reeds (in addition to wood and pitch), can we
be confident that P retained this understanding? I think it is certain that
we can, and it is here that we come to our third basic reason for understanding *qnym* as 'reeds'. This is that the adjacent items mentioned in
Gen. 6.14—both the gopher wood which precedes the *qnym* and the pitch
which follows—refer specifically to materials used in the construction
of the ark, so this would most naturally apply to the *qnym* as well.
Moreover, the actual details of the construction of the ark are reserved
for 6.15-16, introduced by the words 'This is how you shall make it', and
the internal divisions of the ark are not referred to until Gen. 6.16, where
we read of its being built with three decks. This is highly significant,
since we know from elsewhere that P was highly systematic in the order-
ing of his material. Thus, *qnym* must refer to one of the materials used
for making the ark, not to its rooms. A reference to rooms already in v. 14
would be premature and out of place. Interestingly, already over a
hundred years ago, long before the possibility of reading *qānîm*, 'reeds',

---

12. See the first four references to Gordon in n. 3 above.

13. See H.R. (C.) Cohen, *Biblical Hapax Legomena in the Light of Akkadian and
Ugaritic* (Missoula, MT: Scholars Press, 1978), pp. 33-34, with notes on pp. 53-54.

14. It should be noted that later Berossus also makes specific reference to
bitumen towards the end of his account of the Mesopotamian flood story, stating that
'A portion of the ship which came to rest in Armenia still remains on the mountains
of the Korduaians of Armenia, and some of the people, scraping off pieces of
bitumen from the ship, bring them back and use them as talismans'. See S.M.
Burstein, *The* Babyloniaca *of Berossus* (Sources and Monographs: Sources from the
Ancient Near East, 1.5; Malibu, CA: Undena Publications, 1978), p. 21 (quoted on
p. 63 above).

had even been raised, Eduard Sievers, Hugo Winckler and Hermann Gunkel all felt the force of this difficulty, as did Otto Eissfeldt (in *BHS*) somewhat later. Winckler and Gunkel accordingly removed the reference to *qnym* to v. 16, while Sievers and Eissfeldt transferred the reference to the three decks from v. 16 to v. 14.[15] However, as McEvenue noted, these attempts at radical textual surgery have the effect of ruining the threefold symmetry which is present, since vv. 14-16 are constructed of three triplets: gopher wood–reeds–pitch (v. 14), length-breadth-height (v. 15), and roof–door–decks (v. 16).[16] These proposals are therefore forced and *qnym* must remain in v. 14, separate from the reference to the decks. In conclusion, therefore, the evidence supports the view that 'reeds' was not merely in P's *Vorlage* but was also intended by P himself.

How exactly, then, should we translate the passage and how should we understand the role of the reeds? Two of the three modern Bible translations which support understanding 'reeds' here, the NEB and the REB, follow Godfrey R. Driver in translating 'cover it with reeds'.[17] This rendering presupposes that the reeds were laid inside on the hull of the ark as a kind of mat. However, to render the verb *ʿāśâ* as 'cover' seems implausible here; Driver bases this on Arabic *ġašâ* (*w* and *y*), which can mean 'covered', as well as 'plunged into, unexpectedly undertook'.[18] But since the very existence of this meaning of the verb in Biblical Hebrew is highly unlikely, and since moreover this verb clearly has its common meaning 'make' both in the immediately previous phrase, 'Make for yourself an ark of gopher wood' and in the following verse, 'This is how you shall make it', it is only natural to suppose that it also has this meaning in connection with the reeds. The reeds would thus have played a more fundamental role in the construction of the ark than simply providing matting for the floor.

In seeking a more precise translation of the words *qānîm taʿăśeh ʾet-hattēbâ*, the question boils down to whether we should take *ʾet* as a mark

15. E. Sievers, *Metrische Studien* (7 vols.; Leipzig B.G. Teubner, 1901–19 [1904]), II, pp. 18-19, 251-52; H. Winckler, *Altorientalische Forschungen* (3 vols.; Leipzig: E. Pfeiffer, 1893–1906 [1906]), III, pp. 397-98; H. Gunkel, *Genesis übersetzt und erklärt* (HKAT, 1.1; Göttingen: Vandenhoeck & Ruprecht, 3rd edn, 1910), p. 142, ET *Genesis* (trans. Mark E. Biddle; Macon, GA: Mercer University Press, 1997), p. 144; Otto Eissfeldt, in *BHS* at Gen. 6.14.

16. McEvenue, *The Narrative Style of the Priestly Writer*, p. 44 n. 36.

17. Driver, 'Problems and Solutions', p. 243.

18. See too D. Winton Thomas, 'Translating Hebrew *ʿāsāh*', *BT* 17 (1966), pp. 190-93, who similarly argued that this verb can mean 'to cover', and on p. 191 specifically refers to Gen. 6.14. He also finds this meaning in Num. 15.24; Isa. 32.6; Ezek. 32.6; Obad. 6; Pss. 9.16 [ET 15]; 139.15; Prov. 13.16; 26.28; Job 15.27. I have looked through all of Thomas's examples and find none of them compelling.

of the direct object or as the preposition 'with'. Is it 'you shall make *qānîm* with the ark' or 'with *qānîm* you shall make the ark'? The former rendering would be more compatible with taking *qnym* as *qinnîm*, 'rooms', although even then one might expect the text to have read 'in the ark' (*battēbâ*) rather than 'with the ark' (*ʾet-hattēbâ*). If, however, as I have proposed, the context requires that the *qnym* denote one of the ark's materials, namely, reeds, we should undoubtedly translate 'with reeds you shall make the ark'. This corresponds, in fact, with P's style as exemplified elsewhere in his account of the construction of the tabernacle, for example in Exod. 25.29, where we similarly read *zāhāb ṭāhôr taʿᵃśeh ʾōtām*, 'you shall make them of pure gold', and in Exod. 27.1, *wᵉʿāśîtā ʾet-hammizbēaḥ ʿᵃṣê šiṭṭîm*, 'You shall make the altar of acacia wood', where 'pure gold' and 'acacia wood' likewise lack a preceding preposition (cf. too Exod. 30.1). Of all the modern Bible translations, therefore, NJB comes out best with its rendering 'Make it of reeds'.[19]

How, then, should we understand the role of the reeds in the ark? We should surely reject Ullendorff's comparison of Noah's ark with the *tankwas* of Lake Tana in Ethiopia today, boats made of reed, bound with strips of the bark of the fig-tree *warka*, since these only last for a fortnight before becoming waterlogged and eventually sinking.[20] Similarly, Ullendorff's comparison of Noah's ark with the 'vessels of bulrushes' (*kᵉlê gōmeʾ*) of Isa. 18.2 and the 'ships of reed' (*ʾoniyyôt ʾēbeh*) in Job 9.26 seems inappropriate, since these more naturally refer to boats built entirely of reeds. It is, however, interesting to note that the only other object in the Hebrew Bible apart from Noah's ark which is explicitly called a *tēbâ*, 'ark', is the structure which sheltered the baby Moses, and like Noah's ark this was constructed with reeds (*gōmeʾ*), a word parallel with *qāneh* in Isa. 35.7 and covered with pitch (Exod. 2.3), though there was no wood.

19.   Loewenstamm, 'Should Qinnîm (Gen. 6:14) be Amended to Read Qanîm?', p. 136, finds it odd that the verb *ʿāśâ* should be repeated for two different materials of the ark, and feels it more natural for the second occurrence to refer to the manner of the making, that is, with respect to *qinnîm*, 'rooms'. He compares Num. 10.2 (wrongly cited as Num. 10.1), 'Make two silver trumpets; you shall make them of hammered work...' However, Loewenstamm thereby overlooks the crucial point that in Gen. 6.14 the *qnym* are mentioned in between two other materials for the ark (gopher wood and pitch). This is quite different from Num. 10.2.

20.   Ullendorff, 'The Construction of Noah's Ark', p. 96, reprint p. 49. In n. 3 he refers to R.E. Cheesman, *Lake Tana & the Blue Nile* (London: Macmillan, 1936), pp. 90-92 for information about the *tankwas*, information which I have cited above against Ullendorff's comparison.

The suggestion has been made by Strömberg Krantz that the reeds in Gen. 6.14 should be understood as having being placed between the beams of wood as a means of caulking the ark.[21] There is, in fact, considerable evidence of the use of reeds in this way in the ancient world. For example, Herodotus, *Hist.* 2.96 speaks of the beams of wood in Egyptian boats being caulked with papyrus and similarly Pliny the Elder, *Nat. Hist.* 16.64.158 refers to a hard kind of reed being inserted between the joints of boats for caulking by the Belgae. Again, Ezek. 27.9 is widely understood as saying that men from Gebal (Byblos) caulked the seams of the Tyrian boats, which is interesting in view of the fact that Byblos was a noted centre of the papyrus trade, giving its very name to the Greek word for papyrus (*bublos*). However, the fact that the *Vorlage* of Gen. 6.14 is to be sought in the Mesopotamian flood tradition, specifically in the flood hero's boat in the Atrahasis epic, suggests that it is there that we should seek enlightenment on the subject.[22] With regard to Enki's instructions formally addressed to the wall of a reed hut (but meant for Atrahasis's ears) to pull down the house and build a boat (Atrahasis 3.1.20-23; cf. Gilgamesh 11.21-26), Lambert and Millard rightly state that 'the obvious course was to pull up the bundles of reeds which composed the walls of the house and to fasten them to a wooden framework as a boat'.[23] Moreover, the prominence given to the reeds here suggests that they played a more central role in the construction of the ark than simply caulking.[24] Furthermore, the verb 'to caulk' (*peḫû*) is used rather of the pitch (Atrahasis 3.2.51; DT [W]. lines 3-4; U [Assyrian recension], rev. line 3).[25] Similarly, the way Gen. 6.14 is worded, 'Make yourself an ark of gopher wood, with reeds make the ark, and daub it inside and out with pitch', most naturally implies that in Noah's ark too the reeds were part of the ark's basic structure and it was the pitch which was used for caulking.

21. See Strömberg Krantz, *Des Schiffes Weg*, pp. 172-73.

22. I have given detailed reasons for believing that the flood story in P, as well as J, was dependent on some form of the Atrahasis epic, rather than on Gilgamesh, in Chapter 6 above.

23. Lambert and Millard, *Atra-ḥasīs*, p. 12.

24. In one particular version of the Atrahasis epic, only preserved in a small fragment (cited above), the reeds (*qá-ne-e*) even appear to be the only material used in the construction of the boat. See Lambert and Millard, *Atra-ḥasīs*, pp. 126-27 (CBS 13532, lines 6-9, esp. 7).

25. Lambert and Millard, *Atra-ḥasīs*, pp. 92-93, 122-23, 128-29. For the use of bitumen as a means of caulking Mesopotamian boats, see D.T. Potts, *Mesopotamian Civilization: The Material Foundation* (London: Athlone Press, 1997), pp. 130-32.

In conclusion, therefore, a strong case can be made that *qnym* in Gen. 6.14 refers to reeds (*qānîm*) used in the construction of the ark rather than rooms (*qinnîm*). This is supported first, by the fact that the word *qēn* means a bird's nest, and although it is sometimes used metaphorically for a human dwelling, this is only elsewhere in poetry and the bird's nest background is never lost sight of. Nothing comparable to its alleged use in Gen. 6.14 for rooms generally without bird's nest overtones is attested elsewhere in Biblical Hebrew. Secondly, there are repeated parallels in the underlying Mesopotamian flood tradition (both in the Atrahasis and Gilgamesh epics) referring to reeds being used in the construction of the ark, including passages that imply that the reeds were used along-side wood and pitch, exactly as is being proposed for Gen. 6.14. Thirdly, the context within Gen. 6.14-16 indicates that v. 14 is alluding to the materials of the ark, the division into sections being held over till v. 16. The original vocalization and sense of the word *qnym* must therefore have been forgotten sometime between the time of the Priestly writer in the sixth century BCE and the translation of the LXX Pentateuch in the third century BCE, when the word was rendered as 'nests'. Most likely the reeds were fastened to the wooden beams of the ark rather than being used for matting or caulking (the latter role being played by the pitch).

Chapter 8

WHY DOES GOD 'ESTABLISH' RATHER THAN 'CUT' A COVENANT WITH NOAH (AND ABRAHAM) IN THE PRIESTLY SOURCE?

It is a well-known fact that, unlike most of the Old Testament, the Priestly source in the Pentateuch never uses the phrase *kārat berît*, literally 'cut a covenant', when speaking of making a covenant, but rather employs a different expression *hēqîm berît*, 'establish a covenant' (Gen. 6.18; 9.9, 11, 17; 17.7, 19, 21; Exod. 6.4).[1] However, so far as I am aware, no-one hitherto has put forward a satisfactory explanation to account for the Priestly writer's use of this peculiar and distinctive terminology. One suspects that most scholars simply assume that this is just a minor stylistic variation on the part of the Priestly writer which is of no particular significance, and give the matter no further thought. I am conscious that this was my own attitude until a student pointedly asked me, 'But *why* does P say "establish a covenant" rather than "cut a covenant"?', which set me on the path that has finally resulted in this chapter.[2] Certainly, when one reflects on the thoroughness and consistency with which P has avoided the phrase which was almost universal elsewhere in earlier Old Testament works and substituted his own alternative expression, one can only conclude that this was the result of a deliberate and self-conscious policy, so presumably he had some reason for doing so.

---

1. P also uses *nātan berît*, literally 'give a covenant', in Gen. 9.12; 17.2; Num. 25.12.
2. The student in question was Helen Williams of Lady Margaret Hall, Oxford, who raised the point during a Hebrew class on Gen. 6–9 in 1994. Fortunately, I was able to formulate the essence of the answer contained here and communicate it to her and the class within a matter of days, even though it was only with the original publication of this essay in 2003 that I had the opportunity to work out the argument in detail and set it forth in print.

Stated simply, the case which I wish to defend here is as follows. The Priestly writer consistently speaks of establishing a covenant rather than cutting a covenant because for him the only major covenants were those with Noah and Abraham (Gen. 9.8-17; 17.1-21)—there was no covenant mediated by Moses, unlike in J, E and D—and prior to the legislation on Mt Sinai in the time of Moses there was no sacrifice, according to P. Consequently, since the usual expression 'cut a covenant' was redolent of making a covenant by cutting up an animal in sacrifice, it behoved P to avoid the expression 'cut a covenant' and find an alternative phrase which avoided sacrificial overtones, and for this purpose 'establish a covenant' was entirely satisfactory. This account of things—never previously proposed so far as I am aware—has plausibility and seems the natural and obvious explanation, but I shall now attempt to defend it in more detail.

First, we need to note that there is general agreement that there is no sacrifice in the Priestly source until the legislation given to Moses in Leviticus 1–7 (cf. Lev. 8–9 for its first enactment). In marked contrast to J, no sacrifice in P takes place in the Primaeval history, and even more remarkably, unlike in J and E, the patriarchs in P never once build an altar or offer sacrifice to God. This is all the more striking when we consider that the Priestly source is a work for which sacrifice and the cult are hardly marginal affairs, since in P cultic matters form the main substance of the large amount of legislation given to Moses on Mt Sinai. This highlights even further the point that they had no role until that time. The Priestly writer has deliberately suppressed them. Hence it is that, for all P's concern with cultic matters, it is not this source but J which records that Noah offered sacrifice after the flood (Gen. 8.20-21)[3] and

3. This is generally accepted. Terry Fenton, however, in a paper read to the 17th IOSOT Congress in Basel in August 2001 entitled 'Talking Sense about the Flood Stories: Origins, Borrowing, Dating', mentioned in passing his view that this comes from P, since J, unlike P, never elsewhere uses the phrase 'pleasing odour' (Gen. 8.21). However, quite apart from the use of the divine name Yahweh and the fact that there do not appear to be any references to sacrifice in P before Leviticus— points which should not lightly be dismissed—the associated reference to God promising never again to destroy the earth (Gen. 8.21-22) is taken up again in Gen. 9, which seems needlessly repetitive but is perfectly understandable if the passages come from different sources. Furthermore, nowhere else in the Old Testament is God actually said *to smell* the pleasing odour of a sacrifice, but such a marked anthropomorphism would be the kind of thing one would naturally expect from J, but is untypical of P. Behind the reference lies, of course, the allusion in the Mesopotamian flood story to the gods gathering round like flies to smell the pleasing odour of the flood hero's sacrifice following the flood (cf. Atrahasis epic 3.5.34-35; Gilgamesh epic 11.161-63.

which distinguishes between the number of clean and unclean animals going into the ark (Gen. 7.2-3; contrast P in Gen. 6.19-20, for whom the laws about clean and unclean animals were not revealed until Lev. 11). Interestingly, J's account of Noah's sacrifice is intimately connected with his version of God's promise never to destroy the world again. We read, 'And when the Lord smelled the pleasing odour, the Lord said in his heart, "I will never again curse the ground because of man, for the imagination of man's heart is evil from his youth; neither will I ever again destroy every living creature as I have done. While the earth remains, seedtime and harvest, cold and heat, summer and winter, day and night, shall not cease"' (Gen. 8.21-22). This motif is taken up in P's account of God's covenant with Noah in Genesis 9. Note in particular the words of Gen. 9.11, 'I establish my covenant with you, that never again shall all flesh be cut off by the waters of a flood, and never again shall there be a flood to destroy the earth'. However, in P's version of the promise all reference to sacrifice has been suppressed, and I would argue that it is significant in this regard that P speaks of establishing rather than cutting a covenant. Similarly, whereas Genesis 15[4] connects God's covenant with Abraham with an unusual sacrificial rite in which the divine presence passes between the pieces—seemingly an act of self-imprecation (cf. Jer. 34.18-19)—P's version of the Abrahamic covenant in Genesis 17 is totally lacking in any reference to sacrifice. Again, I would argue that this is all of a piece with P's speaking of God's establishing a covenant with Abraham (Gen. 17.7, 19, 21), in contrast to Genesis 15, in which God cuts his covenant with Abraham (Gen. 15.18).

---

4. Traditionally Gen. 15 was seen as the work of J, with possibly some E, but more recent scholarship has tended to see it as a later addition to J. Thus, for example, L. Perlitt, *Bundestheologie im Alten Testament* (WMANT, 36; Neukirchen–Vluyn: Neukirchen Verlag, 1969), pp. 68-77, dates it to the early seventh century BCE and E. Kutsch, *Verheißung und Gesetz: Untersuchungen zum sogenannten »Bund« im Alten Testament* (BZAW, 131: Berlin: W. de Gruyter, 1973), pp. 66-70, dates it to the time of Josiah, between 625 and 609 BCE. Cf. E.W. Nicholson, *The Pentateuch in the Twentieth Century: The Legacy of Julius Wellhausen* (Oxford: Clarendon Press, 1998), p. 142, who proposes a *terminus a quo* of 722 BCE and a *terminus ad quem* of the exile for Gen. 15.9-12, 17-21. J.A. Emerton, 'The Origin of the Promises to the Patriarchs in the Older Sources of the Book of Genesis', *VT* 32 (1982), pp. 14-32 (17, 29-30), agrees with a relatively late date but notes that Deuteronomy knows of an oath to the patriarchs and a *beʳît*, presumably the *beʳît* of Gen. 15, so Gen. 15 must be earlier than Deuteronomy. Accordingly, we may continue to maintain the view that Gen. 15's account of the Abrahamic covenant is earlier than P's version in Gen. 17, which most likely dates from the early post-exilic period.

Next one needs to establish that the expression *kārat b^erît* did indeed come about as a result of covenants being characteristically made through cutting up an animal in sacrifice. This is indeed the usual explanation,[5] the assumption being that the phrase constitutes an elided form of speech, comparable to the English expression 'strike a bargain', which in part arose from the custom of striking ones hands in connection with making a bargain.[6] This viewpoint has in its favour not only the fact that sacrifice is associated with covenant-making on a number of occasions in the Old Testament (cf. Exod. 24.4-8 and Ps. 50.5), but also that there are instances which specifically highlight the cutting up of an animal in connection with covenant-making, namely in Genesis 15 and Jeremiah 34. In Genesis 15 Abraham cuts a heifer, a she-goat and a ram in two (vv. 9-10) and then a smoking fire pot and flaming torch symbolizing God pass between the pieces (v. 17) in connection with the divine covenant with Abraham (v. 18). A similar covenant ritual is implied in Jer. 34.18-19, where we read, 'And the men who transgressed my covenant and did not keep the terms of the covenant which they made (*kār^etû*) before me, I will make like the calf[7] which they cut (*kār^etû*) in two and passed between the parts—the priests of Judah, the princes of Jerusalem, the eunuchs, the priests, and all the people of the land who passed between the parts of the calf'. As will be observed, the relationship between the cutting up of the animal (here a calf) and the covenant-making (lit. 'cutting') is made explicit in the employment of the same verb for 'cut' in both cases. Furthermore, the involvement of animal rites in treaty-making in the ancient Near East is clearly spelled out in a number of extra-biblical texts,[8] for example, an eighteenth-century BCE

---

5.   Already F.H.W. Gesenius, *Thesaurus philologicus criticus linguae Hebraeae et Chaldaeae Veteris Testamenti* (Leipzig: Fr. Chr. Guil. Vogelii, 1829–57), p. 718, cites this as the standard view and notes that it was followed by such distinguished seventeenth-century scholars as S. Bochart and H. Grotius.

6.   According to J.A.H. Murray *et al.* (eds.), *The Oxford English Dictionary* (13 vols.; Oxford: Clarendon Press, 1933), X, p. 1134, the English expression 'to strike a bargain' arose partly from the custom of striking hands in confirmation of a bargain and partly from the Latin expression *ferire foedus*, a term for treaty-making to which I shall make reference shortly. Incidentally, it may be noted that B.W. Jones, 'Cutting Deals and Striking Bargains', *English Today* 46.2 (1996), pp. 35-40, suggests that the slang American expression 'to cut a deal' derives directly from the Hebrew expression *kārat b^erît* via American Jews.

7.   Reading *kā^cēgel*, 'like a calf', for MT *hā^cēgel*, 'the calf', as is generally done.

8.   For a discussion of these as well as some other texts, see, e.g., G.F. Hasel, 'The Meaning of the Animal Rite in Gen. 15', *JSOT* 19 (1981), pp. 61-78 (64-68); J.C. Greenfield, 'An Ancient Treaty Ritual and its Targumic Echo', in *Salvación en*

text from Mari,[9] an eighteenth-century BCE letter from Old Babylonian
Tell al Rimah concerning Zimri-Lim of Mari and Hatnu-rapi of Karana,[10]
the seventeenth-century BCE treaty between Abba-AN and Yarimlim,[11]
and the eighth-century BCE vassal treaty between Asshurnirari V of
Assyria and Mati'ilu of Arpad.[12]

Further support for the ritual origin of the phrase 'cut a covenant' may
be drawn from comparable expressions which are attested for covenant/
treaty making in classical Greek and Latin. Thus, in classical Greek
we find the term *horkia temnein*, literally 'to cut oaths'[13] and *spondas
temnein*, literally 'to cut drink offerings',[14] and similarly in classical
Latin we find *ferire foedus*,[15] *icere foedus*[16] and *percutere foedus*,[17] all of
which mean literally 'to strike a treaty' or the like. There is no doubt
whatsoever that these phrases derive from the custom of cutting up an
animal in connection with swearing oaths or making a treaty. The expression *horkia temnein*, 'to cut oaths', is already attested as early as Homer,
who explicitly records several examples of the swearing of oaths being
attended by the cutting up of an animal in sacrifice.[18] The similarity
between these and other sacrificial expressions in classical and ancient
Near Eastern languages gives good grounds for thinking that they had a

la Palabra: Targum, Derash, Berith; Homenaje al Prof. Alejandro Diez Macho
(Madrid: Cristiandad, 1986), pp. 391-97, reprinted in *ʿAl Kanfei Yonah: Collected
Studies of Jonas C. Greenfield on Semitic Philology* (ed. S.M. Paul, M.E. Stone and
A. Pinnick; 2 vols.; Leiden: Brill, 2001), I, pp. 405-11; A. Viberg, *Symbols of Law:
A Contextual Analysis of Legal Symbolic Acts in the Old Testament* (ConBOT, 34:
Stockholm: Almqvist & Wiksell, 1992), pp. 53-57, as well as D.J. McCarthy, *Treaty
and Covenant* (AnBib, 21A; Rome: Biblical Institute Press, 2nd edn, 1978), *passim.*

9. See *ANET*, p. 482 (translation by W.F. Albright); M. Held, 'Philological Notes
on the Mari Covenant Rituals', *BASOR* 200 (1970), pp. 32-40.

10. See S. Dalley *et al.*, *The Old Babylonian Tablets from Tell al Rimah*
(London: British School of Archaeology in Iraq, 1976) pp. 12-13 (letter 1, lines
11-12).

11. Originally published in D.J. Wiseman, 'Abban and Alalah', *JCS* 12 (1958),
pp. 124-29.

12. See *ANET*, p. 532 (translation by E. Reiner).

13. Cf. Homer, *Il.* 2.124; 3.73, 93, 105, 245-301; 4 155; 19.191; *Od.* 24.483;
Herodotus, *Hist.* 4.201; 7.132; Polybius, *Hist.* 21.24.3; 22.15.

14. Cf. Euripides, *Helena* 1235.

15. Cf. Ennius, *ap.* Macrobius, *Saturnalia* 6.1; Cicero, *Oratio pro Rabiro
Posthumo* 3.6; Virgil, *Aeneid* 10.154.

16. Cf. Cicero, *Oratio in Pisonem* 12.28; *Oratio pro L. Corn. Balbo* 15.34;
Tacitus, *Annals* 12.62.

17. Cf. Justinus, *Epitome of the Philipppic History of Pompeius Trogus* 42.3.4;
43.5.10.

18. Cf. Homer, *Il.* 3.103-107, 271-301; 4.153-59; 19.252-68.

common origin,[19] so the clear sacrificial background of the classical expressions is highly relevant to the origin of the Hebrew expression 'cut a covenant' under discussion here. With regard to 'cut oath(s)', it may be noted that this phraseology is attested in the Semitic world not only in the Old Testament (*krt ᵓlh*, Deut. 29.11, 13 [ET 12, 14]) but also in Phoenician and Aramaic inscriptions. The Phoenician equivalent *krt ᵓlt*, 'cut an oath', is attested on the first amulet from Arlan Tash in Upper Syria, dating to the seventh century BCE, where we read (end of lines 8- 12): 'One has made (lit. "cut") an eternal covenant (lit. "oath") with us, Asshur has made (lit. "cut") (it) with us, as well as all the sons of the gods and the greatest of all our holy ones'.[20] (As Z. Zevit[21] has pointed out, interestingly we have here the notion of a divine covenant being made with human beings, thus paralleling the Old Testament.) The Aramaic equivalent *gzr ᶜdy* is used in connection with the eighth-century BCE treaty between Barga'yah and Mati'el in Sefire treaty text 1A 7, where we read *wᶜdy ᵓln zy gzr brgᵓ[yh]*, 'Now (it is) this treaty (lit. "these oaths") which Barga'[yah] concluded (lit. "cut")'. It is interesting to note that this text also reflects awareness of Aramaic *gzr* in its ritual sense in IA 39-40, where we read, '[Just as] this calf is cut in two, so may Mati'el be cut in two, and may his nobles be cut in two'. It is difficult not to connect the expression *gzr ᶜdy* in line 7 with the ritual referred to in lines 39-40, so it is likely that *gzr ᶜdy* is indeed derivative from that.[22] Though the word *ᶜdy* translates as 'treaty', etymologically it

19.   See J.F. Priest, '"Ορκια in the *Iliad* and Consideration of a Recent Theory', *JNES* 23 (1964), pp. 48-54; M. Weinfeld, 'Covenant Terminology in the Ancient Near East and its Influence on the West', *JAOS* 93 (1973), pp. 190-99.

20.   D. Pardee, 'Les documents d'Arslan Tash: authentiques ou faux?', *Syria* 75 (1998), pp. 15-54, has convincingly shown that the Arslan Tash amulets are authentic, contrary to the allegations of J. Teixidor, 'Les tablettes d'Arslan Tash au Musée d'Alep', *AuOr* 1 (1983), pp. 105-108; *idem, Bulletin d'épigraphie sémitique (1964– 1980)* (BAH, 127; Paris: Geuthner, 1986), pp. 471-72, and P. Amiet, 'Observations sur les "Tablettes magiques" d'Arslan Tash', *AuOr* 1 (1988), p. 109.

21.   Z. Zevit, 'A Phoenician Inscription and Biblical Covenant Theology', *IEJ* 27 (1977), pp. 110-18.

22.   The reference to '*this* calf' suggests that an actual ritual is being carried out. J.A. Fitzmyer, *The Aramaic Inscriptions of Sefire* (BibOr, 19A; Pontifical Institute Press, 1995), p. 69, notes, 'Undoubtedly the rite alluded to in line 40 is the source of the expression [*gzr ᶜdy*]'. There seem no good reasons for following J.C.L. Gibson, *Textbook of Syrian Semitic Inscriptions*. II. *Aramaic Inscriptions* (3 vols.; Oxford: Clarendon Press, 1971–82 [1975]), p. 42), in thinking that a wax model of a calf rather than a literal calf is here in view: although certain objects of wax are included in the list of imprecatory sayings, not all are said to be, and the calf is one of the latter.

probably means 'oaths', according to the distinguished Aramaist J.A. Fitzmyer.[23]

In addition to all the evidence cited above in support of the ritual origin of the expression *kārat bᵉrît*, the point needs to be noted that no other satisfactory explanation of the origin of the phrase has been forthcoming. Thus, E. Kutsch[24] proposed that besides meaning 'to cut', *kārat* could also mean 'to decree' on analogy with the verb *gāzar*, which came to mean 'to decree' as well as 'to cut' (Job 22.28), a meaning which is well attested for its Aramaic cognate *gᵉzar*.[25] However, it may be objected that there is not a single instance elsewhere in the Old Testament where Biblical Hebrew *kārat* means 'decree' rather than 'cut',[26] so it seems more natural to regard the expression *kārat bᵉrît* as meaning 'cut a covenant' and deriving from the custom of cutting up an animal in connection with making a covenant, as argued above.

Granted that the phrase *kārat bᵉrît* arose from the custom of making a covenant by sacrifice, the question remains whether by the time when the Priestly writer wrote—probably in the sixth century BCE—he would still have been aware of this nuance, or whether this was merely a case of archaic etymology which would have long been forgotten. In favour of the view that the original meaning was still in the consciousness of sixth-century BCE Israelites it may be pointed out that Jer. 34.8-22—a sixth-century prose sermon which reflects Deuteronomistic redaction in the exile not far off from the time of the Priestly source[27]—specifically reflects awareness of this understanding in its employment of the verb *kārat* to denote both the covenant-making and the cutting up of the animals (cf. Jer. 34.15, 18).[28] It may also be noted that Genesis 15, which

---

23. Cf. Fitzmyer, *The Aramaic Inscriptions of Sefire*. pp. 58-59.

24. See Kutsch, *Verheißung und Gesetz*, Chapter 3.

25. Kutsch, *Verheißung und Gesetz*, pp. 49-50, prefers to render the verb *gzr* in the expression *gzr ʿdyʾ* in the Sefire treaty noted above as '(he) decreed'. However, as pointed out above, the clear attestation of *gzr* in its ritual meaning of 'cut' in connection with an animal rite in the same treaty tells against this.

26. A point previously made by McCarthy, *Treaty and Covenant*, p. 93 n. 25.

27. Cf. E.W. Nicholson, *Preaching to the Exiles: A Study of the Prose Tradition in the Book of Jeremiah* (Oxford: Clarendon Press, 1970), pp. 63-65.

28. Interestingly, J. Barr, *The Semantics of Biblical Language* (London: Oxford University Press, 1961), who has done so much to make us aware that words develop meaning as well as have etymologies, and who points out how rarely the Old Testament draws attention to the underlying sacrificial overtones of the phrase *kārat bᵉrît*, nevertheless concedes, 'It is true that the original value of *kārat* when combined with *bᵉrît*, continued to be known in the culture, and this is realized in the famous passage Jer 34,18'. So J. Barr, 'Some Semantic Notes on the Covenant',

likewise attests covenant-making in connection with a rite of cutting up of animals while avoiding Jeremiah 34's word play, is now dated by many scholars around the seventh century BCE.[29]

Accordingly, to avoid all sacrificial overtones, it makes sense that P should consistently avoid the expression *kārat bᵉrît*, 'cut a covenant', and use instead the phrase *hēqim bᵉrît*, 'establish a covenant' (Gen. 6.18; 9.9, 11, 17; 17.7, 19, 21; Exod. 6.4), or *nātan bᵉrît*, 'make (lit. "give") a covenant' (Gen. 9.12; 17.2; Num. 25.12). The expression *hēqîm bᵉrît* is found elsewhere in the Old Testament only in Ezek. 16.60, 62, with regard to God's future covenant with Israel (though Ezek. 16.60 does refer back to 'my covenant with you in the days of your youth', presumably with Moses), in H in Lev. 26.9, where one could perhaps render *hēqîm* as either 'establish' or 'confirm', and in Deut. 8.18, where the context clearly implies the confirming of an existing covenant rather than the establishment of a covenant *ab initio*: 'that he may confirm the covenant which he swore to your fathers, as at this day'. In fact, it has occasionally been claimed by some scholars, including W.G. Dumbrell, G.J. Wenham and J. Milgrom,[30] that the above verses in P, generally taken to refer to God's establishing a covenant (*hēqîm bᵉrît*), allude to God's maintaining or confirming a pre-existent covenant rather than establishing a new covenant. However, both with regard to the Noachic covenant in Genesis 9 and the Abrahamic covenant in Genesis 17 this standpoint is clearly forced. In the case of Noah there is no pre-existing covenant to be maintained; Dumbrell's view that there was a pre-existing creation covenant is not attested in the text of Genesis, and the same is true of one of Milgrom's proposals, namely, that a covenant with Adam might be in mind here. Milgrom's alternative proposal is that the verb *hēqîm* might be used with respect to the covenant's being maintained for Noah's descendants, having originally been made (*nātan*) for Noah. However, against this view it may be noted that Noah's descendants are not referred to in every instance of the use of *hēqîm*—indeed they are explicitly mentioned in connection with the covenant only in Gen. 9.9; in

in H. Donner, R. Hanhart and R. Smend (eds.), *Beiträge zur alttestamentlichen Theologie: Festschrift fur Walther Zimmerli zum 70. Geburtstag* (Göttingen: Vandenhoeck & Ruprecht, 1977), pp. 23-38 (27).

29. See above n. 4.

30. W.J. Dumbrell, *Covenant and Creation: A Theology of the Old Testament Covenants* (Exeter: Paternoster Press, 1984), p. 26; G.J. Wenham, *Genesis 1–15* (WBC, 1; Waco, TX: Word Books, 1987), p. 175, and *Genesis 16–50* (WBC, 2; Waco, TX: Word Books, 1994), p. 20; J. Milgrom, *Leviticus 23–27* (AB, 3B; New York: Doubleday, 2001), pp. 2343-46.

Gen. 6.18; 9.11, 17 the covenant is specifically with Noah himself, so it is more natural to understand *hēqîm* here as 'establish' rather than 'maintain'. Furthermore, the translation 'maintain' would be particularly strained in Gen. 6.18, the very first mention of the covenant with Noah, since it would be curious to read of God's maintaining a pre-existing covenant when we have not yet been informed of its establishment in the first place! Accordingly, *hēqîm bᵉrît* must refer to the original establishment of the covenant (like *nātan bᵉrît*). Nor is there any good reason to believe with G.J. Wenham, following a view previously argued by P.A.H. de Boer,[31] that there was an already pre-existing covenant with Noah which the text does not describe. Further, the fact that Gen. 9.12 also employs the verb *nātan*, 'make' (lit. 'give'), in connection with the covenant clearly implies that *hēqîm* means 'establish' rather than 'confirm' here. It should also be noted that the future tense of *hēqîm* is employed in Gen. 6.18 and 9.11 (in addition to the participle applicable to the imminent future in Gen. 9.9) and the perfect tense in Gen. 9.17, and this most naturally implies that the establishment of a new covenant with Noah takes place in the course of Genesis 9. Consequently, it is to be concluded that Genesis 9 is referring to the establishment of a new covenant with Noah rather than a confirmation of a pre-existing covenant.

Again, the view of Dumbrell and Wenham that the covenant with Abraham in Genesis 17 is simply a confirmation of the covenant ratified in Genesis 15 rather than the establishment of a new covenant would only occur to someone desperate to find a consistent synchronic reading in Genesis and who denied or wished to play down the existence of separate sources in the text. As is the case with the covenant with Noah in Gen. 9.12, the covenant with Abraham in Gen. 17.2 also has the verb *nātan*, 'make' (lit. 'give'), used in connection with it, which again suggests that *hēqîm* should be understood as 'establish' rather than 'confirm'.

---

31. P.A.H. de Boer, 'Quelques remarques sur l'Arc dans la Nuée (Genèse 9, 18-17)', in C. Brekelmans (ed.), *Questions disputées d'Ancien Testament: Méthode et Théologie* (BETL, 33; Leuven: Leuven University Press, 1974), pp. 105-14 (105-108). At p. 108 n. 4 de Boer cites E. König, *Die Genesis eingeleitet, übersetzt und erklärt* (Gütersloh: C. Bertelsmann,1925), p. 386, as having already rendered the verb *hēqîm* as 'maintain' ('aufrecht erhalten') in connection with the Noachic covenant. Consultation of König's commentary shows, however, that in contrast to de Boer, while he saw this meaning in Gen. 9.11, he rendered *hēqîm* as 'establish' in Gen. 6.18 and 9.9, 17 (and similarly *nātan* in 9.12). Moreover, in connection with the Abrahamic covenant König also understood *hēqîm* as to denote 'maintain' in Gen. 17.7, while keeping to the translation 'establish' in Gen. 17.19, 21 (and similarly *nātan* in 17.2). Such inconsistency in translation is arbitrary and unconvincing.

P.R. Williamson[32] has recently rightly argued that *hēqîm bᵉrît* refers to God's establishment of a new covenant and he also rightly perceives the sacrificial overtones of the phrase *kārat bᵉrît*, but this leads him to follow the forced view of T.D. Alexander[33] that the covenant established in Genesis 17 is not ratified until after the offering of sacrifice in Genesis 22. However, quite apart from the fact that Genesis 17 and 22 are generally accepted as deriving from different sources, this view fails to explain why the phrase *kārat bᵉrît* is not found in Genesis 22; indeed, the word 'covenant' does not occur there at all. Finally, Milgrom's view that in Genesis 17 the verb *hēqîm* is used of God's maintaining his covenant with Abraham's descendants (vv. 7, 19, 21), in contrast to his original making (*nātan*) of the covenant with Abraham himself (v. 2), is superficially plausible, but becomes untenable in the light of the fact that we have already seen above (in connection with Noah) that the verb *hēqîm* in P refers to the original making of a covenant, not its later maintenance, and so is identical in meaning with the verb *nātan*.

An alternative explanation to the one that I have suggested in order to account for the Priestly writer's abandonment of 'cut a covenant' in favour of 'establish a covenant' might be to claim that it was a way of emphasizing God's unilateral grace in formulating the covenant.[34] However, against the likelihood of this proposal it should be noted that there are various places where Yahweh's grace is emphasized which do nevertheless employ the expression *kārat bᵉrît*, for example Jer. 31.31, where Yahweh promises a new covenant in which he will write his law on human hearts. More particularly, it should be noted that the Genesis 15 version of the Abrahamic covenant, which employs the phrase *kārat bᵉrît*, clearly emphasizes the unilateral gracious nature of Yahweh's act in initiating the covenant more than Genesis 17, since it is purely promissory and lacks the demand for the human response of circumcision which we find in Genesis 17, failure to observe which is regarded by P as a breaking of the covenant and leads to one's being cut off from God's people (Gen. 17.14).

32. P.R. Williamson, *Abraham, Israel and the Nations: The Patriarchal Promise and its Covenantal Development in Genesis* (JSOTSup, 315; Sheffield: Sheffield Academic Press, 2000), Chapter 6.

33. T.D. Alexander, 'Genesis 22 and the Covenant of Circumcision', *JSOT* 25 (1983), pp. 17-22.

34. This view is found in W. Eichrodt, *Theologie des Alten Testaments* (2 vols.; Stuttgart: Klotz, 1957), I, p. 23, ET *Theology of the Old Testament* (2 vols.; London: SCM Press, 1961), I, p. 56.

Yet another suggestion with regard to P's substitution of the expression *hēqîm bᵉrît* for *kārat bᵉrît*, specifically with regard to the Abrahamic covenant, was made by Vawter,[35] who hypothesized that 'The ancient oath rite and its accompanying language may well have seemed too anthropomorphic for the theology of P'. However, since P has studiously eliminated not merely the sacrificial act of Genesis 15 but every single reference to sacrifice prior to the time of Moses, it seems more natural to suppose that P's avoidance of a term having sacrificial overtones should be seen against that broader background. A similar objection pertains to Milgrom's wondering with regarded to P's eschewal of the verb *kārat*, 'Is it because the word originated in the ceremony of passing between the "cut" halves of animals [cf. Gen. 15:17; Jer. 34:18), implying an illegitimate sacrificial rite?'[36] As has already been noted, it was not simply this act but all sacrifice which was regarded by P as illegitimate before the time of Moses, and which presumably therefore led to P's avoidance of a term having sacrificial overtones.

It is generally agreed today that the Priestly source has two main divine covenants, one with Noah and one with Abraham. In the nineteenth century, however, Wellhausen[37] referred to P as Q = *Liber quatuor foederum* (*Vierbundesbuch*), mistakenly believing that P had four covenants, namely with Adam and Moses in addition to Noah and Abraham. The idea of a covenant with Adam is also found earlier in the post-Reformation period in some of the Federal Theologians such as Johannes Cocceius[38] but has no basis in Scripture, let alone in the Priestly source. Wellhausen believed that it was implicit in Gen. 1.28–2.4, but this is far from obvious.

Nor can one appeal to Hos. 6.7, where the MT reads literally, 'But like Adam they transgressed the covenant, there they dealt faithlessly with me',[39] since it is now generally and rightly agreed that we should rather

35. B. Vawter, *On Genesis: A New Reading* (London: Geoffrey Chapman, 1977), p. 220.

36. Milgrom, *Leviticus 23–27*, p. 2344.

37. Cf. J. Wellhausen, *Prolegomena zur Geschichte Israels* (Berlin: G. Reimer, 2nd edn, 1883), p. 9 n. 3, ET *Prolegomena to the History of Israel* (Edinburgh: A. & C. Black, 1885), pp. 8 n. 2; idem, *Die Composition des Hexateuchs und der historischen Bücher des Alten Testaments* (Berlin: G. Reimer, 3rd edn, 1899), p. 1.

38. On Federal Theology's origins, see D.A. Weir, *The Origins of the Federal Theology in Sixteenth-Century Reformation Thought* (Oxford: Clarendon Press, 1990). For Cocceius, see W.J. van Asselt, *The Federal Theology of Johannes Cocceius (1603–1669)* (Studies in the History of Christian Thought; Leiden: Brill, 2001).

39. Cf. AV, ASV, NASV, NIV. The translation 'like Adam' was appealed to by some of the Federal theologians in support of their notion of a covenant with Adam;

translate, 'But at Adam they transgressed the covenant...', understanding Adam as a place name (cf. Josh. 3.16) and reading $b^e\bar{a}d\bar{a}m$ 'at Adam' for $k^e\bar{a}d\bar{a}m$, 'like Adam', since the word 'there' ($\check{s}\bar{a}m$) in the parallel line clearly requires this.[40] As for the covenant with Moses, it is noteworthy that this is completely omitted by the Priestly writer, unlike the other Pentateuchal sources,[41] a point first noted, so far as I am aware, by J.J.P. Valeton.[42] In the light of what has been said earlier about P's suppression of all sacrificial allusions prior to Leviticus, it is readily understandable that the ritual ratification of the covenant described in Exodus 24 should have no role in his presentation. But why should P suppress the Mosaic covenant altogether? In attempting to explain

so, e.g., Thomas Boston. See A.T.B. McGowan, *The Federal Theology of Thomas Boston* (Carlisle: Paternoster Press, 1997), p. 13.

40.   As J. Wellhausen, *Die kleinen Propheten* (Berlin: G. Reimer, 1898), pp. 116-17, himself noted. Since Wellhausen's time the meaning 'at Adam' has been widely followed, including most Bible translations. Cf. J. Day, 'Pre-Deuteronomic Allusions to the Covenant in Hosea and Psalm lxxviii', *VT* 36 (1986), pp. 1-12 (2); E.W. Nicholson, *God and his People: Covenant and Theology in the Old Testament* (Oxford: Clarendon Press, 1986), p. 181.

41.   This is generally admitted. There are, however, those like F.M. Cross, 'The Priestly Work', in *Canaanite Myth and Hebrew Epic* (Cambridge, MA: Harvard University Press, 1973), pp. 293-325, who find it difficult to believe that P rejected the concept of a Mosaic covenant, and envisage P as the redactor of the Pentateuch rather than an independent source, and assume that P simply incorporated the earlier account of the covenant ratification in Exod. 24 into his work. There are, however, compelling objections against seeing P as a mere redactor: see, e.g., J.A. Emerton, 'The Priestly Writer in Genesis', *JTS* NS 39 (1988), pp. 381-400, and Nicholson, *The Pentateuch in the Twentieth Century*, pp. 196-218. P's omission of the Mosaic covenant is also fully understandable in the light of the arguments of W. Zimmerli, 'Sinaibund und Abrahambund: Ein Beitrag zum Verständnis der Priesterschrift', *TZ* 16 (Festgabe für Walther Eichrodt, 1960), pp. 268-80, reprinted in *idem, Gottes Offenbarung: Gesammelte Aufsätze zum Alten Testament* (Munich: Chr. Kaiser, 1963), pp. 205-16, noted in the body of the text shortly. Moreover, if the Mosaic covenant was really important for P, as Cross claims, it is surprising that he did not write his own version of it, as he did in the cases of the covenants with Noah and Abraham. S.L. McKenzie (*Covenant* [Understanding Biblical Themes; St. Louis, MO: Chalice Press, 2000], pp. 46-50) also assumes that P has a Mosaic covenant, but seems unaware of the controversial nature of this notion and makes no attempt to defend it against the usual objections. Presumably, he is simply following Cross.

42.   J.J.P. Valeton, 'Bedeutung und Stellung des Wortes ברית im Priestercodex', *ZAW* 12 (1892), pp. 1-2. I. Knohl, *The Sanctuary of Silence: The Priestly Torah and the Holiness School* (Minneapolis: Fortress Press, 1995), p. 143 n. 79, draws attention to Vaeton's priority, but at p. 141 n. 65 mistakenly gives the year of his article as 1982 and the full page reference as pp. 501-12 instead of pp. 1-22.

this Zimmerli[43] has rightly pointed out that in P it is the Abrahamic covenant which is envisaged as being fulfilled in the time of Moses, not only with regard to the multiplication of the people and the gift of the Promised Land, which are also found in Genesis 15's version of the Abrahamic covenant, but also in the promise that Yahweh should be Israel's God (Gen. 17.8). P takes up this last promise again in Exod. 6.7, and it finds ultimate fulfilment in connection with the Mosaic Tent of Meeting, where Yahweh dwells in the midst of Israel so as to be her God (Exod. 29.45-46). However, it seems that the Holiness Code (H), which has generally been regarded as representing an earlier stage of Priestly theology than that contained in the Priestly document proper, did have the notion of a Mosaic covenant.[44] Thus, although Lev. 26.42 certainly and 26.9 probably[45] refer to the covenant with the patriarchs, Lev. 26.15, 25, 44-45 more naturally allude to the Mosaic covenant. Thus, for example, v. 45 implies that the covenant referred to was with the Exodus generation and v. 15 alludes to the covenant in the context of Yahweh's statutes, ordinances and commandments, which is suggestive of Sinai. A hint of this older Priestly conception is presumably contained in Exod. 31.16, which speaks of the Sabbath as 'a perpetual covenant' (cf. Lev. 24.8, where H similarly describes the shewbread).

There is, however, a third covenant in P, in addition to those with Noah and Abraham, which is often overlooked, though it is of subordinate importance. This is the covenant with Phinehas, the son of Eleazar and grandson of Aaron, attested in Num. 25.12-13, where after Phinehas's averting the divine wrath following the incident at Baal-Peor, we read that God says, 'Therefore say, "Behold, I give to him my covenant of peace; and it shall be to him, and to his descendants after him, the covenant of a perpetual priesthood, because he was jealous for his God,

---

43. Zimmerli, 'Sinaibund und Abrahambund', pp. 268-80, reprinted in *idem*, *Gottes Offenbarung*, pp. 205-16.

44. It has been generally held that H is prior to P. Recently, however, a few scholars, notably I. Knohl, *The Sanctuary of Silence*, and J. Milgrom, *Leviticus 17–22* (AB, 3A; New York: Doubleday, 2000), pp. 1352-55, have argued that H is rather to be seen as subsequent to P, but I find the traditional view more compelling. Thus, unlike P, which presupposes a central sanctuary, Lev. 17 positively demands one (like D), which suggests it is earlier, and H (again like D and unlike P) counters Canaanite idolatry and syncretism (cf. Lev. 18.21; 20.1-5; 26.1), which also suggests it is earlier than P. Further, unlike Knohl and Milgrom, I follow the usual view and do not see P as pre-exilic; see J. Day, 'The Religion of Israel', in A.D.H. Mayes (ed.), *Text in Context: Essays by Members of the Society for Old Testament Study* (Oxford: Oxford University Press, 2000), pp. 428-53 (439-40).

45. Lev. 26.9's association of the covenant with progeny is suggestive.

and made atonement for the people of Israel"'. (The covenant with Phinehas is also alluded to in 1 Macc. 2.54 and Ecclus 45.24; cf. Ecclus 45.7, 15, where there is a covenant with Aaron.) That there was a covenant with the priesthood is also implied in several other passages of the Old Testament, namely Jer. 33.21; Mal. 2.4-5, 8; Neh. 13.29. However, the covenant in Jer. 33.21 is said to be with 'the Levitical priests', reflecting the Deuteronomic language and ideology according to which the priests and Levites are identical, rather than the Priestly notion that the priests are the sons of Aaron and to be distinguished from the rest of the Levites. This is understandable if this passage has undergone Deuteronomistic editing, like other prose sermons in Jeremiah. Similarly Malachi 2 seems to equate the priests and the Levites, and this is of a piece with other evidence in Malachi suggesting strong dependence on the book of Deuteronomy. However, the fact that Mal. 2.8 speaks of the covenant with Levi as 'a covenant of...peace' does suggest a connection with the Priestly tradition in Num. 25.12, which similarly refers to the covenant with Phinehas as 'my covenant of peace'.[46] Nehemiah 13.29 speaks of 'the covenant of the priesthood and the Levites', reflecting awareness of the distinction between them (cf. Neh. 10.38 [ET 39]; 12.47; 13.30). In Num. 25.12-13 this covenant is narrowed down to those Aaronite priests claiming descent from Eleazar and Phinehas, which includes the Zadokite high priesthood (cf. 1 Chron. 5.27-41 [ET 6.1-15]), and the descendants of Aaron's son Ithamar are excluded. The fact that God 'gives' the covenant (Num. 25.12) is, of course, consistent with the Priestly writer's alternative terminology used in connection with the earlier covenants (Gen. 9.12; 17.2). Even though sacrifice has now been inaugurated according to P, we are presumably to understand that sacrifice was not employed in the making of this covenant.

46. Even though the Deuteronomic tradition clearly knew of a covenant with Levi, this does not seem to be the covenant in mind in Deut. 33.9, which states that the Levites 'observed your word, and kept your covenant'. As A.D.H. Mayes, *Deuteronomy* (NCB; London: Oliphants, 1979), p. 403 observes, the covenant referred to there is more likely that between Yahweh and Israel, and as various commentators have noted, Deut. 33.9 is probably referring back to the incident in Exod. 32.26-29. However, even though the word 'covenant' is not specifically mentioned, the divine covenant with Levi does seem to be in mind in 1 Sam. 2.27-28, which alludes to God's original promise of the priesthood to Levi in Egypt. (Cf. too Deut. 10.8.) One may compare 2 Sam. 7, the classic passage concerning the foundation of what is commonly referred to as the Davidic covenant, even though that chapter does not actually use the word 'covenant' in that connection, unlike some other parts of the Old Testament.

Chapter 9

NOAH'S DRUNKENNESS, THE CURSE OF CANAAN,
HAM'S CRIME, AND THE BLESSING OF SHEM AND JAPHETH
(GENESIS 9.18-27)

Genesis 9.18-27, which tells of Noah's drunkenness, Ham's crime, the cursing of Canaan and the blessing of Shem and Japheth, is truly one of the strange stories of the Bible. Martin Luther called it 'a silly and altogether unprofitable little story',[1] and more recently John Gibson roundly declared: 'The distasteful story of the curse of Canaan ought not to be in the Bible'.[2] There was a time in the not so far distant history of the Church when it was used by some as a biblical support for the oppression of the so-called Hamitic, black peoples of the world and against the abolition of slavery. The point has frequently been made, however, that the story does not in fact recount the cursing of Ham at all but rather of his son Canaan, thereby providing an aetiology of the subsequent subordination of the Canaanites to the Israelites. The process by which the cursing of Canaan got attached to Ham instead, and with such devastating effects, is a subject to which we shall return at the end of this chapter. Meanwhile, this short passage raises various other important questions of interpretation on which there is still no consensus. Thus, why is it that it is Canaan who is cursed by Noah when it is rather his father Ham who is allegedly guilty? What exactly is the nature of Ham's crime? What is the significance of the blessing of Japheth (alongside Shem) towards the end of the story? And should we understand Noah's discovery of wine in Gen. 9.20-21 as being positively anticipated in Gen 5.29? These are all questions which will be reconsidered here.

1. Martin Luther, *Luther's Works*. II. *Lectures on Genesis Chapters 6–14* (ed. J. Pelikan; St. Louis: Concordia Publishing House, 1960), p. 166.
2. J.C.L. Gibson, *Genesis* (2 vols.; Daily Study Bible; Edinburgh: Saint Andrew Press, 1981–82 [1981]), I, pp. 201-202.

1. *What Was Ham's Crime?*

On a surface reading Ham's crime was that he saw his drunken father
naked and, unlike his brothers, he merely talked about it and took no
action to rectify the situation. Because to a modern reader this sounds
more like a peccadillo than a major crime, a number of more serious
crimes have been sometimes suggested to account for Noah's curse. All
these alternative interpretations, however, involve reading into the text
what is simply not there. First there is the view that Ham's crime consisted of castrating his father. This is attested in variant forms in a number of rabbinic sources (*b. Sanh.* 70a; *Gen. R.* 36.7; implicit in Targum
Pseudo-Jonathan on Gen. 9.24), though in modern times, so far as I can
see, it has been taken seriously only by Robert Graves and Raphael
Patai,[3] who even speculated that the original castrating instrument was a
pruning-knife from Noah's vineyard! However, A.I. Baumgarten[4] has
shown that the castration motif is not original but was developed to
explain certain features of the biblical text in the second century CE,
when it is first referred to by Theophilus of Antioch (*Ad Autolycum*
3.19), doubtless dependent on Jewish exegesis, with which he was much
familiar. A different rabbinic view (*b. Sanh.* 70a) which has had rather
more support in modern times is that Ham sexually abused his father
Noah. Supporting this view are scholars such as A. Phillips, M. Nissinen
and R.A.J. Gagnon.[5] However, whereas Gagnon emphasizes the act as
one of homosexual rape, Nissinen sees it more as an expression of Ham's
hunger for power. An alternative view first put forward in modern times
is that Ham had heterosexual relations with Noah's wife. Supporting
the heterosexual understanding are scholars such as F.W. Bassett,

---

3.   R. Graves and R. Patai, *Hebrew Myths: The Book of Genesis* (London: Cassell,
1963), pp. 122-24; U. (M.D.) Cassuto, *A Commentary on the Book of Genesis*. II.
From Noah to Abraham (trans. I. Abrahams; Jerusalem: Magnes Press, 1964),
pp. 150-53, rejects this view only after much hesitation.
    4.   A.I. Baumgarten, 'Myth and Midrash: Genesis 9:20-29', in J. Neusner (ed.),
*Christianity, Judaism and Other Greco-Roman Cults: Studies for Morton Smith at
Sixty*. III. *Judaism before 70* (SJLA, 12; Leiden: Brill, 1975), pp. 55-71.
    5.   A. Phillips, 'Uncovering the Father's Skirt', *VT* 30 (1980), pp. 38-43 (41); M.
Nissinen, *Homoeroticism in the Biblical World: A Historical Perspective* (trans. K.
Stjerna; Minneapolis: Fortress Press, 1998), pp. 52-53; R.A.J. Gagnon, *The Bible
and Homosexual Practice: Texts and Hermeneutics* (Nashville: Abingdon Press,
2001), pp. 63-71.

J.S. Bergsma and S.W. Hahn.[6] Both the homosexual and heterosexual interpretations are based on the assumption that the reference to seeing the nakedness of Noah is the same as that of uncovering Noah's nakedness, that is, having sexual intercourse. However, the two expressions are not identical and there is just one place in the Hebrew Bible where they appear to be identical in meaning, namely Lev. 20.17. But this cannot be the case in Genesis 9, since the fact that Shem and Japheth have to walk backwards so as not to see Noah's nakedness makes clear that it is a case of literal seeing. Faced with this problem, Bassett is forced to conclude that the passage about the brothers walking backwards must be a later gloss, but this serves only to highlight the weakness of his case. In fact, not only the heterosexual but also the homosexual and castration interpretations of Ham's deed run counter to the natural interpretation of the text, which clearly implies that Ham's seeing of Noah's nakedness must be a case of literal seeing, since Shem and Japheth are said to have walked backwards in order not to see their naked father. Also the further objection may be made that it was not in the nature of J to be overly coy in his descriptions of sexual relations. Finally, a curious view first put forward in modern times by H. Hirsch Cohen should be noted: this supposes that Ham saw Noah naked while the latter was having sexual intercourse with his wife and that Ham thereby acquired his potency.[7] Consequently, Noah was unable to curse him, so he cursed Canaan instead in order that his potency should not get transferred to him. However, this view, which seems far-fetched, has gained no following.

So we are left with the literal interpretation, which implies that Ham saw his father's nakedness but that this involved a serious lapse of filial obligation on Ham's part. This obligation is clearly spelled out in the Ugaritic Aqhat epic, where one of the duties of the son towards his father is specifically stated to be 'to take his hand in drunkenness, to bear him up [when] full of wine' (*KTU* 1.17.I.30-31). Deutero-Isaiah also refers to this obligation when he says of Jerusalem, drunk with the wrath of God, 'There is no one to guide her among all the sons she has borne; there is no one to take her by the hand among all the sons she has brought up' (Isa. 51.18). So, what the story in Genesis illustrates is not just a peccadillo but a serious failure of filial obligation on Ham's part.

6. F.W. Bassett, 'Noah's Nakedness and the Curse of Canaan: A Case of Incest?', *VT* 21 (1971), pp. 232-37; J.S. Bergsma and S.W. Hahn, 'Noah's Nakedness and the Curse on Canaan (Genesis 9:20-27)', *JBL* 124 (2005), pp. 125-40.

7. H.H. Cohen, *The Drunkenness of Noah* (Tuscaloosa, AL: University of Alabama Press, 1974), pp. 13-30.

2. Why Was Canaan Cursed rather than Ham?

The first question that puzzles the attentive reader is why it should be Canaan who was cursed by Noah when it was rather his father, Ham, who was guilty of seeing him naked, a problem already noted in antiquity, for example, by Philo of Alexandria, *Quaestiones in Genesim* 2.77. Some explanations are bound up with rabbinic and other interpretations of the story that have already been rejected above. Thus, the view that Ham had sexual intercourse with Noah's wife seeks to explain the cursing of Canaan on the basis that he was the offspring of that vile relationship. However, the text suggests that Canaan was already in existence at the time of the curse in the immediate aftermath of Noah's drunkenness (Gen. 9.24-25). Again, the view that Ham castrated Noah sought to explain the cursing of Canaan on the basis that the latter was Ham's fourth son, and so this was fitting retribution for Noah himself having been made unable to beget a fourth son. Further, the notion found in some rabbinic sources that Canaan himself castrated Noah prior to Ham's seeing his nakedness (*PRE* 23) is likewise unfounded in the text. According to another ingenious rabbinic explanation attributed to Rabbi Judah in *Gen. R.* 36.7, Ham could not be cursed because God had previously blessed him (alongside his brothers and father) in Gen. 9.1, and consequently his son Canaan was cursed instead. Interestingly, this interpretation is attested even earlier at Qumran in 4Q252 (4Q Pesher Genesis[a]) 1.2.6-7. However, this will not convince a modern critical scholar, since Gen. 9.1 is from P and Gen. 9.18-27 is from J.

Rather, the old critical arguments that various tensions in the text indicate that it was originally Canaan who was guilty of seeing his father naked, thereby meriting the curse, look extremely convincing.[8] First, there is the important point that in one of the poetic verses (Gen. 9.25) it is Canaan rather than Ham who is declared to be the brother of Shem and Japheth. Secondly, in Gen. 9.24 the one who sees Noah's nakedness is described as 'his youngest son',[9] which contradicts the impression we receive from the constant references elsewhere to 'Shem, Ham and

---

8. E.g. J. Wellhausen, *Die Composition des Hexateuchs und der historischen Bücher des Alten Testaments* (Berlin: G. Reimer, 3rd edn, 1899), pp. 12-13; J. Skinner, *A Critical and Exegetical Commentary on Genesis* (ICC; Edinburgh: T. & T. Clark, 1910), p. 182; G. von Rad, *Das erste Buch Mose: Genesis* (ATD, 2.4; Göttingen: Vandenhoeck & Ruprecht, 5th edn, 1958), p. 112, ET *Genesis* (trans. J.H. Marks; OTL; London: SCM Press, 2nd edn, 1963), pp. 131-32.

9. It has occasionally been suggested that one could circumvent this problem by translating *bᵉnô haqqāṭān* as 'his younger son', but this does not correspond with Hebrew usage.

Japheth', and suggests that Ham was the middle son. Thirdly, it is highly odd that Canaan alone should be cursed, and not Ham directly at all. Although one might try to explain away each of these points individually by saying that the word 'brother' is used in a loose sense, that the names 'Shem, Ham and Japheth' are not in strict order of age, and that Ham and his Canaanite descendants are closely identified, to explain away all three points simultaneously does seem highly forced. It seems far more natural to suppose that behind our current story there was an earlier tradition according to which the three sons were Shem, Japheth and Canaan, with Canaan being the youngest and the one who saw his father's nakedness. This alternative tradition has been imperfecly incorporated into a narrative in which Noah's three sons are now Shem, Ham and Japheth. We should therefore conclude that underlying our text was an earlier version that spoke about 'Canaan' rather than 'Ham, the father of Canaan' (cf. Gen 9.18, 22). However, in the final form of the text it is Ham who sees Noah's nakedness, not Canaan, so the redactor who put the text together as we now have it, admittedly not too cleverly, presumably had some view on the matter. Most probably, the final redactor simply envisaged Ham as being punished through his Canaanite descendants.

3. *The Blessing of Shem*

In Gen. 9.26 we have Noah's blessing of Shem. It is generally accepted that Shem symbolizes Israel, which is supported by the fact that Shem is said to be the father of all the children of Eber (Gen. 10.21), the eponymous ancestor of the Hebrews (*ʿēber*, Eber, being doubtless a back projection from *ʿibrî*, 'Hebrew'). It is further reinforced by the fact that this verse speaks of Yahweh as Shem's God, in contrast to the next verse, where the deity is spoken of merely as Elohim in connection with Japheth.[10] As is widely agreed, the blessing of Shem, which speaks of Canaan's enslavement, clearly provides an aetiology of Israel's enslavement of the Canaanites in the wake of the settlement and rise of the United Monarchy (cf. Josh. 9.27; Judg. 1.28, 30, 33; 1 Kgs 9.20-21).

However, while there is general agreement as to the interpretation, there is some disagreement among scholars regarding the precise translation of the verse. As it stands Gen. 9.26 does not directly speak of the blessing of Shem, but reads, 'Blessed be the Lord God of Shem; and let

---

10. This is comparable to the deliberate use of different divine names in the books of Jonah and Job. See J. Day, 'Problems in the Interpretation of the Book of Jonah', in A.S. van der Woude (ed.), *In Quest of the Past: Studies on Israelite Religion, Literature and Prophetism* (OS, 26; Leiden: Brill, 1990), pp. 32-47 (43-44).

Canaan be his slave'. This reading is universally followed in our Hebrew manuscripts as well as being presupposed in all the ancient Versions. It is thus the traditional rendering (cf. AV, RV), and is still followed in a number of modern translations (NAB, NIV, JB, NJB), and defended by some modern scholars, for example, G. von Rad and W. Zimmerli.[11] However, at first sight there appears to be a problem here in that the context leads one to expect that it will be Shem who is to be blessed, not the God of Shem, in keeping with the parallel blessing of Japheth and curse of Canaan (vv. 25, 27). Initially the simplest way to get round this problem might be to make a slight emendation of the MT, reading *ᵓelōhay* for *ᵓelōhê*, and rendering 'Blessed by the Lord *my God* be Shem' (so RSV, NRSV). However, apart from this lacking any textual support in the ancient Versions or Hebrew manuscripts, it needs to be noted that a perusal of other Old Testament passages involving 'blessed' (*bārûk*) indicates that the name of the person being blessed regularly follows immediately after the word 'blessed', while the one by whom one is blessed should be indicated by the preposition *lᵉ*. These observations would similarly rule out emending to read 'Blessed of the Lord be *the tents* (*ᵓohᵒlê*) of Shem…' (cf. the phrase, 'tents of Shem' in the next verse). The NEB and REB diverge further from the MT by additionally emending the first word *bārûk* to an imperative, 'Bless (*bārēk*), O Lord, the tents of Shem'. But without any versional support this seems too speculative, and the very fact that the previous sentence started with the word 'Cursed' makes it natural to retain 'Blessed' here. These considerations tend to favour the retention of the Masoretic text. In support we may compare a frequently overlooked passage in one of the tribal blessings in the Blessing of Moses in Deuteronomy 33, where God is similarly blessed rather than the tribe directly. This is Deut. 33.20, where we read 'Blessed is the one who enlarges Gad!', that is, God.[12] This further strengthens the plausibility of accepting the Masoretic text in Gen. 9.26, where the implication must surely be that if Shem's God Yahweh is blessed, so too is Shem.[13]

---

11. Von Rad, *Das erste Buch Mose*, p. 114, ET *Genesis*, p. 133; W. Zimmerli, *1. Mose 1–11* (Zürcher Bibelkommentare; Zurich: Zwingli Verlag, 3rd edn, 1967), pp. 355-56.

12. Noted by J.H. Tigay, *Deuteronomy* (JPSTC; Philadelphia: Jewish Publication Society, 1996), p. 331. NRSV translates 'Blessed be the *enlargement* of Gad', and NEB and REB more paraphrastically render, 'Blessed be Gad, *in his wide domain*', but these are not natural renderings of the hiphil participle *marḥîb*, literally 'the one who enlarges'.

13. Many translators in earlier centuries rendered *ᶜebed lāmô* as 'their slave' rather than 'his slave' both here and in v. 27; cf. RV margin. However, while the

4. *The Blessing of Japheth*

Following the curse of Canaan and blessing of Shem we find in Gen. 9.27 Noah's blessing of Japheth, with its evident word play: 'May God make space (*yapt*) for Japheth (*yepet*), and let him live in the tents of Shem; and let Canaan be his slave'. The blessing of Shem is not surprising, since this figure was the ancestor of the Hebrews. There is, however, no unanimity on the subject of the blessing of Japheth. Some older views are now generally rejected since they lack adequate support, and are consequently only rarely discussed by recent commentators. Apart from the old rabbinic (e.g. Targum Pseudo-Jonathan) and patristic interpretation that it refers to the conversion of the gentiles,[14] these include the view that Japheth denotes the Phoenicians,[15] who are clearly inappropriate since they were Canaanites, Sidon being a son of Canaan in Gen. 10.15, whereas Japheth is explicitly contrasted with Canaan; that it refers to the Hittites,[16] though they too are regarded in the Old Testament as being closely bound up with the Canaanite population, Heth being a son of Canaan in Gen. 10.15; or that it signifies the Assyrians or Babylonians,[17] though they did not live in the area denoted by Japheth.

Some commentators nowadays find it too difficult to come to a conclusion about Japheth,[18] while a few do not even bother to discuss the matter.[19] Of views which are currently held, two minority ones may be

expression *lāmô* is capable of meaning both 'to him' and 'to them', the context here suggests the former, since Gen. 9.25 states that Canaan will be a slave to each of his brothers, not to God as well.

14. Still accepted in part by S.R. Driver, *The Book of Genesis* (Westminster Commentaries; London: Methuen Books, 1904), p. 111.

15. K. Budde, *Die biblische Urgeschichte (Gen 1–12,5)* (Giessen: J. Ricker, 1883), pp. 330-65.

16. H. Gunkel, *Genesis* (Göttinger HKAT, 1.1; Göttingen: Vandenhoeck & Ruprecht, 1910), p. 83, ET *Genesis* (trans. M.E. Biddle; Macon, GA: Mercer University Press, 1997), p. 84.

17. J. Hoftijzer, 'Some Remarks on the Tale of Noah's Drunkenness', in B. Gemser *et al.*, *Studies on the Book of Genesis* (OTS 12; Leiden: Brill, 1958), pp. 22-27 (25-26 n. 7). Hoftijzer also concedes that the reference might be to the Philistines, but regards a reference to the Assyrians, or more likely the Babylonians, as most probable.

18. C. Westermann, *Genesis 1–11* (BKAT, 1.1; Neukirchen–Vluyn: Neukirchener Verlag, 1974), p. 660, ET *Genesis 1–11: A Commentary* (trans. J.J. Scullion; London: SPCK, 1984), p. 493; G.J. Wenham, *Genesis 1–15* (WBC, 1; Waco, TX: Word Books, 1987), pp. 202-203.

19. N.M. Sarna, *Genesis* (JPS Torah Commentary; Philadelphia: Jewish Publication Society, 1989), p. 67; B.T. Arnold, *Genesis* (NCBC; New York: Cambridge University Press, 2009), pp. 112-13.

noted. First, W.C. Kaiser and J.J. Scullion still maintain the view earlier attested in *Jub.* 8.18, Philo of Alexandria and certain rabbinic sources (e.g. Targums Neofiti 1 and Onqelos; *Gen. R.* 36.8; *b. Yoma* 10a; Rashi; Ibn Ezra) that the one dwelling in the tents of Shem is not Japheth at all but rather God.[20] This, however, does not seem a natural interpretation, as it is difficult to understand how God's dwelling in the tents of Shem would constitute a blessing on Japheth, and since a wish is expressed for Japheth to expand, it makes sense that it is Japheth who is to dwell in the tents of Shem. Secondly, Van Seters[21] sees here a very late Hellenistic textual expansion referring to the Greeks. However, the existence of such a late gloss in the Pentateuch would be surprising; Num. 24.24 (referring to ships from Kittim coming to afflict the Near East), which Van Seters compares, more naturally refers to the Philistines than the Greeks, since Alexander the Great did not come by ship, whereas the Philistines did, and the overall context of Num. 24.17-24 concerns the conquests of the United Monarchy, so a reference to the Philistines is only to be expected in the original text. (On this passage, see more below.) Moreover, Gen. 9.25-27 speaks of Canaan serving his brothers, which most naturally implies joint rule over Canaan by Shem and Japheth, whereas the Greeks did not share rule over Canaan with Israel but rather conquered Israel.[22]

When a confident view is expressed nowadays it is usually that Japheth represents the Philistines.[23] This makes sense, since Japheth

---

20. W.C. Kaiser, *Toward an Old Testament Theology* (Grand Rapids, MI: Zondervan, 1978), pp. 37-39, 81-82; J.J. Scullion, *Genesis: A Commentary for Students, Teachers, and Preachers* (Old Testament Studies, 6; Collegeville, MN: Liturgical Press [A Michael Glazier Book], 1992), p. 86.

21. J. Van Seters, *Prologue to History: The Yahwist as Historian in Genesis* (Louisville, KY: Westminster/John Knox Press, 1992), pp. 179, 186 n. 22. Further, Van Seters speculatively thinks that Noah's words originally related only to Eber and Canaan, who were subsequently replaced by Shem and Ham. A. Bertholet, *Die Stellung der Israeliten und der Juden zu den Fremden* (Freiburg i.B.: J.C.B. Mohr [Paul Siebeck], 1896), pp. 76-77, 198, and J. Herrmann, 'Zu Gen 9 18-27', *ZAW* 30 (1910), pp. 127-31, similarly saw the blessing of Japheth as a later addition and maintained that the story originally concerned only Shem and Canaan.

22. Presumably Van Seters would maintain that Canaan's serving of Japheth followed on afterwards and replaced his serving of Shem, but this is not the most obvious reading of the biblical text.

23. This view appears to go back to Wellhausen, 'Die Composition des Hexateuchs', p. 403, subsequently taken up in *Die Composition des Hexateuchs*, p. 13; E. Meyer, *Geschichte des Alterthums* (5 vols.; Stuttgart: J.G. Cotta, 1st edn, 1884–1902 [1884]), I, p. 214 n. 1 (tentatively), and *idem, Die Israeliten und ihre Nachbarstämme* (Halle: Max Niemeyer, 1906), p. 221 (more confidently). More recently, this view has been followed by von Rad, *Das erste Buch Mose*, pp. 114-15, ET

clearly denotes the Mediterranean, especially island, nations, in addition to certain parts of western Asia, and it is difficult to envisage any other people from this area other than the Philistines (or associated Sea Peoples) who shared rule with the Israelites over the Canaanites, which is what Genesis 9 appears to have in mind. Although not dependent on it, this view also coheres with the fact that the name Japheth, ancestor of the Mediterranean nations and islands, is plausibly related to that of the Greek mythological Titan called Iapetos,[24] who was the ancestor (great-grandfather) of Hellen, the father of the Hellenic peoples. Interestingly, Japheth was the son of the biblical flood hero, Noah, and Iapetos was the grandfather of the Greek flood hero, Deucalion. (The Greek flood story has clear Near Eastern roots.)

However, so far as I am aware, no one hitherto has succeeded in dealing with two objections to which the Philistine interpretation has sometimes been subject. First, there is the question why the Philistines should be represented as descended from Japheth, when Gen. 10.14 attributes them (and Caphtor, their place of origin) to Ham. In response it may be noted that the reference to the Philistines coming from Caphtor in Gen. 10.14 is a later gloss (as its current misplacing following Casluhim shows).[25] Moreover, in Num. 24.24—which is similarly from

Genesis, pp. 134-35; E.A. Speiser, *Genesis* (AB, 1; Garden City, NY: Doubleday, 1964), pp. 62-63; Zimmerli, *1. Mose 1–11*, p. 359. Similarly, D. Neiman, 'The Date and Circumstances of the Cursing of Canaan', in A. Altmann (ed.), *Biblical Motifs: Origins and Transformations* (Cambridge, MA: Harvard University Press, 1966), pp. 113-34, though he relates the text to the thirteenth or twelfth century BCE, and A.P. Ross, 'The Curse of Canaan', *BSac* 137 (1980), pp. 223-40 (237), and V.P. Hamilton, *The Book of Genesis Chapters 1–17* (NICOT; Grand Rapids, MI: Eerdmans, 1990), pp. 325-27, two conservative scholars who see this as prophetic rather than aetiological.

24. This view is found already in writers from the Renaissance period, and has been quite frequently followed in modern times, by, e.g., D. Neiman, 'The Two Genealogies of Japhet', in H.A. Hoffner (ed.), *Orient and Occident: Essays Presented to Cyrus H. Gordon on the Occasion of his Sixty-Fifth Birthday* (AOAT, 22; Kevelaer: Verlag Butzon & Bercker; Neukirchen–Vluyn: Neukirchener Verlag, 1973), pp. 119-26 (123-25). However, M.L. West, *The East Face of Helicon: West Asiatic Elements in Greek Poetry and Myth* (Oxford: Clarendon Press, 1997), pp. 289-90, feels somewhat sceptical, as he does not see much resemblance in role, in spite of the admitted similarity of name. However, since Iapetos was the ancestor of the Hellenic peoples, there is a similarity here to Japheth.

25. However, G.A. Rendsburg, 'Gen 10:13-14: An Authentic Tradition concerning the Origin of the Philistines', *JNSL* 13 (1987), pp. 89-96, has argued that the MT's reference to the Philistines coming from Casluhim is authentic. He understands Casluhim to refer to Lower Egypt (with Naphtuhim referring to Memphites [Middle

the Yahwist,[26] and a part of the oracles of Balaam alluding to the defeat of Israel's enemies at the time of the United Monarchy—what appear to be the Philistines come in ships from Kittim (Cyprus) to afflict the Near East prior to their defeat.[27] Now according to Gen. 10.4 Kittim was regarded as a son of Japheth. That J in Genesis 9 should designate the Philistines by the name Japheth thus makes sense in the light of J's association of Kittim, a son of Japheth, with the Philistines in Num. 24.24. There is, moreover, some archaeological evidence that the Philistines came to Canaan via Cyprus (Kittim).[28] This is preferable to the view of H. Rouillard and J. Van Seters that the reference in Num. 24.24 to ships coming from Kittim is a late Hellenistic gloss alluding to Alexander the Great,[29] since, as noted, he did not actually invade the Near East by ship.

Egypt] and Pathrusim, as is generally agreed, alluding to Upper Egypt), and claims that the Philistines originally came from there before moving on to Crete. However, all this seems very speculative. Moreover, it is noteworthy that when we delete the reference to the Philistines, Gen. 10 has precisely 70 nations, which is what we should expect in view of the Jewish concept of 70 nations paralleling the 70 sons of God (Deut. 32.8).

    26.   The traditional ascription of the Balaam oracles to the J source has much to be said for it. Note, for example, that both the Balaam oracles and the J source in Genesis have the common anticipation of Israel's becoming a great nation (Gen. 12.1-3; Num. 24.17-24), both refer to Seth (Sheth) and Cain (Kain) in close proximity (Gen. 4.1-17, 24, 25-26; Num. 24.17, 22), and it is only in Gen. 3 and Num. 22 that the Hebrew Bible refers to speaking animals (the Eden serpent and Balaam's ass).

    27.   In Num. 24.24, prior to the demise of their power ('and he also shall perish for ever'), the ships coming from Kittim 'shall afflict Asshur and Eber'. Eber clearly has Israel in mind, but how can the Philistines be envisaged as afflicting Assyria? Here I would note that Rameses III states with regard to the invasion of the Sea Peoples that 'No land could stand before their arms, from Hatti, Kode, Carchemish, Arzawa, and Alashiya on' (*ANET*, p. 262), some of which could be construed as falling within the Assyrian sphere of influence. Similarly, recently discovered texts from Tell Tayinat and Aleppo indicate that there was a powerful kingdom of 'Palistin' with Aegean connections in northern Syria during the Early Iron Age. See J.D. Hawkins, 'Cilicia, Amuq, and Aleppo: New Light on a Dark Age', *Near Eastern Archaeology* 72 (2009), pp. 164-73; T.P. Harrison, 'Neo-Hittites in the '"Land of Palistin": Renewed Investigations at Tell Ta'yinat on the Plain of Antioch', *Near Eastern Archaeology* 72 (2009), pp. 174-89.

    28.   Cf. A. Killebrew, *Biblical Peoples and Ethnicity: An Archaeological Study of Egyptians, Canaanites, Philistines, and Early Israel 1300–1100 B.C.E.* (SBLABS, 9; Leiden: Brill, 2005), pp. 197-245; A. Yasur-Landau, *The Philistines and Aegean Migrations at the End of the Late Bronze Age* (Cambridge: Cambridge University Press, 2010), pp. 334, 339.

    29.   H. Rouillard, *La péricope de Balaam (Nombres 22–24): La prose et les oracles* (Etudes bibliques; Paris: Gabalda, 1985), pp. 462-64, cf. p. 458; Van Seters,

Secondly, it has sometimes been regarded as unlikely that an Israelite writer would represent the Philistines as being the object of a divine blessing. However, what at first might seem a surprisingly positive view of the role of the Philistines is not unparalleled in the Hebrew Bible, for Amos 9.7 similarly presupposes the belief that God was responsible for bringing the Philistines to Canaan (Amos being from a rather similar date to J, in my view[30]). Moreover, as Zimmerli and von Rad have noted, the blessing of Japheth makes excellent sense as an explanation of why the Israelites had not taken control of all the Promised Land, some being left for the Philistines.[31] Noah's words imply that this had been God's intention from the beginning. Thus we remarkably have here, in this seemingly unedifying story, one of the most enlightened and tolerant attitudes towards the Philistines in the whole of the Old Testament.

5. *Noah's Discovery of Wine and Subsequent Drunkenness*

A point that I have not seen highlighted hitherto is the fact that in a number of his stories in Genesis 1–11 the Yahwist offers us not merely one aetiology but several combined. Thus, for example, the story of the Garden of Eden in Gen. 2.4b–3.24 explains not only human beings' acquisition of wisdom and failure to acquire immortality, but also the origins of snakes crawling on their bellies, the traditional female subordination to men, and why men have to engage in laborious work. Again, the story of the tower of Babel in Gen. 11.1-9 explains not merely the scattering of humanity and the multiplication of languages but also the origin of the place name Babel (Babylon). Further, the brief narrative about Nimrod in Gen. 10.8-12 not only offers an account of the first warrior on earth and an explanation of a proverb, but also tells us the origin of various Assyrian cities.[32] Similarly, in the story of Noah under

Prologue to History, p. 186 n. 22. Cf. P.-E. Dion, 'Les *KTYM* de Tel Arad: Grecs ou Phéniciens?', *RB* 99 (1992), pp. 70-97 (94-96), who sees this passage as late but rejects a connection with Alexander.

30. In the J narrative about Nimrod in Gen. 10.12, Calah (modern Nimrud) appears to be called 'the great city'. It was in fact from c. 880–c.700 BCE that Calah was the capital of Assyria. This might suggest that the date of J is most likely in the ninth or eighth century. So far as I can see, this point has not previously been noted; I intend to discuss it in more detail in another place.

31. Von Rad, *Das erste Buch Mose*, p. 115, ET *Genesis*, pp. 134-35; Zimmerli, *1. Mose 1–11*, pp. 361-62.

32. It is sometimes thought that Gen. 6.1-4 likewise gives us an aetiology of the origin of the giant Nephilim (Num. 13.33) as well as of the reduction of human life to 120 years. However, while the latter is surely the case, a careful reading of

consideration here, we have not merely an aetiology of the subordination of the Canaanites to both Israel and the Philistines, but also an account of the discovery of wine. As Gen. 9.20-21 states, 'Noah, a man of the soil (lit. 'ground'), was the first to plant a vineyard. He drank some of the wine and became drunk...' This aspect of the story follows in the train of Gen. 4.17-26, where the Yahwist has already told us of the origin of various other human activities, a narrative thus containing further multiple aetiologies.

It has been widely held that Noah's discovery of wine appears to be anticipated in Gen. 5.29, an extract from J in an overwhelmingly Priestly genealogy, in which we read that Lamech named his son 'Noah, saying "Out of the ground that the Lord has cursed this one shall bring us relief from our work and from the toil of our hands"'.[33] This understanding is surely correct. The verse clearly refers back to Yahweh's cursing of the ground in Gen. 3.17 and the consequent laboriousness of human labour, but predicts that because of Noah there will be some amelioration of human labour. That Noah's discovery of wine is specifically in mind is strongly supported by the fact that it is precisely the cursed ground that is predicted as providing the source of relief, and this very word 'ground' (*ʾªdāmâ*) is actually mentioned in Gen. 9.20 in connection with Noah's discovery of wine. Although the positive side of wine is not highlighted in Genesis 9, it coheres with what is said about wine elsewhere in the Hebrew Bible. Thus, in Ps. 104.15 we read of 'wine to gladden the human heart', and similarly Judg. 9.13 speaks of 'wine that cheers gods and mortals'. Again, Prov. 31.6-7 declares, 'Give strong drink to one who is perishing, and wine to those in bitter distress; let them drink and forget their poverty, and remember their misery no more'. Interestingly, the Hebrew root *nāḥam*, 'comfort, console', used in Gen. 5.29 is explicitly used of wine elsewhere in Jer. 16.17, in connection with the 'cup of consolation' offered to the bereaved.[34]

Gen. 6.4 suggests that J regarded the Nephilim as being already on the earth when the sexual liaisons between the sons of God and daughters of men took place. We must therefore suppose that it was at an earlier stage of the tradition that the Nephilim were regarded as the offspring of the divine/human marriages, and that J has deliberately demythologized the story to a certain extent. See above, Chapter 5.

33.   E.g. Budde, *Die biblische Urgeschichte*, p. 313; von Rad, *Das erste Buch Mose*, p. 113, ET *Genesis*, p. 132; Zimmerli, *1. Mose 1–11*, pp. 259-60; Van Seters, *Prologue to History*, p. 179.

34.   Wine is also associated with consolation in Euripides, *Bacchae* 279-83.

Some scholars, however, have claimed that Gen. 5.29 is not an anticipation of the discovery of wine in Gen. 9.20-21 but rather of what is described in Gen. 8.21-22, where God instigates a new era following the flood.[35] However, against this it may first be objected that Gen. 8.21-22 does not offer any relief of human labour from the ground, such as Gen. 5.29 anticipates, but rather implies that the ground will never be cursed again after the manner of the flood. The Lord there says, 'I will never again curse the ground because of humanity, for the inclination of the human heart is evil from youth, nor will I ever again destroy every living creature as I have done. As long as the earth endures, seedtime and harvest, cold and heat, summer and winter, day and night shall not cease.' Secondly, Gen. 5.29 envisages Noah as the one who provides relief from human labour, whereas the new, post-flood order of Gen. 8.21-22 (which does not speak of human labour) is inaugurated by God himself. These same two objections apply to the view of M. Witte, who has suggested that the fulfilment of Gen. 5.29 is to be seen in the Priestly Noachic covenant of Gen. 9.1-17, in addition to Gen. 8.21-22.[36]

Many readers are understandably surprised by J's depiction of the drunkenness and nakedness of Noah, someone who has previously been so completely righteous that only he and his family among human beings are allowed to survive the flood. In response, it may be argued that if Noah is being depicted as the discoverer of wine, it is entirely natural that he should have to learn from experience that excessive consumption of wine can lead to drunkenness. This is consistent with the fact that the narrative in Gen. 9.20-27 makes no explicit criticism of Noah. Rather, the blame falls squarely on Ham (originally Canaan) for failing to provide him with the necessary assistance. Again, there may be something in the view of A.I. Baumgarten that this post-flood story about Noah, which so much emphasizes his proneness to human weakness, was included as a way of countering the earlier Mesopotamian tradition that the flood hero was taken away to live with the gods after the flood (cf. the Sumerian flood story, a fragment of the Atrahasis flood story from

35. E.g. Driver, *Genesis*, pp. 77-78; R. Rendtorff, 'Genesis 8 21 und die Urgeschichte des Jahwisten', *Kerygma und Dogma* 7 (1961), pp. 69-78 (74); W.A.M. Clark, 'The Flood and the Structure of the Pre-Patriarchal History', *ZAW* 83 (1971), pp. 184-211 (208); N.C. Baumgart, 'Gen 5,29—ein Brückenvers in der Urgeschichte und zugleich ein Erzählerkommentar', *BN* 92 (1998), pp. 21-37 (31-35).

36. M. Witte, *Die biblische Urgeschichte: Redaktions- und theologiegeschichtliche Beobachtungen zu Genesis 1,1–11,26* (BZAW, 265; Berlin: W. de Gruyter, 1998), pp. 207-17. Witte regards Gen. 5.29 as a redactional addition subsequent to both J and P. However, this verse bears every sign of being from J himself.

Ugarit,[37] Gilgamesh 11.203-206, and Berossus).[38] J's rejection of the Mesopotamian tradition of the flood hero's apotheosis at this point is certainly striking when we consider how much the underlying Mesopotamian flood story has been followed in other regards.[39] Far less plausible is the wildly speculative view of H. Hirsch Cohen,[40] who claimed that Noah got drunk in order to facilitate sex and so fulfil God's command to be fruitful and multiply. This over-imaginative suggestion, which has gained no support, overlooks the fact that our narrative is from the J source, whereas the command to be fruitful and multiply comes from the later P source, albeit Cohen rejects the documentary hypothesis.

With this attribution of the discovery of wine to a human being, Noah, we appear to have a break with Israel's ancient Near Eastern background, where this discovery was often attributed to a god. Thus, the Greeks attributed the discovery of wine to Dionysus and the Egyptians to Osiris. Moreover, the Ugaritic texts attribute the drinking of wine to the gods, including the creator god El, who is even depicted getting drunk and needing assistance in one text (*KTU* 1.114.15-19), so presumably the Ugaritians ascribed the discovery of wine to the gods. Philo of Byblos, who claims to preserve Phoenician traditions, does, like Genesis 4, attribute many inventions or discoveries to primaeval human beings rather than gods, but makes no specific reference to wine; the nearest he gets is the discovery of nourishment from trees, which he attributes to the men Aeon and Protogonos (reported in Eusebius, *Praep. Ev.* 1.6.7).

---

37. W.G. Lambert and A.R. Millard, *Atra-ḥasīs: The Babylonian Story of the Flood* (Oxford: Clarendon Press, 1969), pp. 132-33, reverse, lines 1-4.

38. Baumgarten, 'Myth and Midrash: Genesis 9:20-29', pp. 58-61.

39. The Priestly writer appears to have transferred the motif of the flood hero's ascent into heaven to Enoch in Gen. 5.24; cf. J. VanderKam, *Enoch and the Growth of an Apocalyptic Tradition* (CBQMS, 16; Washington, DC: Catholic Biblical Association, 1984), pp. 49-50. This is more likely than the view of R. Borger, 'Die Beschwörungsserie *Bît Mēseri* und die Himmelfahrt Henochs', *JNES* 33 (1974), pp. 183-96, that Enoch's ascent was derived from Utu-abzu, the apkallu (sage) of Enmeduranki. Not only would the Mesopotamian flood-hero myth have been much more familiar to the Israelites than the figure of Utu-abzu, but the verb *lāqaḥ*, 'take', used of Enoch in Gen. 5.24 is directly comparable to the Akkadian verb *leqû*, used in connection with Utnapishtim's apotheosis in Gilgamesh 11.206. (The line numbering in Gilgamesh here and above follows that in A.R. George, *The Babylonian Gilgamesh Epic: Introduction, Critical Edition and Cuneiform Texts* [2 vols.; Oxford: Oxford University Press, 2003], I, pp. 716-17. Some other translations follow a different line numbering.)

40. Cohen, *The Drunkenness of Noah*, pp. 1-12.

6. *A History of Misinterpretation:*
From the Cursing of Canaan to the Cursing of Ham

As noted earlier, the story of the curse of Canaan later got misinterpreted as a curse on Ham, and subsequently on the so-called Hamitic nations of the world, with devastating effects for black people. How exactly did this come about? The beginnings of this process have been traced in detail by David Goldenberg.[41] He is able to show that—in spite of the clear statement of the Bible to the contrary—already in the first millennium CE various Jewish rabbinic, patristic Christian and Muslim sources can be found claiming that Noah's curse affected Ham and/or all Ham's children, and not just Canaan. The sheer unreasonableness of the biblical story in which Ham is the guilty party but his son Canaan is condemned, as well as understandable misremembering of the story, contributed to the idea that it was Ham and/or all Ham's children who were cursed. Further, the Near Eastern environment in which black people were often slaves also tended to encourage the view that it was black people who had been cursed. The notion that Ham himself was black (as one of his sons, Kush, certainly was), though something not implied in the Bible, was encouraged by a false etymology according to which the name Ham was associated either with the Hebrew root *ḥāmam*, 'to be hot', or with *ḥûm*, 'to be dark, black'.[42] This is already reflected in two rabbinic passages, one in the Palestinian Talmud (*y. Ta'an.* 1.6, 64d), which states that 'Ham went forth darkened (*mᵉpûḥām*)' and another in the Babylonian Talmud (*b. Sanh.* 108b), which declares more vaguely that 'Ham was punished in his skin'. However, it should be noted that these two rabbinic statements are totally unrelated to Noah's curse in Genesis 9 but represent rather a punishment for Ham's disobedience in having had sexual relations in the Ark.

41. D.M. Goldenberg, *The Curse of Ham: Race and Slavery in Early Judaism, Christianity, and Islam* (Princeton, NJ: Princeton University Press, 2003), pp. 141-77.

42. Although the precise scientific etymology of the name Ham is unknown, both these proposed etymologies are certainly wrong. Goldenberg notes that the name Ham started with *ḥ*, as is shown by its representation in the LXX by the letter χ, whereas the roots 'to be hot' and 'to be dark, black' both have *ḥ*. Incidentally, Egyptian *km(t)*, 'black', an Egyptian term for Egypt sometimes regarded as the etymology of Ham in more recent times, similarly has the wrong first letter (Egyptian *k* is always represented in Hebrew by kaph or qoph). On all this, see Goldenberg, *The Curse of Ham*, pp. 144-49.

The first explicit connection between Noah's alleged curse of Ham and black slavery is found in Islamic sources from the seventh century onwards, a period which witnessed the Muslim conquest of parts of Africa when native peoples were enslaved by Arabs. We find this connection expressed, for example, by 'Aṭā' (died 732/3) and an anonymous source, both quoted by Ṭabarī (died 923), in a tenth- or eleventh-century work called *Akhbār al-zamān*, and by 'genealogists' cited by Ibn Khaldūn (died 1406).[43] In some Islamic sources Canaan himself is envisaged as the ancestor of black people, a view perhaps influenced by an eastern Christian work, *The Cave of Treasures*, a book originally compiled in Syriac in the third or fourth century CE in which the connection between black people and slavery is implicit, and becoming more explicit in later recensions.[44]

During the later mediaeval period Christian interpretation understood the curse of Canaan as providing an aetiology of serfdom, rather than anything with racial overtones.[45] However, during the sixteenth and especially the seventeenth century Canaan essentially dropped out of the story and it started to become common among Christian biblical commentators and preachers for Noah's curse to be understood as being uttered directly against Ham, who was understood to be black.[46] Coming alongside the development of the African slave trade, this interpretation was to have devastating consequences. Thomas Newton (1704–1782), an English cleric and biblical scholar who eventually became Bishop of Bristol, went so far as to emend the Hebrew text of Gen. 9.25 so as to read 'Ham, the father of Canaan' rather than 'Canaan' as the object of Noah's curse. This was in the first volume of his *Dissertations on the Prophecies*, published in 1754. In support of his view he appealed to the Arabic version of the Bible, certain Septuagint manuscripts, the alleged opinion of the sixteenth-century scholar François Vatablus, and Hebrew metre, but his arguments were weak.[47] Nevertheless, Newton's work was one of those appealed to by Americans in the southern states seeking to defend black slavery. It was indeed in the nineteenth century, up to the

43. For full details, see Goldenberg, *The Curse of Ham*, p. 170, with pp. 350-51 nn. 10-17.
44. See Goldenberg, *The Curse of Ham*, pp. 172-74.
45. See D.M. Whitford, *The Curse of Ham in the Early Modern Era: The Bible and the Justifications for Slavery* (St Andrews Studies in Reformation History; Farnham: Ashgate, 2009), pp. 19-42.
46. See Whitford, *The Curse of Ham*, pp. 77-104.
47. On Newton and the curse of Ham, see Whitford, *The Curse of Ham*, pp. 140-69, who highlights the weaknesses in Newton's arguments on pp. 150-60.

time of the Civil War, that the notion of Noah's curse of Ham became particularly prominent and was highly influential in the American south in providing an apparent scriptural basis for the enslavement of black people.[48] This continued even after the Civil War, as, for example, in the case of Benjamin M. Palmer, a prominent Presbyterian pastor in New Orleans from 1856 to 1902, who proclaimed throughout this period the mental and moral degradation of Ham's black progeny and their divine sentence to perpetual servitude.[49] Over against this, those in favour of the abolition of slavery argued that the use of Genesis 9 in this connection was unjustified, noting among other things that the curse was directed at Canaan rather than Ham, and that it was Kush, not Canaan, who was the ancestor of the black African nations. Moreover, it was pointed out that Nimrod, a grandson of Ham, was a mighty man, and clearly not cursed! However, even in the twentieth century the so-called curse of Ham continued to be appealed to by American segregationists, as well as by some Boers and the Dutch Reformed Church in South Africa in justi-fication of apartheid. All this goes to show how people are capable of finding support in the Bible for anything they fancy, and it also high-lights the necessity for responsible biblical exegesis.

48. On this see especially S.R. Haynes, *Noah's Curse: The Biblical Justification of American Slavery* (Religion in America Series; New York: Oxford University Press, 2001). Other studies include T.V. Peterson, *Ham and Japheth: The Mythic World of Whites in the Antebellum South* (ATLA Monograph Series, 12; Metuchen, NJ: The Scarecrow Press; London: American Theological Library Association, 1978), and S.A. Johnson, *The Myth of Ham in Nineteenth-Century American Christi-anity: Race, Heathens, and the People of God* (New York: Palgrave Macmillan, 2004).

49. On Palmer, see Haynes, *Noah's Curse*, pp. 125-60.

Chapter 10

WHERE WAS TARSHISH (GENESIS 10.4)?

1. *Introduction*

Genesis 10 gives us a list of about seventy names of nations and cities of the world, presented as the descendants of Noah's three sons, Shem, Ham and Japheth. In part of the chapter attributed to the P source, we read the following concerning the descendants of Japheth: 'The descendants of Javan: Elishah, Tarshish, Kittim, and Rodanim' (Gen. 10.4). Javan is a Hebrew form of the name Ionia, the location of the eastern Greeks in western Anatolia.

The last named place, Rodanim, is generally agreed to denote the people of the island of Rhodes, off the south-west coast of Anatolia. Although the Masoretic text has Dodanim, it is generally accepted that this is a simple corruption from Rodanim. The correct form Rodanim is represented by the Septuagint and Samaritan versions and some Hebrew manuscripts, as well as in the parallel list of places in 1 Chron. 1.7.[1]

The name Kittim certainly derives from Kition, a Cypriot city of Phoenician foundation and denotes Cyprus or a part of it in Old Testament passages (Num. 24.24; Isa. 23.1, 12; Jer. 2.10; Ezek. 27.6), though it was subsequently used for Macedonia (1 Macc. 1.1; 8.5) and the Romans (Dan. 11.30; Qumran), doubtless through later reinterpretations of Num. 24.24, which speaks of 'ships of Kittim' coming to attack the Near East.

That Elishah reflects an older name for Cyprus, Alashiya, seems very likely. After many years in which it had been suspected that Alashiya was Cyprus, or a part of Cyprus, because of its abundance of copper (cf. El-Amarna letters 33-36, 40, especially 35, and Papyrus Anastasi IV), this has been decisively proved by a petrographic analysis of the clay of the El-Amarna and Ugaritic tablets sent from Alashiya.[2] That the name

---

1. On G. Garbini's view that we should emend to Donanim, see below.
2. See Y. Goren, I. Finkelstein and N. Na'aman, 'The Location of Alashiya. Petrographic Analysis of the Tablets', *AJA* 107 (2003), pp. 233-55.

Alashiya was still used in the first millennium is shown by a fourth-century BCE Cypriot inscription from Tamassos referring to Apollo Alasiotas. Since Cyprus is represented by two names here and we know that its population consisted of both Phoenicians and Greeks, it is plausible to suppose that J.C. Greenfield was right in conjecturing that Kittim and Elishah designated respectively the Phoenician and Greek parts of Cyprus.[3]

However, E. Lipiński,[4] has suggested that Elishah reflects the name Ulysses, thereby denoting the island of Ithaca whence he came, but we have no evidence that Ithaca was ever called Ulysses. Older views now rejected include that of E. Meyer,[5] who believed Elishah denoted Carthage, and that this was reflected in Dido's alternative name Elissa. However, we likewise have no evidence that Carthage was called Elissa and it is difficult to see why it should be attributed to the Greeks (Gen. 1.4), since it remained a Phoenician site for many centuries until becoming a Roman colony in 146 BCE. Again, F. Schmidtke[6] equated Elishah with Elaiussa, a site on the coast of Cilicia, but this is not attested before the second century BCE. (Schmidtke identified it with Wilusa, a place attested in Hittite texts, but this is now equated with Ilios, i.e. Troy.) There is also nothing to be said for Josephus's equation of Elishah with the Aeolians (*Ant.* 1.127) or the view of P.-R. Berger[7] that it was Lissa in Crete.

But where was Tarshish? This is the first of many references in the Old Testament to the place name Tarshish, the others being in 1 Kgs 10.22; 22.49 (ET 48); Pss. 48.8 (ET 7); 72.10; Jer. 10.9; Ezek. 27.12, 25; 38.13; Jon. 1.3; 4.2; 1 Chron. 1.7; 7.10; 2 Chron. 9.21; 20.36-37; Isa. 2.16; 23.1, 6, 10, 14; 60.9; 66.19. Although a number of locations have been proposed, for a long time the consensus has been that Tarshish was located at Tartessos at the mouth of the Guadalquivir in southern Spain,[8]

3. J.C. Greenfield, 'Elishah', in *IDB* 2, p. 92.

4. E. Lipiński, 'Les Japhétites selon Gen 10,1-4 et 1 Chr 1,5-7', *ZAH* 3 (1990), pp. 40-53 (50-51).

5. E. Meyer, *Geschichte des Alterthums* (5 vols.; Stuttgart: J.G. Cotta, 1884–1902 [1884]), I, p. 341.

6. F. Schmidtke, *Die Japhetiten der biblischen Völkertafel* (Breslauer Studien zur historischen Theologie, 7; Breslau: Müller & Seiffert, 1926), pp. 69-70.

7. P.-R. Berger, 'Ellasar, Tarschich und Jawan, Gn 14 und Gn 10', *WO* 13 (1982), pp. 50-78 (57-60).

8. See, e.g., H. Wildberger, *Jesaja Kapitel 13–27* (BKAT, 10.2; Neukirchen–Vluyn: Neukirchener Verlag, 1978), pp. 869-70, ET *Isaiah 13–27* (trans. T.H. Trapp; Continental Commentary; Minneapolis: Fortress Press, 1997), p. 422; M. Koch, *Tarschisch und Hispanien* (Madrider Forschungen, 14; Berlin: W. de Gruyter, 1984);

but in recent years a number of scholars, including Arie van der Kooij and André Lemaire, have reargued the older view (first attested in Josephus, *War* 7.23; *Ant.* 1.127; 9.208) that it should be equated with Tarsus in Cilicia.[9] H.G.M. Williamson, while referring to Tarshish as being 'across the Mediterranean' in his Chronicles commentary, which possibly indicates that he had Tartessos in mind, has been persuaded that it was Tarsus in his more recent Isaiah commentary.[10] The purpose of the present chapter is to reinvestigate this matter.

2. *Tartessos or Tarsus?*

First I shall consider Psalm 72, a psalm whose implication that Tarshish was in the far west has often been overlooked. Speaking of the universal extent of the king's reign, as ideally conceived, v. 8 declares: 'May he have dominion from sea to sea, and from the river to the ends of the earth'. This is further explicated in vv. 10-11: 'May the kings of Tarshish and the isles render him tribute, may the kings of Sheba and Seba bring gifts. May all kings fall before him, all nations give him service.' Quite clearly Tarshish and the isles on the one hand and Sheba and Seba on the other represent the furthest known parts of the world ('the ends of the earth'). Sheba is Saba in southern Arabia (the modern Yemen) and Seba in east Africa certainly represent the most remote places in a southerly direction. Tarshish and the isles must correspondingly be located in the furthest known western part of the Mediterranean sea, seeing that the Old Testament regularly depicts Tarshish as being in the west (with the

M. Elat, 'Tarshish and the Problem of Phoenician Colonisation in the Western Mediterranean', *OLP* 13 (1989), pp. 55-69; E. Lipiński, *Itineraria Phoenicia* (OLA, 127, Studia Phoenicia, 18; Leuven: Peeters, 2004), pp. 225-65. Although S. Bochart is often said to have been the first to equate Tarshish with Tartessus, this actually goes back much earlier to Hippolytus and others; see Lipiński, *Itineraria Phoenicia*, pp. 233-34.

9. A. van der Kooij, *The Oracle of Tyre: The Septuagint of Isaiah XXIII as Version and Vision* (VTSup, 71; Leiden: Brill, 1998), pp. 40-47; A. Lemaire, 'Tarshish-*Tarsisi*: problème de topographie historique biblique et assyrienne', in G. Galil and M. Weinfeld (eds.), *Studies in Historical Geography and Biblical Historiography Presented to Zecharia Kallai* (VTSup, 81; Leiden: Brill, 2000), pp. 44-62. Cf. too A. Andrew Das, 'Paul of Tarsus: Isaiah 66.19 and the Spanish Mission of Romans 15.24, 28', *NTS* 54 (2008), pp. 60-73.

10. H.G.M. Williamson, *1 and 2 Chronicles* (NCB; Grand Rapids, MI: Eerdmans: Marshall, Morgan & Scott, 1982), p. 235; *idem*, *A Critical and Exegetical Commentary on Isaiah 1–27*. I. *Isaiah 1–5* (ICC; London: T&T Clark International, 2006), pp. 226-27 n. 109.

exception of the late Chronicler). This simply does not fit Tarsus, which could hardly represent one of the most distant parts of the world, being not so far away and more or less due north from Joppa. However, it does fit Tartessos, which was similarly regarded as the furthermost known place in the west (cf. Strabo, *Geog.* 3.2.12). A number of places further west than Tarsus are cited elsewhere in the Old Testament, for example, Crete (Caphtor), Rhodes (Rodanim), Ionia (Javan), Libya (Lubim, Lehabim, Put) and Lydia (Lud), most of which are mentioned in passages that also refer to Tarshish, so we should certainly expect Tarshish to be further west than all of those. Similarly in the book of Jonah we read that in order to avoid his divine call to preach to the Ninevites, the prophet boarded a ship at Joppa going to Tarshish, away from the presence of the Lord. Nineveh, the capital of Assyria, was of course to the north-east of Israel, and if Jonah were heading for Tarsus he would actually have been going nearer to Nineveh than if he had stayed in Joppa! A voyage to the furthest known place in the Mediterranean, as indicated by Psalm 72, would have been far more appropriate for Jonah's purpose. Curiously, the discussions by both van der Kooij and Lemaire of the location of Tarshish fail to discuss these implications of Psalm 72 and Jonah.

The next piece of evidence bearing on the location of Tarshish which I shall consider is an inscription of King Esarhaddon of Assyria, c. 671 BCE,[11] which states that 'All the kings from amidst the sea—from Cyprus, Ionia, as far as Tarsisi—bowed to my feet and I received heavy tribute from them'. It is clear from this that Tarsisi (universally agreed to be Tarshish) must be the most distant place named, and west of Ionia, just as Ionia is west of Cyprus. Consequently it is impossible to equate it with Tarsus, which would rather have been the nearest of these places from Assyria's point of view. Van der Kooij's denial that this is the case is inadmissible, while Lemaire does not adequately discuss the implications of Esarhaddon's statement.[12] Moreover, we know that Tarsus was spelled *trz* (Tarz) in Aramaic on fifth-century BCE coins from Tarsus[13]

11. Cf. R. Borger, *Die Inschriften Asarhaddons, Königs von Assyrien* (AfO, 9; Graz: Im Selbstverlage des Herausgebers, 1956), p. 86. The translation by A.L. Oppenheim in *ANET*, p. 290 reads, 'All the kings from (the islands) amidst the sea—from the country Iadnana (Cyprus), as far as Tarsisi, bowed to my feet and I received heavy tribute from them', omitting the reference to Ionia, but this is clearly a slip.

12. Van der Kooij, *The Oracle of Tyre*, p. 43; Lemaire 'Tarshish-*Tarsis*', pp. 49-50, 53.

13. E. Babelon, *Catalogue des monnaies grecques de la Bibliothèque Nationale: Les Perses Achéménides* (Paris: Rollin & Feuardent, 1893), pp. xxvi, 17-18.

and Tarzi or Tarzu in Neo-Assyrian inscriptions,[14] which further distinguishes it from Tarsisi. Furthermore Tarzi/Tarzu is designated a city and Tarsisi a country in Akkadian. Van der Kooij and Lemaire[15] point out that the Hittite spelling was Tarsha, but this is a non-Semitic spelling dating from the pre-biblical period. Moreover, the Aramaic and Akkadian names (like the Hittite) confirm that *–s* at the end of the Greek form Tarsos (whence we get the form Tarsus) is simply a Greek ending, thus further heightening the difference from Tarshish. It might be thought that Tartessos in Spain was outside the Assyrian sphere of influence.[16] However, reference to tribute being brought from Tartessos becomes intelligible when we recall that Esarhaddon mentions this in the context of his conquest of Tyre: Tartessos was a Phoenician colony, so in conquering Tyre Esarhaddon could lay claim to her dependent colonies as well, even if this was true only in a nominal sense.

It is interesting to observe that in Isaiah 23, which very likely refers to the same fall of Tyre as Esarhaddon's inscription,[17] not only are the ships of Tarshish told to lament (vv. 1, 14), but Tarshish itself is somehow affected by the event (v. 10). Moreover, the inhabitants of Tyre are encouraged to escape to Tarshish (v. 6), just as they are told to flee to Kittim (v. 12). Since Kition, whence the name Kittim derives, was a Phoenician (indeed Tyrian) colony, it makes excellent sense if Tarshish was so too. This was indeed the case with Tartessos, as both classical sources and archaeology attest,[18] but not so with Tarsus, even though the Phoenicians had dealings with it.

It is sometimes claimed[19] that an identification of Tarshish with Tarsus fits better with the references to the places mentioned alongside it in

14. S. Parpola, *Neo-Assyrian Toponyms* (AOAT, 6; Neukirchen–Vluyn: Neukirchener Verlag; Kevelaer: Butzon & Bercker, 1970), p. 349.

15. Van der Kooij, *The Oracle of Tyre*, pp. 44-45; Lemaire, 'Tarshish-*Tarsisi*', p. 54.

16. Van der Kooij, *The Oracle of Tyre*, p. 43; Lemaire, 'Tarshish-*Tarsisi*', p. 52.

17. So Wildberger, *Jesaja Kapitel 13–27*, pp. 864-66, ET *Isaiah 13–27*, pp. 417-19; R.E. Clements, *Isaiah 1–39* (NCB; Grand Rapids, MI: Eerdmans: Marshall, Morgan & Scott, 1982), pp. 191-92.

18. Cf. A. Schulten, *Tartessos* (Hamburg: W. de Gruyter, 1950); Maria E. Aubet, *The Phoenicians and the West* (trans. M. Turton; Cambridge: Cambridge University Press, 2nd edn, 2001); Ann Neville, *Mountains of Silver & Rivers of Gold: The Phoenicians in Iberia* (Oxford: Oxbow Books, 2007); M. Dietler and C. López-Ruiz (eds.), *Colonial Encounters in Ancient Iberia* (Chicago: University of Chicago Press, 2009).

19. E.g. van der Kooij, *The Oracle of Tyre*, pp. 41-43; Lemaire, 'Tarshish-*Tarsisi*', pp. 48-49; Williamson, *Isaiah 1–27*, I, p. 227 n. 109.

Ezek. 27.12-14, Isa. 66.19 and Gen. 10.4. However, with regard to Ezekiel 27, it should be noted that Tarshish is mentioned alongside Ionia (v. 12), and Rhodes is mentioned shortly afterwards in v. 15, just as is Libya (Put) shortly before in v. 10. In the light of Tarshish's reputation as the furthest known western place (Ps. 72.10), Tarshish must be further west than all of these, which simply does not fit Tarsus. Furthermore, we should note that Ezek. 27.12-24 is a distinct unit listing Tyre's trading partners, moving broadly from west to east. It is therefore significant that Tarshish is the very first place mentioned, suggesting it was indeed the furthest west. However, this pattern would be broken if we were to locate Tarshish at Tarsus rather than Tartessos. Moreover, as classical sources attest, the Phoenicians were famous for their trade with Tartessos, so it would be surprising for this place not to be mentioned in Ezekiel 27. As for Isa. 66.19, Tarshish is mentioned alongside Libya (Put[20]) and Lydia (Lud), so Tarshish ought to be to the west of both of those, which again does not fit Tarsus but would cohere with Tartessos.

Finally, returning to Gen. 10.4, I would argue that Tarshish—as the furthest known place in the west—must be to the west of Ionia, Rhodes and Cyprus, which are also mentioned in this verse. Interestingly, the names of the sons of Javan (Ionia) come in two pairs here, 'Elishah and Tarshish, Kittim and Rodanim'.[21] As noted earlier, Elishah and Kittim refer to two different parts of Cyprus, so it is clear that the list is not in strict geographical order, since Tarshish intervenes between them. Rather, P has divided the names into two groups on the basis of their being singular or plural. With regard to these pairings, P.-E. Dion,[22] suggested that Kittim and Rodanim are modernizing terms added by P to explain the preceding names Elishah and Tarshish. In this way he tries to account for there being two references to Cyprus here, but it also follows that he believes Rodanim (Rhodes) is a modernizing term for Tarshish.[23] However, the argument is weak. Not only are there no grounds for

20. The MT has 'Pul', which is otherwise unknown. It is widely accepted that we should follow the LXX in reading 'Put', which is several other times mentioned alongside Lydia (Lud or Ludim, Jer. 46.9; Ezek. 27.10; 30.5), as in Isa. 66.19.

21. The MT has Dodanim, but, as noted above, it is generally accepted that we should read Rodanim with the LXX, Samaritan version and some Hebrew manuscripts, as well as the parallel text in 1 Chron. 1.7.

22. P.-E. Dion, 'Les *KTYM* de Tel Arad: Grecs ou Phéniciens?', *RB* 99 (1992), pp. 70-97 (84-85).

23. However, on p. 84 n. 84 Dion identifies Tarshish with Tarsus, at any rate probably for Isa. 23; regarding this latter, see my arguments in favour of Tartessos above.

believing that Tarshish was regarded as an archaic term—it continued to be used in the post-exilic period in Jonah as well as in different parts of Third Isaiah (in addition to Chronicles)—but it clearly cannot be equated with Rhodes. This is not only because nowhere else in Genesis 10 does P provide two names for the same place—as Dion himself concedes[24]—but also because in Ezekiel 27 the prophet (who is similar in date and outlook to P) refers to Kittim and Elishah as two distinct places (vv. 6, 7), as he also does with regard to Tarshish and Rhodes (vv. 12, 15).[25] On the other hand, G. Garbini[26] has argued that Tarshish in Gen. 10.4 is to be equated with Tarsus, even though he admits that Tarshish was elsewhere equivalent to Tartessos (though he does not discuss which passages). Garbini regards both Elishah and Kittim as representing Cyprus and holds that it would be appropriate for Tarsus in nearby Cilicia to be mentioned alongside them. Dodanim, usually emended to Rodanim (Rhodes; see above n. 21), Garbini prefers to read as Donanim, supposing this likewise to be in Cilicia (cf. *dnnym* in the Karatepe inscription, *KAI* 26). However, this emendation is entirely conjectural, without supporting evidence. Moreover, we have already seen above that the Semitic forms of the name of Tarsus do not cohere with Tarshish. It is more natural to suppose that Tarshish in Gen. 10.4 is the same Tarshish mentioned elsewhere in the Old Testament.

It is to be noted that in Gen. 10.4 Tarshish is listed under the sons of Javan (Ionia), whereas in Isaiah 23 it is closely aligned with Tyre. This is to be explained by the fact that between the mid-seventh century and the time of the Priestly source Tartessos had come under Greek influence, as archaeology attests (cf. Herodotus, *Hist.* 1.163; 4.152).[27] Similarly Kittim is listed as a son of Javan in Gen. 10.4, although its centre, Kition, was originally a Phoenician colony. Contrary to Gordon Wenham,[28] therefore, there is no problem in Tartessos being attributed to the Greeks in Gen. 10.4.

24. Dion, 'Les *KTYM* de Tel Arad', p. 85.
25. In Ezek. 27.15 it is generally agreed that we should read 'Rhodians' (*b^{e}nê rōdān*) with the LXX rather than MT's Dedanites (*b^{e}nê d^{e}dān*). Dedan is mentioned a few verses later in Ezek. 27.20 alongside other Arabian locations. It is therefore out of place in v. 15, where it is immediately followed by a reference to 'many coastlands/islands', phraseology associated elsewhere with the Mediterranean.
26. Cf. G. Garbini, 'Tarsis e Gen. 10,4', *BeO* 7 (1965), pp. 13-19.
27. See Y.B. Tsirkin, 'The Greeks and Tartessos', *Oikumene* 5 (1986), pp. 163-71.
28. G.J. Wenham, *Genesis 1–15* (WBC, 1; Waco, TX: Word Books, 1987), p. 202.

Although I have repeatedly noted above that Tarsus is much too far to the east to accommodate the Old Testament's references to Tarshish, since so many other places further west are also referred to (Libya, Crete, Rhodes, Lydia, Ionia), we still need to provide an answer to Lemaire's question why, if Tarshish is Tartessos, the Old Testament has no references to other western places like Malta, Sicily, Sardinia and Carthage.[29] The answer is, I think, fairly simple. It was only quite late that Carthage came to prominence, and Malta, Sicily and Sardinia were not well known to the Israelites. On the other hand, Tartessos was well known to the Israelites because of its important sources of silver and other metals procured by the Phoenicians. Interestingly, the metals referred to as being extracted from Tarshish agree perfectly with Tartessos. The Old Testament states that Tarshish was the source of silver, iron, tin and lead (Ezek. 27.12), and Jer. 10.9 again singles out especially silver, and it should also be noted that a pre-exilic Hebrew ostracon (variously dated to c. 800 or c. 620 BCE) refers to 'silver of Tarshish for the temple of Yahweh: 3 sh(ekels)'.[30] Probably Isa. 60.9 also associates silver (as well as gold) with Tarshish. Similarly, ancient classical sources highlight Tartessos's wealth of silver in particular (Strabo, *Geog.* 3.2.11; Diodorus Siculus, *Univ. Hist.* 5.35) but also other metals. In addition to silver, Pliny, *Nat. Hist.* 3.3 mentions lead, iron, copper and gold, while Avienus, *Ora Maritima* 293 cites it as a source of tin. However, Lemaire points out that these same metals were also associated with the Taurus mountains north of Tarsus.[31] Against this, however, it may be noted that while the Phoenicians were familiar with Tarsus, ancient classical sources nowhere single it out as a special trading place for metals used by the Phoenicians in the way they do with Tartessos.

Interestingly, the phrase 'ships of Tarshish' (1 Kgs 10.22; 22.49 [ET 48]; Isa. 2.16; 23.1, 14; 60.9; Ezek. 27.25; Ps. 48.8 [ET 7]) is a further indication that Tarshish was a very remote place. The implication of these references that the ships of Tarshish were particularly impressive, going to Ophir and other exotic places, indicates that they were large boats capable of going long distances. Since they are named 'ships of Tarshish' this suggests that Tarshish was a similarly remote place, which fits Tartessos admirably but does not cohere very well with Tarsus.

29. Lemaire, 'Tarshish-*Tarsisi*', p. 52.

30. P. Bordreuil, F. Israel and D. Pardee, 'Deux ostraca paléo-hébreux de la collection Sh. Moussaieff', *Sem* 46 (1996), pp. 49-76 (49-61); H. Shanks, 'Three Shekels for the Lord: Ancient Inscriptions Record Gift to Solomon's Temple', *BARev* 23.6 (1997), pp. 28-32.

31. See Lemaire, 'Tarshish-*Tarsisi*', pp. 55-57.

Strikingly, Herodotus, *Hist.* 1.163 informs us that the Phocaeans, 'the pioneer navigators of the Greeks', used special ships to go to Tartessos. He states: 'They used to sail not in deep, broad-beamed merchant vessels but in fifty-oared galleys'. Such special ships would not have been needed for a journey from Israel to Tarsus, which could be reached by coastal shipping.[32]

It has been widely accepted that the Semitic and Greek names Tarshish and Tartessos[33] are perfectly compatible philologically, though without spelling out why, Lemaire claims they are not. However, *–os* is readily understood as a Greek ending, and of course Greek does not have the letter *sh*, naturally rendering by *s* or *ss*. With regard to the *t* in the middle of Tartessos in place of *sh*, this can be explained if the name is indigenous in origin, with this sound being variously reproduced in Semitic and Greek renderings.

3. *Other Minority Views*

We have concluded that throughout the Old Testament Tarshish is Tartessos in Spain, not Tarsus in Cilicia. However, before we consider the variant location found in the Chronicler, we need briefly to note the objections to various minority viewpoints that have been suggested. Thus C.H. Gordon[34] proposed that Tarshish is not a place at all but a name for the sea. However, the contexts in which the word occurs clearly indicate a definite location, as real as the other places mentioned alongside it. It has also very occasionally been suggested that Tarshish was in India[35] or Ethiopia,[36] but both views conflict with the evidence of the Old Testament and Esarhaddon's inscription that it was somewhere in the west. One minority view that does locate it in the west is that of P.-R. Berger,[37] who thought it was Carthage, as did the Septuagint on a few occasions.[38]

---

32. Cf. Schmidtke, *Die Japhetiten der biblischen Völkertafel*, p. 71.

33. Lemaire, 'Tarshish-*Tarsisi*', p. 52.

34. C.H. Gordon, 'The Wine-Dark Sea', *JNES* 37 (1978), pp. 51-52; similarly S.B. Hoenig, 'Tarshish', *JQR* 69 (1979), pp. 181-82.

35. J.M. Blázquez, *Tartessos y los orígenes de la colonización fenicia en occidente* (Acta Salamanticensia, Filosofía y Letras, 58; Salamanca: Universidad de Salamanca, 2nd edn, 1975), pp. 15-21.

36. Origen, Psalmus LXXI.9 (= LXXII.10), in *PG* 12 (1862), col. 1524, though he says Tarshish in Jonah is Tarsus.

37. Berger, 'Ellasar, Tarschisch und Jawan, Gn 14 und Gn 10', pp. 61-65.

38. Generally the Septuagint transliterates the name, but in Isa. 23.1, 6, 10, 14 it renders it as 'Carthage' and in Ezek. 27.12, 25; 38.13 by 'Carthaginians'. It is significant that in both Isa. 23 and Ezek. 27 the allusions are in connection with the

However, quite apart from its relative unimportance during the period of many of the Old Testament's allusions to Tarshish, it is difficult to understand why Gen. 10.4 should represent Carthage as a son of Javan (Ionia), since it was a Phoenician site for many centuries until becoming a Roman colony in 146 BCE; furthermore, it was never noted for its silver. Another view, proposed by A. Knobel, identified Tarshish in Gen. 10.4 and probably Isa. 66.19 with the habitation of the Etruscans in Italy,[39] though elsewhere he saw Tarshish as Tartessos. However, apart from the fact that there is insufficient evidence to justify distinguishing more than one Tarshish, the name of the Etruscans (Greek Tursenoi), which seems to derive from that of the Tursha, one of the Sea peoples, lacks a final *s* or *sh*, unlike Tarshish. G. Bunnens[40] supposes that the name Tarshish was applied to various places in the far west. However, though the general location is correct, once again there is insufficient evidence to distinguish more than one Tarshish. W.F. Albright,[41] while accepting that the biblical Tarshish and Assyrian Tarsisi are probably Tartessos, believed that the root meaning was 'refinery' and that the name could be applied to various places, including Tarshish in the Nora stone, which he believed was Nora itself, in southern Sardinia. The Nora stone contains a Phoenician inscription dated palaeographically to the ninth or early eighth century BCE. Although the precise translation of the text as a whole is disputed, it is widely agreed that it contains a reference to both 'in Tarshish' and 'in Sardinia'. It appears to refer to someone who was in Tarshish being banished to Sardinia,[42] in which case Tarshish

Phoenician city-state of Tyre, which had extensive trading connections with the west. Moreover, Carthage had an importance in the second century BCE (up till its destruction in 146 BCE), which it did not have at the time of the original composition of Isa. 23 and Ezek. 27. It is therefore understandable how the Septuagint mistook the original meaning of Tarshish here.

39. A. Knobel, *Die Völkertafel der Genesis* (Giessen: J. Ricker, 1850), pp. 86-94; *idem, Die Genesis erklärt* (Kurzgefasstes exegetisches Handbuch zum Alten Testament; Leipzig: S. Hirzel, 2nd edn, 1860), pp. 111-12.

40. G. Bunnens, *L'expansion phénicienne en Méditerranée* (Brussels: Institut historique belge de Rome, 1979), pp. 347-48.

41. W.F. Albright, 'The Role of the Canaanites in the History of Civilization', in G.E. Wright (ed.), *The Bible in the Ancient Near East: Essays in Honor of William Foxwell Albright* (Garden City, NY: Doubleday, 1961), pp. 328-62 (346-47); *idem,* 'New Light on the Early History of Phoenician Colonization', *BASOR* 83 (1941), pp. 14-22 (21). Albright's view that Tarshish means 'refinery', appealing to Akkadian *rašāšu*, 'to melt', has gained little following.

42. On the Nora stone see, e.g., B. Peckham, 'The Nora Inscription', *Or* 41 (1972), pp. 457-68; F.M. Cross, 'An Interpretation of the Nora Stone', *BASOR* 208 (1972), pp. 13-19; G.W. Ahlström, 'The Nora Inscription and Tarshish', *Maarav* 7

is being contrasted rather than equated with Sardinia. Incidentally, we have other evidence linking Tartessos with Sardinia,[43] which might favour Tarshish being Tartessos here.

4. *The Divergent View of the Chronicler*

However, an alternative location is presupposed in the Chronicler, who wrongly supposed that Tarshish was to be reached by going south along the Red Sea. This is clear from both 2 Chron. 9.21 and 20.36-37, where he misunderstood the references in his *Vorlage* in 1 Kings to ships of Tarshish to mean ships going to Tarshish. Thus, in 2 Chron. 20.36-37 King Jehoshaphat of Judah joined King Ahaziah of Israel in building ships at Ezion-geber (on the Red Sea) to go to Tarshish, but the ships were wrecked and so unable to go to Tarshish. The underlying *Vorlage* in 1 Kgs 22.49 (ET 48), however, states explicitly that the ships of Tarshish destroyed at Ezion-geber were intended to go to Ophir, which was located somewhere on the coast of the Arabian peninsula (cf. Gen. 10.29).[44] Similarly, 2 Chron. 9.21 speaks of Solomon's ships going with the servants of Huram [*sic*] every three years to Tarshish, bringing back gold, silver, ivory, apes and peacocks. The nature of some of these objects again indicates a destination reached along the Red Sea, not the Mediterranean (probably Ophir; cf. 1 Kgs 9.26-28 = 2 Chron. 8.17-19), but the Chronicler has again misunderstood a reference in his underlying source in 1 Kgs 10.22 to ships of Tarshish, taking it to mean ships going to Tarshish. This is rightly recognized in both cases by commentators such as H.G.M. Williamson,[45] but whereas Sara Japhet[46] rightly considers the Chronicler to have mislocated Tarshish along the shore of the Red

(1991), pp. 41-49; W.H. Shea, 'The Dedication on the Nora Stone', *VT* 41 (1991), pp. 241-45; A.J. Frendo, 'The Particles *beth* and *waw* and the Periodic Structure of the Nora Stone Inscription', *PEQ* 128 (1996), pp. 8-11.

43. J.B. Tsirkin, 'The Phoenicians and Tartessos', *Gerión* 15 (1997), pp. 243-51 (247).

44. This is widely accepted and supported by the context of the reference to Ophir in Gen. 10.29 and coheres with 1 Kgs 9.26-28 and 22.49 (ET 48), which indicate that it was reached via the Red Sea. I am unconvinced by E. Lipiński, *Itineraria Phoenicia*, pp. 189-223, who dismisses these biblical allusions as unreliable and locates Ophir on the Mediterranean coast of North Africa. Since gold is not actually found there, he proposes that this North African Ophir was merely a distribution point for gold which had been brought overland from West Africa.

45. Williamson, *1 and 2 Chronicles*, pp. 235, 303.

46. Sara Japhet, *1 & II Chronicles* (OTL; London: SCM Press, 1993), pp. 641, 802.

Sea in 2 Chron. 20.36-37, she inconsistently assumes that he places it in the western Mediterranean in 2 Chron. 9.21. Raymond Dillard is worse in that he fails to comment on the location of Tarshish in 2 Chron. 20.36-37, merely referring the reader to his comment on 2 Chron. 9.21, where he states that 'It is not necessary to conclude that the author was ignorant either of the type of the vessel or of the geography'.[47] Dillard does not properly explain how this can be the case, but his comment in the Introduction that 'the Bible does not lie... It is without error in all that it teaches'[48] shows where he is coming from. Anyway, what we have seen in the Chronicler demonstrates that by c. 300 BCE the location of Tarshish was being forgotten.

5. *Conclusion*

The place names mentioned in Gen. 10.4, Elishah, Tarshish, Kittim and Rodanim, are not listed in geographical order, rather, the first two represent Mediterranean place names in the singular and the latter two Mediterranean place names in the plural, the first and third representing different parts of Cyprus and the second and fourth places further west. There is every reason to maintain the traditional view that Tarshish in Gen. 10.4, as well as everywhere else in the Old Testament except in the late Chronicler (who thought it was to be reached down the Red Sea), is to be equated with Tartessos in southern Spain. The recent revival of the old view that Tarshish is Tarsus simply will not do. It is insufficiently far away to satisfy a number of the indications provided by the Old Testament and an inscription of Esar-haddon. It is true that it is rather remote compared with many other places mentioned in the Old Testament, but the Israelites became aware of it because it was an important source of silver and other precious metals brought back by the Phoenicians.

---

47. R.B. Dillard, *2 Chronicles* (WBC, 15; Waco, TX: Word Books), pp. 73, 160.
48. Dillard, *2 Chronicles*, p. xviii.

Chapter 11

THE TOWER AND CITY OF BABEL STORY (GENESIS 11.1-9):
PROBLEMS OF INTERPRETATION AND BACKGROUND

1. *Introduction*

The famous story in Gen. 11.1-9 is constantly referred to as that of 'the tower of Babel'. Curiously enough, this precise phrase never occurs anywhere in the narrative, though it certainly refers to the building of a particularly high tower as well as a city in Babel. What is a little peculiar is that in our English Bibles the word Babel, a simple transliteration of the Hebrew, is used here to denote the place, whereas elsewhere the word is rendered appropriately as Babylon (a form of the name derived from Greek). The only other exception is in the previous chapter, Gen. 10.10, where English Bibles similarly tend to use Babel rather than Babylon to denote one of the Mesopotamian king Nimrod's cities. This curiosity of the English Bible goes back many centuries, and is attested at least as far back as the Wycliffe Bible in the fourteenth century. The same distinction is also found in translations into other European languages (apart, of course, from those for which Babel is the regular term for Babylon anyway). For whatever reason it started, we have to assume that the phrase 'tower of Babel' so caught on that it became normative in English and some other languages to render it thus rather than 'tower of Babylon'.

As mentioned, the narrative actually speaks of a city as well as a tower being built in Babel (Gen. 11.4, 5), while Gen. 11.8 mentions simply the city, stating 'and they left off building the city', though *a fortiori* work on the tower would also have ceased.[1] Years ago Hermann Gunkel argued that our narrative in Gen. 11.1-9 is made up of what were originally two different stories, one about a city and the other about a tower.[2]

1. The Samaritan and LXX versions also include the tower in Gen. 11.8 but this is due to later harmonization, as shown by the fact that the very next sentence continues 'Therefore *it* was called Babel...'

2. H. Gunkel, *Genesis* (HKAT, 1.1; Göttingen: Vandenhoeck & Ruprecht, 3rd edn, 1910), pp. 92-97, ET *Genesis* (trans. M.E. Biddle; Macon, GA: Mercer University Press, 1997), pp. 94-99. Over the years a number of scholars, especially

He saw the story of city building in vv. 1, 3a, 4aαγ, 6aα, 7, 8b and 9a, and the account of tower building in vv. 2, 4aβb, 5, 6aβb, 8a, and 9b. There seems, however, no solid reason to follow this speculation, and it is now generally rejected. The story reads perfectly well as it stands and has none of the contradictions, doublets or other inconsistencies characteristic of composite narratives. Although vv. 5 and 7 both speak of Yahweh coming down, these are not mere doublets but speak of successive events in God's purposes, first to see the city and tower that the men have built, and then in order to confuse the language of the people. Moreover, vv. 8a and 9b would constitute an awkwardly repetitive ending for the tower story, so Gunkel was forced to interpolate between them a hypothetical passage in which the tower was said to be named Pîṣ (Dispersion)!

More recently, Klaus Seybold proposed an alternative view of the redactional growth of Gen. 11.1-9.[3] According to Seybold, the original story is contained within vv. 2-4a, 5-6aαβ, 6aε-7, 8b-9aα. This was followed by a first redaction from J, which saw the addition of vv. 1, 6aγ, 9aβ concerning the confusion of tongues. Finally, a second redaction saw the addition of vv. 4b, 8a, 9b, where the dispersion of humanity is referred to. Again, however, this appears to be all too speculative, without solid evidence. Moreover, there is an inconsistency in Seybold's analysis in that the motif of the confusion of tongues is already mentioned in v. 7, part of his original story, so there is no need to assign the other allusions to it to a later redactor. Most now accept that there is no reason to doubt the essential unity of Gen. 11.1-9.

Within this unified narrative there is a clear division between vv. 1-4, which focus on the human building of the city and tower, and vv. 6-9, which concentrate on the divine reaction. Verse 5 clearly constitutes the turning point between the two halves, in which Yahweh comes down to observe the city and the tower. Now, within Gen. 11.1-9 there is a simple concentric structure as follows:[4]

---

in the German-speaking world, followed Gunkel. Although this view has now gone into serious decline, versions of it were still followed by L. Ruppert, *Genesis. I. Gen. 1,1–11,26* (FzB, 70; Würzburg: Echter Verlag, 1992), pp. 485-94, who thought a city recension was supplemented by a tower recension, and C. Rose, 'Nochmals: Der Turmbau zu Babel', *VT* 54 (2004), pp. 223-38, who maintained the reverse.

3. K. Seybold, 'Der Turmbau zu Babel. Zur Entstehung von Genesis xi 1-9', *VT* 26 (1976), pp. 453-79.

4. Noted, e.g., by Y.T. Radday, 'Chiasm in Tora', *Linguistica Biblica* 19 (1972), pp. 12-23 (15); I.M. Kikawada, 'The Shape of Genesis 11:1-9', in J.J. Jackson and M. Kessler (eds.), *Rhetorical Criticism: Essays in Honor of James Muilenburg* (Pittsburgh Theological Monograph Series, 1; Pittsburgh: Pickwick Press, 1974),

```
        A   vv. 1-2    Narrative
   B    vv. 3-4        Direct Speech
C       v. 5           Narrative Mid-point
   B'   vv. 6-7        Direct Speech
        A'  vv. 8-9    Narrative
```

The narrative in A' represents a reversal of the situation in A, with humanity now having many languages instead of one, and scattered over the whole earth instead of being in one place. Similarly, within the B and B' direct speech of the humans and God, in vv. 3-4 and 6-7 respectively, we can detect a certain symmetry, since both include speech in the cohortative form preceded by *hābâ*, 'come'. On all this there can be no disagreement.

However, there have been various attempts to spell out a more detailed and precise concentric structure. Thus, Jan P. Fokkelman, followed by Gordon J. Wenham, has argued for the following structure.[5]

```
Now the whole earth had one language   A (v. 1)
                          there  B (v. 2)
                 to one another  C (v. 3)
           Come, let us make bricks  D (v. 3)
        Let us build for ourselves  E (v. 4)
            a city and a tower  F (v. 4)
   The Lord came down to see  X (v. 5)
         the city and the tower  F' (v. 5)
      Which the men had built  E' (v. 5)
           Come…let us confuse  D' (v. 7)
            one another's speech  C' (v. 7)
                 from there  B' (v. 9)
(confused) the language of all the earth  A' (v. 9)
```

This structure appears quite striking at first sight. However, on closer observation we notice flaws in the scheme. For example, v. 6, which is rather a long verse, does not form part of the structure at all. Again, we

---

pp. 18-32 (19); W. Brueggemann, *Genesis* (Interpretation; Atlanta: Westminster/ John Knox Press, 1982), p. 98; C. Uehlinger, *Weltreich und «eine Rede»: Eine neue Deutung der sogenannten Turmbauerzählung (Gen 11,1-9)* (OBO, 101; Freiburg: Universitätsverlag; Göttingen: Vandenhoeck & Ruprecht, 1990), pp. 300-301; B.W. Anderson, 'The Tower of Babel: Unity and Diversity in God's Creation', in *idem, From Creation to New Creation* (OBT; Minneapolis: Fortress Press, 1994), pp. 165-78 (169-70); J. Blenkinsopp, *Creation, Un-Creation, Re-Creation: A Discursive Commentary on Genesis 1–11* (London: T&T Clark International, 2011), pp. 164-65.

    5. J.P. Fokkelman, *Narrative Art in Genesis: Specimens of Stylistic and Structural Analysis* (Studia Semitica Neerlandica, 17; Assen: Van Gorcum, 2nd edn, 1975; repr. The Biblical Seminar, 12; Sheffield: JSOT Press, 1991), pp. 11-32 (22-29); G.J. Wenham, *Genesis 1–15* (WBC, 1; Waco, TX: Word Books, 1987), p. 235.

notice that there is nothing from v. 8, and the important theme of the scattering of the people, which features there (v. 8a), as well as in vv. 4b and 9b, is excluded. One also notes that the only parallel in v. 2 is the word 'there'. Pierre Auffret was able to improve on this by pairing 'let us make' in v. 4 with 'to do' (same verb) in v. 6, as well as 'there' in v. 2 with 'from there' in v. 8.[6] However, even then, vv. 2, 6 and 8 have only one Hebrew word each in the scheme, so there is still much content that is excluded. Prior to Fokkelman, Radday had set out a more detailed concentric structure which attempted to include all parallels between the two halves of Gen. 11.1-9, but some of the parallels proved not to be in appropriate equivalent positions.[7] All this just goes to show that, though there is indeed a broad concentric structure within Gen. 11.1-9, it does not encompass everything.

It has also been proposed by Kikawada that there is additionally a sequential parallelism between the two halves of the narrative as follows:[8]

A	(v. 1)	one language
B	(v. 2)	there
C	(v. 3)	each other
D	(v. 4)	let us build a city
E	(v. 4)	a name
F	(v. 4)	lest we be scattered over the face of all the earth
A'	(v. 6)	one language
B'	(v. 7)	there
C'	(v. 7)	each other
D'	(v. 8)	from building the city
E'	(v. 9)	its name
F'	(v. 9)	he scattered them over the face of all the earth

Again, at first sight this looks fairly impressive, but it is to be observed that not everything is included. Only the word 'there' is used from v. 2, and only 'each other' from the whole of v. 3, which is a lengthy verse. Moreover, it is noteworthy that the striking parallel between 'Come' + cohortative in vv. 3 and 4 and 'Come' + cohortative in v. 7 do not form a parallel in Kikawada's scheme.

Alternatively, a slightly different sequential structure has been proposed by Fokkelman:[9]

6. P. Auffret, *La sagesse a bati sa maison* (OBO, 49; Fribourg: Editions universitaires; Göttingen: Vandenhoeck & Ruprecht, 1982), p. 74.
7. Radday, 'Chiasm in Torah', p. 15.
8. Kikawada, 'The Shape of Genesis 11:1-9', p. 26. This is followed by Wenham, *Genesis 1–15*, p. 235. Cf. Auffret, *La sagesse*. pp. 74-80.
9. Fokkelman, *Narrative Art in Genesis*, pp. 20-22.

A (v. 1) One language and the same words
B (v. 3) Come + cohortative (× 2)
C (v. 4) Let us build
D (v. 4) Let us make a name
E (v. 4) otherwise we shall be scattered abroad upon the face of the
          whole earth
A' (v. 6) they are one people, and they have all one language
B' (v. 7) Come + cohortative
C' (v. 8) and they left off building
D' (v. 9) its name Babel
E' (v. 9) the Lord scattered them abroad over the face of all the earth

Once again, however, we find that this does not encompass everything. Whereas, unlike Kikawada's, this sequential scheme is able to include the parallelism between 'Come' + cohortative in vv. 3 and 7, this is at the cost of having to omit the parallelism between "each other" in these same verses. Also, unlike all the other verses in the first half, v. 2 is not paralleled at all in the second half of the narrative.

2. The Tower as the Ziggurat at Babylon

According to Gen. 11.2, Babel is set in a plain in the land of Shinar (cf. Herodotus, *History* 1.178, where Babylon is similarly said to lie 'in a great plain'). We read that the inhabitants of the earth reached it by apparently journeying eastwards (*bᵉnosᶜām miqqedem*). Translators vary according to whether they translate *miqqedem* as 'from the east' (AV, Moffatt, RSV, NRSV, NJPS) or 'eastward(s)' (JB, NJB, NIV), 'east' (RV), or 'in the east' (NEB, REB, NAB). The problem is the preposition *min*. Although this most commonly means 'from', and 'from the east' is indeed followed in all the ancient Versions, scrutiny of the Hebrew Bible indicates that elsewhere *miqqedem* can mean 'eastward(s)' (Gen. 13.11), 'in the east' (Gen. 2.8) or 'on the east' (Zech. 14.4). The closest analogy is just two chapters later in another J narrative in Gen. 13.11, which similarly uses the verb *nsᶜ* with *miqqedem*, and here the meaning is indisputably 'eastward(s)', since it is used of Lot's journeying towards the plains of the Jordan, in contrast to Abram's settling in the land of Canaan (v. 12). A strong case can therefore be made that people journeyed eastwards to Shinar in Gen. 11.2. Compare the passage paralleling Gen. 11.2 in *Jub.* 10.19, 'For they departed from the land of Ararat *toward the east* into Shinar…'[10]

---

10. Cf. E.G. Kraeling, 'Miqqedem in Genesis XI 2', *JQR* 38 (1947–48), pp. 161-65, who defends the translation 'eastward(s)', as do BDB, KB and the new Gesenius dictionary. Contrast *HALAT (HALOT)* and *DCL*, which prefer 'from the east'.

As for the land of Shinar, it is generally agreed that this refers to Babylonia, since not only did it include the city of Babylon in our passage (Gen. 11.8), and the cities of Babylon, Erech, and Accad in Gen. 10.10, but it was also the place where Nebuchadrezzar II deported the king of Judah and the Jerusalem temple vessels in Dan. 1.2 (cf. Isa. 11.11, where Shinar is likewise one of the places of exile in a list which otherwise excludes Babylonia). Other references to Shinar are also compatible with this location (Gen. 14.1, 9; Josh. 7.21; Zech 5.11), and there is also considerable support in the ancient Versions for the equation of Shinar with Babylonia. Although at one time it was thought that the name Shinar was somehow connected to that of Sumer, this is difficult to defend philologically.[11] It is more satisfactory, as Ran Zadok has argued, to see it as equivalent to Akkadian *Šanḫara* and Egyptian *Sngr*, a name which appears to have originated in the Kassite period as a designation for Babylonia by those living west of the Euphrates, but was not employed in Mesopotamia itself.[12]

Many scholars accept that the tower of Babel is a reflection of the ziggurat at Babylon, which was by far the most impressive high building there, standing out above everything else. A ziggurat (a word ultimately deriving from Akkadian *zaqāru*, 'to be high') was a high temple tower constructed of several storeys, and was conceived as a staircase for the gods to ascend and descend between heaven and the earth or underworld, with the deity's dwelling at the top. Over thirty ziggurats are known from ancient Mesopotamia and its environs (mostly in modern Iraq, but also extending into Iran and Syria), the best preserved today being that at Ur.[13]

---

11.   A.H. Sayce, 'Assyriological Notes: No. 1', *PSEA* 18 (1896), pp. 173-74 (173) mentions that the Sumer view was originally proposed by 'Dr Haigh'. This must be Daniel Henry Haigh (1819–1879), who occasionally wrote on ancient Near Eastern topics, even though he was primarily an authority on Anglo-Saxon antiquities, history and literature. This view was later defended by Anton Deimel, 'Šumer = שִׁנְעָר', *Bib* 2 (1921), pp. 71-74.

12.   See R. Zadok, 'The Origin of the Name Shinar', *ZA* 74 (1984), pp. 240-44; similarly G. Wilhelm, 'Šanḫara', in *RLA* 12 (Berlin: W. de Gruyter, 2009), pp. 11-12. This equation was first made by A.H. Sayce, *Patriarchal Palestine* (London: SPCK, 1895), pp. 67-68; *idem*, 'Assyriological Notes. No. 1', pp. 173-74.

13.   For detailed studies of ziggurats, see A. Parrot, *Ziggurats et tour de Babel* (Paris: Albin Michel, 1949); T.A. Busink, 'L'origine et l'évolution de la ziggurat babylonienne', *JEOL* 21 (1970), pp. 91-142. There is also some useful information about ziggurats generally in J.H. Walton, 'The Mesopotamian Background of the Tower of Babel Account and its Implications', *BBR* 5 (1995), pp. 155-75, in spite of its flawed conservative theological perspective. For an annotated map of over thirty ziggurat sites, see M.A. Beek, *Atlas of Mesopotamia* (ed. H.H. Rowley; trans. D.R. Welsh; London: Nelson, 1962), map 21.

The idea that the tower of Babel was a ziggurat is not simply a notion of modern scholarship. For many centuries both local and Jewish tradition identified the tower with the ziggurat at Borsippa called Birs Nimrud (known as Ezida in Akkadian and dedicated to Nabu), which is eleven miles south-west of Babylon. Doubtless this site was preferred to that of Babylon because the remains of the ziggurat at Borsippa were much more impressive, as they still are today.[14] In its time the ziggurat at Babylon would have been impressive, but owing to quarrying over the years only its base is left today.[15] But over the last century it has become common for scholars to accept that the tower of Babel was a reflection of the ziggurat at Babylon, in view of the fact that the name Babel undoubtedly denotes Babylon elsewhere in the Bible.

Moreover, J clearly had some accurate knowledge about the ziggurat at Babylon, for Nabopolassar (626–605 BCE) gives some strikingly similar details in his account of the renovation of the ziggurat at Babylon, Etemenanki, 'House of the Foundation of Heaven and Earth'. Just as Gen. 11.3 highlights the typically Babylonian and un-Palestinian use of bricks and bitumen in the building ('they had brick for stone, and bitumen for mortar') and Gen. 11.4 refers to it as 'a tower with its top in the heavens', so Nabopolassar refers to the ziggurat of Babylon as having its top in the heavens and being made of baked bricks and bitumen. He states:

> At that time my lord Marduk told me in regard to Etemenanki, the ziggurat of Babylon, which before my day was (already) very weak and badly buckled, to ground its bottom on the breast of the netherworld, to make its top vie with the heavens... I had them shape mud bricks without number and mould baked bricks like countless raindrops. I had the river Arahtu bear asphalt and bitumen like a mighty flood.[16]

However, a few scholars, including Otto E. Ravn, Claus Westermann, and Christoph Uehlinger have questioned the connection of the tower of Babel with the ziggurat at Babylon, on the grounds that nothing is

---

14. That the Borsippa ziggurat was in view in Gen. 11 was still maintained by E.G. Kraeling, 'The Tower of Babel', *JAOS* 40 (1920), pp. 276-81; J.P. Peters, 'The Tower of Babel at Borsippa', *JAOS* 41 (1921), pp. 57-59.

15. On the ziggurat at Babylon, see E. Klengel-Brandt, *Der Turm von Babylon. Legende und Geschichte eines Bauwerkes* (Berlin: Koehler & Amelang, 2nd edn, 1992); H. Schmid, *Der Tempelturm Etemenanki in Babylon* (Baghdader Forschungen, 17; Mainz: Philipp von Zabern, 1995); W. Seipel (ed.), *Der Turmbau zu Babel* (2 vols.; Vienna: Kunsthistorisches Museum, 2003), I; A.R. George, 'The Tower of Babel: Archaeology, History and Cuneiform Texts', *AfO* 51 (2005–2006), pp. 75-95.

16. This translation of Nbp 1 I 30-ii 11 is taken from George, 'The Tower of Babel', pp. 83-84 (with minor orthographic changes).

implied about a religious or cultic role for the tower in Genesis 11.[17] It is certainly true that the Yahwist presents the construction of the tower as a grandiose act of hubris and symbol of strength (Gen. 11.4), so the view that Gen 11.1-9 is a direct piece of polemic against Babylonian religion or an attack on the futility of idolatry is to be rejected.[18] However, that does not mean that the Babylonian ziggurat does not lie behind our story. As already noted, the ziggurat stood out as Babylon's one truly impressively high building, the Yahwist clearly had good knowledge of the Babylonian building materials, and his statement that the tower was planned to have its top in the heavens reflects language actually used of the ziggurat, ultimately going back to its religious function as a link between heaven and earth. In addition to the argument just rejected, Uehlinger claims that the writer should have used an Akkadian loanword if a ziggurat were in mind.[19] But it may be argued that this was unnecessary when a perfectly good Hebrew word *migdāl* was available.

Uehlinger's above claims are part of a massive work presenting a radically new thesis about Gen. 11.1-9 as a whole, which we must now consider. On his understanding, the original narrative, dating from c. 700 BCE, consisted only of Gen. 11.1a, 3aα, 4αβγε̌, 5, 6, 7 and 8b, and referred not to Babylon but to Sargon II's incomplete new capital city at Dur-Sharrukin (Khorsabad), which Uehlinger claims was abandoned after his death. In the original story, therefore, the narrative described Yahweh's judgment on this Assyrian imperial building project.[20] Uehlinger argues that the reference to the people having one speech originally did not allude to their having one language, but rather reflected Neo-Assyrian political rhetoric which spoke of the people having 'one mouth' (*pû ištēn*), implying their unity under the Assyrian world ruler.[21]

17. O.E. Ravn, 'Der Turm zu Babel', *ZDMG* 9 NF 16 (1937), pp. 352-72 (369); C. Westermann, *Genesis 1–11* (BKAT, 1.1; Neukirchen–Vluyn: Neukirchener Verlag, 1974), pp. 720-21, ET *Genesis 1–11: A Commentary* (trans. J.J. Scullion; London: SPCK, 1984), 541; Uehlinger, *Weltreich*, 231.

18. For these two views, see H.D. Preuss, *Verspottung fremder Religionen im Alten Testament* (BWANT, 92; Stuttgart: Kohlhammer, 1971), pp. 51-52; R.B. Laurin, 'The Tower of Babel Revisited', in G.A. Tuttle (ed.), *Biblical and Near Eastern Studies: Essays in Honor of William Sanford LaSor* (Grand Rapids, MI: Eerdmans, 1978), pp. 142-45. It should also be noted that rabbinic sources envisaged an idol on the top of the tower; cf. Targums Neofiti and Pseudo-Jonathan on Gen. 11.4 and *Gen. R.* 38.8.

19. Uehlinger, *Weltreich*, p. 233.

20. Uehlinger, *Weltreich*, pp. 514-36.

21. Uehlinger, *Weltreich*, pp. 406-513.

For Uehlinger, it was only in a second redaction (which added Gen. 11.1b, 3aβγ, 4aα, 9a), dating from the exile in the sixth century BCE after the death of Nebuchadrezzar II, that references to Mesopotamian building materials and Babylon were added, thereby relating it to the building works there, though he is undecided whether the Babylonian ziggurat, Etemenanki, was specifically intended by the 'tower' in this redaction. It was also in this redaction that 'one speech' now came to mean one language.[22] Then, in a third redaction, when the story was taken up into J's Primaeval narrative, but before its union with P, Gen. 11.2 was added, making the story an episode in the early history of humanity.[23] Finally, in the Persian period, the passages about the scattering of the people in Gen. 11.4b, 8a, and 9b were inserted.[24]

What are we to make of all this? Uehlinger's book is certainly the most thorough study in existence of the story of the tower of Babel and its background, and we must be grateful for the voluminous information and references that it provides on a host of matters. However, the book's central thesis, just delineated, resembles the tower of Babel itself, a magnificent construction but seriously doomed to failure.[25] Among the objections that may be made are first, the whole thesis of a complex fourfold redaction of Gen. 11.1-9 seems highly speculative and based on flimsy evidence, since Gen. 11.1-9 very much reads as an artistically constructed unity, as noted earlier. Uehlinger's case for seeing different redactions is dependent on finding 'incoherences' in the text which have generally failed to convince.[26] Secondly, Uehlinger's comparison of the people's having 'one lip' in Genesis 11 with Akkadian 'one mouth' is

---

22. Uehlinger, *Weltreich*, pp. 546-58.

23. Uehlinger, *Weltreich*, pp. 558-62.

24. Uehlinger, *Weltreich*, pp. 572-83.

25. For critical evaluations, see R.S. Hendel, Review of Uehlinger, *Weltreich und «eine Rede»: Eine neue Deutung der sogenannten Turmbauerzählung (Gen 11,1-9)* (OB101; Freiburg: Universitätsverlag, and Göttingen: Vandenhoeck & Ruprecht, 1990), *CBQ* 55 (1993), pp. 785-87; P.J. Harland, 'Vertical or Horizontal: The Sin of Babel', *VT* 48 (1998), pp. 515-33 (517-19); H. Seebass, *Genesis*. I. *Urgeschichte (1,1–11,26)* (Neukirchen–Vluyn: Neukirchener Verlag, 3rd edn, 2009), esp. pp. 280-81. See too the works cited below in n. 26.

26. Even van der Kooij, who is one of the few scholars to accept Uehlinger's thesis that Gen. 11.1-9 has anything to do with Sargon II's building works at Dur-Sharrukin, finds Uehlinger's textual 'incoherences' invalid and maintains the unity of Gen. 11.1-9. See A. van der Kooij's lengthy review of Uehlinger, 'The Story of Genesis 11:1-9 and the Culture of Ancient Mesopotamia', *BO* 53 (1996), pp. 28-38, and his article, 'The City of Babel and Assyrian Imperialism: Genesis 11:1-9 Interpreted in the Light of Mesopotamian Sources', in A. Lemaire (ed.), *Congress Volume: Leiden 2004* (VTSup, 109; Leiden: Brill, 2006), pp. 1-17 (8-11).

unconvincing, since in Neo-Assyrian sources the latter is used with regard to the enforced unity of the people under the world-ruling king and occurs in military contexts, both of which are completely lacking in Genesis 11. We should therefore assume that 'one lip' meant 'one language' from the start, employing a meaning for 'lip' well attested elsewhere in the Old Testament (cf. Isa. 19.18; 33.19; Ezek. 3.5, 6). Thirdly, having rejected the notion that *migdāl* was an appropriate term to use for a ziggurat, Uehlinger is inconsistent when he leaves open the possibility that the word might have designated the Babylonian ziggurat after all in the sixth-century redaction of the story. Fourthly, since Sargon's building works at Dur-Sharrukin started only in 706 and ceased shortly afterwards on his death in 705 BCE, it would be surprising if the people of Judah were much aware of them; moreover, it does not appear that Khorsabad was actually abandoned after Sargon's death, contrary to Uehlinger's statement.[27]

In recent years it has become somewhat fashionable in certain circles to suppose that the story of the tower and city of Babel dates from the period of the sixth century, when Babylon was at the height of its power and when the Jews in exile would have become familiar with Babylon.[28] However, although superficially plausible, there is a problem with this view which I have not previously seen noted. This is the fact that the story in Genesis 11 appears to be an aetiological account of Babylon at a time when the city and its tower were in an incomplete state. This stands in stark contrast to the exilic period, since by then Nebuchadrezzar II had completed the rebuilding of Babylon and its ziggurat Etemenanki, and both were in their full splendour.

John Van Seters notes that the name Etemenanki is first mentioned in the Erra epic (1.128).[29] The precise date of this epic is debated, W.G. Lambert and L. Cagni, for example, dating it to the first half of the ninth century BCE and W. von Soden (followed by Van Seters) to c. 765 BCE[30] However, von Soden goes on to speculate that the tower was

27. On Khorsabad's continuing existence, see J.A. Brinkman, *Prelude to Empire: Babylonian Politics and Society, 747–626 B.C.* (Occasional Papers of the Babylonian Fund, 7; Philadelphia: University Museum, 1984), p. 54 n. 254. I am grateful to Stephanie Dalley for drawing this to my attention.

28. E.g. J. Van Seters, *Prologue to History: The Yahwist as Historian in Genesis* (Louisville, KY: Westminster/John Knox Press, 1992), pp. 180-85, with notes on pp. 186-87.

29. Van Seters, *Prologue to History*, p. 182.

30. W.G. Lambert, Review of F. Gössmann, *Das Era-Epos* (Würzburg: Augustinus, 1956), *AfO* 18 (1957–58), pp. 395-401 (400); *idem*, 'A Catalogue of Texts and Authors', *JCS* 16 (1962), pp. 59-77 (76); L. Cagni, *L'epopea di Erra*

constructed in the time of Nebuchadrezzar I (c. 1126–1103 BCE), though, as Andrew George has argued, Babylon probably had a ziggurat much earlier in the second millennium BCE.[31] Anyway, Enuma elish 6.62-64, dating to no later than 1100 BCE, does already attest the presence of a ziggurat in Babylon then. It states, 'They raised the head of Esagila on high, the counterpart to Apsu, they built the upper ziggurat (*zi-qur-rat*) of Apsu, for Anu-Enlil-Ea they founded his…and dwelling'.[32] It will be noted that the allusion in Enuma elish suggests that the term Esagila (which means 'the house whose head is lifted') originally referred to the ziggurat of Babylon or alternatively to the entire temple complex that included the ziggurat; Etemenanki was probably a later designation for the tower. It seems going too far, however, to follow E.A. Speiser in thinking that Genesis 11's reference to the tower of Babel is specifically dependent on this passage of Enuma elish.[33] Although Enuma elish (6.58, 60) has just previously referred to bricks, it makes no mention of bitumen, which Gen. 11.3 correctly mentions (cf. Naboplassar), suggesting first-hand knowledge of the tower rather than merely literary borrowing from Enuma elish.

Sennacherib claims to have torn down the ziggurat, but his successors Esarhaddon and Asshurbanibal started rebuilding it. This was continued by the Babylonian king Nabonidus and finalized by his successor, Nebuchadrezzar II.[34]

(Rome: Istituto di Studi del Vicino Oriente dell'Università, 1969), pp. 37-42; *idem*, *The Poem of Erra* (Sources from the Ancient Near East, 1.3; Malibu, CA: Undena Publications, 1977), pp. 20-21; W. von Soden, 'Etemenanki vor Asarhaddon nach der Erzählung vom Turmbau zu Babel und dem Erra-Mythos', *UF* 3 (1971), pp. 253-64, repr. in H.-P. Müller (ed.), *Bibel und alter Orient: Altorientalische Beiträge zum Alten Testament von Wolfram von Soden* (BZAW, 162; Berlin: W. de Gruyter, 1985), pp. 134-47; Van Seters, *Prologue to History*, p. 182.

31. Von Soden, *loc. cit.*; contrast George, 'The Tower of Babel', pp. 87-88.

32. The translation is from B.R. Foster, *Before the Muses: An Anthology of Akkadian Literature* (Bethesda, MD: CDL Press, 3rd edn, 2005), 471. The context clearly implies that the ziggurat was intended for Marduk. As Foster, *Before the Muses*, p. 471 n. 3, explains, the reference to 'Anu-Enlil-Ea' implies the syncretism of Marduk with these deities, and we may compare tablet 7, lines 136 and 140, where Marduk is explicitly given the names of Enlil and Ea.

33. E.A. Speiser, 'Word Plays on the Creation Epic's Version of the Founding of Babylon', *Or* 25 (1956), pp. 317-23, repr. in J.J. Finkelstein and M. Greenberg (eds.), *Oriental and Biblical Studies: Collected Writings of E.A. Speiser* (Philadelphia: University of Pennsylvania Press, 1967), pp. 53-61.

34. See references and discussion in George, 'The Tower of Babel', pp. 79-86.

According to Herodotus, *History* 1.181, the tower at Babylon still existed in his day (c. 460 BCE) and he gives the following description, though he speaks of it rather as a series of towers:

> ...and in the midmost of the other [division of the city] is still to this day the sacred enclosure of Zeus-Belus, a square of two furlongs each way, with gates of bronze. In the centre of this enclosure a solid tower has been built, of one furlong's length and breadth; a second tower rises from this, and from it yet another, till at last there are eight. The way up to them mounts spirally outside all the towers; about halfway in the ascent is a halting place, with seats for repose, where those who ascend will sit down and rest. In the last tower there is a great shrine; and in it a great and well-covered couch is laid, and a golden table set hard by. But no image has been set up in the shrine, nor does any human creature lie therein for the night, except one native woman, chosen from all women by the god, as say the Chaldaeans, who are priests of this god.[35]

However, there are certain errors in this account: the length and breadth of the ziggurat are grossly exaggerated, it did not have a spiral staircase, and it had seven, not eight stages. Many scholars doubt that Herodotus had actually ever visited Babylon himself.[36] Just before Herodotus's time, it appears that Xerxes I had disabled the ziggurat in 484 BCE, while later the site was levelled by Alexander the Great and his successors with a view to rebuilding, though this never took place.[37] Even later, after the tower lay in ruins, Diodorus Siculus, *Universal History* 2.9 still knew that it had been high and built of bitumen and bricks, but Strabo, *Geography* 16.1.5, who likewise knew it had been high, built of baked brick and ascended by a stairway, mistakenly referred to it as the tomb of Belus.

For authentic information in Akkadian we are dependent on the so-called Esagila tablet.[38] This was written c. 229 BCE but is a copy of an older text found at Borsippa. According to this Etemenanki was 91 metres square at the base, which corresponds closely to what archaeological excavations have revealed. The Esagila tablet also tells us that it

35. The translation is taken from A.D. Godley, *Herodotus Books I–II* (LCL; Cambridge, MA: Harvard University Press, rev. edn, 1926), pp. 225-27.

36. See, e.g., R. Rollinger, *Herodots babylonischer Logos* (Innsbruck: Verlag des Instituts für Sprachwissenschaft der Universität Innsbruck, 1993). Contrast O.E. Ravn's earlier study, *Herodotus' Description of Babylon* (Copenhagen: Nyt Nordisk Forlag, 1942), which concluded that Herodotus did go to Babylon

37. See references and discussion in George, 'The Tower of Babel', pp. 89-92.

38. I say so-called, since it is primarily concerned with Etemenanki. For text and commentary, see A.R. George, *Babylonian Topographical Texts* (OLA, 40; Leuven: Peeters, 1992), pp. 109-19, 414-34.

was 91 metres high and consisted of seven stages. Interestingly, a fairly recently discovered Neo-Babylonian stele, now in the Schøyen Collection, depicts a king (almost certainly Nebuchadrezzar II) standing before a seven-staged ziggurat called 'Etemenanki, ziggurat of Babylon'.[39]

3. *The Confusion of Languages and Scattering of Humanity*

The Genesis 11 account starts in v. 1 with the sentence, 'Now the whole earth had one language and the same words', and concludes in v. 9 with the confusion of the language of all the earth and the associated scattering of the nations. This makes clear that the writer saw the change from one world language to many languages as the central theme of the story.

However, as has often been observed, one problem posed by Genesis 11 is that the multiplicity of nations and languages is already presupposed in Genesis 10 (cf. vv. 5, 20, 31, 32). Some attempt to get round this problem by claiming that the account in ch. 11 is a flashback to the time before Genesis 10, while others note that the references cited above implying a multiplicity of languages and nations in Genesis 10 are from P, while Gen. 11.1-9 is from J. Both points are surely true. In the final form of the text we may indeed suppose that Gen. 11.1-9 is intended to describe events prior to Genesis 10. At the same time it is the case that the above-mentioned references in Genesis 10 come from P, who appears to have had a different concept of the origin of many languages from J, as he did in some other matters. P in Genesis 10 even uses a different word for 'language' (*lāšôn*, lit. 'tongue') from that which J uses in Genesis 11 (*śāpâ*, lit. 'lip'). Moreover, whereas in the J account in Genesis 11 humanity's dispersion throughout the world is a divine reaction to the building of Babylon and its tower, in P the dispersion of humanity in Genesis 10 is a natural consequence of obedience to the divine command to be fruitful and multiply and fill the earth (cf. Gen. 9.1, 7, reiterating Gen 1.28).

Not all of Genesis 10 is from P, however. The insertion about Nimrod in Gen. 10.8-12 is from J and presupposes that Babylon already exists (alongside some other Mesopotamian cities; Babylon and the other cities of v. 10, unlike the Assyrian cities of v. 11, are not stated to have been built by Nimrod). This stands in contrast to Gen. 11.1-9, which describes the building of Babylon as a new event, thus further indicating that Genesis 10 follows 11.1-9 chronologically. Possibly the redactor wished

39. See J.-L. Montero-Fenellós, 'La tour de Babylone, repensée', in B. André-Salvini (ed.), *Babylone* (Paris: Hazan and Musée du Louvre, 2008), pp. 229-30; George, 'The Tower of Babel', p. 76.

to end the Primaeval narrative on a negative note, so as to set the scene for the new beginning with Abram in Genesis 12. Originally in J's narrative, however, Gen. 11.1-9 would have followed fairly soon after the flood. This would interestingly cohere with Berossus who, following the landing of the ark in Armenia, recounts, 'When these people came to Babylon, they dug up the writings at (the city) of the Sipparians and founded many cities and rebuilt shrines and founded anew Babylon'.[40] It could well be that Berossus and J were dependent on a common Babylonian tradition. However, whereas J was speaking of the foundation of Babylon for the first time, Berossus was envisaging the restoration of a city that had previously existed before the flood (cf. Enuma elish 6.57-68, where it was founded by the Anunnaki just after the creation of the world).

A suggestion of Cyrus H. Gordon and Victor P. Hamilton that attempts to avoid seeing tension between Genesis 10 and 11.1-9 is that the latter is merely implying that there was a common *lingua franca* (which they suppose to be Sumerian) rather than literally one language in the world, and that it is this which now ceases.[41] This, however, is forced, reading into the narrative something that is not there. Moreover, it is at Gen. 11.9 that the scattering of the people over the earth begins, so there is still a tension with Genesis 10, where this division of nations already exists.

Genesis 11.9 contains a marvellous pun, in keeping with J's penchant for such things (cf. Gen. 4.1, 25; 5.29; 9.27), but unfortunately most English Bible translations fail to represent it adequately in their renderings, generally translating as 'Therefore it was called Babel (*bābel*), because there the Lord confused (*bālal*) the language of all the earth…', or suchlike. The obvious way of representing the pun is curiously followed by only two of the major English Bible translations, the NEB and REB, in addition to Moffatt and the little-known God's Word translation, which all render something like 'the Lord there *made a babble* of the language of all the world'.[42] Scholars often state that the name of

---

40. The translation is from S.M. Burstein, *The Babyloniaca of Berossus* (Sources from the Ancient Near East, 1.5; Malibu, CA: Undena Publications, 1978), p. 21.

41. C.H. Gordon advocated this in various places, including 'Ebla and Genesis 11', in M.L. Peterson (ed.), *A Spectrum of Thought: Essays in Honor of Dennis F. Kinlaw* (Wilmore, KY: Francis Asbury, 1982), pp. 125-34 (129-30); Victor P. Hamilton, *The Book of Genesis Chapters 1–17* (NICOT; Grand Rapids, MI: Eerdmans, 1990), pp. 350-51.

42. In fact, one might have imagined that the word 'babble' derived from 'Babel', but J.A.H. Murray *et al.*, *The Oxford English Dictionary* (13 vols.; Oxford: Clarendon Press, 1933), I, p. 604, states that 'No direct connexion with *Babel* can be traced; though association with that may have affected the senses'. Rather, it con-

Babylon actually means 'gate of God' (*bab-ilim*). However, what is less often observed is that Assyriologists believe that this latter may itself be a popular etymology, and that the original meaning of the name, possibly Babil, is uncertain.[43]

The Sumerologist S.N. Kramer argued in 1968 that we have a Sumerian precursor to Genesis 11's multiplication of languages in the epic known as 'Enmerkar and the Lord of Aratta'.[44] For him, part of lines 145-55 read, 'The whole universe, the people in unison (?), to Enlil in one tongue...Enki[...]the leader of the gods...changed the speech in their mouths, [brought (?)] contention into it, into the speech of man that (until then) had been one'. In Kramer's view this implies that all humanity originally spoke the same language (Sumerian), until Enki changed people's speech. However, Bendt Alster argued that the text is actually envisaging a future time when all humanity would speak the same language.[45] On this understanding the text should rather read: 'The

cludes: 'Probably formed (with frequentative suffix *–le*; cf. prattle) on the repeated syllable *ba*, *ba*, one of the earliest articulate sounds made by infants, fitly used to express childish prattle'.

43. Cf. I.J. Gelb, 'The Name of Babylon', *Journal of the Institute of Asian Studies* 1 (1955), pp. 1-4. Already much earlier, Gunkel, *Genesis*, p. 95, ET *Genesis*, p. 97, had suggested that *Bab-ili*, 'gate of God', might be a folk etymology. On a different track, F.M.T. Böhl, 'Die Etymologie von "Babel"', Genesis 11 9', *ZAW* 36 (1916), pp. 110-13 thought that a popular Babylonian etymology from *babālu* (= *abālu*), 'to scatter', might lie behind the Hebrew text, which J had to change to *bālal*, 'confuse', as the former verb did not exist in Hebrew.

44. S.N. Kramer, 'The "Babel of Tongues": A Sumerian Version', *JAOS* 88 (1968), pp. 108-11. Cf. J. van Dijk, 'La confusion des langues: Notes sur le lexique et sur la morphologie d'Enmerkar, 147-55', *Or* NS 39 (1970), pp. 302-10; C. Mittermayer, *Enmerkara und der Herr von Arata. Ein ungleicher Wettstreit* (OBO, 239; Fribourg: Academic Press; Göttingen: Vandenhoeck & Ruprecht, 2009), pp. 57-62, 122-23, reprinted in R.S. Hess and D.T. Tsumura (eds.), *"I Studied Inscriptions from before the Flood": Ancient Near Eastern, Literary, and Linguistic Approaches to Genesis 1–11* (Sources for Biblical and Theological Study, 4; Winona Lake, IN: Eisenbrauns, 1994), pp. 278-82.

45. B. Alster, 'An Aspect of "Enmerkar and the Land of Aratta"', *RA* 67 (1973), pp. 101-109. This view was subsequently followed by H. Schmökel, in W. Beyerlin (ed.), *Religionsgeschichtliches Textbuch zum Alten Testament* (Grundrisse zum Alten Testament, 1; Göttingen: Vandenhoeck & Ruprecht, 1975), pp. 112-13, ET *Near Eastern Religious Texts Relating to the Old Testament* (trans. J. Bowden; London: SCM Press, 1978), p. 87; H. Vanstiphout, *Epics of Sumerian Kings: The Matter of Aratta* (SBL Writings from the Ancient World, 20; Atlanta: SBL, 2003), p. 65; J. Black in *The Electronic Text Corpus of Sumerian Literature* (accessible at http://etcsl.orinst.ox.ac.uk). I wish to thank Andrew George, who on balance favours this view, for discussing this passage with me.

whole universe, the well-guarded people—May they all address Enlil together in a single language! ... Enki[...]the expert of the gods...shall change the speech in their mouths, as many as he had placed there, and so the speech of mankind is truly one.'[46]

Although the interpretation of the text is difficult, Alster's view does seem more natural. The words form part of a passage seeking the submission of the foreign Lord of Aratta (in Iran) to Enmerkar of Uruk, so the narrative flow makes it more likely that the tense is future: if all nations are to bow down to Enlil and speak Sumerian, the Lord of Aratta will have to do so too. This passage would then provide an interesting parallel not to Gen. 11.1-9 but rather Zeph. 3.9, which similarly envisages a future time when all nations will worship Yahweh in a common language (Hebrew). We there read, 'At that time I will change the speech of the peoples to a pure speech, that all of them may call on the name of the Lord, and serve him with one accord'.

Overall, the story in Gen. 11.1-9 provides multiple aetiologies: not only for human beings having many different languages, but also for the dispersal of humanity throughout the earth, and for the origin of the place name Babel. This offering of multiple aetiologies in one story is characteristic of the Yahwist in the Primaeval narrative, as also is the word play in Gen. 11.9 previously noted. Also characteristic, of course, is the use of the tetragrammaton for the divine name, in addition to its being a story of crime and punishment, that the divine intervention is accompanied by divine words before the judgment is inflicted (Gen. 11.6-7; cf. 3.22; 4.9-12; 6.3), that this includes a first person plural address to the divine council (Gen. 11.7; cf. 3.22), the fact that the narrative ends with an expulsion (Gen. 11.8-9; cf. 3.22-24; 4.11-16), the anthropomorphic depiction of God exemplified by his coming down to see the tower (Gen. 11.5, 7; cf. 2.7, 8; 3.8; 7.16b), and the way in which the story is concerned with the transcending of boundaries (Gen. 11.4, 7; cf. 3.22; 6.2-3).[47] Further typical of J are the use of the verb *ḥālal*,

---

46. Translation taken from *The Electronic Text Corpus of Sumerian Literature*.

47. Regarding the transcendence of boundaries, J.M. Sasson, 'The Tower of Babel as a Clue to the Redactional Structuring of the Primeval History (Gen. 1.1–11.9)', in G.A. Rendsburg, R. Adler. M. Arfa, and N.H. Winter (eds.), *The Bible World: Essays in Honor of Cyrus H. Gordon* (New York: Ktav, 1980), pp. 211-19 (218-19), has claimed that the redactors have organized Gen. 1–11 into two parallel sections, Gen. 1.1–6.8 and 6.9–11.9, with the Babel story in Gen. 11.1-9 corresponding to Gen. 6.1-8. However, although both these passages do involve the transcendence of boundaries (in opposite directions), Sasson's overall structure is unconvincing, since his parallels are too general, the Garden of Eden story is left without a parallel in the second half, and the ten generations after the flood (Gen. 11.10-32) are

'begin', in Gen. 11.6 (cf. 4.26; 6.1; 9.20; 10.8), of the noun *šēm*, 'name', in the sense of 'reputation' in Gen. 11.4 (cf. 6.4; 12.2), and of the interjection *hēn*, 'behold', in Gen. 11.6 (cf. 3.22; 4.14). There seems no good reason, therefore, to deny this narrative to the Yahwist.[48]

4. *The Yahwist's Perspective:*
A Story of Pride and Punishment or Something Else?

The traditional interpretation of the narrative about Babel in Gen. 11.1-9 is that it is a story of hubris and the divine punishment that comes upon it. This interpretation is already found, for example, in *Jubilees* and the *Sybilline Oracles* (for more on which see below), and then in the rabbis and Church Fathers, through the Reformers and right up to the present day in many works. Such a view is suggested by the reference to the people of Babel (the human race as it then was) wishing to build a city with a tower having its top in the heavens so as to make a name for themselves (Gen. 11.4). In recent years, however, this interpretation has been questioned by scholars such as Ellen van Wolde and Theodore Hiebert.[49] Van Wolde prefers to see the story as one about the dispersion

left out, although they provide a clear parallel to the ten antediluvian generations in Gen. 5.1-32, the latter (together with Gen. 4.17-26) being made rather to parallel Gen. 10 in Sasson's scheme.

48. However, D.M. Carr, *Reading the Fractures of Genesis: Historical and Literary Approaches* (Louisville, KY: Westminster/John Knox Press, 1996), p. 248; *idem, The Formation of the Hebrew Bible: A New Reconstruction* (New York: Oxford University Press, 2011), pp. 459-60; M. Witte, *Die biblische Urgeschichte: Redaktions- und theologiegeschichtliche Beobachtungen zu Genesis 1,1–11,26* (BZAW, 265; Berlin: W. de Gruyter, 1998), pp. 87-99; and J.C. Gertz, 'Babel in Rücken und das Land vor Augen: Anmerkungen zum Abschluß der Urgeschichte und zum Anfang der Erzählungen von den Erzeltern Israels', in A. Hagedorn and H. Pfeiffer (eds.), *Die Erzväter in der biblischen Tradition: Festschrift für Matthias Köckert* (BZAW, 400; Berlin: W. de Gruyter, 2009), pp. 9-34, see the non-P material in Gen. 11.1-9 as a later supplement to the text. All three see the other transcending of boundaries passages in Gen. 3.22, 24; 6.1-4 as also redactional. All this seems arbitrary to me, but quite apart from these parallels, there are sufficient other parallels to J in Gen. 11.1-9 noted above to justify the attribution of the passage to this source.

49. E. van Wolde, *Words Become Worlds: Semantic Studies in Genesis 1–11* (BibInt, 6; Leiden: Brill, 1994), pp. 84-89; *eadem, Stories of the Beginning: Genesis 1–11 and Other Creation Stories* (trans. J. Bowden; London: SCM Press, 1996), pp. 162-69; T. Hiebert, 'The Tower of Babel and the Origin of the World's Cultures', *JBL* 126 (2007), pp. 29-58; *idem*, 'Babel: Babble or Blueprint? Calvin, Cultural Diversity, and the Interpretation of Genesis 11:1-9', in W.N. Alston and M. Welker (eds.), *Reformed Theology: Identity and Ecumenicity. II. Biblical Interpretation in the Reformed Tradition* (Grand Rapids, MI: Eerdmans, 2007), pp. 127-45.

of humanity in reaction to the tower builders' desire to stay in one place, as opposed to a story of human hubris. But surely these two elements are both true and not mutually exclusive: the people of Babel do wish to stay in one place but at the same time their desire to build a tower with its top in the heavens is an act of hubris. Van Wolde's approach succeeds in completely flattening the tower! Again, Hiebert maintains that the multiplication of languages is not depicted as a judgment on human hubris but rather reflects Yahweh's preference for cultural diversity. But it is difficult not to regard God's extreme alarm at the danger of humans getting out of control in v. 6 as being inspired particularly by the building of the tower previously mentioned in v. 4.[50] The people there declare, 'Come let us build ourselves a city, and a tower with its top in the heavens, and let us make a name for ourselves...' The heavens were where God was believed to dwell, so attempting to encroach on that exalted realm would surely have been seen as an act of hubris. The attempt to reach heaven is thus meant literally (contrast the hyperbole of Deut. 1.28; 9.1), and so still reflects something of the original Babylonian understanding of the ziggurat as a link between heaven and earth. Moreover, the scattering over the earth that the builders of Babel feared (Gen. 11.4)—something which ironically came upon them—must have been from God himself, since the inhabitants of Babel constituted at that point the whole world (Gen. 11.1) and there were no other humans to fear. This therefore implies a note of defiance towards God in their attitude.

The traditional interpretation involving hubris is also favoured by observing the striking parallels between Gen. 11.1-9 and the story in Genesis 3, in both of which divine disapproval is expressed of humans transcending the divine/human boundaries, and God makes reference to the heavenly court by speaking in the first person plural (Gen. 3.22; 11.7). Moreover, in both of these God expresses the fear of worse if the humans continue along their current course, with common use of *hēn*... *we'attâ*. Compare Gen. 3.22, 'Behold (*hēn*), the man has become like us knowing good and evil; and now (*we'attâ*), lest he reach out his hand and take also from the tree of life, and eat, and live for ever' with Gen. 11.6, 'Behold (*hēn*), they are one people, and they all have one language; and

50. See too the critiques in J.T. Strong, 'Shattering the Image of God: A Response to Theodore Hiebert's Interpretation of the Story of the Tower of Babel', *JBL* 127 (2008), pp. 625-34; A. LaCocque, 'Whatever Happened in the Valley of Shinar? A Response to Theodore Hiebert', *JBL* 128 (2009), pp. 29-41; *idem, The Captivity of Innocence: Babel and the Yahwist* (Eugene, OR: Cascade Books, 2010), pp. 30-31, 67.

this is only the beginning of what they will do; and now (*w^{e c}attâ*) nothing that they propose to do will be impossible for them'.[51]

Peter Harland concedes that for J Gen. 11.1-9 is indeed a story about human hubris *vis-à-vis* God, but claims that if we read it as part of Genesis 1–11 in its final canonical form, it is now to be understood as illustrating disobedience to God's command to be fruitful, multiply, and fill the earth (Gen. 1.28; 9.1, 7). In response, one might argue that, as sophisticated final-form readers, we might care to read it that way, but is there really any evidence that the redactor of Genesis 1–11 so intended it? After all, the hubristic elements within Gen. 11.1-9 are still there, and indeed were emphasized by the earliest Jewish interpreters, while the commands to fill the earth are set within the context of humanity being fruitful and multiplying, something which there is every reason to believe the people of Genesis 11 had been doing in view of their apparently large numbers so soon after the flood (Gen. 11.1).

On another track, W. von Soden, Klaus Seybold, Hubert Bost and Gunther H. Wittenberg have all envisaged the account of the tower of Babel as containing an implied critique of Solomon's building works, a view bound up with the dating of J to the tenth century which is now out of favour.[52] This understanding was elaborated in most detail by Wittenberg, who not only interpreted the tower of Babel narrative as containing an implicit attack on Solomon's oppressive building works, but also saw the division of the peoples as mirroring the division of the kingdom following Solomon's death. However, it seems bizarre to suppose that the foreign city of Babylon would be employed to symbolize the Israelite Solomon, and the division of the kingdom into two is quite different from the scattering of the peoples all over the world. Also, this reading leaves no role for the confusion of languages, which is so central

---

51. There is a striking parallel with Job 42.2 in terms of both vocabulary and idea here. Just as God says of the people of Babel, 'nothing that they propose (*yāz^emû*) to do will be withheld (*yibbāṣēr*) from them', so Job declares to God, 'I know that no purpose (*m^ezimmâ*) of yours can be thwarted (*yibbāṣēr*)'.

52. W. von Soden, 'Verschlüsselte Kritik an Salomo in der Urgeschichte des Jahwisten?', *WO* 7 (1974), pp. 228-40 (236-37), reprinted in H.-P. Müller (ed.), *Bibel und alter Orient. Altorientalische Beiträge zum Alten Testament von Wolfram von Soden* (BZAW, 162; Berlin: W. de Gruyter, 1985), pp. 174-86 (82-83); K. Seybold, 'Der Turmbau zu Babel. Zur Enstehung von Genesis 11,1-9', *VT* 26 (1976), pp. 453-79 (469); Hubert Bost, 'La tour de Babel. Gen 11,1-9', in *La ville dans le Proche-Orient ancien* (Les cahiers du CEPOA, 1; Leuven: Peeters, 1983), pp. 231-38 (235-36); G.H. Wittenberg, *King Solomon and the Theologians* (Pietermaritzburg: University of Natal Press, 1988), p. 16. This view is rightly rejected by Van Seters, *Prologue to History*, p. 186 n. 32.

to the story, something which Wittenberg unconvincingly supposed symbolized the growth in misunderstanding between social groups in Israel. Moreover, although Babylon is condemned for its oppressive acts in certain prophetic passages (cf. Isa. 47; Hab. 1 12-17), this is not the emphasis of the Yahwist in Gen. 11.1-9, for whom there were no other people around on the earth at the time to be oppressed, and the building of the tower represented rather a direct act of hubris towards Yahweh himself.

5. *The* Nachgeschichte *of the Story*

Finally, we shall discuss the *Nachgeschichte* of this story. First, is it the case that the story of the tower of Babel is referred to anywhere else in the Hebrew Bible? It is possible, though not certain, that there is an allusion to it in Jer. 51.53, where we read in the course of this exilic oracle against Babylon, 'Though Babylon should mount up to heaven, and though she should fortify her strong height, from me destroyers would come upon her, says the Lord'. Interestingly, the verb *bṣr* occurs in both Gen. 11.6 and Jer. 51.53, which might appear to support a connection, but on the other hand the verb's meaning is clearly different in each case, the former being in the niphal, 'be withheld', and the latter in the piel, 'fortify'. If the occurrence of this verb is a coincidence, Jer. 51.53 will have to be explained without reference to Genesis 11 as simply a development of Isa. 14.12-15, an oracle about the shining one, son of the dawn (symbolizing the king of Babylon), who seeks to rise up into heaven but is subsequently cast down to Sheol.[53]

Yair Zakovitch has claimed that the account of Jacob's dream at Bethel in Genesis 28, in which angels ascended and descended on a staircase between heaven and earth, reflected knowledge of the story of the tower of Babel in Genesis 11.[54] However, this seems unlikely. What is true, however, and cannot have been deduced from Genesis 11, is that the staircase (not ladder) in Jacob's dream seems to reflect the form and function of a Mesopotamian ziggurat up and down which gods and goddesses ascend and descend between heaven and earth (for *sullām*, cf. Akkadian *simmiltu*), though it is now a case of angels rather than

53. On the myth in Isa. 14.12-15 and the historical situation alluded to, see my discussion in J. Day, *Yahweh and the Gods and Goddesses of Canaan* (JSOTSup, 265; Sheffield: Sheffield Academic Press, 2000), pp. 165-84.

54. Y. Zakovitch, *Through the Looking Glass: Reflection Stories in the Bible* (Tel Aviv: Hakibbutz Hameuchad, 1995 [Hebrew]), pp. 60-62.

deities.[55] Victor Hurowitz has further suggested that Genesis 28 is dependent specifically on the ziggurat at Babylon.[56] Among other things, he points out that the term 'gate of heaven' (Gen. 28.17) recalls the name Babylon as 'the gate of god'.

Genesis 11 does not say that God destroyed the tower of Babel, merely that work on building the city of Babel ceased following God's intervention to disperse the people. Nevertheless, the notion that God destroyed the tower did arise in antiquity. Thus, according to *Jub.* 10.18-26, *Sib. Or.* 3.97-109 and Josephus, *Ant.* 1.4.3 (who quotes the Sibyl), God overturned the tower with a great wind. Further, in *Midrash Tanḥuma*, Noaḥ 18 it is stated that one third of the tower was burnt, one third swallowed up, and one third was left standing.

Interestingly, by conflating the references to Babel in Genesis 10 and 11 the view later came about among the Jews that Nimrod was actually involved in the building of the tower and city of Babel, indeed was its instigator. This idea, already found in Philo, *Quaestiones in Genesim* 2.81-82 and Josephus, *Ant.* 1.4.3, was later taken up by the Talmud and Christian sources, and is reflected in the Arabic name of the ziggurat at Borsippa, Birs Nimrud, which as noted earlier, was long considered the site of the tower of Babel. In contrast, according to Targum Pseudo-Jonathan on Gen. 10.11, Nimrod actually opposed the building of the tower.

It is not surprising that the rabbis thought that the original language of humanity implied by the story of the tower of Babel was Hebrew (Targum Neofiti and Fragment Targum on Gen. 11.1; *y. Meg.* 1.11; *Midr. Tanḥ.* 28a). However, according to the ninth-century Muslim historian al-Ṭabarī, in his *History of the Prophets and Kings*, it was rather Syriac, a notion already found in the Syriac *Cave of Treasures* (W) 24. Coming to the Qur'an, it is possible that this contains a garbled allusion to the tower of Babel in Surah 28.38, where we read that in the time of Moses Pharaoh instructed his minister Haman to kindle a fire, bake mud and build a high tower in order that he might see Moses's god, whom he

55. Cf. A.R. Millard, 'The Celestial Ladder and the Gate of Heaven (Genesis xxviii.12, 17)', *ExpTim* 78 (1966), pp. 86-87.

56. V.A. Hurowitz, 'Babylon in Bethel—New Light on Jacob's Dream', in S.W. Holladay (ed.), *Orientalism, Assyriology and the Bible* (Hebrew Bible Monographs, 10; Sheffield: Sheffield Phoenix Press, 2006), pp. 436-48. An earlier version of this article was published in M. Heltzer and M. Malul (eds.), *Tᵉshûrôt laAvishur: Studies in the Bible and the Ancient Near East, in Hebrew and Semitic Languages. Festschrift Presented to Prof. Yitzhaq Avishur on the Occasion of his Sixty-Fifth Birthday* (Tel Aviv: Archaeological Center Publications, 2004), pp. 184-94 (Hebrew).

suspects is a liar. There is a similar passage in Surah 40.36-37, which speaks of this tower reaching the heavens. It is generally accepted by critical scholars that Muhammad has here confused Pharaoh's minister with Haman, minister of Ahasuerus in the book of Esther, so there is no reason why he should not similarly inadvertently have transplanted the tower of Babel from Babylon to Egypt.

As for the tower of Babel within Christianity, there is no reference to it within the New Testament. Nevertheless, it has often been supposed that the events of the day of Pentecost in Acts 2, in which visitors from various nations could all understand the apostles' words, are to be understood as a reversal of the story of Babel in Gen. 11.1-9, in which languages are multiplied and people scattered.[57] However, although this is a popular Christian notion up to the present time, there is little evidence that Luke himself consciously intended this in Acts 2, as there is no obvious reference back to Genesis 11 within the text. Most scholarly New Testament commentaries on Acts 2 fail even to mention Genesis 11, and the few that do dismiss the influence of this text for lack of evidence.[58] It would appear rather that this idea was simply an imaginative creation of the early Church Fathers. Although this has sometimes been attributed to Origen, it was actually Acts 4.32 that he contrasted with Gen. 11.1-3, where the early Church is said to have been of one heart and spirit; cf. Origen, *On Genesis*, c. 1 (*PG*, 12, col. 112). The earliest of the Fathers to relate Genesis 11 specifically to Acts 2 that we know of was Gregory of Nazianzus (*Oration* 41, 16 [*PG* 36, col. 449]), and this idea was subsequently followed by John Chrysostom (*Homily 2 on Pentecost*, 2 [*PG* 50, col. 467]), and others such as Augustine (*Narration on Psalm 54*, verse 11 [*PL* 36, col. 636], and *Sermon 271* [*PL* 38, col. 1245]) and Gregory the Great (*Homily on the Gospels*, Book 2, Homily 30, 4 [*PL* 76, col. 1222]).

Later, within Christian Europe, the depiction of the tower of Babel became common in art as a symbol of the nemesis of hubris.[59] The most famous is one of two extant paintings on this theme by the sixteenth-century Flemish artist Peter Bruegel the Elder, now present in the

---

57. E.g. J.G. Davies, 'Pentecost and Glossolalia', *JTS* 3 NS (1952), pp. 228-31 (228-29).

58. Cf. I.H. Marshall, *The Acts of the Apostles: An Introduction and Commentary* (Leicester: Inter-Varsity Press; Grand Rapids, MI: Eerdmans, 1980), p. 68; C.K. Barrett, *The Acts of the Apostles* (ICC; Edinburgh: T. & T. Clark, 1994), p. 112.

59. See Parrot, *Ziggurats et tour de Babel*, pp. 169-93; M.J. Seymour in I.L. Finkel and M.J. Seymour (eds.), *Babylon: Myth and Reality* (London: British Museum Press, 2008), pp. 132-41.

Kunsthistorisches Museum, Vienna.[60] At the front left of this painting there is a depiction of a king, with typical anachronism wearing the royal regalia of a later age, who is inspecting the building of the tower, which clearly reflects the tradition (possibly derived by Bruegel from Josephus) that Nimrod was the instigator of the tower.[61]

Even in our own era the story of the tower of Babel lives on in the popular consciousness: some decades ago George Steiner chose to give his famous book on language and translation the title *After Babel*,[62] and just as I write *Babel* is the name of a rock band's album riding high in the UK charts.

60. Bruegel's second painting ('The "Little" Tower of Babel') is in the Museum Boijmans van Beuningen, Rotterdam. He also painted a third picture of the tower of Babel but it is no longer preserved.

61. This painting has often been reproduced on the Internet. Cf. A. Parrot, *La tour de Babel* (Cahiers d'archéologie biblique, 2; Neuchâtel: Delachaux & Niestlé, 1953), where it is depicted on the front cover, ET *The Tower of Babel* (trans. E. Hudson; Studies in Biblical Archaeology, 2; London: SCM Press, 1955), where it appears as the frontispiece.

62. G. Steiner, *After Babel: Aspects of Language and Translation* (Oxford: Oxford University Press, 1975). For a critical survey of this work by a noted Semitist, see Edward Ullendorff's review in *BSOAS* 39 (1976), pp. 403-20.

BIBLIOGRAPHY

Abou-Assaf, A., P. Bordreuil and A.R, Millard, *La statue de Tell Fekherye et son inscription assyro-araméenne* (Etudes assyriologiques, 7; Paris: Editions Recherche sur les civilisations, 1982).

Adler, W., and P. Tuffin, *The Chronography of George Synkellus: A Byzantine Chronicle of Universal History from the Creation* (Oxford: Oxford University Press, 2002).

Ahlström, G.W., 'The Nora Inscription and Tarshish', *Maarav* 7 (1991), pp. 41-49.

Albright, W.F., 'The Land of Damascus between 1850 and 1750 B.C.', *BASOR* 83 (1941), pp. 30-36.

—'New Light on the Early History of Phoenician Colonization', *BASOR* 83 (1941), pp. 14-22.

—'The Role of the Canaanites in the History of Civilization', in G.E. Wright (ed.), *The Bible in the Ancient Near East: Essays in Honor of William Foxwell Albright* (Garden City, NY: Doubleday, 1961), pp. 328-62.

Alexander, P.S., 'The Targumim and Early Exegesis of "Sons of God" in Genesis 6', *JJS* 23 (1972), pp. 60-71.

Alexander, T.D., 'Genesis 22 and the Covenant of Circumcision', *JSOT* 25 (1983), pp. 17-22.

Alster, B., 'An Aspect of "Enmerkar and the Land of Aratta"', *RA* 67 (1973), pp. 101-109.

Alter, R., *Genesis* (New York: W.W. Norton, 1996).

Amiet, P., 'Observations sur les "Tablettes magiques" d'Arslan Tash', *AuOr* 1 (1988), p. 109.

Anderson, B.W., 'The Tower of Babel: Unity and Diversity in God's Creation', in *idem*, *From Creation to New Creation* (OBT; Minneapolis: Fortress Press, 1994), pp. 165-78.

Armstrong, G.T., *Die Genesis in der alten Kirche* (Promotionsarbeit, Heidelberg; Tübingen: J.C.B. Mohr [Paul Siebeck], 1962).

Arnold, B.T., *Genesis* (NCBC; Cambridge: Cambridge University Press, 2009).

Ashleigh, T.R., *The Book of Numbers* (NICOT; Grand Rapids, 1993).

Asselt, W.J. van, *The Federal Theology of Johannes Cocceius (1603–1669)* (Studies in the History of Christian Thought; Leiden: Brill, 2001).

Atwell, J., 'An Egyptian Source for Genesis 1', *JTS* 51 (2000), pp. 441-77.

Aubet, M.E. *The Phoenicians and the West* (trans. M. Turton; Cambridge: Cambridge University Press, 2nd edn, 2001).

Auffret, P., *La sagesse a bati sa maison* (OBO, 49; Fribourg: Editions universitaires, and Göttingen: Vandenhoeck & Ruprecht, 1982).

Babelon, E., Catalogue des monnaies grecques de la Bibliothèque Nationale: Les Perses Achéménides (Paris: Rollin & Feuardent, 1893).

Bailey, L.R., *Genesis, Creation, and Creationism* (Mahwah, NJ: Paulist Press, 1993).
—*Noah: The Person and the Story in History and Tradition* (Columbia, SC: University of South Columbia Press, 1989).
Bal, M., *Lethal Love: Feminist Literary Readings of Biblical Love Stories* (Indiana Studies in Biblical Literature; Bloomington, IN: Indiana University Press, 1989).
Barker, D.G., 'The Waters of the Earth: An Exegetical Study of Psalm 104:1-9', *Grace Theological Journal* 7 (1986), pp. 57-80.
Barker, M., *The Older Testament: The Survival of Themes from the Ancient Royal Cult in Sectarian Judaism and Early Christianity* (London: SCM Press, 1987).
—'Some Reflections upon the Enoch Myth', *JSOT* 15 (1980), pp. 7-29.
Barr, J., *Biblical Chronology: Legend or Science?* (Ethel M. Wood Lecture; London: University of London, 1987).
—*The Garden of Eden and the Hope of Immortality* (London: SCM Press, 1992).
—'Is God a Liar? (Genesis 2–3)—and Related Matters', *JTS* 57 (2006), pp. 1-22.
—'Is Hebrew קן "Nest" a Metaphor?', in A.S. Kaye (ed.), *Semitic Studies in Honour of Wolf Leslau* (Wiesbaden: Otto Harrassowitz, 1991), pp. 150-61.
—'Man and Nature—The Ecological Controversy and the Old Testament', *BJRL* 55 (1972), pp. 9-32.
—Review of E. Ullendorff, *Is Biblical Hebrew a Language?*, *JSS* 26 (1981), pp. 115-22.
—*The Semantics of Biblical Language* (London: Oxford University Press, 1961).
—'Some Semantic Notes on the Covenant', in H. Donner, R. Hanhart and R. Smend (eds.), *Beiträge zur alttestamentlichen Theologie: Festschrift für Walther Zimmerli zum 70. Geburtstag* (Göttingen: Vandenhoeck & Ruprecht, 1977), pp. 23-38.
—' "Thou art the Cherub": Ezekiel 28.14 and the Post-Ezekiel Understanding of Genesis 2–3', in E.C. Ulrich *et al.* (eds.), Priests, *Prophets and Scribes: Essays on the Formation and Heritage of Second Temple Judaism in Honour of Joseph Blenkinsopp* (JSOTSup, 140: JSOT Press, 1992), pp. 213-22.
—'Was Everything that God Created Really Good? A Question in the First Verse of the Bible', in T. Linafelt and T.K. Beal (eds.), *God in the Fray: A Tribute to Walter Brueggemann* (Minneapolis: Fortress Press, 1998), pp. 55-65.
—'Why the World was Created in 4004 B.C.: Archbishop Ussher and Biblical Chronology', *BJRL* 67 (1984–85), pp. 565-608.
Barrett, C.K., *The Acts of the Apostles* (ICC; Edinburgh: T. & T. Clark, 1994).
—*From First Adam to Last: A Study in Pauline Theology* (London: A. & C. Black, 1962).
Bartelmus, R., *Heroentum in Israel und seiner Umwelt: Eine traditionsgeschichtliche Untersuchung zu Gen. 6, 1-4 und verwandten Texten im Alten Testament und der altorientalischen Literatur* (AThANT, 65; Zurich: Theologischer Verlag, 1979).
Barton, G.A., *Christ and Evolution: A Study of the Doctrine of Redemption in the Light of Modern Knowledge* (Philadelphia: University of Pennsylvania Press, 1934).
Barton, S.C., and D. Wilkinson, *Reading Genesis after Darwin* (Oxford: Oxford University Press, 2009).
Bassett, F.W., 'Noah's Nakedness and the Curse of Canaan: A Case of Incest?', *VT* 21 (1971), pp. 232-37.
Bauer, H., and P. Leander, *Historische Grammatik der hebräischen Sprache des Alten Testaments* (Halle: Niemeyer, 1922).

Baumgart, N.C., 'Gen 5,29—ein Brückenvers in der Urgeschichte und zugleich ein Erzählerkommentar', *BN* 92 (1998), pp. 21-37.

Baumgarten, A.I., 'Myth and Midrash: Genesis 9:20-29', in J. Neusner (ed.), *Christianity, Judaism and Other Greco-Roman Cults: Studies for Morton Smith at Sixty*. III. *Judaism before 70* (SJLA, 12; Leiden: Brill, 1975), pp. 55-71.

—*The Phoenician History of Philo of Byblos: A Commentary* (Etudes préliminaires aux religions orientales dans l'empire romain; Leiden: Brill, 1981).

Becking, B., and M.C.A. Korpel, 'To Create, to Separate or to Construct: An Alternative for a Recent Proposal as to the Interpretation of ברא in Genesis 1.1–2.4a', *JHS* 10 (2010), article 3.

Beek, M.A., *Atlas of Mesopotamia* (trans. D.R. Welsh; ed. H.H. Rowley; London: Nelson, 1962).

Berger, P.-R., 'Ellasar, Tarschich und Jawan, Gn 14 und Gn 10', *WO* 13 (1982), pp. 50-78.

Bergsma, J.S., and S.W. Hahn, 'Noah's Nakedness and the Curse on Canaan (Genesis 9:20-27)', *JBL* 124 (2005), pp. 125-40.

Bernstein, M.J., 'לאידור רוחי באדם לעולם: Biblical Text or Biblical Interpretation?', *RevQ* 16 (1994), pp. 421-27.

Berry, G.R., 'The Interpretation of Gen. 6:3', *AJSL* 16 (1899–1900), pp. 47-49.

Bertholet, A., *Die Stellung der Israeliten und der Juden zu den Fremden* (Freiburg i.B.: J.C.B. Mohr [Paul Siebeck], 1896).

Beyerlin, W. (ed.), *Religionsgeschichtliches Textbuch zum Alten Testament* (Grundrisse zum Alten Testament, 1; Göttingen: Vandenhoeck & Ruprecht, 1975), ET *Near Eastern Religious Texts Relating to the Old Testament* (trans. J. Bowden; London: SCM Press, 1978).

Black, M., *The Book of Enoch or 1 Enoch: A New English Edition with Commentary and Textual Notes* (SVTP, 7; Leiden: Brill, 1985).

Blau, L., *Das altjüdische Zauberwesen* (Budapest: Landes-Rabbinerschule, 1898).

Blázquez, J.M., *Tartessos y los orígenes de la colonización fenicia en occidente* (Acta Salamanticensia, Filosofía y Letras, 58; Salamanca: Universidad de Salamanca, 2nd edn, 1975).

Blenkinsopp, J., *Creation, Un-Creation, Re-Creation: A Discursive Commentary on Genesis 1–11* (London: T&T Clark International, 2011).

Blum, E., 'Von Gottesunmittelbarkeit zu Gottesähnlichkeit: Überlegungen zur theologischen Anthropologie der Paradieserzählung', in G. Eberhardt and K. Liess (eds.), *Gottes Nähe im Alten Testament* (SBS, 202; Stuttgart: Katholisches Bibelwerk, 2004), pp. 9-29.

Böhl, F.M.T., 'Die Etymologie von "Babel", Genesis 11 9', *ZAW* 36 (1916), pp. 110-13.

Bordreuil, P., F. Israel and D. Pardee, 'Deux ostraca paléo-hébreux de la collection Sh. Moussaieff', *Sem* 46 (1996), pp. 49-76.

Borger, R., 'Die Beschwörungsserie *bīt mēseri* und die Himmelfahrt Henochs', *JNES* 33 (1974), pp. 183-96, reprinted in English translation as 'The Incantation Series *Bīt Mēseri* and Enoch's Ascension to Heaven' in R.S. Hess and D.T. Tsumura (eds.), *"I Studied Inscriptions from before the Flood": Ancient Near Eastern, Literary, and Linguistic Approaches to Genesis 1–11* (Sources for Biblical and Theological Study, 4; Winona Lake, IN: Eisenbrauns, 1994), pp. 234-53.

—*Die Inschriften Asarhaddons, Königs von Assyrien* (AfO, 9; Graz: Im Selbstverlage des Herausgebers, 1956).

Bost, H., 'La tour de Babel. Gen 11,1-9', in *La ville dans le Proche-Orient ancien* (Les cahiers du CEPOA, 1; Leuven: Peeters, 1983), pp. 231-38.

Bremmer, J.N., 'Paradise: From Persia, via Greece, into the *Septuagint*', in G.P. Luttikhuizen (ed.), *Paradise Interpreted: Representations of Biblical Paradise in Judaism and Christianity* (Themes in Biblical Narrative, 2; Leiden: Brill, 1999), pp. 1-20.

Brinkman, J.A., *Prelude to Empire: Babylonian Politics and Society, 747–626 B.C.* (Occasional Papers of the Babylonian Fund, 7; Philadelphia: University Museum, 1984).

Brooke, G.J., 'Some Remarks on 4Q252 and the Text of Genesis', *Textus* 19 (1998), pp. 1-25.

Brown, W.P., *The Seven Pillars of Creation: The Bible, Science, and the Ecology of Wonder* (Oxford: Oxford University Press, 2010).

Brueggemann, W., *Genesis* (Interpretation; Atlanta: Westminster/John Knox, 1982).

Budde, K., *Die biblische Urgeschichte (Gen. 1–12,5)* (Giessen: J. Ricker, 1883).

Bunnens, G., *L'expansion phénicienne en Méditerranée* (Brussels: Institut historique belge de Rome, 1979).

Burstein, S.M., *The* Babyloniaca *of Berossus* (Sources and Monographs: Sources from the Ancient Near East, 1.5; Malibu, CA: Undena, 1978).

Busink, T.A., 'L'origine et l'évolution de la ziggurat babylonienne', *JEOL* 21 (1970), pp. 91-142.

Cagni, L., *L'epopea di Erra* (Rome: Istituto di Studi del Vicino Oriente dell'Università, 1969).

—*The Poem of Erra* (Sources and Monographs: Sources from the Ancient Near East, 1.3; Malibu, CA: Undena Publications, 1977].

Calmet, A., *Commentaire litteral sur tous les livres de l'Ancien et du Nouveau Testament* (16 vols.; Paris: Pierre Emery, 2nd edn, 1709–30).

Calvin, J., *Commentaries on the First Book of Moses Called Genesis* (trans. J. King; 2 vols.; Calvin Translation Society; Edinburgh: The Edinburgh Printing Co., 1847–60).

Carr, D.M., *Reading the Fractures of Genesis: Historical and Literary Approaches* (Louisville: Westminster/John Knox, 1996).

—*The Formation of the Hebrew Bible: A New Reconstruction* (New York: Oxford University Press, 2011).

Cassuto, U. (M.D.), *A Commentary on the Book of Genesis. I. From Adam to Noah, Genesis 1–VI 8* (trans. I. Abrahams; Jerusalem: Magnes Press, 1961).

—*A Commentary on the Book of Genesis. II. From Noah to Abraham* (trans. I. Abrahams; Jerusalem: Magnes Press, 1964).

—'The Episode of the Sons of God and the Daughters of Men', in *idem*, *Biblical and Oriental Studies* (2 vols.; trans. I. Abrahams; Jerusalem: Magnes Press, 1973–75 [1973]), I, pp. 17-28.

Charlesworth, J.H., *The Good and Evil Serpent* (Anchor Yale Bible Reference Library; New Haven: Yale University Press, 2010).

Cheesman, R.E., *Lake Tana & the Blue Nile* (London: Macmillan, 1936).

Childs, B.S., *Myth and Reality in the Old Testament* (SBT, 27; London: SCM Press, 2nd edn, 1962).

Clark, W.A.M., 'The Flood and the Structure of the Pre-Patriarchal History', *ZAW* 83 (1971), pp. 184-211.

—'A Legal Background to the Yahwist's Use of "Good and Evil" in Genesis 2–3', *JBL* 88 (1969), pp. 266-78.

Clements, R.E., *Isaiah 1–39* (NCB; Grand Rapids, MI: W.B. Eerdmans; London: Marshall, Morgan & Scott, 1982).

Cline, E.H., *From Eden to Exile: Unravelling Mysteries of the Bible From Eden to Exile* (Washington, DC: National Geographic, 2007).

Clines, D.J.A., 'The Image of God in Man', *TynBul* 19 (1968), pp. 53-103, reprinted as 'Humanity as the Image of God', in *idem, On the way to the Postmodern: Old Testament Essays, 1967–98* (2 vols.; JSOTSup, 292-93 [293]; Sheffield: Sheffield Academic Press, 1998), II, pp. 447-97.

—'The Significance of the "Sons of God" Episode (Genesis 6:1–4) in the Context of the "Primeval History" (Genesis 1–11)', *JSOT* 13 (1979), pp. 33-46.

—*The Theme of the Pentateuch* (JSOTSup, 10; Sheffield: JSOT Press, 2nd edn, 1997).

—'What Does Eve Do to Help? And Other Irredeemably Androcentric Orientations in Genesis 1–3', in D.J.A. Clines, *What Does Eve Do To Help? And Other Readerly Questions to the Old Testament* (JSOTSup, 94; Sheffield: JSOT Press, 1990), pp. 25-48.

Coats, G.W., *Genesis with an Introduction to Narrative Literature* (FOTL; Grand Rapids, MI: W.B. Eerdmans, 1983).

Cohen, H.H., *The Drunkenness of Noah* (Tuscaloosa, AL: University of Alabama Press, 1974).

Cohen, H.R. (C.), *Biblical Hapax Legomena in the Light of Akkadian and Ugaritic* (SBLMS, 37; Missoula, MT: Scholars Press, 1978).

Collins, J.J., *The Bible after Babel: Historical Criticism in a Postmodern Age* (Grand Rapids, MI: W.B. Eerdmans, 2005).

—'The Sons of God and the Daughters of Men', in M. Nissinen and R. Uro (eds.), *Sacred Marriages: The Divine–Human Sexual Metaphor from Sumer to Early Christianity* (Winona Lake, IN: Eisenbrauns, 2008), pp. 259-74.

Cooke, G., 'The Sons of (the) God(s)', *ZAW* 76 NF 35 (1964), pp. 22-47.

Coppens, J., *La connaissance du bien et du mal at le péché du paradis* (Gembloux: J. Duculot, 1948).

Cross, F.M., *Canaanite Myth and Hebrew Epic* (Cambridge, MA: Harvard University Press, 1973).

—'An Interpretation of the Nora Stone', *BASOR* 208 (1972), pp. 13-19.

Dalley, S., *Myths from Mesopotamia* (Oxford: Oxford University Press, 1989).

Dalley, S., *et al., The Old Babylonian Tablets from Tell al Rimah* (London: British School of Archaeology in Iraq, 1976).

Das, A. Andrew, 'Paul of Tarsus: Isaiah 66.19 and the Spanish Mission of Romans 15.24, 28', *NTS* 54 (2008), pp. 60-73.

Davidson, R., *Genesis 1–11* (CBC; Cambridge: Cambridge University Press, 1973).

Davies, E.W., *Numbers* (NCB; London: Marshall Pickering, 1995).

Davies, J.G., 'Pentecost and Glossolalia', *JTS* NS 3 (1952), pp. 228-31.

Davies, P.R., 'And Enoch was Not, for Genesis Took Him', in C. Hempel and J.M. Lieu (eds.), *Biblical Traditions in Transmission: Essays in Honour of Michael A. Knibb* (Leiden: Brill, 2006), pp. 97-107.

—'Sons of Cain', in J.D. Martin and P.R. Davies (eds.), *A Word in Season: Essays in Honour of William McKane* (JSOTSup, 42; Sheffield: Sheffield Academic Press, 1986), pp. 35-56.

Day, J., 'Cain and the Kenites', in G. Galil, M. Geller and A.R. Millard (eds.), *Homeland and Exile: Biblical and Ancient Near Eastern Studies in Honour of Bustenay Oded* (VTSup, 130; Leiden: Brill, 2009), pp. 335-46.

—'The Flood and the Ten Antediluvian Figures in Berossus and in the Priestly Source in Genesis', in J.K. Aitken, K.J. Dell and B.A. Mastin (eds.), *On Stone and Scroll: A Festschrift for Graham Ivor Davies* (BZAW, 420; Berlin: W. de Gruyter, 2011), pp. 211-23.

—'The Genesis Flood Narrative in Relation to Ancient Near Eastern Flood Accounts', in K.J. Dell and P.M. Joyce (eds.), *Biblical Interpretation and Method: Essays in Honour of Professor John Barton* (Oxford: Oxford University Press, 2013), pp. 74-88.

—*God's Conflict with the Dragon and the Sea: Echoes of a Canaanite Myth in the Old Testament* (UCOP, 35; Cambridge: Cambridge University Press, 1985).

—'Pre-Deuteronomic Allusions to the Covenant in Hosea and Psalm lxxviii', *VT* 36 (1986), pp. 1-12.

—'Problems in the Interpretation of the Book of Jonah', in A.S. van der Woude (ed.), *In Quest of the Past: Studies on Israelite Religion, Literature and Prophetism* (OTS, 26; Leiden: Brill, 1990), pp. 32-47.

—'Psalm 104 and Akhenaten's Hymn to the Sun', in S. Gillingham (ed.), *Jewish and Christian Approaches to the Psalms: Conflict and Convergence* (Oxford: Oxford University Press, 2013), pp. 211-28.

—*The Recovery of the Ancient Hebrew Language: The Lexicographical Writings of D. Winton Thomas* (Sheffield: Sheffield Phoenix Press, 2013).

—'The Religion of Israel', in A.D.H. Mayes (ed.), *Text in Context: Essays by Members of the Society for Old Testament Study* (Oxford: Oxford University Press, 2000), pp. 428-53.

—*Yahweh and the Gods and Goddesses of Canaan* (JSOTSup, 265; Sheffield: Sheffield Academic Press, 2000).

Day, J. (ed.), *William Robertson Smith: Lectures on the Religion of the Semites, Second and Third Series* (JSOTSup, 183; Sheffield: Sheffield Academic Press, 1995).

de Boer, P.A.H., 'Quelques remarques sur l'Arc dans la Nuée (Genèse 9, 18-17)', in C. Brekelmans (ed.), *Questions disputées d'Ancien Testament: Méthode et Théologie* (BETL, 33; Leuven: Leuven University Press, 1974), pp. 105-14.

Deimel, A., 'Šumer = שִׁנְעָר', *Bib* 2 (1921), pp. 71-74.

Delcor, M., 'Le mythe de la chute des anges et de l'origine des géants comme explication du mal dans le monde dans l'apocalyptique juive. Histoire des traditions', *RHR* 190 (1976), pp. 3-53.

Delitzsch, Franz, *Neuer Commentar über die Genesis* (Leipzig: Dörffling & Franke, 1887).

Delitzsch, Friedrich, *Wo lag das Paradies?* (Leipzig: J.C. Hinrichs, 1881).

Delumeau, J., *Une histoire du Paradis: le jardin des délices* (Paris: Fayard, 1992), ET *History of Paradise: The Garden of Eden in Myth and Tradition* (trans. M. O'Connell; New York: Continuum, 1995).

Dexinger, F., 'Jüdisch-Christliche Nachgeschichte von Gen 6,1–4', in S. Kreuzer and K. Luthi (eds.), *Zur Aktualität des Alten Testaments: Festschrift für Georg Sauer zum 65. Geburtstag* (Frankfurt: Peter Lang, 1992), pp. 155-75.

—*Sturz der Göttersöhne oder Engel vor der Sintflut? Versuch eines Neuverständnisses von Genesis 6,2–4 unter Berückschtigung der religionsvergleichenden und exegesegeschichtlichen Methode* (Wiener Beiträge zur Theologie, 13; Vienna: Herder, 1966).

Dhorme, E., *Le livre de Job* (Etudes bibliques; Paris: V. Lecoffre, 1926), ET *A Commentary on the Book of Job* (trans. H. Knight; London: Thomas Nelson, 1967).

Dietler, M., and C. López-Ruiz (ed.), *Colonial Encounters in Ancient Iberia* (Chicago: University of Chicago Press, 2009).

Dietrich, M., 'Das biblische Paradies und der babylonische Tempelgarten: Überlegungen zur Lage des Garten Eden', in B. Janowski and B. Ego (eds.), *Das biblische Weltbild und seine altorientalischen Kontexte* (Tübingen: Mohr Siebeck, 2001), pp. 281-323.

Dijk, J. van, 'La confusion des langues: Notes sur le lexique et sur la morphologie d'Enmerkar, 147-55', *Or* NS 39 (1970), pp. 302-10.

Dillmann, A., *Die Genesis* (Kurzgefasstes exegetisches Handbuch zum Alten Testament; Leipzig: S. Hirzel, 5th edn, 1886).

Dimant, D., 'Use and Interpretation of Mikra in the Apocrypha and Pseudepigrapha', in M.J. Mulder (ed.), *Mikra: Text, Translation, Reading of the Hebrew Bible in Ancient Judaism and Early Christianity* (Assen: Van Gorcum, 1988), pp. 404-406.

Dion, P.-E., 'Les *KTYM* de Tel Arad: Grecs ou Phéniciens?', *RB* 99 (1992), pp. 70-97.

Dittenberger, W., 'Daisios', in Georg Wissowa (ed.), *Paulys Real-Encyclopädie der classischen Altertumswissenschaft* 4 (Stuttgart: J.B. Metzlerscher Verlag, 1901), cols. 2014-15.

Driver, G.R., 'L'interprétation masorétique à la lumière de la lexicographie hébraïque', *ETL* 26 (1950), pp. 337-53.

—'Problems and Solutions', *VT* 4 (1954), pp. 225-45.

Driver, S.R., *Genesis* (Westminster Commentaries; London: Methuen, 1904).

Drower, E.S., and R. Macuch, *A Mandaic Dictionary* (Oxford: Clarendon Press, 1963).

Dumbrell, W.J., *Covenant and Creation: A Theology of the Old Testament Covenants* (Exeter: Paternoster Press, 1984).

Dundes, A. (ed.), *The Flood Myth* (Berkeley: University of California Press, 1988).

Durand, J.M., 'Le mythologème du combat entre le dieu de l'orage et la mer en Mésopotamie', *Mari: Annales de Recherches Interdisciplinaires* 7 (1993), pp. 41-61.

Dykgraaf, C., 'The Mesopotamian Flood Epic in the Earliest Texts, the Bible, and the Qur'an', in R. Sterman Sabbath (ed.), *Sacred Tropes: Tanakh, New Testament and Qur'an as Literature and Culture* (BibInt Series, 98: Leiden: Brill, 2009), pp. 233-43.

Ebach, J., *Weltentstehung und Kulturentwicklung bei Philo von Byblos* (BWANT, 108; Stuttgart: W. Kohlhammer, 1979), pp. 278-354.

Edelman, D., 'The "Ashurites" of Eshbaal's State', *PEQ* 117 (1985), pp. 85-91.

—'Saul's Battle against Amaleq', *JSOT* 35 (1986), pp. 71-84.

Eichrodt, W., *Theologie des Alten Testaments* (2 vols.; Stuttgart: Klotz, 1957), ET *Theology of the Old Testament* (2 vols.; London: SCM Press, 1961).

Elat, M., 'Tarshish and the Problem of Phoenician Colonisation in the Western Mediterranean', *OLP* 13 (1989), pp. 55-69.

Emerton, J.A., 'The Date of the Yahwist', in J. Day (ed.), *In Search of Pre-Exilic Israel: Proceedings of the Oxford Old Testament Seminar* (JSOTSup, 406; London: T&T Clark International, 2004), pp. 107-29.

—'An Examination of Some Attempts to Defend the Unity of the Flood Narrative in Genesis', *VT* 37 (1987), pp. 401-20.

—'An Examination of Some Attempts to Defend the Unity of the Flood Narrative in Genesis. Part II', *VT* 38 (1988), pp. 1-21.

—'The Origin of the Promises to the Patriarchs in the Older Sources of the Book of Genesis', *VT* 32 (1982), pp. 14-32.

—'The Priestly Writer in Genesis', *JTS* NS 39 (1988), pp. 381-400.

—'Some Difficult Words in Genesis 49', in P.R. Ackroyd and B. Lindars (eds.), *Words and Meanings: Essays Presented to David Winton Thomas* (Cambridge: Cambridge University Press, 1968), pp. 81-93.

Engnell, I., '"Knowledge" and "Life" in the Creation Story', in M. Noth and D.W. Thomas (eds.), *Wisdom in Israel and in the Ancient Near East Presented to Professor Harold Henry Rowley* (VTSup, 3; Leiden: Brill, 1955), pp. 103-19.

Eph'al, I., *The Ancient Arabs* (Jerusalem and Leiden: Magnes Press and Brill, 1982).

Erffa, H.M. von, *Iconologie der Genesis: die christlichen Bildthemen aus dem Alten Testament und ihre Quellen* (2 vols.; Munich: Deutscher Kunstverlag, 1989–95 [1989]).

Eslinger, L., 'A Contextual Identification of the *bene ha'elohim* and *benoth ha'adam* in Genesis 6:1–4', *JSOT* 13 (1979), pp. 65-73.

Ewald, H., 'Erklärung der Biblischen urgeschichte. 4. Die geschlechter des ersten Weltalters', *Jahrbücher der Biblischen wissenschaft* [sic] 6 (1853–54), pp. 1-19.

Fenton, T., 'Chaos in the Bible? Tohu vabohu', in G. Abramson and T. Parfitt (eds.), *Jewish Education and Learning: Published in Honour of Dr David Patterson on the Occasion of His Seventieth Birthday* (London: Harwood Academic Publishers, 1994), pp. 203-19.

Finkelstein, J.J., 'The Antediluvian Kings: A University of California Tablet', *JCS* 17 (1963), pp. 39-54.

Fitzmyer, J.A., *The Aramaic Inscriptions of Sefire* (BibOr, 19A; Pontifical Institute Press, 1995).

Fockner, S., 'Reopening the Discussion: Another Contextual Look at the Sons of God', *JSOT* 32 (2008), pp. 435-56.

Fokkelman, J.P., *Narrative Art in Genesis: Specimens of Stylistic and Structural Analysis* (Studia Semitica Neerlandica, 17; Assen: Van Gorcum, 2nd edn,1975; repr. The Biblical Seminar, 12; Sheffield: JSOT Press, 1991).

Foster, B.R., *Before the Muses: An Anthology of Akkadian Literature* (Bethesda, MD: CDL, 3rd edn, 2005).

Frendo, A.J., 'The Particles *beth* and *waw* and the Periodic Structure of the Nora Stone Inscription', *PEQ* 128 (1996), pp. 8-11.

Friedman, R.E., *Who Wrote the Bible?* (London: Cape, 1988).

Frymer-Kensky, T., 'The Atrahasis Epic and its Significance for Understanding Genesis 1–9', *BA* 40 (1977), pp. 147-55, reprinted in A. Dundes (ed.), *The Flood Myth* (Berkeley: University of California Press, 1988), pp. 61-73.

Gagnon, R.A.J., *The Bible and Homosexual Practice: Texts and Hermeneutics* (Nashville: Abingdon, 2001).

Garbini, G., 'Tarsis e Gen. 10,4', *BeO* 7 (1965), pp. 13-19.

Gardiner, A.H., *Egyptian Grammar* (Oxford: Griffith Institute, Ashmolean Museum, 3rd edn, 1957).

Garr, W.R., *In His Own Likeness: Humanity, Divinity, and Monotheism* (CHANE, 15; Brill: Leiden, 2003).

Gaster, T.H., *Myth, Legend, and Custom in the Old Testament* (London: Duckworth, 1969).

Gelb, I.J., 'The Name of Babylon', *Journal of the Institute of Asian Studies* 1 (1955), pp. 1-4.

George, A.R., *The Babylonian Gilgamesh Epic: Introduction, Critical Edition and Cuneiform Texts* (2 vols.; Oxford: Oxford University Press, 2003).

—*Babylonian Topographical Texts* (OLA, 40; Leuven: Peeters, 1992).

—*The Epic of Gilgamesh* (London: Penguin Books, 1999).

—'The Tower of Babel: Archaeology, History and Cuneiform Texts', *AfO* 51 (2005–2006), pp. 75-95.

Gertz, J.C., 'Babel in Rücken und das Land vor Augen: Anmerkungen zum Abschluß der Urgeschichte und zum Anfang der Erzählungen von den Erzeltern Israels', in A. Hagedorn and H. Pfeiffer (eds.), *Die Erzväter in der biblischen Tradition: Festschrift für Matthias Köckert* (BZAW, 400; Berlin: W. de Gruyter, 2009), pp. 9-34.

—'Von Adam zu Enosch: Überlegungen zur Entstehungsgeschichte von Genesis 2–4', in M. Witte (ed.), *Gott und Mensch im Dialog: Festschrift für Otto Kaiser zum 80. Geburtstag* (BZAW, 345.1; Berlin: W. de Gruyter, 2004), pp. 215-36.

Gese, H., 'Der bewachte Lebensbaum und die Heroen: Zwei mythologische Ergänzungen zur Urgeschichte der Quelle J', in H. Gese and H.P. Rüger (eds.), *Wort und Geschichte: Festschrift für Karl Elliger zum 70. Geburtstag* (AOAT, 18; Neukirchen–Vluyn: Neukirchener Verlag, 1973), pp. 77-85.

Gesenius, F.H.W., *Thesaurus philologicus criticus linguae Hebraeae et Chaldaeae Veteris Testamenti* (Leipzig: Fr. Chr. Guil. Vogelii, 1829–57).

Gibson, J.C.L., *Genesis* (2 vols.; Daily Study Bible; Edinburgh: Saint Andrew Press, 1981–82).

—*Textbook of Syrian Semitic Inscriptions* (3 vols.; Oxford: Clarendon Press, 1971–82).

Ginzberg, L., *Legends of the Jews* (7 vols.; Philadelphia: Jewish Publication Society of America, 1968).

Glassner, J.-J., *Mesopotamian Chronicles* (SBL Writings from the Ancient World; Leiden: Brill, 2004).

Gmirkin, R.E., *Berossus and Genesis, Manetho and Exodus: Hellenistic Historians and the Date of the Pentateuch* (LHBOTS, 433; London: T&T Clark International, 2006).

Godley, A.D., *Herodotus Books I–II* (LCL; Cambridge, MA: Harvard University Press, rev. edn, 1926).

Goldenberg, D.M., *The Curse of Ham: Race and Slavery in Early Judaism, Christianity, and Islam* (Princeton: Princeton University Press, 2003).

Gordon, C.H., 'Ebla and Genesis 11', in M.L. Peterson (ed.), *A Spectrum of Thought: Essays in Honor of Dennis F. Kinlaw* (Wilmore, KY: Francis Asbury, 1982), pp. 125-34.

—'Homer and Bible: The Origin and Character of East Mediterranean Literature', *HUCA* 26 (1955), pp. 43-108, reprinted as *Homer and Bible: The Origin and Character of East Mediterranean Literature* (Ventnor, NJ: Ventnor Publishers, 1967).

—*Introduction to Old Testament Times* (Ventnor, NJ: Ventnor Publishers, 1953), reprinted as *The Ancient Near East* (New York: W.W. Norton, 3rd edn, 1969), and C.H. Gordon and G.A. Rendsburg, *The Bible and the Ancient Near East* (New York: W.W. Norton, 4th edn, 1997).

—*Ugaritic Literature* (Rome: Pontifical Biblical Institute, 1949).

—'The Wine-Dark Sea', *JNES* 37 (1978), pp. 51-52.

Gordon, R.P., 'The Ethics of Eden: Truth-Telling in Genesis 2–3', in K.J. Dell (ed.), *Ethical and Unethical in the Old Testament: God and Humans in Dialogue* (LHBOTS, 528; T&T Clark International, 2010), pp. 11-33.

Goren, G., I. Finkelstein and N. Na'aman, 'The Location of Alashiya. Petrographic Analysis of the Tablets', *AJA* 107 (2003), pp. 233-55.

Görg, M., 'Die Sünde Salomos. Zeitkritische Aspekte der jahwistischen Sünden-fallerzählung', *BN* 16 (1981), pp. 42-59.

—'Weisheit als Provokation: Religionsgeschichtliche und theologische Aspekte der Sündenfallerzählung', in A.E. Hierold *et al.* (eds.), *Die Kraft der Hoffnung. Gemeinde und Evangelium. Festschrift für Alterzbischof DDr. Josef Schneider zum 80. Geburtstag* (Bamberg: St. Otto-Verlag, 1986), pp. 19-34.

Grabbe, L.L., *Comparative Philology and the Text of Job: A Study in Methodology* (SBLDS, 34; Missoula, MT: Scholars Press, 1977).

—Review of R.E. Gmirkin, *Berossus and Genesis, Manetho and Exodus: Hellenistic Historians and the Date of the Pentateuch* (LHBOTS, 433; London: T&T Clark International, 2006), *Society for Old Testament Study Book List 2007* (London: Sage, 2007), p. 117.

Graves, R., and R. Patai, *Hebrew Myths: The Book of Genesis* (London: Cassell, 1963).

Greenfield, J.C., 'An Ancient Treaty Ritual and its Targumic Echo', in *Salvación en la Palabra: Targum, Derash, Berith; Homenaje al Prof. Alejandro Diez Macho* (Madrid: Cristiandad, 1986), pp. 391-97, reprinted in ʿ*Al Kanfei Yonah: Collected Studies of Jonas C. Greenfield on Semitic Philology* (ed. S.M. Paul, M.E. Stone and A. Pinnick; 2 vols.; Leiden: Brill, 2001), I, pp. 405-11.

—'Elishah', *IDB* 2, p. 92.

—'A Touch of Eden', in *Acta Orientalia J. Duchesne-Guillemin emerito oblata* (Acta Iranica, 23; Leiden: Brill, 1984), pp. 219-24, reprinted in ʿ*Al Kanfei Yonah: Collected Studies of Jonas C. Greenfield on Semitic Philology* (ed. S.M. Paul, M.E. Stone and A. Pinnick; 2 vols.; Leiden: Brill; Jerusalem: Magnes Press, 2001), II, pp. 750-55.

Guillaume, P., *Land and Calendar: The Priestly Document from Genesis 1 to Joshua 18* (LHBOTS, 391; New York: T&T Clark International, 2009).

Gunkel, H., *Genesis* (HKAT, 1.1; Göttingen: Vandenhoeck & Ruprecht, 3rd edn, 1910), ET *Genesis* (trans. M.E. Biddle; Macon, GA: Mercer University Press, 1997).

—*Schöpfung und Chaos in Urzeit und Endzeit* (Göttingen: Vandenhoeck & Ruprecht, 1895), ET *Creation and Chaos in the Primeval Era and the Eschaton: A Religio-Historical Study of Genesis 1 and Revelation 12* (trans. K.W. Whitney, Jr; Grand Rapids, MI: W.B. Eerdmans, 2006).

Hamilton, V.P., *The Book of Genesis Chapters 1–17* (NICOT; Grand Rapids, MI: W.B. Eerdmans, 1990).

—*Die Psalmen* (HKAT, 11.2; Göttingen: Vandenhoeck & Ruprecht, 1925–26).

Hamori, E., *"When Gods Were Men": The Embodied God in Biblical and Near Eastern Literature* (BZAW, 384; Berlin: W. de Gruyter, 2008).

Hanson, P.D., 'Rebellion in Heaven, Azazel, and Euhemerist c Heroes in 1 Enoch 6–11', *JBL* 96 (1977), pp. 195-233.

Harland, P.J., 'Vertical or Horizontal: The Sin of Babel', *VT* 48 (1998), pp. 515-33.

Harrison, T.P., 'Neo-Hittites in the "Land of Palistin": Renewed Investigations at Tell Ta'yinat on the Plain of Antioch', *Near Eastern Archaeology* 72 (2009), pp. 174-89.

Hartman, L., 'Sin in Paradise', *CBQ* 20 (1958), pp. 26-40.

Hasel, G.F., 'The Genealogies of Gen 5 and 11 and their Alleged Babylonian Background', *AUSS* 16 (1978), pp. 361-74.

—'The Meaning of the Animal Rite in Gen. 15', *JSOT* 19 (981), pp. 61-78.

Haupt, P., 'Wo lag das Paradies?', in *Ueber Land und Meer* 15 (1894–95), pp. 3-8.

Hawkins, J.D., 'Cilicia, Amuq, and Aleppo: New Light on a Dark Age', *Near Eastern Archaeology* 72 (2009), pp. 164-73.

Haynes, S.R., *Noah's Curse: The Biblical Justification of American Slavery* (Religion in America Series; New York: Oxford University Press, 2001).

Heidel, A., *The Babylonian Genesis* (Chicago: University of Chicago Press, 2nd edn, 1951).

—*The Gilgamesh Epic and Old Testament Parallels* (Chicago: University of Chicago Press, 2nd edn, 1949).

Held, M., 'Philological Notes on the Mari Covenant Rituals', *BASOR* 200 (1970), pp. 32-40.

Hendel, R.S., '"Begetting" and "Being Born" in the Pentateuch: Notes on Historical Linguistics and Source Criticism', *VT* 50 (2000), pp. 38-46.

—*Genesis 1–11* (Anchor Yale Bible, 1A; New Haven: Yale University Press, forthcoming).

—'A Hasmonean Edition of MT Genesis? The Implications of the Editions of the Chronology in Genesis 5', *HeBAI* 1 (2012), pp. 448-64.

—'Historical Context', in C.A. Evans, J.N. Lohr and D L. Petersen, *The Book of Genesis: Composition, Reception, and Interpretation* (VTSup, 152; Leiden: Brill, 2012), pp. 51-81.

—'The Nephilim were on the Earth: Genesis 6:1-4 and its Ancient Near Eastern Context', in C. Auffarth and L.T. Stuckenbruck (eds.), *The Fall of the Angels* (Themes in Biblical Narrative: Jewish and Christian Traditions, 6; Leiden: Brill, 2004), pp. 11-34.

—'Of Demigods and the Deluge: Towards an Interpretation of Genesis 6:1-4', *JBL* 106 (1987), pp. 13-26.

—'Other Edens', in J.D. Schloen (ed.), *Exploring the Long Durée: Essays in Honor of Lawrence E. Stager* (Winona Lake, IN: Eisenbrauns, 2008), pp. 185-89.

—Review of C. Uehlinger, *Weltreich und «eine Rede»: Eine neue Deutung der sogenannten Turmbauerzählung (Gen 11,1-9)* (OBO, 101; Freiburg: Universitätsverlag, and Göttingen: Vandenhoeck & Ruprecht, 199)), *CBQ* 55 (1993), pp. 785-87.

—*The Text of Genesis 1–11: Textual Studies and Critical Edition* (New York: Oxford University Press, 1998).

Herder, J.G. von, *Älteste Urkunde des Menschengeschlechts* (2 vols.; ed. J.G. Müller; Tübingen: J.G. Cotta, 1806).

Herrmann, J., 'Zu Gen 9 18-27', *ZAW* 30 (1910), pp. 127-31.

Hess, R.S., and D.T. Tsumura (eds.), *"I Studied Inscriptions from before the Flood":
Ancient Near Eastern, Literary, and Linguistic Approaches to Genesis 1–11*
(Sources for Biblical and Theological Study, 4; Winona Lake, IN: Eisenbrauns,
1994).

Heyde, H., *Kain, der erste Jahwe-Verehrer* (Stuttgart: Calwer Verlag, 1965).

Hiebert, T., 'Babel: Babble or Blueprint? Calvin, Cultural Diversity, and the Interpreta-
tion of Genesis 11:1-9', in W.N. Alston and M. Welker (eds.), *Reformed Theology:
Identity and Ecumenicity.* II. *Biblical Interpretation in the Reformed Tradition*
(Grand Rapids, MI: W.B. Eerdmans, 2007), pp. 127-45.

——'The Tower of Babel and the Origin of the World's Cultures', *JBL* 126 (2007), pp. 29-
58.

Higgins, J.M., 'The Myth of Eve: The Temptress', *JAAR* 44 (1976), pp. 639-47.

Hilion, G., *Le déluge dans la Bible et les inscriptions akkadiennes et sumériennes* (Paris:
Geuthner, 1925).

Hoenig, S.B., 'Tarshish', *JQR* 69 (1979), pp. 181-82.

Hoffner, H., 'The Elkunirsa Myth Reconsidered', *Revue hittite et asianique* 23 (1965),
pp. 5-16.

Hoftijzer, J., 'Some Remarks on the Tale of Noah's Drunkenness', in B. Gemser *et al.*,
Studies on the Book of Genesis (OS, 12; Leiden: Brill, 1958), pp. 22-27.

Holter, K., 'The Serpent in Eden as a Symbol of Israel's Political Enemies: A Yahwistic
Criticism of the Solomonic Foreign Policy?', *SJOT* 4 (1990), pp. 106-12.

Humbert, P., 'La relation de Genèse 1 et du Psaume 104 avec la liturgie du Nouvel-An
israëlite', *RHPR* 15 (1935), pp. 1-27.

Hurowitz, V.A., 'Babylon in Bethel—New Light on Jacob's Dream', in S.W. Holloway
(ed.), *Orientalism, Assyriology and the Bible* (Hebrew Bible Monographs, 10;
Sheffield: Sheffield Phoenix Press, 2006), pp. 436-48. An earlier version of this
article was published in M. Heltzer and M. Malul (eds.), *Tᵉshûrôt laAvishur:
Studies in the Bible and the Ancient Near East, in Hebrew and Semitic Languages.
Festschrift Presented to Prof. Yitzhaq Avishur on the Occasion of his Sixty-Fifth
Birthday* (Tel Aviv: Archaeological Center Publications, 2004), pp. 184-94
(Hebrew).

Husser, J.-M., 'Entre mythe et philosophie: La relecture sapientielle de Genèse', *RB* 107
(2000), pp. 232-59.

Huxley, G.L., 'Nikolaos of Damascus on Urartu', *Greek, Roman and Byzantine Studies* 9
(1968), pp. 319-20.

Hvidberg, F.F., 'The Canaanitic Background of Gen. i–iii', *VT* 10 (1960), pp. 285-94.

Izre'el, S., *Adapa and the South Wind: Language Has the Power of Life and Death*
(Winona Lake, IN: Eisenbrauns, 2001).

Jacob, B., *Das erste Buch der Tora: Genesis übersetzt und erklärt* (Berlin: Schocken,
1934), ET *The First Book of the Bible: Genesis Interpreted* (abridged, edited and
translated by E.I. Jacob and W. Jacob; New York: Ktav, 1974; reprinted Jersey
City, NJ: Ktav, 2007).

Jacobsen, T., 'The Battle between Marduk and Tiamat', *JAOS* 88 (1968), pp. 104-108.

——'The Eridu Genesis', *JBL* 80 (1981), pp. 513-29, reprinted in R.S. Hess and D.T.
Tsumura (eds.), *"I Studied Inscriptions from before the Flood": Ancient Near
Eastern, Literary, and Linguistic Approaches to Genesis 1–11* (Sources for Biblical
and Theological Study, 4; Winona Lake, IN: Eisenbrauns, 1994), pp. 129-42.

—*The Sumerian King List* (Assyriological Studies, 11; Chicago: University of Chicago Press, 1939).

Jacoby, F., *Die Fragmente der griechischen Historiker* 3C 1 (14 vols.; Leiden: Brill, 1923–58 [1958]).

Janowski, B., and A. Krüger, 'Gottes Sturm und Gottes Atem. Zum Verständnis von רוּחַ אֱלֹהִים in Gen 1,2 und Ps 104,29f', in *Jahrbuch für Biblische Theologie* 24 (2009), pp. 3-29.

Japhet, S., *1 & II Chronicles* (OTL; London: SCM Press, 1993).

Jennings, W.H., *Storms over Genesis: Biblical Battleground in America's Wars of Religion* (Minneapolis: Fortress Press, 2007).

Jobling, D., 'The Myth Semantics of Genesis 2.4b–3.24', *Semeia* 18 (1980), pp. 41-49.

Johnson, S.A., *The Myth of Ham in Nineteenth-Century American Christianity: Race, Heathens, and the People of God* (New York: Palgrave Macmillan, 2004).

Joines, K.R., *Serpent Symbolism in the Old Testament* (Haddonfield, NJ: Haddonfield House, 1974).

Jones, B.W., 'Cutting Deals and Striking Bargains', *English Today* 46.2 (1996), pp. 35-40

Jónsson, G.A., *The Image of God: Genesis 1:26-28 in a Century of Old Testament Research* (ConBOT, 26; Stockholm: Almqvist & Wiksell, 1988).

Joosten, J., 'The Operation of Syntactic Rule in Classical Biblical Hebrew and in Hebrew Inscriptions of the Monarchic Period', in J.K. Aitken, K.J. Dell and B.A. Mastin (eds.), *On Stone and Scroll: A Festschrift for Graham Ivor Davies* (BZAW, 420; Berlin: W. de Gruyter, 2011), pp. 493-505.

Kaiser, W.C., *Toward an Old Testament Theology* (Grand Rapids, MI: Zondervan, 1978).

Kaminski, C.M., 'Beautiful Women or "False Judgment?" Interpreting Genesis 6.2 in the Context of the Primaeval History', *JSOT* 32 (2008), pp. 457-73.

Kiepert, H., *Formae Orbis Antiqui* (Berlin: D. Reimer, 1902).

Kikawada, I.M., 'The Shape of Genesis 11:1-9', in J.J. Jackson and M. Kessler (eds.), *Rhetorical Criticism: Essays in Honor of James Muilenburg* (Pittsburgh Theological Monograph Series, 1; Pittsburgh: Pickwick Press, 1974), pp. 18-32.

Killebrew, A., *Biblical Peoples and Ethnicity: An Archaeological Study of Egyptians, Canaanites, Philistines, and Early Israel 1300–1100 B.C.E.* (SBLABS, 9; Leiden: Brill, 2005).

Kilmer, A.D., 'The Mesopotamian Concept of Overpopulation and its Solution as Reflected in the Mythology', *Or* 41 (1972), pp. 160-77.

—'The Symbolism of the Flies in the Mesopotamian Flood Myth and Some Further Implications', in Francesca Rochberg-Halton (ed.), *Language, Literature, and History: Philological and Historical Studies Presented to Erica Reiner* (AOS Series, 67; New Haven, CT: American Oriental Society, 1987), pp. 175-80.

Klein, J., 'The "Bane" of Humanity: A Lifespan of One Hundred and Twenty Years', *Acta Sumerologica* 12 (1990), pp. 58-70.

Klein, R.W., 'Archaic Chronologies and the Textual History of the Old Testament', *HTR* 67 (1974), pp. 255-63.

Klengel-Brandt, E., *Der Turm von Babylon. Legende und Geschichte eines Bauwerkes* (Berlin: Koehler & Amelang, 2nd edn, 1992).

Kline, M.G., 'Divine Kingship and Genesis 6:1-4', *WTJ* 24 (1962), pp. 187-204.

Knauf, E.A., *Midian: Untersuchungen zur Geschichte Palästinas und Nordarabiens am Ende des 2. Jahrtausends v. Chr.* (Abhandlungen der deutschen Palästinavereins; Wiesbaden: O. Harrassowitz, 1988).

Knights, C.M., 'Kenites = Rechabites? 1 Chronicles ii 55 Reconsidered', *VT* 43 (1993), pp. 1-18.

Knobel, A., *Die Genesis erklärt* (Kurzgefasstes exegetisches Handbuch zum Alten Testament; Leipzig: S. Hirzel; 2nd edn, 1860).

—*Die Völkertafel der Genesis* (Giessen: J. Ricker, 1850), pp. 86-94.

Knohl, I., *The Sanctuary of Silence: The Priestly Torah and the Holiness School* (Minneapolis: Fortress Press, 1995).

Koch, M., *Tarschisch und Hispanien* (Madrider Forschungen, 14; Berlin: W. de Gruyter, 1984).

Koenig, Y., 'Les textes d'envoûtement de Mirgissa', *Revue d'Egyptologie* 41 (1990), pp. 101-25.

Komoróczy, G., 'Berossus and the Mesopotamian Literature', *Acta Antiqua* 21 (1973), pp. 125-52.

König, E., *Die Genesis eingeleitet, übersetzt und erklärt* (Gütersloh: C. Bertelsmann, 1925).

Kooij, A. van der, 'The City of Babel and Assyrian Imperialism: Genesis 11:1-9 Interpreted in the Light of Mesopotamian Sources', in A. Lemaire (ed.), *Congress Volume: Leiden 2004* (VTSup, 109; Leiden: Brill, 2006), pp. 1-17.

—Review of C. Uehlinger, 'The Story of Genesis 11:1-9 and the Culture of Ancient Mesopotamia', *BO* 53 (1996), pp. 28-38.

—'The Story of Paradise in the Light of Mesopotamian Culture and Literature', in K.J. Dell, G.I. Davies and Y.V. Koh (eds.), *Genesis, Isaiah and Psalms: A Festschrift to Honour Professor John Emerton for His Eightieth Birthday* (VTSup, 135; Leiden: Brill, 2010), pp. 1-22.

Kraeling, E.G., 'Miqqedem in Genesis XI 2', *JQR* 38 (1947–48), pp. 161-65.

—'The Tower of Babel', *JAOS* 40 (1920), pp. 276-81.

—'Xisouthros, Deucalion and the Flood Traditions', *JAOS* 67 (1947), pp. 177-83.

Kramer, S.N., 'The "Babel of Tongues": A Sumerian Version', *JAOS* 88 (1968), pp. 108-11.

Kupper, J.R., 'Sutéens et Ḫapiru', *RA* 55 (1961), pp. 197-205.

Kutsch, E., *Verheißung und Gesetz: Untersuchungen zum sogenannten »Bund« im Alten Testament* (BZAW, 131: Berlin: W. de Gruyter, 1973).

Kvanvig, H.S., *Primeval History: Babylonian, Biblical, Enochic* (JSJSup, 149; Leiden: Brill, 2011).

—*Roots of Apocalyptic: The Mesopotamian Background of the Enoch Figure and of the Son of Man* (WMANT, 61; Neukirchen–Vluyn: Neukirchener Verlag, 1988).

LaCocque, A., *The Captivity of Innocence: Babel and the Yahwist* (Eugene, OR: Cascade Books, 2010).

—*The Trial of Innocence: Adam, Eve, and the Yahwist* (Eugene, OR: Cascade Books [Wipf & Stock], 2006).

—'Whatever Happened in the Valley of Shinar? A Response to Theodore Hiebert', *JBL* 128 (2009), pp. 29-41.

Lambert, W.G., 'A Catalogue of Texts and Authors', *JCS* 16 (1962), pp. 59-77.

—'Enmeduranki and Related Matters', *JCS* 21 (1967), pp. 126-38.

—'A New Look at the Babylonian Background of Genesis', *JTS* NS 16 (1965), pp. 287-300, reprinted in R.S. Hess and D.T. Tsumura (eds.), *"I Studied Inscriptions from before the Flood": Ancient Near Eastern, Literary, and Linguistic Approaches to Genesis 1–11* (Sources for Biblical and Theological Study, 4; Winona Lake, IN: Eisenbrauns, 1994), pp. 96-113.

—'Note brève, Niṣir or Nimuš', *RA* 80 (1986), pp. 185-86.

—Review of F. Gössmann, *Das Era-Epos* (Würzburg: Augustinus, 1956), *AfO* 18 (1957–58), pp. 395-401.

—'The Theology of Death', in B. Alster (ed.), *Death in Mesopotamia: Papers Read at the XXVI⁰ Rencontre assyriologique internationale* (Copenhagen: Akademisk forlag, 1980), pp. 52-66.

Lambert, W.G., and A.R. Millard, *Atra-ḫasīs: The Babylonian Story of the Flood* (Oxford: Clarendon Press, 1969).

Lanfer, P.T., *Remembering Eden: The Reception History of Genesis 3:22-24* (New York: Oxford University Press, 2012).

Laurin, R.B., 'The Tower of Babel Revisited', in Garry A. Tuttle (ed.), *Biblical and Near Eastern Studies: Essays in Honor of William Sanford LaSor* (Grand Rapids, MI: Eerdmans, 1978), pp. 142-45.

Leder, H.-G., 'Arbor Scientiae: Die Tradition vom paradiesischen Apfelbaum', *ZNW* 52 (1961), pp. 156-89.

Lemaire, A., 'Tarshish-*Tarsisi*: problème de topographie historique biblique et assyrienne', in G. Galil and M. Weinfeld (eds.), *Studies in Historical Geography and Biblical Historiography Presented to Zecharia Kallai* (VTSup, 81; Leiden: Brill, 2000), pp. 44-62.

Levenson, J.D., *Creation and the Persistence of Evil: The Jewish Drama of Divine Omnipotence* (San Francisco: Harper & Row, 1988).

—*Sinai and Zion: An Entry into the Jewish Bible* (Minneapolis: Winston, 1985).

Levias, C., 'Blau on Ancient Jewish Magic', *AJSL* 15 (1898–99), pp. 191-92.

Levine, B.A., *Numbers 21–36* (AB, 4A; New York: Doubleday, 2000).

Levison, J.R., 'Is Eve to Blame? A Contextual Study of Sirach 25:24', *CBQ* 47 (1985), pp. 617-23.

—*Portraits of Adam in Early Judaism: From Sirach to 2 Baruch* (JSOTSup, 1; Sheffield: JSOT Press, 1988).

Lichtheim, M., *Ancient Egyptian Literature* (3 vols.; Berkeley: University of California Press, 1973–80).

Lightfoot, J.L., *Lucian, On the Syrian Goddess* (Oxford: Oxford University Press, 2003).

Lim, J.T.K., 'Did the Scholar(s) Get it Right?', in R. Boer, M. Carden and J. Kelso (eds.), *The One Who Reads May Run: Essays in Honour of Edgar W. Conrad* (LHBOTS, 553; London: T&T Clark International, 2012), pp. 69-79.

—*Grace in the Midst of Judgment: Grappling with Genesis 1–11* (BZAW, 314; Berlin: W. de Gruyter, 2002).

Lim, T.J., 'Biblical Quotations in the Pesharim', in E.D. Herbert and E. Tov (eds.), *The Bible as a Book: The Hebrew Bible and the Judaean Desert Discoveries* (London: The British Library, 2002), pp. 72-79.

Lipiński, E., 'El's Abode: Mythological Traditions Related to Mount Hermon and to the Mountains of Armenia', *OLP* 2 (1971), pp. 13-69.

—*Itineraria Phoenicia* (OLA, 127, Studia Phoenicia, 18; Leuven: Peeters, 2004), pp. 225-65.

—'Les Japhétites selon Gen 10,1-4 et 1 Chr 1,5-7', *ZAH* 3 (1990), pp. 40-53.

Liverani, M., *Studies in the Annals of Ashurnasirpal II*, 2: *Topographical Analysis* (Quaderni di Geografia Storica, 4; Rome: Università di Roma 'La Sapienza', Dipartimento di Scienze storiche, archeologiche e antropologiche dell'Antichità, 1992).

Loewenstamm, S., 'The Flood', in *idem*, *Comparative Studies in Biblical and Oriental Literature* (AOAT, 204; Neukirchen–Vluyn: Neukirchener Verlag, 1980), pp. 93-121.

—'Should Qinnîm (Gen. 6:14) be Amended to Read Qanîm?', in *Beer-Sheva* 1 (Jerusalem: Kiryat Sepher, 1973), pp. 135-36 (Hebrew).

Luther, M., *Luther's Works. II. Lectures on Genesis Chapters 6–14* (ed. J. Pelikan; St. Louis: Concordia Publishing House, 1960).

Marcus, R. (trans. and ed.), *Philo Supplement I. Questions and Answers on Genesis* (LCL; London: William Heinemann, 1953).

Marshall, I.H., *The Acts of the Apostles: An Introduction and Commentary* (Leicester: Inter-Varsity Press; Grand Rapids, MI: W.B. Eerdmans, 1980).

Mayes, A.D.H., *Deuteronomy* (NCB; London: Oliphants, 1979).

McCarthy, D.J., *Treaty and Covenant* (AnBib, 21A; Rome: Biblical Institute Press, 2nd edn, 1978).

McEvenue, S.E., *The Narrative Style of the Priestly Writer* (AnBib, 50; Rome: Biblical Institute Press, 1971).

McGowan, A.T.B., *The Federal Theology of Thomas Boston* (Carlisle: Paternoster Press, 1997).

McKenzie, S.L., *Covenant* (Understanding Biblical Themes; St. Louis, MO: Chalice Press, 2000).

McKeown, J., *Genesis* (Two Horizons OT Commentary; Grand Rapids, MI: W.B. Eerdmans, 2008).

McNamara, M., *Targum Neofiti 1: Genesis Translated, with Apparatus and Notes* (The Aramaic Bible, 1A; Edinburgh: T. & T. Clark, 1992).

Mettinger, T.N.D., *The Eden Narrative: A Literary and Religio-Historical Study of Genesis 2–3* (Winona Lake, IN: Eisenbrauns, 2007).

Meyer, E., *Geschichte des Alterthums* (5 vols.; Stuttgart: J.G. Cotta, 1884–1902).

—*Die Israeliten und ihre Nachbarstämme* (Halle: Max Niemeyer, 1906).

Meyers, C.L., *Discovering Eve: Ancient Israelite Women in Context* (New York: Oxford University Press, 1988).

Middleton, J.R., *The Liberating Image: The* Imago Dei *in Genesis 1* (Grand Rapids, MI: Brazos Press, 2005).

Milgrom, J., *Leviticus 17–22* (AB, 3A; New York: Doubleday, 2000).

—*Leviticus 23–27* (AB, 3B; New York: Doubleday, 2001).

—*Numbers* (JPS Torah Commentary; Philadelphia: Jewish Publication Society, 1990).

Milik, J.T. (ed. with the collaboration of M. Black), *The Book of Enoch: Aramaic Fragments of Qumrân Cave 4* (Oxford: Clarendon Press, 1976).

Millard, A.R., 'The Celestial Ladder and the Gate of Heaven (Genesis xxviii.12, 17)', *ExpTim* 78 (1966), pp. 86-87.

—'The Etymology of Eden', *VT* 34 (1984), pp. 103-106.

—'A New Babylonian "Genesis" Story', *TynBul* 18 (1967), pp. 3-18, reprinted in R.S. Hess and D.T. Tsumura (eds.), *"I Studied Inscriptions from before the Flood": Ancient Near Eastern, Literary, and Linguistic Approaches to Genesis 1–11* (Sources for Biblical and Theological Study, 4; Winona Lake, IN: Eisenbrauns, 1994), pp. 114-28.

Miller, P.D., *Genesis 1–11: Studies in Structure & Theme* (JSOTSup, 8; Sheffield: Department of Biblical Studies, University of Sheffield, 1978).

Mittermayer, C., *Enmerkara und der Herr von Arata. Ein ungleicher Wettstreit* (OBO, 239; Fribourg: Academic Press; Göttingen: Vandenhoeck & Ruprecht, 2009).

Moberly, R.W.L., 'Did the Interpreters Get it Right?', *JTS* 59 (2008), pp. 22-40.

—'Did the Serpent Get it Right?', *JTS* 39 (1988), pp. 1-27.

Montero-Fenellós, J.-L., 'La tour de Babylone, repensée', in B. André-Salvini (ed.), *Babylone* (Paris: Hazan and Musée du Louvre, 2008), pp. 229-30.

Moran, W.L., 'Atrahasis: The Babylonian Story of the Flood', *Bib* 52 (1971), pp. 51-61.

Mowinckel, S., *The Two Sources of the Predeuteronomic Primeval History (JE) in Gen. 1–11* (Avhandlinger utgitt av Det Norske Videnskaps-Akademi i Oslo, II. Hist.-Filos. Klasse 1937, No. 2; Oslo: J. Dybwad, 1937).

Murray, J.A.H. *et al.*, *The Oxford English Dictionary* (13 vols.; Oxford: Clarendon Press, 1933).

Neiman, D., 'The Date and Circumstances of the Cursing of Canaan', in A. Altmann (ed.), *Biblical Motifs: Origins and Transformations* (Cambridge, MA: Harvard University Press, 1966), pp. 113-34.

—'The Two Genealogies of Japhet', in H.A. Hoffner (ed.), *Orient and Occident: Essays Presented to Cyrus H. Gordon on the Occasion of His Sixty-Fifth Birthday* (AOAT, 22; Kevelaer: Verlag Butzon & Bercker; Neukirchen–Vluyn: Neukirchener Verlag, 1973), pp. 119-26.

Neumann-Gersolke, U., *Herrschen in den Grenzen der Schöpfung: ein Beitrag zur alttestamentlichen Anthropologie am Beispiel von Psalm 8, Genesis 1 und verwandten Texten* (WMANT, 101; Neukirchen–Vluyn: Neukirchener Verlag, 2004).

Neville, A., *Mountains of Silver & Rivers of Gold: The Phoenicians in Iberia* (Oxford: Oxbow Books, 2007).

Nicholson, E.W., *God and His People: Covenant and Theology in the Old Testament* (Oxford: Clarendon Press, 1986).

Nickelsburg, G.W.E., 'Apocalyptic and Myth in 1 Enoch 6–11', *JBL* 96 (1977), pp. 383-405.

—*Preaching to the Exiles: A Study of the Prose Tradition in the Book of Jeremiah* (Oxford: Clarendon Press, 1970).

Nissinen, M., *Homoeroticism in the Biblical World: A Historical Perspective* (trans. K. Stjerna; Minneapolis: Fortress Press, 1998).

Nöldeke, T., *Ueber die Amalekiter und einige andere Nachbarvölker der Israeliten* (Göttingen: Dieterich, 1864).

Numbers, R.L., *The Creationists: From Scientific Creationism to Intelligent Design* (Cambridge, MA: Harvard University Press, 2006).

Oded, B., 'Ish-bosheth', *Encyclopaedia Judaica* (Detroit: Thomson Gale [22 vols.; Macmillan Reference USA], 2nd edn, 2007), X, pp. 80-81.

—*Mass Deportations and Deportees in the Neo-Assyrian Empire* (Wiesbaden: O. Harrassowitz, 1979).

Oden, R.A., 'Divine Aspirations in Atrahasis and in Genesis 1–11', *ZAW* 93 (1981), pp. 197-216.

—*Studies in Lucian's De Syria Dea* (HSM, 125; Missoula, MT: Scholars Press, 1977).

Oppert, J., 'Chronology (I)', in *The Jewish Encyclopedia* (12 vols.; New York: Funk & Wagnalls, 1903–1906 [1903]), IV, pp. 64-68.

—'Die Daten der Genesis', *Nachrichten von der Königlichen Gesellschaft der Wissenschaften in Göttingen* (1877), pp. 201-23.

Orlinsky, H.M., 'The Plain Meaning of ruaḥ in Gen. 1.2', *JQR* 48 (1957–58), pp. 174-82.

Otten, H., 'Ein kanaanäischer Mythus aus Boğazköy', *MIO* 1 (1953), pp. 125-50.

Ottosson, M., 'Eden and the Land of Promise', in J.A. Emerton (ed.), *Congress Volume: Jerusalem 1986* (VTSup, 40; Brill, 1986), pp. 177-86.

Page, H.R., *The Myth of Cosmic Rebellion: A Study of its Reflexes in Ugaritic and Biblical Literature* (VTSup, 65; Leiden: Brill, 1996).

Pardee, D., 'Les documents d'Arslan Tash: authentiques ou faux?', *Syria* 75 (1998), pp. 15-54.

Parpola, S., *Neo-Assyrian Toponyms* (AOAT, 6; Neukirchen–Vluyn: Neukirchener Verlag, and Kevelaer: Butzon & Bercker, 1970).

Parrot, A., *La tour de Babel* (Cahiers d'archeologie biblique, 2; Neuchatel: Delachaux & Niestle, 1953), ET *The Tower of Babel* (trans. E. Hudson; Studies in Biblical Archaeology, 2; London: SCM Press, 1955).

—*Ziggurats et tour de Babel* (Paris: Albin Michel, 1949).

Peckham, B., 'The Nora Inscription', *Or* 41 (1972), pp. 457-68.

Perlitt, L., *Bundestheologie im Alten Testament* (WMANT, 36; Neukirchen–Vluyn: Neukirchener Verlag, 1969).

—*Riesen im Alten Testament* (Nachrichten von der Akademie der Wissenschaften in Göttingen, Philologisch-Historische Klasse, 1990, Nr. 1; Göttingen: Vandenhoeck & Ruprecht, 1990).

Peters, J.P., 'The Tower of Babel at Borsippa', *JAOS* 41 (1921), pp. 57-59.

Pettinato, G., 'Die Bestrafung des Menschengeschlechts durch die Sintflut: die erste Tafel des Atramḥasīs-Epos eröfffnet eine neue Einsicht in die Motivation dieser Strafe', *Or* NS 37 (1968), pp. 165-200.

Peterson, T.V., *Ham and Japheth: The Mythic World of Whites in the Antebellum South* (ATLA Monograph Series, 12; Metuchen, NJ: The Scarecrow Press; London: American Theological Library Association, 1978).

Phillips, A., 'Uncovering the Father's Skirt', *VT* 30 (1980), pp. 38-43.

Pope, M.H., *Job* (AB, 15; Garden City, NY: Doubleday, 3rd edn, 1973).

Posener, G., *Princes et pays d'Asie et de Nubie* (Brussels: Fondation égyptologique reine Elisabeth, 1940).

Potts, D.T., *Mesopotamian Civilization: The Material Foundation* (London: Athlone Press, 1997).

Preuss, H.D., *Verspottung fremder Religionen im Alten Testament* (BWANT, 92; Stuttgart: W. Kohlhammer, 1971).

Priest, J.F., '῞Ορκια in the *Iliad* and Consideration of a Recent Theory', *JNES* 23 (1964), pp. 48-54.

Rad, G. von, *Das erste Buch Mose: Genesis* (ATD, 2.4; Göttingen: Vandenhoeck & Ruprecht, 5th edn, 1958), ET *Genesis* (trans. J.H. Marks; OTL; London: SCM Press, 2nd edn, 1963).

Radday, Y.T., 'Chiasm in Tora', *Linguistica Biblica* 19 (1972), pp. 12-23.

Ravn, O.E., 'Der Turm zu Babel', *ZDMG* 9 NF 16 (1937), pp. 352-72.

—*Herodotus' Description of Babylon* (Copenhagen: Nyt Nordisk Forlag, 1942).

Reicke, B., 'The Knowledge Hidden in the Tree of Paradise', *JSS* 1 (1956), pp. 193-202.

Rendsburg, G.A., 'The Biblical Flood Story in the Light of the Gilgameš Flood Account', in J. Azize and N. Weeks (eds.), *Gilgameš and the World of Assyria: Proceedings of the Conference Held at Mandelbaum House, The University of Sidney, 21–23 July 2004* (Ancient Near Eastern Studies, Supplement 21; Leuven: Peeters, 2007), pp. 115-27.

—'Gen 10:13-14: An Authentic Tradition concerning the Origin of the Philistines', *JNSL* 13 (1987), pp. 89-96.

Riem, J.K.R., *Die Sintflut in Sage und Wissenschaft* (Hamburg: Agentur des Rauhen Hauses, 1925).

Rogerson, J., 'The Creation Stories: Their Ecological Potential and Problems', in D.G. Horrell, C. Hunt, C. Southgate and F. Stavrakopoulou (eds.), *Ecological Hermeneutics: Biblical, Historical and Theological Perspectives* (London: T&T Clark International, 2010), pp. 21-31.

Rollinger, R., *Herodots babylonischer Logos* (Innsbruck: Verlag des Instituts für Sprachwissenschaft der Universität Innsbruck, 1993).

Rooker, M.F., *Biblical Hebrew in Transition: The Language of the Book of Ezekiel* (JSOTSup, 90; Sheffield: JSOT Press, 1990).

Rose, C., 'Nochmals: Der Turmbau zu Babel', *VT* 54 (2004), pp. 223-38.

Ross, A.P., 'The Curse of Canaan', *BSac* 137 (1980), pp. 223-40.

Rouillard, H., *La péricope de Balaam (Nombres 22–24): La prose et les oracles* (Etudes bibliques; Paris: Gabalda, 1985).

Rowley, H.H., *The Faith of Israel* (London: SCM Press, 1956).

—*Job* (NCB; London: Thomas Nelson, 1970).

Ruppert, L., *Genesis. I. Gen. 1,1–11,26* (FzB, 70; Würzburg: Echter, 1992).

Rüterswörden, U., *Dominum Terrae: Studien zur Genese einer alttestamentlichen Vorstellung* (BZAW, 215; Berlin: W. de Gruyter, 1993).

Salvesen, A., *Symmachus in the Pentateuch* (JSSM, 15. Manchester: Manchester University, 1991).

Samuel, A.E., *Greek and Roman Chronology: Calendars and Years in Classical Antiquity* (Handbuch der Altertumswissenschaft, 1.7; Munich: C.H. Beck, 1972), pp. 139-44.

Sandmel, S., 'Parallelomania', *JBL* 81 (1962), pp. 1-13.

Sarna, N.M., *Genesis* (JPS Torah Commentary; Philadelphia: Jewish Publication Society, 1989).

Sasson, J.M., 'A Genealogical "Convention" in Biblical Chronography?', *ZAW* 90 (1978), pp. 171-85.

—'Generation, Seventh', in *IDBSup*, pp. 354-56.

—'The Tower of Babel as a Clue to the Redactional Structuring of the Primeval History (Gen. 1.1–11.9)', in G. Rendsburg, R. Adler, M. Arfa and N.H. Winter (eds.), *The Bible World: Essays in Honor of Cyrus H. Gordon* (New York: Ktav, 1980), pp. 211-19.

Sayce, A.H., 'Assyriological Notes. No. 1.', *PSBA* 18 (1895), pp. 173-74.

—'Balaam's Prophecy (Numbers xxiv.17-24) and the God Sheth', *Hebraica* 4 (1887), pp. 1-6.

—'The Cuneiform Inscriptions of Van, Deciphered and Translated', *JRAS* 14 (1882), pp. 377-732.

—*The Early History of the Hebrews* (London: Rivingtons, 1897).

—'Eden', in J. Hastings (ed.), *Dictionary of the Bible* (5 vols.; Edinburgh: T. & T. Clark, 1898–1904 [1898]), I, pp. 643-44.

—*Patriarchal Palestine* (London: SPCK, 1895).

—'Ur of the Chaldees', *ExpT* 13 (1901–1902), pp. 64-66.

Scafi, A., *Mapping Paradise: A History of Heaven on Earth* (London: British Library, 2006).

Scharbert, J., 'Traditions- und Redaktionsgeschichte von Gn 6,1–4', *BZ* NF 11 (1967), pp. 66-78.

Schmid, H., *Der Tempelturm Etemenanki in Babylon* (Baghdader Forschungen, 17; Mainz: Philipp von Zabern, 1995).

Schmid, K., 'Loss of Immortality: Hermeneutical Aspects of Genesis 2–3 and its Early Reception', in *idem* (ed.), *Beyond Eden: The Biblical Story of Paradise (Genesis 2–3) and its Reception History* (FAT, 2.34; Tübingen: Mohr Siebeck, 2008), pp. 58-78.

Schmidt, H., *Die Erzählung von Paradies und Sündenfall* (Tübingen: J.C.B. Mohr [P. Siebeck], 1931).

Schmidt, W.H., *Die Schöpfungsgeschichte der Priesterschrift* (WMANT, 17; Neukirchen–Vluyn: Neukirchener Verlag, 1964).

Schmidtke, F., *Die Japhetiten der biblischen Völkertafel* (Breslauer Studien zur historischen Theologie, 7; Breslau: Müller & Seiffert, 1926).

Schnabel, P., *Berossos und die babylonisch-hellenistische Literatur* (Leipzig: B.G. Teubner, 1923).

Schüle, A., 'The Divine–Human Marriages (Genesis 6:1–4) and the Greek Framing of the Primeval History', *TZ* 65 (2009), pp. 116-28.

Schulten, A., *Tartessos* (Hamburg: W. de Gruyter, 1950).

Schwartz, M., 'Qumran, Turfan, Arabic Magic, and Noah's Name', in R. Gyselen (ed.), *Charmes et sortilèges: Magie et magiciens* (Res Orientales, 14; Bures-sur-Yvette: Groupe pour l'Etude de la Civilisation du Moyen-Orient, 2002), pp. 231-38.

Scroggs, R., *The Last Adam: A Study in Pauline Anthropology* (Oxford: Blackwell, 1966).

Scullion, J.J., *Genesis: A Commentary for Students, Teachers, and Preachers* (Old Testament Studies, 6; Collegeville: Liturgical Press [A Michael Glazier Book], 1992).

Seebass, H., *Genesis. I. Urgeschichte (1,1–11,26)* (Neukirchen–Vluyn: Neukirchener Verlag, 3rd edn, 2009).

Seipel, W. (ed.), *Der Turmbau zu Babel* (2 vols.; Vienna: Kunsthistorisches Museum, 2003).

Sethe, K., *Die Ächtung feindlicher Fürsten, Völker und Dinge auf altägyptischen Tongefässscherben der mittleren Reiches* (Berlin: Akademie der Wissenschaften in Kommission bei W. de Gruyter, 1926).

Seybold, K., 'Der Turmbau zu Babel. Zur Entstehung von Genesis xi 1-9', *VT* 26 (1976), pp. 453-79.

Seymour, M.J., in I.L. Finkel and M.J. Seymour (eds.), *Babylon: Myth and Reality* (London: British Museum Press, 2008), pp. 132-41.

Shanks, H., 'Three Shekels for the Lord: Ancient Inscriptions Record Gift to Solomon's Temple', *BARev* 23.6 (1997), pp. 28-32.

Shea, W.H., 'The Dedication on the Nora Stone', *VT* 41 (1991), pp. 241-45.

Sievers, E., *Metrische Studien* (7 vols.; Leipzig: B.G. Teubner, 1901–19).

Sjöberg, Å.W., 'Eve and the Chameleon', in W.B. Barrick and J.R. Spencer (eds.), *In the Shelter of Elyon: Essays on Ancient Palestinian Life and Literature in Honor of G.W. Ahlström* (JSOTSup, 31; Sheffield: JSOT Press, 1984), pp. 217-25.

Skinner, J., *A Critical and Exegetical Commentary on Genesis* (ICC; Edinburgh: T. & T. Clark, 1910).

Smith, G., 'The Chaldean Account of the Deluge', *TSBA* 2 (1873), pp. 213-34. Reprinted in A. Dundes, *The Flood Myth* (Berkeley: University of California Press, 1988), pp. 29-48.

Smith, M.S., 'Light in Genesis 1:3—Created or Uncreated: A Question of Priestly Mysticism?', in C. Cohen, V.A. Hurowitz, A. Hurvitz, Y. Muffs, B.J. Schwartz and J.H. Tigay (eds.), *Birkat Shalom: Studies in Bible, Ancient Near Eastern Literature, and Postbiblical Judaism Presented to Shalom M. Paul on the Occasion of His Seventieth Birthday* (2 vols.; Winona Lake, IN: Eisenbrauns, 2008), I, pp. 125-34.

—*The Priestly Vision of Genesis 1* (Minneapolis: Fortress Press, 2010).

—*The Rituals and Myths of the Feast of the Goodly Gods of KTU/CAT 1.23: Royal Constructions of Opposition, Intersection, Integration, and Domination* (SBL Resources for Biblical Study, 51; Atlanta: SBL, 2006).

—*The Ugaritic Baal Cycle*. I. *Introduction with Text, Translation and Commentary on KTU 1.1–1.2* (VTSup, 55; Leiden: Brill, 1995).

Snyder, J., 'Jan van Eyck and Adam's Apple', *Art Bulletin* 58 (1976), pp. 511-15.

Soden, W. von, 'Etemenanki vor Asarhaddon nach der Erzählung vom Turmbau zu Babel und dem Erra-Mythos', *UF* 3 (1971), pp. 253-64, reprinted in H.-P. Müller (ed.), *Bibel und alter Orient: Altorientalische Beiträge zum Alten Testament von Wolfram von Soden* (BZAW, 162; Berlin: W. de Gruyter, 1985), pp. 134-47.

—'Verschlüsselte Kritik an Salomo in der Urgeschichte des Jahwisten?', *WO* 7 (1974), pp. 228-40, reprinted in H.-P. Müller (ed.), *Bibel und alter Orient: Altorientalische Beiträge zum Alten Testament von Wolfram von Soden* (BZAW, 162; Berlin: W. de Gruyter, 1985), pp. 174-86.

Soggin, J.A., 'The Fall of Man in the Third Chapter of Genesis', in *idem*, *Old Testament and Oriental Studies* (Rome: Biblical Institute Press, 1975), pp. 88-111.

—*Genesis 1–11* (Commentario storico ed esegetico all'Antico e al Nuovo Testamento, AT 1.1; Turin: Marietti, 1991).

—'The Reign of ʾEšbaʿal, Son of Saul', *Old Testament and Oriental Studies* (BibOr, 29; Rome: Biblical Institute Press, 1975), pp. 31-49.

Spar, I., and W.G. Lambert (eds.), *Cuneiform Texts in the Metropolitan Museum of Art*. II. *Literary and Scholastic Texts of the First Millennium B.C.* (Metropolitan Museum of Art, New York: Brepols, 2005).

Speiser, E.A., *Genesis* (AB, 1; Garden City, NY: Doubleday, 1964).

—'The Rivers of Paradise', in R. von Kienle, A. Moortgat, H. Otten, E. von Schuler and W. Zaumseil (eds.), *Festschrift Johannes Friedrich* (Heidelberg: Carl Winter, Universitätsverlag, 1959), pp. 473-85, reprinted in J.J. Finkelstein and M. Greenberg (eds.), *Oriental and Biblical Studies: Collected Writings of E.A. Speiser* (Philadelphia: University of Pennsylvania Press, 1967), pp. 23-34.

—'Southern Kurdistan in the Annals of Ashurnasirpal and Today', *AASOR* 8 for 1926–27 (1928), pp. 1-41.

—'Word Plays on the Creation Epic's Version of the Founding of Babylon', *Or* 25 (1956), pp. 317-23, reprinted in J.J. Finkelstein and M. Greenberg (eds.), *Oriental and Biblical Studies: Collected Writings of E.A. Speiser* (Philadelphia: University of Pennsylvania Press, 1967), pp. 53-61.

—'*YDWN*, Gen 6:3', *JBL* 75 (1956), pp. 126-29, reprinted in J.J. Finkelstein and M. Greeenberg (eds.), *Oriental and Biblical Studies: Collected Writings of E.A. Speiser* (Philadelphia: University of Pennsylvania Press, 1967), pp. 35-40.

Spek, R.J. van der, 'Berossus as a Babylonian Chronicler and Greek Historian', in R.J. van der Spek (ed.), *Studies in Ancient Near Eastern World View and Society: Presented to Marten Stol on the Occasion of His 65th Birthday* (Bethesda, MD: CDL Press, 2008), pp. 277-318.

Stade, B., 'Das Kainszeichen', *ZAW* 14 (1894), pp. 250-318.

Stadelmann, L.I.J., *The Hebrew Conception of the World* (AnBib, 39; Rome: Biblical Institute Press, 1970).

Stager, L.E., 'Jerusalem and the Garden of Eden', in B.A. Levine, P.J. King, J. Naveh and E. Stern (eds.), *Eretz-Israel* 26 (Frank Moore Cross Volume; Jerusalem: Israel Exploration Society, 1999), pp. 183*-94*.

—'Jerusalem as Eden', *BARev* 20.3 (May/June 2000), pp. 37-47, 66.

Steck, O.H., *Der Schöpfungsbericht der Priesterschrift* (FRLANT, 115; Göttingen: Vandenhoeck & Ruprecht, 1975).

Steiner, G., *After Babel: Aspects of Language and Translation* (Oxford: Oxford University Press, 1975).

Stordalen, T., *Echoes of Eden: Genesis 2–3 and Symbolism of the Eden Garden in Biblical Hebrew Literature* (Contributions to Biblical Exegesis and Theology, 25; Leuven: Peeters, 2000).

Strömberg Krantz, E., *Des Schiffes Weg mitten im Meer: Beiträge zur Erforschung der nautischen Terminologie des Alten Testaments* (ConBOT, 19; Lund: C.W.K. Gleerup, 1982).

Strong, J.T., 'Shattering the Image of God: A Response to Theodore Hiebert's Interpretation of the Story of the Tower of Babel', *JBL* 127 (2008), pp. 625-34.

Stuckenbruck, L.T., *The Book of the Giants from Qumran* (Texte und Studien zum Antiken Judentum, 63; Tübingen: Mohr Siebeck, 1997).

Teixidor, J., *Bulletin d'épigraphie sémitique (1964–1980)* (BAH, 127; Paris: Geuthner, 1986).

—'Les tablettes d'Arslan Tash au Musée d'Alep', *AuOr* 1 (1983), pp. 105-108.

Tengström, S., *Die Toledotformel und die literarische Struktur der priesterlichen Erweiterungsschicht im Pentateuch* (ConBOT, 17; Lund: Gleerup, 1982).

Tennant, F.R., *The Sources of the Doctrines of the Fall and Original Sin* (Cambridge: Cambridge University Press, 1903).

Thomas, D.W., 'Translating Hebrew *'āsāh*', *BT* 17 (1966), pp. 190-93.

Thomas, M.A., *These are the Generations: Identity, Covenant, and the* toledot *Formula* (LHBOTS, 551; New York: T&T Clark International, 2011).

Tigay, J.H., *Deuteronomy* (JPS Torah Commentary; Philadelphia: Jewish Publication Society, 1996).

—*The Evolution of the Gilgamesh Epic* (Philadelphia: University of Pennsylvania Press, 1982).

Titus, P.J., *The Second Story of Creation (Gen 2:4–3:24): A Prologue to the Concept of the Enneateuch?* (European University Studies, 23.9 2; Frankfurt: Peter Lang, 2011).

Treidler, H., 'Βάρις ὄρος', in K. Ziegler and W. Sontheimer (eds.), *Der kleine Pauly Lexikon der Antike* (5 vols.; Stuttgart: A. Druckenmüller, 1964–75), I, pp. 825-26.

Trible, P., *God and the Rhetoric of Sexuality* (OBT; Philadelphia: Fortress Press, 1978).

Tsirkin, J.B. [Y.B.], 'The Phoenicians and Tartessos', *Gerión* 15 (1997), pp. 243-51.

Tsirkin, Y.B. [J.B.], 'The Greeks and Tartessos', *Oikumene* 5 (1986), pp. 163-71.

Tsumura, D.T., *Creation and Destruction: A Reappraisal of the* Chaoskampf *Theory in the Old Testament* (Winona Lake, IN: Eisenbrauns, 2005).

Uehlinger, C., *Weltreich und «eine Rede»: Eine neue Deutung der sogenannten Turmbauerzählung (Gen 11,1-9)* (OBO, 101; Freiburg: Universitätsverlag, and Göttingen: Vandenhoeck & Ruprecht, 1990).

Ullendorff, E., 'The Construction of Noah's Ark', *VT* 4 (1954), pp. 95-96, reprinted in *idem, Is Biblical Hebrew a Language? Studies in Semitic Languages and Civilizations* (Wiesbaden: Otto Harrassowitz, 1977), pp. 48-49.

—Review of George Steiner, *After Babel: Aspects of Language and Translation* (Oxford: Oxford University Press, 1975), *BSOAS* 39 (1976), pp. 403-20.

Ulrich, E., *et al., Qumran Cave 4.IX. Deuteronomy, Joshua, Judges, Kings* (DJD, 14; Oxford: Clarendon Press, 1995).

Ussher, J., *Annales veteris testamenti, prima mundi origine deducti* (London: J. Flesher, 1650), ET *The Annals of the World* (London: E. Tyler, 1658).

Valeton, J.J.P., 'Bedeutung und Stellung des Wortes ברית im Priestercodex', *ZAW* 12 (1892), pp. 1-22.

VanderKam, J.C., *Enoch and the Growth of an Apocalyptic Tradition* (CBQMS, 16; Washington, DC: Catholic Biblical Association of America, 1984).

Van Seters, J., 'The Creation of Man and the Creation of the King', *ZAW* 101 (1989), pp. 333-42.

—'The Primeval Histories of Greece and Israel Compared', *ZAW* 100 (1988), pp. 1-21.

—*Prologue to History: The Yahwist as Historian in Genesis* (Louisville, KY: Westminster/John Knox, 1992).

—Review of R.E. Gmirkin, *Berossus and Genesis, Manetho and Exodus: Hellenistic Historians and the Date of the Pentateuch* (LHBOTS, 433; London: T&T Clark International, 2006), *JTS* 59 (2008), pp. 212-14.

Vanstiphout, H., *Epics of Sumerian Kings: The Matter of Aratta* (SBL Writings from the Ancient World, 20; Atlanta: SBL, 2003).

Vaulx, J. de, *Les Nombres* (Sources bibliques; Paris: J. Gabalda, 1972).

Vawter, B., *On Genesis: A New Reading* (London: Geoffrey Chapman, 1977).

Velikovsky, I., *Ages in Chaos* (London: Sidgwick & Jackson, 1953).

Verbrugghe, P., and J.M. Wickersham, *Berossos and Manetho, Introduced and Translated; Native Traditions in Ancient Mesopotamia and Egypt* (Ann Arbor: University of Michigan Press, 1996).

Vermeylen, J., 'Le récit du paradis et la question des origines du Pentateuque', *Bijdragen: Tijdschrift voor filosofie en theologie* 41 (1980), pp. 230-50.

Vervenne, M., 'All They Need is Love: Once More Genesis 6.1-4', in J. Davies, G. Harvey and W.G.E. Watson (eds.), *Words Remembered, Texts Renewed: Essays in Honour of John F.A. Sawyer* (JSOTSup, 195; Sheffield: Sheffield Academic Press, 1995).

Viberg, A., *Symbols of Law: A Contextual Analysis of Legal Symbolic Acts in the Old Testament* (ConBOT, 34: Stockholm: Almqvist & Wiksell, 1992), pp. 53-57.

Vischer, W., *Jahwe der Gott Kains* (Munich: Chr. Kaiser, 1929).

Vollers, K., 'Zur Erklärung des יָדוֹן Gen 6,3', *ZA* 14 (1899), pp. 349-56.

Voort, A. van der, 'Genèse I, 1 à II, 4a et le Psaume 104', *RB* 58 (1951), pp. 321-47.

Walcot, P., *Hesiod and the Near East* (Cardiff: University of Wales Press, 1966).

Wallace, H., *The Eden Narrative* (HSM, 32; Atlanta: Scholars Press, 1983).

Walton, J.H., 'The Antediluvian Section of the Sumerian King List and Genesis 5', *BA* 44 (1981), pp. 207-208.

—*Genesis 1 as Ancient Cosmology* (Winona Lake, IN: Eisenbrauns, 2011).

—*The Lost World of Genesis One: Ancient Cosmology and the Origins Debate* (Downers Grove, IL: IVP Academic, 2009).

—'The Mesopotamian Background of the Tower of Babel Account and its Implications', *BBR* 5 (1995), pp. 155-75.

Watson, R.S., *Chaos Uncreated: A Reassessment of the Theme of "Chaos" in the Hebrew Bible* (BZAW, 341; Berlin: W. de Gruyter, 2005).

Weinfeld, M., 'Covenant Terminology in the Ancient Near East and its Influence on the West', *JAOS* 93 (1973), pp. 190-99.

—'Sabbath, Temple, and the Enthronment of the Lord—The Problem of the Sitz in Leben of Genesis 1:1–2:3', in A. Caquot and M. Delcor (eds.), *Mélanges bibliques et orientaux en l'honneur de M. Henri Cazelles* (AOAT, 212; Neukirchen–Vluyn: Neukirchener Verlag, 1981), pp. 501-12.

Weir, D.A., *The Origins of the Federal Theology in Sixteenth-Century Reformation Thought* (Oxford: Clarendon Press, 1990).

Wellhausen, J., *Die Composition des Hexateuchs und der historischen Bücher des Alten Testaments* (Berlin: G. Reimer, 3rd edn, 1899).

—*Die kleinen Propheten* (Berlin: G. Reimer, 1898).

—*Prolegomena zur Geschichte Israels* (Berlin: G. Reimer, 2nd edn, 1883), ET *Prolegomena to the History of Israel* (Edinburgh: A. & C. Black, 1885).

Wenham, G.J., *Genesis 1–15* (WBC, 1; Waco, TX: Word Books, 1987).

—*Numbers* (Tyndale Commentary; Leicester: Inter-Varsity Press, 1981).

—'Sanctuary Symbolism in the Garden of Eden Story', in *Proceedings of the Ninth World Congress of Jewish Studies, Division A: The Period of the Bible* (Jerusalem: World Union of Jewish Studies, 1985), pp. 19-25, reprinted in R.S. Hess and D.T. Tsumura (eds.), *"I Studied Inscriptions from before the Flood": Ancient Near Eastern, Literary, and Linguistic Approaches to Genesis 1–11* (Sources for Biblical and Theological Study, 4; Winona Lake, IN: Eisenbrauns, 1994), pp. 399-404.

West, M.L., *The East Face of Helicon: West Asiatic Elements in Greek Poetry and Myth* (Oxford: Clarendon Press, 1997).

—'The Flood Myth in Ovid, Lucian, and Nonnus', in Juan Antonio López Férez (ed.), *Mitos en la literatura griega helenística e imperial* (Madrid: Ediciones Clásicas, 2003), pp. 245-59.

—*The Hesiodic Catalogue of Women: Its Nature, Structure, and Origins* (Oxford: Clarendon Press, 1985).

Westermann, C., *Genesis 1–11* (BKAT, 1.1; Neukirchen–Vluyn: Neukirchener Verlag, 1974), ET *Genesis 1–11: A Commentary* (trans. John J. Scullion; London: SPCK, 1984).

White, L., 'The Historical Roots of our Ecologic Crisis', *Science* 155, no. 3767 (1967), pp. 1203-1207.

Whitford, D.M., *The Curse of Ham in the Early Modern Era: The Bible and the Justifications for Slavery* (St. Andrews Studies in Reformation History; Farnham: Ashgate, 2009).

Wickham, L.R., 'The Sons of God and Daughters of Men: Genesis vi 2 in Early Christian Exegesis', in A.S. van der Woude (ed.), *Language and Meaning: Studies in Hebrew Language and Biblical Exegesis* (OS, 19; Leiden: Brill, 1974), pp. 135-47.

Wifall, W., 'Asshur and Eber, or Asher and Heber? A Commentary on the Last Balaam Oracle, Num 24 21-24', *ZAW* 80 (1970), pp. 110-14.

—'Genesis 6:1–4—A Royal Davidic Myth', *BTB* 5 (1975), pp. 294-301.

Wildberger, H., 'Das Abbild Gottes. Gen. I, 26-30', *TZ* 21 (1965), pp. 245-59, 481-501, reprinted in H. Wildberger, *Jahwe und sein Volk: Gesammelte Aufsätze zum Alten Testament. Zu seinem 70. Geburtstag am 2. Januar 1980* (eds. H.H. Schmid and O.H. Steck; TBü, 66; Munich: Chr. Kaiser, 1979), pp. 110-45.

—*Jesaja Kapitel 13–27* (BKAT, 10.2; Neukirchen–Vluyn: Neukirchener Verlag, 1978), ET *Isaiah 13–27* (trans. T.H. Trapp; Continental Commentary; Minneapolis: Fortress, 1997).

Wilensky-Lanford, B., *Paradise Lust: Searching for the Garden of Eden* (New York: Grove Press, 2011).

Wilhelm, G., 'Šanhara', in *RLA* 12 (Berlin: W. de Gruyter, 2009), pp. 11-12.

Williams, N.P., *The Ideas of the Fall and Original Sin: A Historical and Critical Study* (London: Longmans, Green & Co., 1927).

Williamson, H.G.M., *1 and 2 Chronicles* (NCB; Grand Rapids, MI: Eerdmans: Marshall, Morgan & Scott, 1982).

—*A Critical and Exegetical Commentary on Isaiah 1–27. I Isaiah 1–5* (ICC; London: T&T Clark International, 2006).

Williamson, P., *Abraham, Israel and the Nations: The Patriarchal Promise and its Covenantal Development in Genesis* (JSOTSup, 315; Sheffield: Sheffield Academic Press, 2000).

Wilson, R.McL., 'The Early History of the Exegesis of Gen 1:28', *Studia Patristica* 1 (1957), pp. 420-37.

Winckler, H., *Altorientalische Forschungen* (3 vols.; Leipzig: E. Pfeiffer, 1893–1906).

Wiseman, D.J., 'Abban and Alalah', *JCS* 12 (1958), pp. 124-29.

Witte, M., *Die biblische Urgeschichte: Redaktions- und theologiegeschichtliche Beobachtungen zu Genesis 1,1–11,26* (BZAW, 265; Berlin: W. de Gruyter, 1998).

Wittenberg, G.H., *King Solomon and the Theologians* (Pietermaritzburg: University of Natal Press, 1988).

Wolde, E. van, *Reframing Biblical Studies: When Language and Text Meet Culture, Cognition and Context* (Winona Lake, IN: Eisenbrauns, 2009).

—*Stories of the Beginning: Genesis 1–11 and Other Creation Stories* (trans. J. Bowden; London: SCM Press, 1996).

—'Why the Verb ברא Does Not Mean "To Create" in Genesis 1.1–2.4a', *JSOT* 34 (2009), pp. 3-23.

—*Words Become Worlds: Semantic Studies in Genesis 1–11* (BibInt, 6; Leiden: Brill, 1994).

Wolde, E. van, and R. Rezetko, 'Semantics and the Semantics of ברא: A Rejoinder to the Arguments Advanced by B. Becking and M. Korpel', *JHS* 11 (2011), article 9.

Wood, J.R., Review of R.E. Gmirkin, *Berossus and Genesis, Manetho and Exodus: Hellenistic Historians and the Date of the Pentateuch* (LHBOTS, 433; London: T&T Clark International, 2006), *JHS* 8 (2008).

Wright, R.M., *Linguistic Evidence for the Pre-Exilic Date of the Yahwistic Source* (LHBOTS, 419; London: T&T Clark International, 2005).

Wyatt, N., 'Interpreting the Creation and Fall Story in Genesis 2–3', *ZAW* 93 (1981), pp. 10-21.

Yahuda, A.S., *Die Sprache des Pentateuch in ihren Beziehungen zum Aegyptischen* (Berlin: W. de Gruyter, 1929), ET *The Language of the Pentateuch in its Relation to Egyptian* (London: Oxford University Press, 1933).

Yasur-Landau, A., *The Philistines and Aegean Migrations at the End of the Late Bronze Age* (Cambridge: Cambridge University Press, 2010).

Younker, R.W., and R.M. Davidson, 'The Myth of the Solid Heavenly Dome: Another Look at the Hebrew רָקִיעַ (*RĀQÎAʿ*)', *AUSS* 49 (2011), pp. 125-47.

Zadok, R., 'The Origin of the Name Shinar', *ZA* 74 (1984), pp. 240-44.

Zakovitch, Y., *Through the Looking Glass: Reflection Stories in the Bible* (Tel Aviv: Hakibbutz Hameuchad, 1995 [Hebrew]).

Zevit, Z., 'A Phoenician Inscription and Biblical Covenant Theology', *IEJ* 27 (1977), pp. 110-18.

Zeynder, H., 'Kainszeichen, Keniter und Beschneidung', *ZAW* 18 (1898), pp. 120-25.

Zimmerli, W., *1. Mose 1–11* (Zürcher Bibelkommentare; Zurich: Zwingli Verlag, 3rd edn, 1967).

—'Sinaibund und Abrahambund: Ein Beitrag zum Verständnis der Priesterschrift, *TZ* 16 (Festgabe für Walther Eichrodt, 1960), pp. 268-80, reprinted in *idem, Gottes Offenbarung: Gesammelte Aufsätze zum Alten Testament* (Munich: Chr. Kaiser, 1963), pp. 205-16.

Zimmern, H., 'Die altbabylonischen vor- (und nach-)sintlichen Könige nach neuen Quellen', *ZDMG* 78 NF 3 (1924), pp. 19-35.

—'Urkönige und Uroffenbarung', in Eberhard Schrader (ed.), *Die Keilinschriften und das Alte Testament* (Giessen: Reuther & Reichard, 3rd edn, 1902–1903), pp. 530-43.

INDICES

INDEX OF REFERENCES

Genesis (cont.)		*Exodus*		26.25	135
17	125, 130-32	2.3	118, 120	26.42	135
		3.1	57	26.44-45	135
17.1-21	124	6.4	123, 130	26.45	135
17.2	123, 130-32, 136	6.6	53		
		6.7	135	*Numbers*	
17.7	123, 125, 130-32	6.14	56	3.1	18
		9.30	25	10.1	120
17.8	135	12.2	65	10.2	120
17.14	132	15.16	53	10.29	57
17.19	123, 125, 130-32	17.8-16	58	13.32	54
		18.1	57	13.33	81, 83, 86, 97, 147
17.21	123, 125, 130-32	20.11	4, 17		
		24	134	15.24	119
17.22	16	24.4-8	126	16.39 ET	3
19.30-38	53	25.11	113	17.4	3
22	132	25.29	120	22	146
22.17	115	27.1	120	22.22-30	35
24.19	16	29.45-46	135	24	55
25.3	52	30.1	120	24.17-24	144, 146
25.4	56, 59	31.12-17	17	24.17	33, 35, 55, 56, 146
25.12	18	31.16	135		
25.19	18	32.26-29	136	24.20	58
27.28	38	39–40	5	24.21-22	52
27.40	49	39.3	3	24.21	114
28	185, 186	40.33	16	24.22	33, 35, 52, 53, 55, 146
28.17	186				
29.34	54	*Leviticus*		24.24	53, 144-46, 154
29.35	54	1–7	124		
33	48	1.9	104	25.12-13	135, 136
33.3	48	8–9	124	25.12	123, 130, 136
33.10	48	11	125		
36	59	16.29-30	65	26.5	56
36.1	18	17	135	29.2	104
36.4	18	18.21	135	33.52	13
36.9	18	20.1-5	135		
36.12	58	20.17	139	*Deuteronomy*	
36.16	58	23.5	65	1.28	183
37.2	18	23.6	65	1.39	43
39.9	90	23.27	65	2.9	53
39.23	90	23.34	65	2.10-12	83
46.9	56	23.39	65	2.10-11	97
49.16	89	24.8	135	2.10	81
49.17	89	25.9	65	2.19	53
49.25	20	26.1	135	2.20-23	83
		26.9	130, 135	2.20-21	81
		26.15	135		

INDEX OF AUTHORS